GENDER, WRITING, AND PERFORMANCE

Gender, Writing, and Performance

Men Defending Women in Late Medieval France, 1440–1538

HELEN J. SWIFT

CLARENDON PRESS · OXFORD

OXFORD

UNIVERSITY PRESS

Great Clarendon Street, Oxford OX2 6DP

Oxford University Press is a department of the University of Oxford.
It furthers the University's objective of excellence in research, scholarship,
and education by publishing worldwide in

Oxford New York

Auckland Cape Town Dar es Salaam Hong Kong Karachi
Kuala Lumpur Madrid Melbourne Mexico City Nairobi
New Delhi Shanghai Taipei Toronto

With offices in

Argentina Austria Brazil Chile Czech Republic France Greece
Guatemala Hungary Italy Japan Poland Portugal Singapore
South Korea Switzerland Thailand Turkey Ukraine Vietnam

Oxford is a registered trade mark of Oxford University Press
in the UK and in certain other countries

Published in the United States
by Oxford University Press Inc., New York

British Library Cataloguing in Publication Data

Data available

Library of Congress Cataloging in Publication Data

Data available

Typeset by Laserwords Private Limited, Chennai, India
Printed in Great Britain
on acid-free paper by
Biddles Ltd., King's Lynn, Norfolk

ISBN 978–0–19–923223–9

1 3 5 7 9 10 8 6 4 2

Preface

This book explores the poetics of literary works written by men in defence of women in late medieval and early modern France. It fills an important lacuna in studies of this polemic in imaginative literature by bridging the gap between Christine de Pizan (d. *c.*1430) and a later generation of women writers and male, Neoplatonist writers who have recently all received due critical attention. I re-evaluate male-authored texts composed between 1440 (Martin Le Franc) and 1538 (Jean Bouchet), hitherto dismissed as 'insincere' or 'intellectual games', by proposing reading strategies that engage with their particular rhetorical and historical contexts. Venturing beyond modern criticism's neglect or dismissal of these allegedly monotonous, repetitive works, I aim both to understand the contemporary popularity of the case for women (*la querelle des femmes*) as literary subject matter, and to show how these texts hold considerable interest for modern audiences. The contemporary context is constructed in part through codicological evidence of manuscript and incunable production, layout, and circulation. The book's key conceptual concerns, gender, writing, and performance, are also examined through interrelated theories of performativity. Such theories provide reading strategies to help modern audiences appreciate the medieval texts in innovative ways. These strategies make explicit in a modern idiom the diverse sorts of interpretative engagement that I believe to have been expected, even demanded, by *querelle* writers and their contemporary audiences. This book's ultimate aim is thus to foster a new, more nuanced perspective on the question of a male author's 'sincerity' when composing a literary text advancing arguments in favour of women. Its arguments and varied critical approaches seek to interest, not only literary scholars of the pan-European *querelle*, but also literary theorists and historians of the book. It is hoped that the intellectual and cultural scope of the book will justly embed the 'lost century' of the *querelle* in late medieval vernacular poetics.

I should like briefly to acknowledge various institutions, groups, and individuals whose resources, guidance, and support have been invaluable in ensuring the completion of this book. I offer thanks to the Bodleian Library, Taylor Institution Library, and Sackler Library in Oxford, as well as to the John Rylands University Library of Manchester. Further afield, I was fortunate enough to spend five months pursuing research at the Bibliothèque nationale de France, and I am also grateful to the Bibliothèque Municipale in Grenoble for the one-off loan of a microfilm of the Grenoble manuscript of Martin Le Franc's *Le Champion des dames*, to which this book accords special attention. I express my gratitude for financial support provided by the Arts and Humanities Research Council (AHRC), and also by the Faculty of Medieval and Modern Languages, Oxford, and Magdalen College, Oxford, whose occasional grants enabled me to attend, and participate in, a number of national and international conferences during the course of my graduate study.

Amongst the many individuals whose help and expertise has been invaluable, I owe the greatest debt of gratitude to my supervisor, Jane Taylor, for her expert guidance and constant encouragement. For their comments and suggestions, I am most grateful to my examiners Adrian Armstrong and Terence Cave, and to the OUP readers. I also offer special thanks for the scholarly generosity of Catherine Attwood, Margaret Bent, Jennifer Britnell, Cynthia J. Brown, Mary Carruthers, Elizabeth L'Estrange, Sandra Hindman, Tony Hunt, Sarah Kay, Sophie Marnette, Roger Middleton, Jason O'Rourke, Nigel Palmer, Roger Pensom, Philip Schwyzer, and Robin Chapman Stacey. I thank Adrian Armstrong and Emma Cayley for allowing me to read their unpublished work, and to refer to it in the preparation of this book. Other thanks go to my colleagues at St Hilda's for their encouragement and guidance.

I should like also to acknowledge the comments and suggestions I have received at various conferences and seminars where I presented as papers earlier versions of parts of this book. I offer particular thanks to colleagues at the British Branch Meeting of the International Courtly Literature Society (ICLS) in Durham, 2003; the International Medieval Congress in Leeds, 2003; the Medieval Academy of America Meeting in Seattle, 2004; the Early Modern French Seminar at the University of Durham; the Medieval Cultures Seminar at Queen's University, Belfast; the Medieval European Research Seminar at the University of Manchester; the Medieval Graduate Seminar at the University of Cambridge, and the Medieval Graduate Seminar in Oxford.

Finally, I offer deepest thanks to my husband and to my parents for their unfailing emotional and material support in upholding the case for this particular woman.

H.J.S

Acknowledgements

The author would like to thank the following for permission to reproduce their copyright material:

Bibliothèque nationale de France, Paris (BnF, MS fr. 841; BnF, RES YE–27; BnF, RES YE–4031).

Bibliothèque Municipale de Grenoble (MS 352 Rés.).

Contents

List of Plates

All illustrations are positioned at the end of the chapter in which reference is made to them. For the sigla of manuscripts of *CD* and the *Nobles femmes*, see Appendix 2.

Conventions of Transcription

When quoting directly from a manuscript, an incunable, or an early printed book, I distinguish between *i* and *j*, *v* and *u*, I expand abbreviations, such as those denoted by the tilde and superior letters in contractions, I modernize punctuation, and I normalize the long *s*, the ampersand, and the Tironian sign to modern usage. My editorial practice follows Foulet and Speer 1979, except that I add the additional diacritical mark of the grave accent on the vowels *a* and *u* in cases where homography may result in confusion (e.g. *la/là, ou/où*). When quoting from a pre-existing critical edition of a text, I respect the conventions observed by the modern editor in question.

Abbreviations

Full bibliographical details are given in the list of references. All translations from foreign languages are the given editor/translator's own, unless stated otherwise.

BHR	*Bibliothèque d'Humanisme et Renaissance*
BL	British Library
BnF	Bibliothèque nationale de France, Département des Manuscrits (division occidentale)
BR	Bibliothèque Royale, Brussels
C	Martin Le Franc, *La Complainte du livre du Champion des dames à maistre Martin Le Franc son acteur*
CD	Martin Le Franc, *Le Champion des dames*
De casibus	Giovanni Boccaccio, *De casibus virorum illustrium*
De la louenge	*Le Livre de Jehan Bocasse de la louenge et vertu des nobles et cleres dames*
Des cas	Laurent de Premierfait, *Des cas des nobles hommes et femmes*
fr.	fonds français
FT	Jacques Milet, *La Forest de Tristesse*
GD	*Le Giroufflier aulx dames*
JP	Jean Bouchet, *Le Jugement poetic de l'honneur femenin*
MFJ	*Monologue fort joyeulx auquel sont introduictz deux avocatz et ung juge, devant lequel est plaidoyé le bien et le mal des dames*
MS	Manuscript
NDV	Symphorien Champier, *La Nef des dames vertueuses*
Nobles femmes	*Le Livre de Jehan Boccace des cleres et nobles femmes*
PFP	*Le Procès des femmes et des pulces, composé par ung frère mineur pèlerin, retournant des Hirrelendes, où il apprint la vraye recepte pour prendre et faire mourir les pulces, laquelle sera déclarée cy après à la diffinitive dudict procès*
PHF	Pierre Michault, *Le Procès d'Honneur Féminin*
PND	Jean Dupré, *Le Palais des nobles dames*

RD	Bertrand Desmarins de Masan, *Le Rousier des dames, sive le pèlerin d'amours*
Recueil	Anatole de Montaiglon and James de Rothschild (eds.), *Recueil de poésies françoises des XVe et XVIe siècles: morales, facétieuses, historiques*
RR	Guillaume de Lorris and Jean de Meun, *Le Roman de la rose*
S	Julia Kristeva, *Semiotikè: recherches pour une sémanalyse*
SM	Jacques Derrida, *Spectres de Marx: l'état de la dette, le travail du dueil et la nouvelle Internationale*
SoM	Jacques Derrida, *Specters of Marx: The State of the Debt, the Work of Mourning, and the New International*
VDA	Jean Marot, *La Vraye disant advocate des dames*
Vies	Antoine Dufour, *Les Vies des femmes célèbres*

STANDARDIZATIONS

I use the following modernized and standardized spellings to refer to the appearances in different texts of popular personification allegories: Amour/dieu d'Amour; Bel Accueil; Honneur Féminin; Malebouche; Vérité.

Introduction

Tant a l'en fait qu'il m'a falu
Demourer seulet en la mue,
De mousse et de pouldre velu
Comme ung viez aiz qu'on ne remue. (*C*, vv. 145–8)

(As a result of their actions I was locked up on my own, and had to
stay there gathering mould and dust, like an old abandoned axe.)[1]

In a verse debate between a Book and its Author, *La Complainte du livre
du Champion des dames à maistre Martin Le Franc son acteur*, Martin
Le Franc complains that his pro-feminine debate poem, *Le Champion
des dames* (*c.*1442), was unjustly rejected by the Burgundian Duke,
Philip the Good, whose patronage it sought to secure.[2] Left on a shelf
all alone to gather dust, the prosopopoeic Livre bemoans a fate which
seems, in modern criticism as opposed to the medieval Burgundian

---

[1] English translations are my own.

[2] The *Complainte* features uniquely in the second, revised codex of the poem, which
was presented to Philip in *c.*1451 after his apparent rejection of the first presentation
copy, offered *c.*1442. The complaining Book suggests that the Duke's advisers felt
that the *Champion* should be burnt on account of the 'poisons' it contained (*C*, vv.
141–2): the pro-feminine poem's debate between woman's Champion and her detractors
mobilizes virulent criticism of Philip's treatment of Joan of Arc, his decision to withdraw
from the Council of Basel, and his subsequent refusal to accept the doctrine of the
Immaculate Conception. The Book's suggestion might, I argue, have been intended to
help promote the *Champion*—if it *was* rejected—by marketing it as a sensational text,
whetting the appetite of potential readers to tackle the 24,000-line poem. However, since
there is no external evidence to corroborate the first manuscript's rejection, and given
that the revised codex is the most complete witness of the poem and its sequel, we might
conjecture that the book never did fail on its first presentation, and that the *Complainte*
was simply an additional promotional stratagem; after all, the diegetic outcome of the
Book's debate with its Author in the *Complainte* is that it should return to court entirely
unchanged. See Swift 2006. I list all the *Champion*'s extant witnesses in Appendix 2A.

court, to have befallen most imaginative literature written in defence of women that is now ranged under the umbrella term 'la querelle des femmes'.[3] Notwithstanding Livre's complaint, literary defences enjoyed considerable popularity in fifteenth- and early sixteenth-century France and Burgundy: they featured frequently amongst the commissions made by two generations of prominent female patrons at the princely and royal courts; they were amongst the first works to go to press with the advent of printing in Lyons, and were subsequently reproduced copiously in Paris in the 1520s and early 1530s. One of the most richly illustrated and frequently reproduced works was, in fact, the *Champion des dames*, to which this book will accord special attention; its date-span traces the *Champion*'s production history in manuscript, incunable, and print. Indeed, it is possible to read Le Franc's *Complainte*, not as an admission of failure, but as a shrewd strategy of self-promotion, seeking to boost the *Champion*'s popularity at Philip's court in line with the Duke's burgeoning bibliophilia.[4] In recognition of such contemporary success, this book aims less to mount a defence of unfairly neglected, dusty defences of women than to flesh out more assertively the now lesser-known history of the *querelle des femmes* between the well-known reference points of Christine de Pizan and the mid-sixteenth century. My principal aim is thus to persuade modern, scholarly audiences that this lacuna in studies of the *querelle* is worth filling by proposing a number of reading strategies as possible, more fruitful new ways of approaching texts from Martin Le Franc's *Champion des dames* (*c*.1440–2) to Jean Bouchet's *Jugement poetic de l'honneur femenin* (1538).

The reading strategies I offer marry the interests of reception history and critical reading; they communicate dynamically to modern scholarship the aspects of these texts that were of key interest to contemporary audiences. We can deduce these sites of interest from evidence that is both internal and external to the text: the cultivation of certain intertextual relationships, as well as the evidence of textual reception provided by programmes of book illustration and patterns of

---

[3] I use this term throughout to refer specifically to literary works written in *defence* of women; this is the sense in which it was understood contemporaneously by Le Franc in his prologue to the *Champion*, when he declares his intention to advance 'the most highly esteemed case for women (*querelle des femmes*)' (*CD* 3, English translations are my own). For a history of the term's genesis and its use in modern criticism, see Zimmermann 1999: 80–3, 85. The best, recent survey of the pan-European, pre-/early modern *querelle* is provided by Bock and Erler 2002.

[4] Philip came late in life to bibliophilia: McKendrick 2003a: 68.

publication. My new strategies of approach help to overcome two principal obstacles that have, I believe, limited hitherto the scope of research in this area. One practical obstacle has been the restricted availability of primary sources. This has improved in recent years with the publication of critical editions of selected longer texts (Le Franc's *Champion*, Pierre Michault's *Procès d'Honneur Féminin* (*c*.1461), Antoine Dufour's *Vies des femmes célèbres* (1504), Jean Marot's *Vraye disant advocate des dames* (*c*.1506), Bouchet's *Jugement*), and the digitization of sources undertaken by the Bibliothèque nationale's on-line text resource, Gallica, which has made instantly accessible both early imprints not yet available in modern editions (those of the *Champion*, Symphorien Champier's *Nef des dames vertueuses* (1503), and Jean Dupré's *Palais des nobles dames* ([1534])), and nineteenth-century anthologies (especially de Montaiglon and de Rothschild's thirteen-volume *Recueil de poésies françoises des XVe et XVIe siècles* (1855–78)) containing transcriptions of several shorter, singularly fascinating texts, such as the anonymous *Giroufflier aulx dames* and *Rousier des dames*. The disparate nature of the sources has, however, meant that critical studies have generally followed one of two paths: either being content to provide a summary—and not always accurate—catalogue, merely listing different works, often without bibliographical information;[5] or, more fruitfully, in the introductory notes to certain recent critical editions and in a few outstanding studies, looking at a single work in its individual contexts of production and reception, or engaging in some measure of comparison.[6]

The originality of the present study lies in its purpose to synthesize. It aims not only to identify a corpus of literary defences of women, but also to define connections between them, to read them in relation to one another, both synchronically and diachronically. It explores common features shared by works from each end of the period, such as the vocabulary used to represent women's gender identity, but also considers how a feature evolves through different texts during the period, like the use of legal process as a fictional framework. The validity of this approach is grounded in the way that systems of cross-referencing and intertextual quotation figure prominently in *querelle*

---

[5] Bock 2002: 1–31; Albistur and Armogathe 1977; Angenot 1977; Telle 1969; Kelso 1956; Richardson 1929. See Zimmermann's review of the secondary literature: 1999: 85–7.

[6] See entries for Armstrong, Blamires, Brown, and Zimmermann in the References.

texts themselves; this occurs, for example, in courtroom fictions which often cite previous defences—and also attacks on women, especially Jean de Meun's *Roman de la rose*—as 'evidence' to support the pro- or anti-feminine case. The texts clearly invite a critical approach that privileges intertextual dialogue, presenting themselves as part of an ongoing discussion; to ignore this dialectical dimension would be to misrepresent the nature of *querelle* textuality.

This synthesizing approach applies also to the extratextual aspect of contemporary literary production: the second part of my first chapter focuses on one work, Le Franc's *Champion*, a particularly richly illus- trated text, and reads its history of illustration across its manuscript, incunable, and early printed witnesses. In the case of its sixteenth- century imprint, it considers material evidence for the circulation of its woodcuts between editions of works with which the *Champion*'s text engages intertextual dialogue; it examines how these material links might be related to the critical connections I—and contemporary literary commentators—make between these texts.

The second obstacle my reading strategies surmount is the accu- mulated body of critical presuppositions about the *querelle des femmes* which have discouraged research, not simply in this area, but, more specifically, in my chosen period. These presuppositions are twofold, and relate to what we might call the 'ethical' and 'aesthetic' dimensions of the texts. The period addressed here is currently a lacuna in studies of the pro-feminine polemic in imaginative literature; it is perceived as a time of stagnation in *querelle* poetics, when writers were simply rehashing the same pro-feminine wine in old poetic bottles.[7] With a few important exceptions,[8] there is scant criticism bridging the gap between Christine de Pizan (d. *c*.1430), who was recently dubbed 'First Lady of the Middle Ages',[9] and a later generation of women writers (such as Marguerite de Navarre) and male Neoplatonist writers, who have all been valued for introducing new things into the *querelle*'s subject matter: the vital novelty of a female perspective in the case of Christine, the first known woman to address the status of women, and the innovation of a new, philosophical dimension in the case of Neoplatonists, with

---

[7] See McLeod 1991: 139; Lazard 1985: 12. Several critics touch on my period of the *querelle* as background to, or a springboard for, the study of French and/or English Renaissance writing on the subject: Benson 1992; Jordan 1990; Woodbridge 1984; Guillerm-Curutchet et al. 1971.

[8] Especially the work of Armstrong, Badel 1996, and Maclean.

[9] Altmann 2002: 17.

the so-called *querelle des amyes*,[10] and the influence of a pro-feminine treatise by Henricus Cornelius Agrippa.[11] Literary defences written by men in the intervening years were found wanting on two counts that we might classify loosely as ethical and aesthetic areas of weakness. First, on ethical grounds, they were entirely eclipsed by Christine; the merit of a male author's perspective—which was prejudged, at bottom, 'really' misogynistic anyway—was automatically discounted in the face of a real woman's viewpoint. The principal criterion for assessing *querelle* works was thus sincerity, with this factor inevitably working to the detriment of all, 'naturally' insincere, male writers. A gendered opposition arose between sincerity and rhetoric, what is 'heartfelt' and what is 'literary',[12] with male-authored defences dismissed either for their presumed *in*sincerity as 'dubious',[13] even facetious, constructions of women, or for being rhetorical flights of fancy that are somehow 'indifferent' to their subject matter and simply 'prescribed exercises on a set subject'.[14] This criterion, set against the gold standard of Christine, resulted in a second alleged weakness being identified in male-authored contributions. Because sincerity, an ethical measure of accomplishment, had primacy, the aesthetic attributes of the texts were discounted; they were rapidly concluded either to be of negligible interest, given the supposed monotony and homogeneity of *querelle* arguments,[15] or to be of so disparate and uneven a nature that they defied comparative investigation.[16]

This book aims to redress these presuppositions by re-evaluating the artistic interest of literary defences. The synthesizing approach discussed above will be complemented by close analyses of texts. This level of close reading, undertaken here for the first time in the case of most of the corpus, uncovers the intriguing, often highly entertaining,

---

[10] Angenot discusses this 'seconde *Querelle des femmes*': 1977: 21.

[11] One of the most popular treatises in favour of women of the early sixteenth century, *De nobilitate et praecellentia foeminei sexus* ('On the nobility and excellence of the female sex'), is believed to have been written (at least in part) as early as 1509 but was only first published in 1529, then a year later translated into French. Composed under the patronage of Maximilian I, it is dedicated also to his daughter, Margaret of Austria. *De nobilitate* comes out of a certain humanist current of treatise-writing that, with the exception of a catalogue by Foresti (see Chapter 3), I omit from consideration in this study in order to focus on the particularities of consciously literary defences. See Agrippa 1996: 20–3.

[12] Kelly 1984: 75. See also Lazard 1985: 11.   [13] Kelly 1984: 75.

[14] Gray 2000: 19; Solterer 1995: 146; Mann 1990: 30.

[15] Gray 2000: 11; Lazard 1985: 11; Albistur and Armogathe 1977: 114.

[16] Maclean 1977: 25–6.

hermeneutic complexity of works which deserve to be more widely appreciated. The importance I accord to artistic concerns is reflected in my decision, discussed more fully below, to divide material between my book chapters according to shared rhetorical or structural features. As a further means of refreshing modern perspectives on the late medieval *querelle*, I engage a critical theoretical framework to illuminate my understanding and explanation of the rhetorical strategies and hermeneutic concerns of male writers. This framework is anchored in a deconstructive, performative approach to issues of writing, rhetoric, and gender, an approach I believe to chime with the concerns of late medieval writers representing women in the *querelle*: their awareness of their own materials as inherently intertextual with, we might say haunted by, prior texts, and their presentation of rhetorical action upon these texts as performative remakings of received material; a similar awareness on the part of early publishers of the way a given text may perform its meaning according to the bibliographical company it keeps and the illustrative programme it is accorded; a remarkable attention on the part of several writers to the art of debate itself, representing the rhetoric of *disputatio* as verbal 'doing', situating such debate in quite sophisticated juridical frameworks, and exploring the interplay between legal procedure and armed struggle as a further manifestation of rhetoric's performative force; the degrees to which certain authors can be seen to conceive of gender roles as discursive positions, open to being done and undone. This approach thus draws on the ideas of Derrida, Austin, and Butler in the theoretical arguments developed in Chapters 1, 2, and 3 respectively.

In sum, the new reading strategies I apply to the *querelle des femmes* may be expressed as three types of necessary contextualization. First, in the sense that I bring together a number of texts from the period to be studied synthetically as a group, in detail and in comparison. Secondly, stemming from this, I situate them both individually and collectively in relation to their historical conditions of composition, production, and (where discernible) reception. In terms of composition, each text has a 'time of insertion' into rhetorical and linguistic tradition, to use Sarah Kay's felicitous phrase.[17] This time of insertion is of crucial significance since, generally speaking, each work defines its position in relation to one of two threads of literary tradition: to the catalogue form stemming from Boccaccio's *De mulieribus claris*, and its French translations,[18]

---

[17] 1990: 4.   [18] I explore this derivation in Chapter 3.

or to the debate tradition which takes issue with the alleged literary misogynists Jean de Meun and Matheolus, and which thus participates in the reception history of the late medieval best seller *Le Roman de la rose*.[19] The time of rhetorical insertion also reveals the intellectual foundations of the *querelle*: its engagement with scholastic forms of *disputatio*, its creative fusion of types of rhetoric,[20] and its interactions with other contemporary discourses,[21] specifically the procedures and terminology of law.[22] This sort of cultural context also embraces the circumstances of textual presentation, namely the manuscript matrix or print series that furnishes the text with a paratextual apparatus; the insertion of marginal labels and the composition and distribution of miniatures or woodcuts provide valuable evidence of contemporary reader response and publishing strategy. The third context brought to bear, as indicated above, is that of my own, twenty-first-century critical skills, which are used to direct critical attention towards the under-explored artistic dimension of male-authored defences of women. I pursue these strategies as fruitful methods of building up some coherent picture of the poetics of the *querelle* corpus, that is, the literary and rhetorical systems they seem to work by, which potentially stimulate as much interest now as they did in fifteenth- and sixteenth-century France and Burgundy.

The temporal parameters of this study are determined by two, complementary factors, one negative and one positive. On the negative side, the dates 1440 to 1538 cover, as conceded above, the period that has suffered most from critical neglect. More positively, they span a time of flourishing literary production, of especial interest on account of the transition it charts between manuscript and print cultures; specifically, the period encloses the intersecting publication histories of Martin Le Franc's *Champion des dames* and that key source of *querelle* intertextuality, the *Roman de la rose*. This intersection receives particular focus in the second part of Chapter 1.

The nature of the texts included in this synthesis I referred to above as 'imaginative literature'. To explain what this designation entails in medieval terms, I return briefly to the false distinction identified above between female and male authorship of defences of women as

---

[19] This line of descent is my focus in Chapters 1 and 2.
[20] Mathieu-Castellani 1998: 30.
[21] Blamires 1997: 63–5. Note also that Le Franc's *Champion* has received greatest critical attention in medieval musicology: see Bent 2004.
[22] I address these issues in Chapter 2.

'sincere' and 'rhetorical' enterprises. This opposition is false to the nature of *querelle* works in two related respects. First, it misrepresents and actually underestimates the importance of rhetoric in these texts, if we consider the rhetorical ambition of writers like Le Franc,[23] whose *Champion des dames* is one of few late medieval vernacular verse fictions to rival in scope, and exceed the length of, the text it challenges, the *Roman de la rose*. Secondly, this opposition fails both to acknowledge any distinction between imaginative fiction and doctrine, and to recognize the nuanced nature of this distinction in contemporary literature. Literary contributions to the *querelle* are often perceived by its critics to be transparent, albeit sometimes ambiguous, windows onto authorial intention,[24] with a male author's 'real' opinion of women typically presumed negative.[25] It is only very recently that the literariness of literary defences has begun to be valorized as an essential aspect of *querelle* texts' meaning.[26] Central to this literariness is the way pro-feminine discourse constitutes an inherently intertextual, reflexive language focused on the art of its own composition, responding to existing representations of women, both positive and negative:

La représentation y est lisible en quelque sorte au second degré, puisque ce discours prend pour objet des discours.[27]

(This representation should in a way be read reflexively, since this discourse takes as its object other discourses.)

A second aspect of literariness concerns the deliberate artifice *querelle* writers espouse by devising fictional frameworks, notably around the *locus* of the courtroom that I explore in Chapter 2. The positive constructions of feminine gender identity that these fictions relay, such as the promotion of women exercising legal office, are intended as imaginative experiments. They thereby exploit a contemporary fascination with fiction as a space for representing possibility, for transforming a 'what if' hypothesis into an 'as if' proposition.[28] The pro-feminine writers in the corpus, whatever their personal opinion of woman's status, opt for a

---

[23] We are addressing, after all, the period and court milieux in which the *grands rhétoriqueurs* flourished in France and Burgundy; recent re-evaluation of *rhétoriqueur* poetics is provided by Armstrong 2000.

[24] Richardson 1929: 37. An important exception is Woodbridge 1984: 4–6.

[25] Kelly 1984.   [26] Armstrong 2002; Zimmermann 1999.

[27] Mathieu-Castellani 1998: 9. English translations are my own. Cf. Angenot 1977: 159.

[28] Solterer 2002: 153–5.

vehicle of imaginative literature rather than an academic treatise to stage their defence of the case for women as a response to the potency of literary representation: the capacity of fiction to change how people—here women or, conversely, writers deemed guilty of slandering women—are evaluated by refashioning the 'discours' in which they are represented.[29] Furthermore, literary representation appears to have enjoyed a particular purchase on historical reality in the fifteenth century, if we recall how the *Roman de la rose* and Alain Chartier's *Belle Dame sans mercy* are works of fiction that provoked sustained controversies, and that the debates around these texts developed in large part through the medium of fiction.[30] In this light, we might see Le Franc's fictionalization of his *Champion*'s reception in the *Complainte* as a means of playing with this interface between rhetoric and reality: the imagined spectacle of the Book's failure is devised as a spur to encourage the work's success amongst its historical audience. Given that seven further manuscript copies and two printed editions followed, this stratagem seems to have borne fruit.

These aspects of literariness—reflexivity, the potency of representation, and the nature of imaginative literature as a field for experimentation—are germane to this study's aim of furnishing possible reading strategies for opening up the poetics of the *querelle des femmes*. Their centrality to *querelle* poetics is revealed by a literary work that is usually held to be the most significant early contribution to the case for women, Christine de Pizan's *Livre de la cité des dames* (1404–5). The principal agenda of this female-authored defence has, I argue, nothing to do with any pro-feminine 'sincerity' understood to be determined by the author's sexual identity, and everything to do with her work's time of insertion into historical, literary, and linguistic tradition, and with its status as a discourse 'au second degré', to quote Mathieu-Castellani (1998:9). Christine sets out to represent and re-present a misrepresented sex, correcting relationships between women and men by correctively rewriting portraits of women transmitted by Jean de Meun, Matheolus, and Boccaccio in order to make them accord with her lived experience as a woman. Her project is effected through the medium of a literary

---

[29] By highlighting the reflexivity of pro-feminine rhetoric, I imply a definition of 'the case for women' that echoes Blamires's view that it is 'a mode of discourse which aims to build a positive representation of women in response to either specified or implicit accusations': 1997: 8–9.

[30] I address the relationship between the so-called *querelle du 'Roman de la rose'* the *querelle de 'la Belle Dame sans mercy'* and the *querelle des femmes* in Chapter 2.

fiction; we recall here that her first step in challenging Jean de Meun was to rebut him, not in a treatise or epistle, as she would proceed to do in the *'Rose' querelle* proper, but through the fictional form of her *Epistre au dieu d'amours* (1399). Moreover, in the opening passage of the *Cité*,[31] the aim of Christine's narrator's now-famous conversation with Dame Raison is, I argue, to equip her with strategies of reading that will enable her to assert herself as an informed, autonomous reader. For example, Raison advises her to make use of 'a grammatical figure known as *antifrasis*';[32] by tactically and systematically taking misogynist writers' words to mean the opposite of what they say, she is hermeneutically empowered to reclaim their arguments for her own cause:

> Si te conseille que tu faces ton prouffit de leurs dis et que l'entendes ainsi, quelque fut leur entente es lieux ou ilz blasment des femmes.[33]
>
> (So I recommend that you turn their writings to your advantage in those places where they defame women, and interpret them thus [= antiphrastically], whatever the writers' intentions.)

Her narrator functions as a diegetic echo of extradiegetic Christine's facility and subtlety in reading and reappropriating the often ambivalent *vitae* of Boccaccio's *De mulieribus claris* which form the foundations of her city/*Cité*.

The focus of this book is, therefore, imaginative literature, a focus which, as I have hinted above, allows critical attention to be directed primarily at the form in which arguments are represented rather than at the content of the arguments themselves. Recent scholars are quite correct to assert that the arguments advanced in support of woman change little in the period, but are wrong to infer from this that the aesthetic dimension of these works' rhetorical structure fails to merit attention, concluding that 'il est inutile de s'appesantir sur l'aspect rhétorique de la *querelle*'.[34] I argue on the contrary that the manner of the material's presentation is, in fact, what is principally at stake in the *querelle*, and in a way that actually binds together form and content in a sophisticated relationship.[35] This bond is forged principally through the

---

[31] Christine de Pizan 1997: 46–50.
[32] Ibid.: 48. English translations are my own.   [33] Ibid.
[34] 'There is no point in dwelling on the rhetorical aspect of the *querelle*': Albistur and Armogathe 1977: 114. English translations are my own. See also McLeod 1991: 139, but cf. Blamires 1997.
[35] Cf. Cerquiglini-Toulet 1993a; Angenot 1977: 152. We may relate this privileging of manner above matter to late medieval developments in rhetorical theory. Thanks, at

act of rewriting—and thus also recontextualizing—literary inheritance; itself motivated by an act of reading, this rewriting performed by medieval authors thus goes hand in hand with my study's central theme of reading and can be seen, perhaps, as the (re-)creative complement to the strategies of textual reception I offer the interpreting modern reader.

In this light, I structure my study around literary form rather than content as the more fruitful means of approaching *querelle* poetics and of bringing together texts to entertain relations with each other that approximate the relations they may have enjoyed in their contemporary context of production. This structure offers the opportunity for appreciating their differences and for comparing nuanced treatments of the same characters and/or arguments. At the same time, it enables some sort of collective, synthesizing perspective to evolve, and thereby overcomes the difficulty, identified by several critics, of approaching these texts in terms of shared formal characteristics.[36] As stated above, no comprehensive catalogue of fifteenth- and early sixteenth-century *querelle* texts has yet been compiled. This is, I believe, due not only to the limited accessibility of the corpus,[37] but also to the difficulty of finding a methodology to introduce some order into this array of often undated and/or anonymous works. Attempts hitherto have often been inadequate: they decline to impose any structural or thematic order,[38] or try to organize chronologically or by content,[39] or, in the case of Albistur and Armogathe, adopt a means of division referring partly to form and partly to content. Albistur and Armogathe arrange texts into three groups: 'polemical writings', 'doctrinaire and didactic writings', and 'literary sources';[40] this grouping entails a further (false) distinction between a 'serious side' and a 'ludic side', with all

least in part, to the arts of versification spawned by the *Seconde Rhétorique*, late medieval rhetoric focused on *dispositio*, *elocutio*, and *actio* rather than *inventio*, the presentation of a given matter rather than the 'finding' of the matter itself: Murphy 2001: pp. xv–xxi; Meyer 1999: 91–2.

[36] Lazard 1985: 12; Maclean 1977: 26.

[37] This is improving: since 1999 scholarly editions have appeared of *CD*, *VDA*, and *JP*, to supplement the *Vies* (1970) and *PHF* (1978). *GD*, *MFJ*, *NDV*, *PND*, *PFP*, and *RD* are now accessible via Gallica, the digitized, on-line text resource of the BnF. Scholarly editions of *NDV* and *PND* are forthcoming in 2007 with Champion.

[38] See Kelso's alphabetically ordered list of 891 sixteenth-century texts on the subject of women: 1956.

[39] Piaget 1993; Angenot 1977; Richardson 1929. A chronological list for the period (see Appendix 1A) must also take into account the appearance of manuscript works in print and the re-edition of certain imprints in the sixteenth century (see Appendix 1B).

[40] 1977: 81–3. In this, they follow Guillerm-Curutchet et al. 1971.

literary texts seemingly consigned to the latter category.[41] As one might expect from my discussion of the complex understanding of imaginative literature in the period, Albistur's and Armogathe's classification system gives rise to strange anomalies which expose its limitations. Most strikingly, perhaps, whilst two works that present themselves with deliberate artifice as literary fictions, Jean Bouchet's *Jugement poetic de l'honneur femenin* (1538) and the anonymous *Chevalier des dames du Dolent fortuné* (before 1477),[42] are deemed 'polemical', a vernacular translation of Boccaccio's *De mulieribus* is adjudged 'literary', but a contemporary reworking of the same work is classified as 'polemical'.[43] It rapidly becomes clear that a shifting confluence of considerations—content, form, intention, and context—is provoking this confusion, which devalues the usefulness of this system for imposing order upon *querelle* texts.

Working solely with literary texts, my own system for grouping these texts rests on form, addressing the debate, *jugement*, and catalogue in turn, whilst acknowledging some inevitable overlap between these basic structures: for example, they often share narrative and rhetorical features in the ways that they are fleshed out by fictional frameworks involving dreams, personification allegories, and/or narrative journeys. This division between forms concerns equally the principal hermeneutic issues that each form raises: questions of intertextuality, linguistic performance, and the construction/constructedness of gender identity. I pause here briefly to insert a parenthesis explaining my chosen term for denoting the case for women: the 'pro-feminine' cause. This choice is made in light of recent critical debate regarding the preferred core, '-feminist' or '-feminine', and its corresponding prefix, 'proto-' or 'pro-', by Armstrong, Aughterson, Blamires, and Lazard. Seeking to avoid anachronism, I follow Blamires's logic that 'pre-modern texts which develop constructions of "woman" which are positive according to the cultural ideology of their period ought logically to be called not "profeminist" but *profeminine*'.[44] However, I wish also to acknowledge as informing influences on the way I use my chosen term important

[41] Albistur and Armogathe 1977: 81. See also Abensour 1979: 9.

[42] See Armstrong 1999; Taylor 1999.

[43] I address both the translation in question, *Le Livre de Jehan Bocasse de la louange et vertu des cleres et nobles dames* (1493), and the reworking, Foresti's *De plurimis claris selectisque mulieribus* (1497), in Chapter 3.

[44] 1997: 11–12. Similarly, therefore, I refer to 'misogynistic' or 'anti-feminine/-woman', and not 'anti-feminist', writings. Cf. Lazard 1985: 7.

points raised by Armstrong and Aughterson, who prefer the core '-feminist'. Arguing for the aptness of 'proto-feminist', Aughterson reasons that

we may find voices, arguments, strategies, and accounts of the gendered construction of power which are recognizable as essential to later feminist positions [. . .] even when fragmentary [. . .] or used by male authors; they provide readers with female voices and models of argumentation, when they are used by later women in their own right.[45]

The methodological implication of her argument, that these 'strategies' may yet be susceptible to analysis in terms of modern theories of gender representation, brings us to address the broader question of the theoretical lenses through which I have chosen to read *querelle* poetics within this book.

Running through this book's principal concerns of gender, writing, and performance, one may perceive a common thread of performativity. My approach to *querelle* poetics through complementary theories of performativity will enable us to conceive and formulate in new ways our appreciation of what is at stake in this domain of late medieval literature. Each chapter introduces a different, yet related, theoretical concept in order to tackle a different aspect of *querelle* poetics: its particularly fomenting intertextuality, broached in Chapter 1 through a literary appropriation of Jacques Derrida's 'spectropolitics', which conceives of troubling intertextual relations as processes of 'haunting'; the dynamics of the *querelle*'s presentation in debate form, illuminated in Chapter 2 by Austinian linguistic performativity, which was itself a significant influence on Derrida's ideas of performance; the constructedness of women's gender identity present in catalogues of ladies, explored in Chapter 3 through the lens of Judith Butler's work on gender performativity. Butler's reflections on the slippery relationship between an individual identity and its prior models, how it repeats but may also be different from them in an empowering way, are themselves informed by both Austin and Derrida. In each case, my recourse to modern critical models is driven by a twofold aim. First, acting in response to particular puzzles thrown up by the texts' formal features, such as a particular insistence upon resurrecting Jean de Meun to stand trial for his alleged crime of slander in the *jugement* fictions of Chapter 2, I enlist these models to provide methodological 'in-roads' to help undo these fascinating

---

[45] 1995: 261. See Armstrong's view in Bouchet 2006: 31–2. Cf. Benson 1992: 2.

knots and locate individual textual analyses in some sort of conceptual framework. Secondly, I engage with theory as a way of encouraging modern scholarship both to look afresh at *querelle* works and to explore their textuality (and visuality, in the case of illustrated copies) in greater detail than hitherto. The nexus of ideas of performativity that broadly unifies the theoretical models enlisted here allows us to advance at least one provisional conclusion about this period of *querelle* imaginative literature. Such a conclusion relates to the literary self-consciousness of *querelle* writers. The reflexivity inherent in their concerns with the rewriting of existing texts, and specifically the rewriting of gender identities, is complemented by an acute awareness of the contingencies of their literary activity outside the text: its interaction with political and cultural actuality, as well as their personal status as a writer. Each author appears aware of a dual status characterizing his literary performance: it is a merely transient event in the course of a discourse's development, but is also a vital moment for speaking out, reinterpreting, and carving his niche in the history of the *querelle des femmes*.

The concerns pursued through ideas of performativity, centred on writing, gender, and performance, develop through three chapters. Chapter 1 introduces perhaps the most radical of the three theoretical frameworks of performativity that this study engages. Starting from a deconstructionist understanding of performance, it explores the innovative intertextual dimension of the *querelle* tradition: how these works consciously respond to one another in a debate between texts. It shows how successive manifestations of an established *querelle* character, such as Dido or Malebouche, may usefully be seen as performances in the ways they creatively remake their literary predecessors. These performances, it would seem, respond to analysis in terms of a new critical model more fruitfully than to existing discourses of intertextuality, influence, or appropriation. The model I propose is one of 'spectropoetics', my own appropriation for literary criticism of Jacques Derrida's hermeneutic discourse of 'spectropolitics', expounded in his *Spectres de Marx*. This is introduced through an initial analysis of how, in Jean Bouchet's innovative presentation of Dido through a first-person epitaph, Dido's rhetoric appears troubled by and yet dependent upon, we might say 'haunted' by, her literary ancestor, Virgil's *infelix Dido*. This idea is extrapolated through several debate poems to develop a theory of interpersonal intertextuality in terms of 'spectropoetics': pro-feminine authors portray themselves and their writings as being 'haunted' by the misogynistic writers they strive to refute, specifically the spectre of the most influential and (allegedly) misogynistic of authorities, Jean de Meun's *Roman de la rose*. This haunting effect is studied in both text and paratext (marginal labels and miniatures/woodcuts) in several manuscript and printed editions of Martin Le Franc's *Champion des dames*.

As a complement to the previous chapter's intertextual focus, Chapter 2 looks at performance on an intratextual level and in a linguistic and dramatic context regarding the verbal 'doings' of *querelle* judgement debates (*jugements*) by Le Franc, Pierre Michault, and Jacques Milet. Aiming to reactivate critical interest in verse debate, which has often been perceived as a tired and dull convention, its first main section falls into two halves, proposing the twofold nature of debate rhetoric as performance. First, I investigate the performative force of language, what speech-act theorists call its 'illocutionary force', which I see harnessed in *querelle* writers' representation of the potency of the spoken word. Secondly, I consider the way disputations are staged in both text and image in certain *querelle* manuscripts as dramatic exchanges; in the case of the *Champion des dames*, we find close attention in the text to aspects of voice, gesture, and audience reaction; in the miniatures of several codices, the dispute's verbal dynamism and acoustic liveliness find their visual equivalent in theatricalized images of animated debate. The second section of Chapter 2 examines how one particular theatre of debate (or field of battle), the fictionalized courtroom and its procedures, is turned creatively to account in Le Franc's, Michault's, and Milet's *jugements*. The imaginary courtroom is used strikingly by pro-feminine advocates to put on trial a 'resurrected' Jean de Meun or Matheolus for their alleged crimes of misogynistic writing. At the nub of debate is the writer's authorial intention as a sort of *mens rea*, hence the focus of these courtroom fictions on prosecuting the person of the *Rose*-continuator as a resurrected personality, and not simply his text. I consider how the *querelle des femmes* appears to appropriate for its own literary invention aspects of the use of forensic oratory in imaginative literature that were already a valuable currency in contemporary literary debates, namely the *querelle du 'Roman de la rose'* and the *querelle de 'la Belle Dame sans mercy'* Both these debates, addressing the authorial intention of Jean de Meun and Alain Chartier respectively, feed into the *querelle des femmes*, and are often deliberately invoked by pro-feminine writers.

Chapter 3 introduces to the previous chapters' focus on writing and rhetoric as performance the sort of performativity associated with the representation—the doing and undoing[46]—of gender identity. It demonstrates how male *querelle* writers necessarily possessed a keen gender consciousness, discernible not least from the ways they dedicate their work to female patrons. I concentrate on two central issues of representation that may fruitfully be discussed as types of 'transvestism' in order to uncover certain writers' awareness of the constructedness of gender roles—the roles of the women they praise, as well as their own discursive positions as implied male speakers. The first issue concerns the implications of a male author defending woman's cause by ventriloquizing her voice; the second explores how he constructs her identity—her status as a woman worthy of honour—through a particular vocabulary of gender behaviour, regarding the 'wearing' of masculine or feminine external or internal characteristics, from cross-dressing clothes to putting on a man's or a woman's heart. This exploration occurs through comparative analysis of the use of collocative phrases (such as 'cueur d'homme') and of the connotations implied by gendered adjectives ('masculin'/'féminin') in the representation of selected women by *querelle* writers compiling catalogues of women after the seminal example of Boccaccio's *De mulieribus claris*: Christine de Pizan, Antoine Dufour (*Les Vies des femmes célèbres* (1504)), and Jean Bouchet (*Le Jugement poetic de l'honneur femenin*). I focus on women whose virtue derives from their fulfilment of an active role, such as the warrior queen Fredegonde, which might be expected to assimilate them automatically to a masculine ideal of conduct, taking on man's attire, heart, and/or mind. Engaging with Judith Butler's reflections on how a woman must negotiate a position for ('perform') her identity in relation to established models, I show how different authors problematize *querelle* women's gender identity as regards the extent to which they handle critically or challenge the 'feminine'- and/or 'masculine'-encoded characteristics they deploy. I consider how both inherited literary traditions of representing active women as well as extratextual factors, especially the character of a desired female patron, may be seen to inform these writers' linguistic choices in their representations of active women.

My conclusion brings together several threads. It considers the usefulness to a modern audience of the approaches to *querelle* texts proposed by the preceding chapters. It addresses first the dividing up of texts on the

---

[46] The allusion is to the title of Butler's most recent work on gender performativity, *Undoing Gender* (2004).

basis of formal characteristics as a means of focusing attention on artistic structure. Such an approach enables the modern reader to recognize, and engage in lively fashion with, what is principally at stake in literary defences of women, namely the sophisticated manner in which their matter is manipulated. Evidence of manuscript and printed production indicates that this ante was shared by contemporary audiences, and is represented, for example, in miniaturists' responses to the text they illustrate. The second aspect of 'approach' concerns the specific ideas of performativity I have associated with different forms: the gesture of intertextual reinterpretation for debate poems composed in the tradition of the *Roman de la rose*; the linguistic, even theatrical, performances of debates, especially *jugements*; and the discursive constructedness of identity relative to both the women represented in *querelle* catalogues and the authorial and narrative positions of the implied male writer. I conclude by offering a reading of a little-known but ingenious text, *Le Rousier des dames* (*c*.1510), to demonstrate how the hermeneutic tools offered by the foregoing chapters have provided a necessary and valuable initiation into new, more fruitful ways of reading male-authored defences of women in the *querelle des femmes*.

1

Haunting Text and Paratext: Performing Intertextuality in *Querelle* Debates

Tu mes Bel Accueil a l'escole
D'une Viellasse rassotee
Qui le gaste, pert et affole.
[. . .]
Il m'est advis quant je l'escoute
Que ce soit une maquerelle,
Laquelle a ung genoul s'acoute
Assise au feu sur une selle.
Et presche une jone pucelle
Et si lui dit: 'Mon enfant tendre,
Car je vous voy plaisant et belle,
Il vous fault ung petit aprendre!
(*CD*, vv. 14393–5, 14401–8)

(You entrust Fair Welcome to the tutelage of a drivelling Old Crone who leads him to ruin, dishonour, and debauchery. [. . .] It seems to me, when I listen, that there's an old pimp kneeling on a bench by the fireside. She is preaching to a young girl, saying: 'My sweet child, as you look so kind and pretty, there's a fair amount you need to learn!)[1]

The *Champion des dames* is a debate poem in five books by the Provost of Lausanne and secretary to Amadeus VIII of Savoy, Martin Le Franc.[2] The poem presents a series of exchanges between the ultimately

---

[1] English translations of the *Champion* are my own.

[2] For further biographical details, see Piaget 1993. For the textual tradition of the poem, see my Appendix 2A. No other verse narrative by Le Franc survives (except the *Complainte*: see Introduction, p. 1), although he did write a highly successful prosimetrum, a Boethian-inspired debate, *L'Estrif de Fortune et de Vertu* (1447–8),

triumphant pro-feminine Champion, Franc Vouloir, and five adversaries representing the Champion's arch-enemy, Malebouche. Towards the end of his debate with Trop Cuidier, at the close of Book III, the Champion takes issue both directly and indirectly with the totemic figure of late medieval literary misogyny, Jean de Meun, the late thirteenth-century continuator of Guillaume de Lorris's *Roman de la rose*. As a direct attack, countering his adversary's too-ready belief ('trop cuidier') in the unimpeachable authority of 'irreproachable Meun' (v. 13542), Franc Vouloir rebukes the author in person: he criticizes the way he uses the character of La Vieille to corrupt the innocence of young Bel Accueil by instructing the neophyte to cast wide the net of her 'franchise' (v. 14440)[3] and use her feminine charms to exploit men while she can. The Champion's *in*direct assault upon La Vieille's teachings, which he reproves for perpetuating the misogynistic stereotype of woman's voracious sexuality, operates through a performative reading of Jean de Meun's text: the Champion relays the scene that his own reading experience of the *Rose* conjures up in his imagination ('Il m'est advis . . .'), and the act of relaying replays to his inscribed audience[4] his interpretative restaging of that scene.

The synaesthetic layering of this whole performance is quite complex. His act of reading consists in hearing the diegetic voice of Jean de Meun's ventriloquized feminine speaker ('quand je l'escoute'), whose speech triggers a visual image of the old woman's physical situation, in which the listener to her speech is fourfold: Bel Accueil, within the *Rose*'s diegesis; Franc Vouloir, as extradiegetic commentator on her words; Franc Vouloir's diegetic audience in the *Champion* who hear his ventriloquistic appropriation of La Vieille's voice; and the extradiegetic audience of the *Champion*, who hear or read how Le Franc rewrites his model through a creative rereading of two of its characters. The Champion's reinterpretative action upon the *Rose* is discernible in two respects. First, he chooses to read Bel Accueil as female—as an extension of the rose-maiden—despite the masculinity presupposed

---

which survives in thirty manuscripts; both the *Champion* and *Estrif* are dedicated to Philip the Good.

[3] In La Vieille's terms, *franchise* signifies a woman's right to 'choose freely' a lover: *RR*, vv. 13879–970.

[4] As a helpful means of differentiating between the different audiences involved in textual reception, those internal and those external to the diegesis, I use throughout this book the useful, ad hoc taxonomy of audience types devised by Strohm 1983. The fictional auditors imagined here are the witnesses to the Champion's debate with Trop Cuidier, namely Malebouche's cohort in the College of Envy.

by the grammatical gender of the character's personified identity; he maintains this interpretation at the same time as citing La Vieille's term of address to a male Bel Accueil: 'My dear sweet son' (*CD*, v. 14433).[5] Secondly, the Champion re-ventriloquizes La Vieille, recasting her speech in terms that cut to the chase of her doctrine of self-prostitution. He uses a transparent sexual metaphor to highlight the vulgarity of her celebration of the mercantile 'prouffit' to be gained from sexual congress:

> Laissez maint homme sejourner
> Devant vostre huis . . .
>
> (vv. 14429–30)[6]

(Let any man who wishes stay awhile at your doorway . . .)

The performance constituted by the Champion's imaginative encounter with the *Rose* is played out on three levels: his envisioned restaging of the episode, his own interpretative rereading of that scene, and the response of his diegetic and extradiegetic audiences as they appreciate his creative glossing of the *Champion*'s key model, Jean de Meun's *Rose*. It thus stands as a performance in both deconstructionist and dramatic senses of the term: troubling the relationship between the original text and its derivative (here through an act of interpretative recasting), as well as presenting this disruption as an act to be experienced and applauded by an audience.[7]

This chapter takes a performative approach to rereading the allegedly static, monotonous nature of *querelle* debate poems, like the *Champion*, in their repeated recourse to the same cast of characters: the same personified debaters, examples of famous women, and despised misogynistic writers. Although new to *querelle* scholarship, this approach may be seen to find resonance with evidence of the works' contemporary reception; it may thus help recover for a modern readership the enjoyment of these texts that was experienced by late medieval audiences. The notion of performance enlisted here may be divided between two axes: the inter*text*ual and the intra*text*ual, corresponding, for present purposes, to the distinction between deconstructionist, and linguistic and dramatic understandings of performance. Chapter 2 will take up the intratextual axis. It will explore how the texts and miniatures of certain debate poems in the *querelle* corpus express a performative, pragmatic force of forensic

---

[5] *RR*, v. 13502.   [6] Cf. *RR*, vv. 12838–40.
[7] I address this distinction below. See also Parker and Sedgwick 1995: 1–18.

rhetoric and adumbrate an almost theatrical dimension of performance in their presentation of the diegetic *agôn* as a dramatic contest.

The current chapter falls into two interlinked parts, exploring the intertextual axis operative in both text and paratext. The first part's focus on textual activity shows how successive manifestations of an established *querelle* character—whether a personification allegory, such as Malebouche, or a legendary woman, like Dido—may usefully be seen as 'performances' in the manner in which they creatively refresh and dynamically re-present their literary inheritance. This textual analysis will be prefaced with a brief consideration of the *querelle*'s omission from recent studies of medieval intertextuality, which will suggest that it is to the medieval texts themselves that we should look for testimony that creative textual recycling was at the fore of *querelle* writers' concerns. In this light, I shall analyse the innovative way the Poitevin writer and jurist Jean Bouchet (arguably better known today as a chronicler)[8] presents women's posthumous perspectives on their own lives in first-person epitaphs decorating a 'palace made for illustrious ladies' (*JP*, v. 1268) in his narrative poem, *Le Jugement poetic de l'honneur femenin* (1538).[9] I take the example of Dido, who appears troubled by, and yet dependent upon—we might say 'haunted' by—her Virgilian literary ancestry. By tracing rhetoric describing intertextual activity through several *querelle* contributions, it will be possible to extrapolate the metaphor of haunting to develop a theory of interpersonal intertextuality in terms of spectrality: pro-feminine authors seem to portray themselves and their writings as 'haunted' by the ghosts of misogynistic literature in the way that they seek both to conjure up and reject the spectres of Jean de Meun and of his *Rose* through acts of what I shall call 'performative interpretation'.[10] In the second part, I apply this haunting effect to the bibliographical dimension of *querelle* works' production, turning from a critical reading of texts to an examination of evidence of their contemporary reception provided by the paratext (marginal notes and illustrations) of various manuscripts and printed editions of the *Champion des dames*. Taking the chapter as a whole, its composite evidence of text and paratext will show how contemporary audiences practised a sophisticated 'reading for the intertext', to use Sylvia Huot's phrase,[11] as an essential element of their hermeneutic engagement with *querelle* works.

---

[8] See Britnell 1986.   [9] English translations are my own.
[10] I borrow the phrase from Derrida, as I explain in detail below, p. 35.
[11] 1993b: 199.

PERFORMING INTERTEXTUALITY:
THE DYNAMICS OF REWRITING

Le Franc's *mise en abyme* of contemporary *Rose* reception that I explored in detail above serves as a useful introduction to the concept of performative interpretation in relation to the particular intertextuality that underpins this chapter.[12] The act of performance lies with both the *querelle* writer, as audience of the antecedent text, and his reader, as audience of the interplay between *querelle* text and antecedent. Franc Vouloir's textual expertise in interpretatively recasting his reading of La Vieille thus triggers the *Champion*'s audience's intertextual competence to deduce in what meaningful way the Champion is engaging with the *Rose*. The way he reworks La Vieille's speech to communicate his condemnation of Jean de Meun's voice through the personification's discourse may usefully be seen to constitute what one performance theorist, Elin Diamond, calls a 'resistant performance'.[13] Diamond builds on the essential iterability of performance, the way that any performance must consist in a repetition of a previous performance in order for it to be comprehensible in terms of existing sign systems.[14] She insists on the possibility of innovative agency that inheres in every new performance, and can be exploited as a force of resistance:

While a performance embeds traces of other performances, it also produces experiences whose interpretation only partially depends on previous experience. This creates the terminology of 're' in discussions of performance, as in

---

[12] I use 'intertextuality' in the sense established by Riffaterre's (1990) development of Kristeva's founding concept of the transformative relationship between any sign system and a later sign system. Riffaterre's intertextuality foregrounds the agencies of transformation, emphasizing the interpretative, potentially creative interaction between two texts that is performed by both writer and reader. I address Kristeva below, pp. 25–6, 36–8.

[13] 1996: 4.

[14] The essential iterability of performance was introduced to the study of (specifically linguistic) performance by Derrida (1982). In his revision of J. L. Austin's founding concept of performative speech, Derrida identifies how an utterance's capacity to signify depends upon its 'general iterability', its impurity, as it were, as a performance that treads the ground between repetition and alterity. He thereby valorizes what Austin dismissed as the 'etiolations' of language (1975: 22), the 'pastness' of performance, that he and also John R. Searle (1969) excluded from performativity. In the specific context of gender performativity (for which, see Chapter 3), Judith Butler advances the same founding premiss, that the performance of gender is historical, 'open to a continual remaking' (2004: 3, 9–10).

*re*embody, *re*inscribe, *re*configure, *re*signify. 'Re' acknowledges the pre-existing discursive field, the repetition—and the desire to repeat—within the performative present, while 'embody', 'configure', 'inscribe', 'signify' assert the possibility of materializing something that exceeds our knowledge, that alters the shape of sites and imagines other as yet unsuspected modes of being.[15]

In the specific case of the textual performance that I propose to be constituted by the Champion's reworking of La Vieille, 'resistant performance' denotes the friction generated between the *querelle* text and its antecedent that is a source of hermeneutic excitement for the *Champion*'s audience. Franc Vouloir's creative reiteration of the pre-existing *Rose* episode can be seen to occur as a dynamic textual performance across a 'contested space'[16] of literary conflict with the prior work. Le Franc effectively calls upon his audience's intertextual competence to 'exceed' the *Rose* episode, challenging them to reorient their attitude to the *Rose* through his hermeneutic action upon La Vieille.

Diamond's reflections on resistant performance offer an appropriate light in which to reconsider the especially dynamic nature of *querelle* intertextualities, which have remained unrecognized in recent scholarship on late medieval poetics. First, in the specific domain of literary defences of women, we recall the charges of monotony frequently levelled against successive *querelle* works' repetition of the same material. I reject such summary dismissals of *querelle* writers' treatment of their material, and focus specifically in this chapter on the innovative intertextualities involved in Bouchet's rewriting of exemplary women, and on certain writers'—particularly Martin Le Franc's—dynamic engagement with the arch-misogynist, Jean de Meun. Secondly, although much critical energy has been invested in re-evaluating the sophisticated poetics of late medieval and early modern intertextualities, notably in studies of literary rhetoric and textual reception,[17] the *querelle*'s peculiar fecundity has not been broached.

Recent recognition that a dynamic reading process is appropriate, not to say necessary, to a full appreciation of this period's intertextuality has focused predominantly on the poetics of the *Rose* and *Rose* reception.[18] Very recently, it has been absorbed by scholarship on the *querelle de 'la Belle Dame sans mercy'*,[19] but it has not yet been integrated into a reading

---

[15] Diamond 1996: 2.   [16] Ibid. 4.   [17] Such as Copeland 1995.
[18] See Taylor 2003; Huot 1993a.   [19] See Cayley 2006: chapter 4, part I.

of the *querelle des femmes*.[20] This latter literary debate is fuelled both by contemporary reworkings and discussion of the *Rose*—notably the famous *querelle du 'Roman de la rose'*—and by literary offshoots of the controversy sparked by Alain Chartier's polemical *Belle Dame*.[21] Arguing from a critical perspective and from the imbricated manuscript tradition of the *Belle Dame* cycle, Jane Taylor and Emma Cayley have highlighted the poetic of engagement exemplified by this succession of poems, whose writers manifest 'textual precision and intellectual investment'[22] in the detailed, intertextual conversations they maintain with Chartier's original and with each other. It is this sort of dynamic that is at work in the *querelle* corpus, and is discernible through modern reading strategies that privilege the performative aspect of a reader/writer's hermeneutic engagement with a prior text. My discussion of *querelle* texts' contestatory reworkings of the *Rose* will build on the literary and bibliographical scholarship discussed above, and will highlight the significant concurrence in date between the appearance in print of certain works in this study's corpus and the early printing history of the *Rose*, of which some twenty-one editions appeared between 1481 and 1538.[23] The intertextual poetic proposed here will be shown to operate throughout the period delineated by this study; indeed, it is the writers at the two extremities, Le Franc and Bouchet, who appear most strikingly to thematize their approaches to creative intertextuality within their poems' diegeses. Having discussed Le Franc's treatment of this subject at the opening of this chapter, I now discuss briefly Bouchet's thematization of intertextual artistry to preface my analysis of the *Jugement*'s epitaphs.

In the *Jugement poetic de l'honneur femenin et sejour des illustres, claires et honnestes dames*, to give the work its full title, a first-person narrator, Le Traverseur,[24] undertakes a fictional journey to the Underworld where the merits of the late Louise of Savoy (the deceased mother of Bouchet's patron, François I) are assessed by three infernal judges who determine

---

[20] Exceptions to this rule address either Christine de Pizan's revision of Boccaccio in her *Cité des dames* (see Chapter 3, n. 80), or Jean Le Fèvre's response to the *Rose* in his *Lamentations de Matheolus* and *Livre de leesce*, such as Pratt 1999. I discuss Le Fèvre in Chapter 2.

[21] It is not the purpose of the present study to trace how this 'fuelling' evolved, although I address the influence of both earlier *querelles* in Chapter 2.

[22] Taylor 2001: 10.   [23] Hult 1997a.

[24] This is the pseudonym habitually adopted by Bouchet throughout his *œuvre*: Britnell 1986: 3. There is only one extant edition of the *Jugement* (Poitiers: De Marnef, 1538), which has received an excellent critical edition by Armstrong: Bouchet 2006.

whether she deserves a place in the 'palais des cleres dames', the 'sejour' to which the work's title alludes, which already houses the first-person epitaphs of 126 Hebrew, pagan, and Christian women from Eve to Margaret of Austria; naturally, she is deemed sufficiently worthy of honour. The narrator turns scribe and copies down as many of these epitaphs as possible before leaving the palace. Bouchet uses the activity of his diegetic persona to highlight his authorial method of compilation in structuring his *vitae* of illustrious women. At the *Jugement*'s conclusion, the Traverseur is seen sifting through an anthology of epitaphs written in praise of Louise of Savoy by various authors, and 'assembled all together' in 'a very fine little book' (*JP*, vv. 3751, 3737).[25] There is one significant difference between the Traverseur's and Bouchet's materials, however: whilst his narrator is juggling only positive portraits of Louise, Bouchet frequently has to contend with both positive and negative images for some of his women speakers. In the case of these ambivalent women, he points up the particular, conflictual strands of textual legacy from which their *vitae* have been woven through the way these women perform their identity in their epitaph.

Bouchet's promotion of himself as an adept juggler of inherited narratives is especially apparent in the cases of three ambivalent women: Dido, Mantho, and Medusa—women whom Bouchet presents in a positive light, but whose intertextual histories are ambiguous, with each woman being susceptible to appropriation as an example both of virtue and of vice.[26] In the *Jugement*, their self-representations are contrived in such a way as to show each woman to be haunted by the spectre of their negative, vice-laden image. The rhetorical patterns of their epitaphs all reveal what I shall call 'intertextual pressure points', that is, points in their self-presentation which seem to the informed *querelle* reader, who is acquainted with different versions of each woman's legend, to be rhetorically 'charged', as if the speaker were suffering as it were the anxiety of her own influence.[27] The pressure is 'intertextual', to refer back to Kristeva's formulation, in that it derives from an unidentified

---

[25] For a suggested identification of this 'petit livre', see Bouchet 2006: 415 n. 531.

[26] For the literary sources of these *vitae*, see Bouchet 2006: 445–7, 441–2. For reasons of space, I deal uniquely with Dido here. For discussion of Dido's epitaph in the context of the *Jugement*'s narrative framework, see Swift 2008.

[27] The function of these 'pressure points' is identical to the phenomenon Riffaterre defines as 'agrammaticalités' (1981), namely textual incongruities that signal the latent, implicit presence of an intertext and demand that the current text be read in dialogue with this antecedent. I introduce the term 'pressure point' to denote a particular type of incongruity translating both the diegetic speaker's anxious attempt to suppress this

prior text that might best be understood, not as a specific textual legacy, but as one possible element in a 'multiple textual space' that constitutes the context in which the epitaph—the 'signifié poétique' in question—should be read:

> Il se crée, ainsi, autour du signifié poétique, un espace textuel multiple dont les éléments sont susceptibles d'être appliqués dans le texte poétique concret. Nous appellerons cet espace *intertextuel*. Pris dans l'intertextualité, l'énoncé poétique est un sous-ensemble d'un ensemble plus grand qui est l'espace des textes appliqués dans notre ensemble. (*S* 194)[28]

(Thus, around the poetic signified, a multiple textual space is created whose constituent elements may be applied in the concrete poetic text. We shall call this space *intertextual*. Read intertextually, the poetic utterance is a sub-group of a larger group that is the space of those texts applied in our group.)

Each epitaph thus holds in tension a range of possible versions of each woman. It thereby engages the reader in what Kristeva calls a *paragrammatic* reading process, identifying how the current text situates itself in relation to other, prior possibilities occupying the same textual space (*S* 194–6).[29]

As we shall see in the example of Dido, such a relationship of anonymous textual interrelation does not preclude the use conjointly of specific quotation. Dido opens her performance by textualizing herself and providing her own gloss on her life: 'Des vefves suys la doctrine et l'exemple.'[30] By moralizing her own history, echoing the way catalogue compilers such as Boccaccio use her *vita* as an *exemplum* of 'unsullied widowhood',[31] she seems to adopt a detached, globalizing viewpoint on

---

antecedent's influence and the extradiegetic author's desire to promote his audience's awareness of this thwarted attempt.

[28] English translations are my own. The anonymity involved in Kristeva's model is very appropriate in the context of Bouchet's first-person speakers, who do not identify their textual sources.

[29] Cf. Riffaterre's belief that, when intertextuality occurs through substitution of one term for another, 'the item substituted for remains *praesens in absentia* in the intertext': 1990: 75.

[30] 'Amongst widows I am/follow the model and the example': *JP*, v. 1900. The meaning of *suys* is interestingly ambiguous: interpretable as the first-person present indicative of either *estre* or *suivre*, it disrupts from the epitaph's outset the relationship between Dido and her antecedents: which sets the precedent, which is the derivative, and where does authority lie?

[31] Her opening line echoes Boccaccio: 'O viduitatis infracte venerandum eternumque specimen, Dido!' ('O Dido, venerable and eternal model of unsullied widowhood') (2001: 174, 175). As Jordan notes, Boccaccio follows Petrarch rather than Virgil and Dante in his portrait of the widowed queen: 1987: 35.

herself that is facilitated by the posthumous perspective of Bouchet's epitaph form. Her viewpoint thus entails a special twist, which we could call, in narratological terms, a sort of reflexive metalepsis: Bouchet's Dido's knowledge extends beyond her own lifespan into her literary legacy. She introduces into the story of her life's actions the knowledge of another level of activity, namely the evolution of her reputation after her death, and this increased scope of knowledge implies that a shift in narrative level should have occurred.[32]

Having taken the long view on herself as an *exemplum*, Dido proceeds to recount chronologically the narrative of her *vita* until she reaches her arrival in Carthage:

> Riche mourut de plus d'un million,
> Dont feiz bastir la cité de Carthage:
> Je voulu vivre en honneste vefvage
> Me contentant du premier chaste lict,
> Et par autant que par force et oultrage
> Ung Roy voullut m'avoir en mariage
> Me mys à mort pour fuÿr ce delict.
>
> (*JP*, vv. 1905–11)

(He [= Sychaeus] died wealthy, possessing more than a million that I used to build the city of Carthage. I wanted to live in honourable widowhood, contenting myself with the first, chaste bed; and because a king wanted to take me in marriage by violent force, I killed myself to escape this offence.)

A notable shift occurs in her rhetorical manner of self-presentation: whereas no first-person pronouns appear before v. 1905, after this point, in the account of her life in Carthage, they feature prominently and with anaphoric emphasis, starting with a pronounced expression of will (v. 1907), followed by a line-initial reflexive pronoun (v. 1908), and concluding in the deferred principal verb that relates her suicide (v. 1911). Within the economy of the epitaph, this rhetorical insistence upon the first person might be read simply as Dido's attempt at self-preservation through the inscription of her self-image, like any other woman in the palace. However, there are already cues in the epitaph which gesture towards a different, broader framework of interpretation. Given that Dido herself has taken the long view, and that she is immediately at pains to establish clearly and definitively the ideological

---

[32] Genette 1972: 243–4. See also the epitaph of Faustina, who describes how she has come to hear of her renown after her own death: *JP*, vv. 2196–7.

context of her own exemplum, namely chastity, I would suggest that this overdetermined 'self-defence' is a pressure point. Dido is responding to the competing discursive force of alternative, negative representations of her character from other sources, with the pressure being exerted, of course, by the Virgilian antecedent: the spectre of *infelix Dido*, who did not die a chaste widow.

It is true that Virgil does not present a wholly damning portrait of her. In Book I of the *Aeneid*, he recognizes quite happily the virtue of Dido's desire to build Carthage: 'instans operi regnisque futuris', but in Book IV he roundly condemns her, 'varium et mutabile semper | femina', for her debauchery ('luxus') with Aeneas.[33] The medieval pro-feminine tradition, after the example of Boccaccio who praised her unimpeachable widowhood, habitually rehabilitated the Virgilian memory of Dido, in two ways: first, it included in its accounts a counter-memory of *pre*-Virgilian Dido, leader of Carthage and widow of Sychaeus; secondly, it exposed Virgil's allegation of debauchery as a falsehood ('la mensonge de Virgille'),[34] by reasoning that the meeting of Dido and Aeneas was a historical impossibility.[35] It is this sort of dual riposte that I believe Bouchet intended his readers, familiar with the *querelle* tradition of Dido portraiture, to discern in the second half of her epitaph through the pressure points of her insistent self-definition. Each statement of self-definition articulates further the key affirmation of her epitaph's opening line, that she epitomizes virtuous widowhood. It is thus her rhetorical activity that *makes* Dido a chaste widow by suppressing or transforming negative representations of her. The audience is intended to see this activity as an essential part of her (and, by implication, Bouchet's) performative interpretation of herself as a figure constantly troubled by, and in dialogue with, her antecedents.[36]

It is possible to identify in Dido's epitaph more precise intertextual interactions with Virgil's text and also, perhaps, with Ovid's *Heroides*, a work comprising twenty-one epistolary laments by mythological women abandoned by their lovers; these can be seen as 'triggers' for

---

[33] 1978: I. i.504 ('pressing on the work of her rising kingdom'); I. iv.569–70 ('a fickle and changeful thing is woman ever'), 193.

[34] *Vies* 1970: 54. See also *PND*, fols. H1ᵛ–2ʳ.

[35] See Desmond 1994: 33, 55–73.

[36] Armstrong considers Bouchet's Dido to be a diminished version of the dynamic and complex character present in Foresti and Boccaccio: Bouchet 2006: 446. Alternatively, one could see the apparent paucity of detail in her *vita* as a strategy designed to provoke the reader to consider more closely and applaud the dexterous manner in which Dido juggles the various threads of her intertextual inheritance.

Dido's protestation of chastity. In the *Aeneid*, in Dido's epitaph in Book IV, the lines immediately following her declaration 'urbem praeclaram statui, mea moenia vidi',[37] lament and curse her liaison with Aeneas. In the lines following the corresponding declaration of civic pride in the *Jugement* (v. 1906), Bouchet has his Dido inscribe her will differently from her literary ancestor, affirming her chastity in widowhood ('Je voulu. . .' (v. 1907)). This shift expresses Bouchet's Dido's resistance to the speech that *infelix Dido* carries in the baggage of her intertextual memory. Likewise, her concluding affirmation that she took her own life (v. 1911) can be read as a subtle recasting of the brief, third-person epitaph she writes for herself in *Heroides* VII:

> praebuit Aeneas et causam mortis et ensem;
> ipsa sua dido concidit usa manu.[38]

(From Aeneas came the cause of her death, and from him came the blade; from the hand of Dido herself came the stroke by which she fell.)

Bouchet's Dido kills herself, but effaces Aeneas as the cause. Her epitaph's pressure points are thus, equally, points of resistance: they perform a neutralizing or recuperative transformation of the implicit Virgilian or Ovidian model such that Dido is placed in a position of rhetorical control over her own reputation. The brevity of Bouchet's epitaph form showcases this virtuoso performance in the compact density of Dido's dialogue with her accumulated, inherited narratives.[39]

Bouchet's three ambivalent *vitae* highlight a peculiarity of *querelle des femmes* intertextuality which makes intertextual relations an intrinsic part of the case for women. The express purpose of pro-feminine works is to defend women against their previous, misogynistic treatment at others' literary hands. The antecedent is, therefore, always already there, and its relationship to the present text is always conflictual. For example, in the preface to the first book of his *Nef des dames vertueuses* (1503), a complex four-part treatise dedicated to Anne of France,[40] the Lyonnaise

---

[37] 'A noble city I have built; my own walls I have seen': 1978: I. iv.655.

[38] Ovid 1986: VII.195.

[39] We may note that the spectre of Virgilian Dido is not forgotten by the *Jugement* as a whole; when the Traverseur likens Honour to 'Cupid, who so bombarded Dido on Aeneas's behalf' (vv. 3498–9), he is, in fact, explicitly enlisting the ghost that Bouchet's epitaph for her strives to lay.

[40] The *Nef* comprises: a catalogue of women (*la fleur des dames*), a treatise on marriage (*le regime de mariage*), a book of *propheties des sibilles*, and a philosophical treatise (*le livre de vraye amour*). The second book is dedicated, not to Anne, but to her daughter,

physician Symphorien Champier states that he is writing in response to accusations made by an unidentified host of pre-existing misogynists:

Mais il y a ung tas de gens qui, par une malice de langue envenimee, ont voulu dire que les plus grans et enormes pechez anciens ont esté perpetrez par femmes [. . .] Ausquelz je respons . . . (*NDV*, fol. B4ʳ)

(But there are numerous individuals who, with malice and venomous tongue, have wanted to state that the biggest and gravest sins of all time have been committed by women [. . .] And to them I respond . . .)

The examples of feminine virtue which follow in his catalogue of virtuous ladies, 'the best (*fleur*) of ladies', are thus, in the case of ambivalent women, implicit responses to previous maliciously drawn portraits. Champier counters these negative representations by omitting them entirely; Dido, for example, is simply said to be a model of 'fidelity' (*NDV*, fol. E2ᵛ).[41] However, alongside the actual image that Champier projects, the informed *querelle* reader 'knows' the potential, negative element that is silenced. The prior text is always there as a ghostly presence making each woman inherently intertextual and her portrait a necessary playing off of counter-memory against memory. It is this inherent intertextuality of plural, competing legacies into which Bouchet creatively taps, and with which he adroitly engages when he enables the rhetorical patterns of his epitaphs to conjure up the ghosts his ladies strive to lay. Their potential, misogynist-inspired images simmer just below the rhetorical surface of the actual, resistant performances through which they reconfigure their identity in a positive, pro-feminine light.[42]

Bouchet's and, to a certain extent, Champier's pro-feminine catalogues can thus be seen as particular products of a drive to play texts off against each other: to filter out selected threads of textual legacy in a manner sufficiently striking and innovative that the author can lay claim to a given portrait as his own, unique performance of that woman's identity. For example, Bouchet signs off from the 'brief epitaphs (*Epigrammes*)' (*JP*, v. 3770) of his *Jugement* with the punning

Suzanne of Bourbon: see Jordan 1990: 95–104. For notes on the textual tradition of the *Nef*, see Chapter 3, n. 28.

[41] Although it is not quite clear with respect to whom her fidelity is praised, since, before commending her for her rejection of Byarbas's advances, Champier notes, almost parenthetically, that she 'got married to Aeneas, who went off to Italy, to whom she remained most faithful' (fol. E2ᵛ).

[42] This rhetorical activity or 'doing' recalls again Butler's idea of performance as Bouchet's ventriloquized women construct themselves by negotiating with pre-existing cultural constructions of their identity: see Chapter 3, pp. 198–201.

authorial signature: ' "Ha bien touché" ' (v. 3773), or 'Ah, well treated!', an anagram that stamps his creative presence on the epitaphs as his own hermeneutic performances of the women's biographies.

The essence of a *querelle* catalogue's merit—the quality that secures it patronage and gains it popularity—is the manner of its composition; the debate's matter is a given. This applies especially in the sixteenth-century *querelle*, whose writers have to hand as works of reference several anthologies of exemplary women compiled by Italian humanists. Different possible legacies are spawned, for example in the case of Dido, and the principal task of the author-compiler is to shape these possibilities by filtering them. As Bouchet thematizes his compilatory activity through his first-person narrator, so the image of filtering out a textual legacy is used by the pro-feminine advocate of Pierre Michault's *querelle* debate poem, *Le Procès d'Honneur Féminin*, as he affirms how sibylline prophecies have successfully filtered through to the present:

> . . . moult firent escriptures subtilles,
> Tant qu'au jour d'uy en distillent les gouttes.
>
> (*PHF* 41)[43]

(. . . they composed such fine prophecies that droplets still filter through today.)

Le Franc expresses a similar concept of derivation when his Champion depicts Ovid's intertextual debt to the Muses in terms of 'tracing':

> Aussy dés sa tendre jouvence
> Monta et ala par les places
> De Parnasus ou souef vente,
> Et des muses suÿ les traces.
>
> (*CD*, vv. 18569–72)[44]

(Thus from his earliest youth he ascended Parnassus and wandered around its sites in the mild breeze, following the tracks of the Muses.)

Ovid's metaphoric journey up Mount Parnassus to the summit of artistic achievement represents his inheritance of the Muses' gift. The metaphor of following their tracks also highlights how the Muses' personal identity is indissociable from their words; this connection, adumbrating

---

[43] English translations are my own. I address *PHF* in detail below, pp. 47–8.

[44] Cf. the author of the late fifteenth-century rhetorical treatise *L'Instructif de la seconde rhétorique*, known only as L'Infortuné, sketches a literary genealogy of medieval vernacular writers, starting with Alain Chartier and going on to describe how ' . . . maistre Arnoul Greban suit bien sa trace': *Jardin de plaisance* 1910–25: i (1910), fol. B5ᵛ, v. 36.

an interpersonal dimension to intertextuality that I shall develop below, is spelt out clearly in the sixteenth century by the rhetorician Pierre de Courcelles. De Courcelles explains the motivation behind imitation:

> Imitation est par laquelle [. . .] sommes esmus et totalement incités d'estre semblables à ceux desquelz nous voulons affectueusement suyvre la trace et belle maniere de parler.[45]
>
> (Imitation is what [. . .] moves us and wholly incites us to emulate those whose traces and fine rhetorical style we wish affectionately to follow.)

The interpersonal dimension remains active, I argue, even when imitation occurs not 'affectionately' but in an antagonistic challenge to a prior author/work.

The potency that such textual 'droplets' (*gouttes*) or 'traces' (*traces*) can possess is revealed in Bouchet's Dido's thwarted attempts to omit certain intertextually transmitted details from her self-portrait: none is ever totally filtered out or erased. Riffaterre theorizes thus a textual trace's power to mark ineradicably a later text:

> L'intertexte laisse dans le texte une trace indélébile, une constante formelle qui joue le rôle d'un impératif de lecture, et gouverne le déchiffrement du message dans ce qu'il a de littéraire.[46]
>
> (The intertext leaves an indelible trace in the text, a formal constant that acts as an imperative to the reader, and dictates how the literary aspect of the message should be decoded.)

The imperative Riffaterre identifies forms a hermeneutic bridge between the prior text and the audience of the current text, a bridge which explains how Dido's misogynistic inheritance, although present only potentially or spectrally in her epitaph, can condition and enhance the reader's experience of the rhetorical strategies Dido deploys in her attempt at having it out with her negative reputation: an opportunity to answer back, but also a risk of raising the ghost. It is not so much a question of intertextual presence or absence in her epitaph, as of a conflict between remembering and forgetting her Virgilian legacy: had she forgotten it entirely—like Champier's Dido—it would not hold the same power as a hermeneutic imperative to the audience; her desire to forget it is itself a sort of recollection since it inescapably constitutes part of her identity of memory and counter-memory. Le Franc's Champion addresses the issue

---

[45] 1557: fol. A3^r. English translation is my own.
[46] 1980: 5. English translations are my own. Cf. Goyet's critique of this 'imperative': 1987: 315.

of remembrance in terms most apposite to Dido's dilemma; discussing the nature of mourning he affirms:

> Que les choses en conscience
> Et en courage ymaginees
> Sont nostres comme s'en presence
> Les veyons ou mortes ou nees.

(CD, vv. 12749–52)

(Things that are seen in mind and heart are ours just the same as if we saw them physically present, whether dead or alive.)

Bouchet's Dido is incapable of banishing the *infelix* spectre that she carries in her textual 'conscience'. She is thus doomed to mourn imperfectly her misogynist legacy: as long as she mourns it, its existence is prolonged in the psyche represented by the rhetoric of her intertextual pressure point.[47] Dido's mourning work remains necessarily incomplete, her performance of identity necessarily impure, since the *querelle* requires her to live on intertextually shackled by her Virgilian burden.

READING INTERTEXTUALITY: A 'SPECTROPOETIC' APPROACH

The sort of intertextuality manifested by Dido's epitaph anticipates the sort of relationship with Jean de Meun's *Rose* that I shall show certain *querelle* writers to entertain: a multi-levelled relationship that is both conflictual and essential. While Bouchet's and Le Franc's diegetic speakers—Dido and Franc Vouloir—express a desire to be rid of Virgil's or the *Rose*'s misogyny, it is in the extradiegetic author's interest to sustain a conversation with these texts on two counts. First, these texts furnish the *raison d'être* of the pro-feminine text, whose objective is to counter those misogynistic arguments that are the necessary pendant to the positive feminine portrait or the anti-*Rose* rhetoric proposed by the *querelle* text. Secondly, the prior text as stimulant for the current poet's activity provides an opportunity for showcasing his rhetorical skill in the sophisticated way he engages with, refutes, or recasts the *Rose*.

---

[47] The Freudian discourse of mourning could be a further light in which to view Dido's rhetoric. Intertextualities are often discussed in terms of a psychoanalytic model: Riffaterre 1990: 77.

A fruitful theoretical discourse for articulating the peculiar dynamic of *querelle* intertextual relations, and an approach whose rhetoric resonates with my discussion of intertextual imperatives, textual traces, haunting, mourning work, and the 'double bind' which binds pro- and anti-feminine strands ineluctably together, is provided by Jacques Derrida's work of political philosophy *Spectres de Marx* (1993).[48] It is my appropriation for *querelle* textuality of Derrida's concept of spectrality that will underpin (indeed, haunt) my readings of intertextual relationships with the *Rose*.[49] Derrida's work offers a critique of the new world order and 'end of history' celebrated triumphantly in post-1989 Western democracies, focusing on jubilation at the death of Marx and Marxism.[50] The insistent nature of this triumphalism gives Derrida pause: if something is dead, why be disturbed by it? Why make such a noise about it? He discerns in this paradox a contradictory gesture of attempted exorcism or a 'work of mourning' (*travail du deuil*): a certain continuation is granted to the spirit of Marx by those still living, who are bound to carry the trace of his thought within their own thoughts even in the very act of refuting him; it is a necessary condition of the work of mourning. They may reject their Marxist inheritance, but they cannot erase it, and must define their own position in relation to it, and thus to its totemic author, Marx himself. A complex negotiation with spectres of Marx ensues, and Derrida takes his cue for this discourse of spectrality from the opening line of the *Communist Manifesto*: 'A spectre is haunting Europe—the spectre of communism.' I transpose Derrida's 'spectropolitics'—'une politique de la mémoire, de l'héritage et des générations'[51]—into what I shall call a 'spectropoetics' of intertextual memory and literary inheritance which can be seen operating in the context of a new *literary* order, so to speak, of pro-feminine triumph. *Querelle* writers repeatedly celebrate the death of Jean de Meun by trying him and pronouncing his guilt, as I show in Chapter 2, and stress their triumph over his *Rose* continuation by rewriting this key late medieval

---

[48] A subsequent symposium on *Spectres* (hereafter *SM*) generated several responses from Marxist scholars to the notion of 'spectralité', to which Derrida responded in turn: Sprinker 1999.

[49] For a critical review of the different ways spectrality has been deployed as a theoretical approach, see Davis 2005.

[50] For further details of the political and scholarly contexts of Derrida's *Spectres*, which was originally a series of lectures before being compiled into a book, see Magnus's and Cullenberg's introduction to Kamuf's translation: Derrida 1994: pp. vii–xi.

[51] *SM*: 15. 'A politics of memory, of inheritance, and of generations.' I follow Kamuf's translations: 1994 (hereafter *SoM*): p. xix.

model in their new works; the spectre haunting the late medieval *querelle des femmes* is, indisputably, the ghost of the *Rose*'s misogyny.

Derrida's concept of spectrality, of the inevitable, irresistible return (*revenance*) of the dead authority, can be seen as a reformulation of his deconstructionist notion of iterability: tensions between the drift (*dérive*) structurally inherent in all language, as the orphaned word cut off from its original progenitor and context, and the guiding force of a discourse's *dérivation* from its paternal root.[52] It is a reformulation which is especially troubled by this latter force of influence. The ghosts of Marx and of his words may metamorphose and experience wear and tear (*usures*) but they will always be identifiable with Marx and Marxism, hence the perceived need amongst his heirs to dislocate the spectres that are still felt to be 'his' through acts of performative interpretation. Derrida describes

cette dimension de l'interprétation performative, c'est-à-dire d'une interprétation qui transforme cela même qu'elle interprète [. . .] Voilà une définition du performatif qui est [. . .] peu orthodoxe au regard de la *speech act theory*. (*SM* 89)

(this dimension of performative interpretation, that is, of an interpretation that transforms the very thing it interprets [. . .] [Here is] a definition of the performative [that is] [. . .] unorthodox with regard to speech act theory. (*SoM* 51))

I shall shortly demonstrate, through close readings of several hermeneutic performances on individual words and phrases, as well as on larger structural units (characters or episodes), how both an intertextuality of orphaned words—the textual equivalent of *dérive*—and an idea of influence as the anxiety-inducing progenitor are pertinent to the late medieval *querelle*'s inheritance of Jean de Meun's *Rose* continuation. We recall here how Le Franc's Champion recasts La Vieille's speech as free-floating language, but is also bound to address her as Jean de Meun's creation. *Querelle* writers not only invite their audience to engage intellectually with the negotiation between prior and current texts that the writer performed in producing his new work, but also call upon them to feel an almost emotive response to the troubling influence of the arch-misogynist Jean de Meun. Again, we recall how the Champion impugns 'Jan de Meün':

---

[52] Thomas M. Greene observes a similar marriage or 'interplay between drift and evolution, between *dérive* and *dérivation*' in the literary uses of *imitatio* in the Renaissance: 1982: 16. I am indebted to his discussion of iterability.

> . . . , halas comment
> Onques osas Bel Accueul mettre
> Sous la Vielle en gouvernement?
> (*CD*, vv. 14498–500)

(. . . , alas! How dare you commit Fair Welcome to the tutelage of the Old Woman?)

His exclamation ('halas') reinforces the vitriolic manner in which he lambastes the *Rose* continuator in person.

Two factors set Derrida's hermeneutic tool apart from the classic formulation of intertextuality provided by Julia Kristeva and picked up by Roland Barthes, and render it a more appropriate, adequate discourse for articulating relationships between *querelle* texts: first, the way Derrida subjectivizes the relationship between text and spectral antecedent, and, secondly, the specifically troubling nature of this relationship that concerns me here. Kristeva and Derrida explain the founding tenets of their theories in similar ways. Building on Bakhtin's notion of language's 'dialogism' and 'ambivalence', Kristeva affirms:

Tout texte se construit comme mosaïque de citations [. . .] et le langage poétique se lit, au moins, comme *double* (*S* 84)[53]

(Every text is constructed as a mosaic of quotations [. . .] and poetic language is read as being at least *double*),

while Derrida asserts through the metaphor of inheritance an analogous state of essential interrelatedness:

Nous *sommes* des héritiers, cela ne veut pas dire que nous *avons* ou que nous *recevons* ceci ou cela, que tel héritage nous enrichit un jour de ceci ou cela, mais que l'*être* de ce que nous sommes *est* d'abord héritage, que nous le voulions et le sachions ou non. (*SM* 94)[54]

(That we *are* heirs does not mean that we *have* or that we *receive* this or that, some inheritance that enriches us one day with this or that, but that the *being* of what we are *is* first of all inheritance, whether we like it or know it or not. (*SoM* 54))

The task of inheritance that Derrida assigns an heir, since 'l'héritage n'est jamais un *donné*, c'est toujours une tâche',[55] develops into a subjectively

---

[53] Italics are Kristeva's own emphases. Cf. Barthes: 'Every text is a new tissue of recycled citations [. . .] The intertext is a field of anonymous formulae whose origin is rarely recoverable': quoted in Orr 2003: 33.

[54] All italics in quotations from *SM* are Derrida's own emphases.

[55] 'Inheritance is never a *given*, it is always a task': *SoM* 54.

performed activity the processes of absorption and transformation that Kristeva uses to denote the state of one text in relation to a prior text: 'tout texte est absorption et transformation d'un autre texte.'[56] The theorists diverge in the two respects that I noted above. First, whilst Kristeva eliminates all subjectivity from intertextuality ('A la place de la notion d'intersubjectivité s'installe celle d'*intertextualité*'[57]), Derrida represents as integral to textual inheritance the response provoked in the inheritor by the pressure exerted by his or her predecessor, a response that is subjective in the extent to which it represents an individual consciousness's awareness of the responsibility inherent in being an heir. The perceived pressure is almost embodied, rendered interpersonal; it is, after all, to the examples of Hamlet's dead father and Marx that Derrida has recourse to illustrate his spectrality effect. This pressure gives inheritance its potency, its capacity to haunt, trouble, and promote anxiety amongst its heirs. We need only look at the terms used by medieval linguistic translators to refer to their position vis-à-vis their authoritative Latin sources to see this anxiety in action. They speak consistently of their *angoisse* ('anxiety'), of the *fardeau* ('burden') weighed upon them by the *grant œuvre* they must translate, and describe their communication with this source as a 'negotiation' (*negoce*).[58] I demonstrate this potency in action both later in this chapter and, concerning specifically the ghost of the author in person, in Chapter 2's exploration of courtroom fictions. The second difference from Kristeva arises out of the first, in that the anxiety Derrida addresses characterizes a specifically troubling intertextual relationship: the inheriting agent is striving to reject rather than to absorb, in full awareness that absolute resistance to an antecedent's penetration is impossible; rejection is itself an act performed on that very antecedent within the new text. Kristeva's model of intertextuality certainly allows for such trouble, but Derrida's formulation privileges the double bind it provokes in a way that resonates more precisely with the intertextual dynamic present in *querelle* texts, as they endeavour to rebuff the spectres of Virgil and of Jean de Meun's *Rose*. Derrida formulates this double bind through wordplay on the polysemy of the French *conjurer*, with its possible nominalizations as 'conjuration' and 'conjurement' (*SM* 89). He argues

---

[56] *S* 84.

[57] Ibid. 'In place of the idea of intersubjectivity there is introduced the notion of *intertextuality*.'

[58] See Bérier 1988: 238–40.

that it is impossible to con*jure* a spectre, to overturn its power, without first conjuring it up.

The discourse of spectres and inheritance is also useful to the extent that, as I suggested in earlier discussion of *dérive* and *dérivation*, it offers an approach that overcomes the problematic terminological difference between 'intertextuality' and 'influence' that has preoccupied recent reappraisals of Kristeva's founding concept.[59] The language of haunting that I propose operates at a general level of intertextual relations, as witnessed in Dido's epitaph; it also addresses an individual spectre, specifically Jean de Meun, who is shown to be have been perceived as an *auctor* rather than simply an *auctoritas*, as a personalized influence with whom psychic battle must be joined in a proto-Bloomian relationship of anxiety and emulation. The outcome of both types of relationship is an appropriation of the prior text achieved through the act of rewriting, which can be seen most fruitfully as the task of inheritance or work of mourning that I discussed above.

In the context of the *querelle* and of the two specific spectres of misogyny, Virgil and Jean de Meun, the creative work of pro-feminine writers like Bouchet and Le Franc is conditioned by their position as readers of the anti-woman texts that provide the impetus for their own compositions. Likewise, the informed reader of the *querelle* text is obliged (and expected) to read it against its opposite. This habit of reading can be deduced from the publishing tradition of pro- and anti-feminine works, which were often grouped together in manuscript and early printed anthologies,[60] or, when they reappeared in print, were published in tandem, with shared paratextual features, so as to weave an

---

[59] See Orr 2003: 171; Lack 1990.

[60] The juxtaposition of *pro* and *contra* is already established in the twelfth century in Marbod of Rennes's *Liber decem capitulorum*, which sets its third chapter, *De meretrice*, before a pro-feminine piece, *De matrona* or *De muliera bona*. Amongst manuscript anthologies it is demonstrated by the thirteenth-century panegyric *Le Bien des fames* and the contemporary invective *Le Blasme des fames*, which were sometimes arranged as a complementary pair to resemble a debate: Fenster and Lees 2002: 1–18 (p. 4). In the late fifteenth century, Christine de Pizan's *Cité* was twice bound together with a French translation of *De mulieribus* (MSS ex-Phillipps 3648; Chantilly 856: see Appendix 2B), perhaps indicating that they were meant to be read against each other, though the sort of relationship intended—complementary or oppositional—is open to speculation. In early print culture, a sixteenth-century compilation claiming to contain Guillaume Coquillart's *œuvre* (now London, BL, C.107.a.9) also reflects this trend, juxtaposing, for example, the satirical *Leaulté des dames* (fols. 86^r–87^r) with the panegyric *La Louange des dames* (fols. 90^r–99^r). I return to the question of what these anthologies tell us about literary production, as well as reception, in Chapter 2.

intertextual dialectic of praise and blame.[61] In this light, the speech of Bouchet's anti-Virgilian Dido can be seen to carry a 'memorial trace', to quote Derrida, of the ghost it strives to lay, since the spectre of *infelix Dido* forms an inescapable part of its literary inheritance: 'l'*être* de ce que nous sommes *est* d'abord héritage' (*SM* 94). The dead letter lives on in this way, possessed of what Derrida calls 'une *sur-vie*, à savoir une trace dont la vie et la mort ne seraient elles-mêmes que des traces et des traces de traces'.[62] Derrida's double meaning for *conjurer*, described above, encapsulates succinctly this paradox of unwanted yet unavoidable survival: it cannot be conjured without first being conjured up.

A similar paradox seems to underpin Jacques Milet's use of the term *conjurer* in the second half of his *Forest de Tristesse* (1459),[63] an allegorical narrative in two parts: the first describes his dreamer-narrator's journey through the eponymous forest, and the second depicts his voyage, guided by Subtilité, to the court of Dame Justice, where he witnesses a juridical debate to determine the sentences that Jean de Meun and Matheolus should face for their crimes committed against the 'chief des dames', the embodiment of woman's honour. Noble Vouloir, the lady's advocate, declares what punishment should befall anyone who defames women:

> On en devroit faire justice
> Et les conjurer et mauldire
> Comme fol mal disant et nice.
>
> (*FT*, fol. 220ʳ)

(One should bring them to justice by denouncing and condemning/convoking and condemning them as defamers and foolish madmen.)[64]

---

[61] See below, pp. 81–7, for discussion of this sharing of woodcuts and layout. For an intratextual manifestation of the dialectic of praise and blame, see Chapter 2, pp. 113–15.

[62] *SM* 17. 'A *living-on*, namely, a trace of which life and death would themselves be but traces and traces of traces': *SoM*, p. xx. Chapter 2 illustrates how this idea of inheritance as a question of life after death is animated within the courtroom fiction of certain *querelle* texts which 'resurrect' misogynists to try them posthumously for their crimes.

[63] No critical edition exists for this work, nor has any medieval manuscript been uncovered; its textual tradition can be traced solely through its appearance in all seven early printed editions of the famous poetic anthology *Le Jardin de plaisance et fleur de rethorique* (1501). The Parisian Milet was much praised by his contemporaries, but is known today only for his *Istoire de la destruction de Troye la grant*, a vast mystery play dedicated to Charles VII.

[64] *Conjurer* here features as part of a binomial expression, as a synonym of *mauldire* (Godefroy 1969: ii. 240–1), and in its specific legal sense of 'summoning': Ragueau 1704: 285. English translations are my own.

The ambivalence of *conjurer* is played out in the ensuing courtroom action: the two prisoners and their texts—Noble Vouloir brandishes Matheolus' 'livre mauldit' (fol. 220^v) before the jury—are convoked in order to be revoked,[65] that is, banished from the kingdom of Love over which the court presides. Their sentence is not, however, definitive; exile does not mean complete exorcism, and Derrida comments further on the peculiarity of triumphal conjuring:

Le cadavre n'est peut-être pas aussi mort, aussi simplement mort que la conjuration tente de le faire accroire. Le disparu paraît toujours *là*, et son apparition n'est pas rien. Elle ne fait pas rien [. . .] Un mort doit pouvoir travailler. Et faire travailler. (*SM* 160)

(The cadaver is perhaps not as dead, as simply dead as the conjuration tries to delude us into believing. The one who has disappeared appears still to be *there*, and his apparition is not nothing. It does not do nothing [. . .] The dead must be able to work. And to cause to work. (*SoM* 97))

As I shall explain in greater detail in Chapter 2, an awareness amongst certain *querelle* writers of a 'double bind' that ties them to their misogynist forebears, who are always 'there', can be seen to explain the inconclusive nature of their trial narratives: the way that, for example, the sentence of death initially passed on Milet's convicts by Dame Justice is mitigated by the King of Love to a punishment which does not preclude the possible return of Jean de Meun. His sustained presence may be understood to obtain in the poem's structure: its use of the personified voices of Reason and the King of Love and the very pretext for the poem's trial narrative are indebted to the *Rose* continuator. Spectral 'thereness' is thus twofold, engaging both the personal and textual levels of intertextual relationships. On the one hand, in courtroom fictions, it is principally the person of the author who 'paraît toujours *là*'. On the other, 'thereness' also helps articulate how the misogynist writer's words are equally perceived as a ghostly presence or 'corps verbal' (*SM* 88), as occurred in the case of Bouchet's Dido's intertextual pressure point: the implicit 'thereness' of *infelix Dido* provokes Dido's mourning work, the rhetorical act of self-defence that I described above.[66] Likewise, the spectre of the

---

[66] The reiterative nature of performance, in that it necessarily brings back the past to unsettle the present, especially with regard to the performance of identity, has led several performance theorists to flirt with the language of 'spectrality': see Carlson 2001; Franko and Richards 2000: 2. No literature scholar has developed a parallel theory, although several have enlisted the language of haunting incidentally when discussing

Rose as a text is felt palpably; its verbal body possesses a certain 'densité spectrale' that excites 'angoisse devant le fantôme' (*SM* 177). Such anxiety in the face of the ghost is expressed in the *Forest* by the 'chief des dames', who, kneeling in prayer to the Virgin Mary, laments the weight exerted upon her soul by a certain section ('chapitre') of the *Rose*:

> Me fait tant de mal sur mon ame
> Qu'au vray dire je n'en puis plus.
>
> (*FT*, fol. 208ʳ)[67]

(It so pains my soul that, to speak true, I can't take any more.)

Oppressed by this misogynist inheritance, wishing to conjure it away, she swiftly addresses the crux of the matter:

> Dame, vous sçavez mon affaire
> Et les choses que j'ay affaire
> Pour trouver remede en ce cy.
> Je ne puis honneur reffaire
> Sans leur mauldiz livres deffaire
> Et leurs escriptz: il est ainsi.
>
> (Ibid.)

(Madam, you know my position and what I need to do in order to resolve this business. I cannot rebuild my honour without undoing/destroying their wretched books and their writings; that's how it must be.)

Through *traductio* on verbs of 'making', 'remaking', and 'unmaking', she hits the hermeneutic nail squarely on the head by acknowledging the necessity of tackling misogynist texts in order to refute them. Standing as a diegetic echo of Milet himself as a pro-feminine writer, his 'chief des dames' recognizes the imperative issued by the prior text and experiences it as an almost palpable burden.[68] Derrida theorizes thus this weighty injunction: 'Peser [. . .] c'est aussi charger, taxer, imposer, endetter, accuser, assigner, enjoindre.'[69] The books and writings of Jean de Meun and Matheolus impose upon the 'chief des dames' their task

intertextuality, quotation, or influence: see Atwood 2002, esp. chapter 6; Blamires 1997: 5; Compagnon 1979: 243; cf. Davis 2005.

[67] The contentious 'chapitre' is the misogynistic tirade voiced by the Mari Jaloux (*RR*, vv. 8459–9496): see below, pp. 43, 51–2.

[68] Jean Le Fèvre articulates in similar terms his necessary struggle against the weight of misogynist tradition: 1905: vv. 745–6.

[69] *SM* 177. 'To weigh is also to charge, tax, impose, indebt, accuse, assign, enjoin': *SoM* 109.

of inheritance, their obligation, Derrida would say, to 'have it out with' (*s'expliquer avec*) the spectre in question, since 'il faut parler *du* fantôme, voire *au* fantôme et *avec* lui'.[70] Milet's lady cannot restore ('reffaire') her honour without engaging with the text of the *Rose*; by doing so, however, she contaminates herself in the same way that her advocate, Noble Vouloir, is troubled by the stain that is caused upon his rhetoric by repeating the language of Jean de Meun, conjuring his verbal body, before Justice's court:

> Et reciter grant mal me fait
> Tes villains motz entre mes ditz,
> Mais pour racompter ton meffait
> Aux dames de quoy tu mesdis
> Je parle aussi comme tu dis.
>
> (*FT*, fol. 220ᵛ)[71]

(It pains me greatly to rehearse your ignoble language amongst my own speech, but in order to recount your offence to the ladies whom you've defamed I use your very words.)

The term *deffaire* employed by Milet's lady to denote her treatment of the *Rose* has two related meanings, both of which are at play in her speech. First, and in anticipation of the poem's trial sequence, during which it will be agreed that at least one of the misogynists' books be burnt, it means 'to destroy'. Noble Vouloir uses the term twice in this sense concerning the death sentence he wants to be passed on Jean de Meun: 'I pray to God that you be destroyed (*qu'on te defface*)', and on both authors: 'may they be killed and destroyed (*deffaiz*)' (fols. 221ʳ, 221ᵛ). However, as Milet's King of Love seems to acknowledge when he attenuates Jean de Meun's sentence, the slippery *Rose* is always, indestructibly 'there'. It is in this context that the second meaning of 'deffaire' comes into play, namely its etymological sense 'to unmake/undo', which is, I argue, pointed up in Milet's lady's speech by its juxtaposition in rhyme position with other compounds of 'faire', especially 'reffaire' ('remake'/'redo'). What she identifies here is the way in which pro-feminine authors may set about rewriting the *Rose*. The notion of 'undoing' implicit in her speech brings us back to the idea of

---

[70] *SM* 15. 'It is necessary to speak *of the* ghost, indeed *to the* ghost, and *with* it': *SoM*, p. xix.

[71] This impurifying effect is addressed by Derrida as he describes how the haunted individual oppressed by a spectre 'no longer has [. . .] a pure identity to itself': *SoM* 109.

resistant performance, and can be seen to be activated in Noble Vouloir's speech quoted above, as he has it out with the *Rose* through 'repetition' (*reciter*) of its arguments that he then counters with a pro-feminine view. To give but one example of how Noble Vouloir rereads the *Rose* through a resistant performance, he takes issue with the precise terms of the Mari Jaloux's contention that a good woman is rarer than a phoenix, and reverses the misogynist character's assertion to create a positive statement about women:

> Dit des femmes trop ville chose.
> En son livre dit et propose
> Qu'ilz sont trop meschantes en personne,
> Mais quant à moy je m'y oppose:
> Il ment comme ung desloyal homme.
> *Prudentes femmes, par saint Denys,*
> Gracieuses et secourables
> *Voit on trop plus que de fénix*
> *Que sont belles et honnorables.*
>
> (*FT*, fols. 220ᵛ–221ʳ (my italics))

(He says a most ignoble thing about women. In his book he remarks and proposes that they are all very wicked, but, as for me, I oppose that argument: he lies like a faithless man. By St Denis, one sees far more honest, gracious, and caring women, who are beautiful and honourable, than one sees phoenixes.)

Noble Vouloir's ironic echo of the Mari Jaloux's oath—

> *Preudefame, par saint Denis!*
> *Dont il est mains que de phenis,*
> Si com Valerius tesmoingne
>
> (*RR*, vv. 8691–3 (my italics))[72]

(By St Denis, there are fewer honest women than there are phoenixes, as Valerius can testify)

—serves as a signpost, what Riffaterre calls a 'connective', to tap his mention of the phoenix specifically into the *Rose* as textual ancestor. Indeed, one might see the self-regenerating mythical beast as a particularly apt metaphor or cue for this textual resurfacing—the Derridean 'sur-vie'—of the *Rose*.

---

[72] English translations are my own. Jean de Meun's source here is the antimatrimonial 'Valerius' of Walter Map's *Dissuasio Valerii ad Ruffinum philosophum ne uxorem ducat* (*c*.1180).

Noble Vouloir's resistant performance of the *Rose* introduces a further dimension of the spectropoetic dilemma of being double bound to the *Rose*, of needing to 'recite' in order to rewrite; this is the dimension of audience response, which brings into play the multi-levelled nature of the double bind to which I alluded earlier. In order for Noble Vouloir's refutation of the Mari Jaloux's allegation to be meaningful and appreciated as a skilful subversion of the *Rose*'s misogyny, its debt to the *Rose* must be visible. In other words, if the fate of Jean de Meun's text expressly desired by Noble Vouloir—that it be destroyed—were to be realized, there would no longer be an intertextual competence amongst Milet's readership that could fully appreciate his performative rereading of the *Rose*. This dilemma is recognized by Martin Le Franc, who addresses it directly in terms of whether or not the *Rose* should be read. Like Milet's pro-feminine advocate, Le Franc's Champion experiences the anxiety of responsibility for 'reciting' the *Rose*, lamenting at one point, when he is inextricably mired in its language: 'I'm saying too much, this language is ignoble (*ce parler est ort*)' (*CD*, v. 12289). He turns this anxiety upon his inscribed audience, the courtiers of the God of Love who witness his debate with Trop Cuidier, enjoining them: 'True lovers, don't read his book' (v. 12113), before issuing the opposite imperative moments later:

> Veez le ribault en son livre
> A quel fin Amours a mené.
>
> (*CD*, vv. 12249–50)

(Look in his book and see to what end the scoundrel has made Love lead.)

This contradictory behaviour discloses the crux of the matter: whilst it is Franc Vouloir's and Le Franc's explicit purpose to condemn and defeat Jean de Meun, it is in both their interests that his *Rose* should be appreciated in tandem with, or as a spectre consistently haunting, the Champion's arguments and the *Champion* itself. Pragmatically, it is in Le Franc's professional interests to foster an acquaintance with the *Rose* if his audience are to possess the competence to be able to applaud his innovative dialogue with the poem. This dialogue will, he hopes, enhance his status as a poet in the same way that, diegetically, it enhances Franc Vouloir's standing as a skilled and successful advocate when he is crowned with a laurel wreath at the poem's conclusion.[73]

---

[73] I address this episode in Chapter 2, pp. 117–18, 130.

Franc Vouloir's concern about repeating the *Rose*'s pernicious language manifests a further intertextual anxiety: that the sustained spectre of Jean de Meun will serve only to propagate the *Rose*'s popularity, a popularity which, although contrary to the express wishes of the diegetic Champion, is in fact profitable to the extradiegetic interests of the poet, Le Franc. This further double bind of promotion-through-denunciation which complicates or haunts *querelle* writers' intertextual engagement with the *Rose* is first pinpointed by Pierre Col writing to Christine de Pizan in the '*Rose*' *querelle*:

Toy et aultres—qui s'efforcent comme toy a impugner ce tres noble escrivain Meung—le loués plus en le cuidant blasmer que je ne pouroye le louer pour y user tous mes membres.[74]

(You and others who strive with you to impugn this most noble writer Jean de Meun. You will perhaps praise him more in thinking to condemn him than I would be able to praise him if all my members were [. . .] employed at the task. (p. 92))[75]

By emphasizing how nefarious Jean de Meun's writings are, his detractors inadvertently accord his work additional publicity that is more sensational because it is adverse. Le Franc sets up Franc Vouloir in just such a trap when the character is denouncing man's sexual voracity:

> Meün assez et trop vous monstre
> La maniere de les happer.
> [. . .]
> Qui voulez femmes attraper
> Lisez son livre, si sçaurez
> Tendre les filez et juper
> Aprez elles, et en aurez.
> (*CD*, vv. 8113–14, 8117–20)

(Meun shows you quite clearly enough how to catch them. [. . .] Those of you who want to entrap women, read his book, then you'll know how to pull the strings and cry out to them, and will get them.)

However steeped in irony, his words reveal more than they conceal, and thus propagate by their titillating allusiveness the contents of the condemned book. A similar state of affairs arises in the *Forest* in Subtilité's observation of how Jean de Meun and Matheolus receive universal condemnation in Love's kingdom:

---

[74] Hicks 1977: 89.   [75] I follow the translation by Baird and Kane 1978.

> Ces deux prisonniers sont haïz
> De toutes ces gens de ce païs.
>
> (*FT*, fol. 219^r)

(These two prisoners are hated by all the people of this kingdom.)

Whether loved or loathed, their universal renown is assured as authors of *succès à scandale*.

REWRITING THE *ROSE*: NEGOTIATING WITH SPECTRES

How are Le Franc's and Milet's diegetic pro-feminine advocates able to respond in any effective way to the ineradicable spectre that haunts them? What rhetorical path is open to them when they stand caught in two double binds: anxious about being held morally accountable for the language of the misogynist ghost they conjure up in order to con*jure* it, and fearing the risk of promoting this text through the very act of denouncing it? At one point in the *Champion*, the logic of Franc Vouloir's argument leads to silence as the only option:

> Honneur ne voulsist maintenant
> Qu'a tous tes dis je respondisse,
> Car jamais n'est appartenent
> Que d'omme honneste ort parler isse.
> Pour ce Vergongne la faitisse
> M'a tousjours conseillié le taire.
>
> (*CD*, vv. 8697–702)

(Honour does not want me to reply to everything you've said, since it is never proper for ignoble speech to issue from an honourable man. For this reason elegant Decorum has always advised me to be silent on such matters.)

In a debate situation, however, such decorum ('vergongne') is of little practical use. In his modern, spectropolitical context Derrida concludes, on the one hand, that the heir to Marx is trapped in the double bind of his debt, ultimately able only to bear witness to it ('en *témoigner*' (*SM* 94)). On the other hand, however, Derrida stands by the imperative obliging that heir to engage actively with the debt in a mobilization ('mobilisation' (p. 88)) to struggle against it by performing the task of inheritance, just as we saw Bouchet's Dido perform her mourning work in an attempt to exorcize Virgil's spectre: to expel its legacy from her epitaph and from her intertextual memory. This task is worthwhile, according to Derrida, because of the 'necessary heterogeneity' of an inheritance; the inheritance delivers an injunction: 'Choisis et décide dans ce dont tu hérites, dit-elle toujours'.[76] Through the process of selecting different threads or traces, the inheritor acquires a certain interpretative latitude, albeit within circumscribed discursive limits—the limits imposed by what is inherited. We may recall here the additional meaning I suggested for Milet's 'deffaire' as a verb denoting the dismantling of an authority, but still constrained within the obligation to 'reciter'. The heir is obliged to choose from a limited range:

Il *faut* filtrer, cribler, critiquer, il faut trier entre plusieurs des possibles qui habitent la même injonction. (*SM* 40)

(*One must* filter, sift, criticize, one must sort out several different possibles that inhabit the same injunction. (*SoM* 16))

But this can be an enabling obligation: it enables Bouchet's Dido, for example, to assess and reject her Virgilian inheritance on account of its historical inconsistency.

In comparing Kristeva's intertextuality with Derrida's theory of spectral inheritance above, I noted that the latter entailed a specifically antagonistic sort of 'absorption' and 'transformation' of an anterior text, and involved an appropriative 'task' which privileges the active agency of the heir. It is on such acts of performative interpretation of the *Rose* in favour of the pro-feminine cause, the most innovative and radical way in which *querelle* poets 'have it out with' misogynist spectres, that I shall focus for the remainder of this part of the current chapter. The inescapable doubleness of pro-feminine discourse that I highlighted above as the condition that bedevils *querelle* intertextuality can, I propose here, be viewed positively as an enabling rather than a crippling rhetorical precondition. This precondition is spelt out in the courtroom fiction of Pierre Michault's allegorical debate *Le Procès d'Honneur Féminin* (*c*.1461).[77] In this prosimetrum, a pro-feminine

---

[76] *SM* 40. 'Choose and decide from among what you inherit': *SoM* 16.

[77] We know little of Michault's life, save that he was attached professionally to the Burgundian court: see Chapter 2, n. 94. As a poet, he composed a *Complainte sur la mort d'Ysabeau de Bourbon*, the late wife of Duke Charles the Bold, and a *Dance aux aveugles* (1464). He is best known for his more scholastic, didactic treatise *Le Doctrinal du temps present* (1466), for which ten manuscripts and four early editions survive. The only printed record of the *Procès* is, like Milet's *Forest*, the *Jardin de plaisance*; one manuscript witness exists, in a late fifteenth-century poetic anthology (Paris, Arsenal, MS 3521, fols. 195^r–218^v): Cayley 2006: 200.

prosecuting counsel, Vray Rapport ('True Report'), accuses misogynists, represented by the devious barrister Faux Parler ('False Speaking'), of having assaulted his noble client Honneur Féminin. It is, with ironic aptness, Faux Parler who explains succinctly the doubleness of pro-feminine discourse, which, in his eyes, irreparably flaws the case for women. He responds to Vray Rapport's accusation that

> Tous maux entassés,
> Tous biens rabaissiez,

(You pile up everything that's bad and knock down everything that's good),

with smug irony:

> On en parle assés
> Mais, serez ou tassés,
> Fault que vous passés
> Par notre langaige.
>
> (*PHF* 58)

(So they say, but, whether packed tightly or heaped up, you have to pass through our language.)

He need not be so smug, however, since the pro-feminine speaker's obligation to 'pass through' villainous anti-feminine discourse, crafting his arguments in woman's defence in relation to, and on the terms dictated by, misogynistic allegations, does not preclude the possibility that he may perform some transformative or recuperative hermeneutic action upon the rhetoric in question, as we saw at the very beginning of this chapter in the *Champion* and, later, in the speech of Noble Vouloir in the *Forest*. There is, therefore, a constant oscillation between enablement and constriction in the inheritor's use of discourse. The only sort of revolution he can perform through language is double bound, and Derrida expresses this bedevilling catch in terms which resonate strikingly with Michault's diegetic speaker:

Il faut passer par le pré-héritage [what I call the 'precondition' of pro-feminine discourse's doubleness], fût-ce en le parodiant, pour s' approprier la vie d'une nouvelle langue ou faire la révolution. (*SM* 181)

(One must pass through the pre-inheritance, even if it is to parody it, in order to appropriate the life of a new language or make the revolution. (*SoM* 110))

One may detect irony in Derrida's reference to revolution; indeed, it may be understood to evoke, not a revolutionary impulse in the sense of radical change, but an inevitable repetition of the same circuit of meaning. Nonetheless, he still holds out the possibility of creatively reconstructing the discourse to which one is heir: re-membering as one remembers. In manner akin to *querelle* poets, Derrida recognizes that forgetting the spectre is not only impossible, but also undesirable:

Car ce qu'on doit oublier aura été indispensable [. . .] Il faut donc ne pas l'oublier, il faut se le rappeler mais en l'oubliant assez, dans cette mémoire même. (*SM* 181)

(For what one must forget will have been indispensable [. . .] So one must not forget it, one must remember it while forgetting it enough, in this very memory. (*SoM* 110))

The spectre can be sufficiently forgotten through what Derrida calls its 'living appropriation' (*SM* 180; *SoM* 110), but, by the same token, and especially for *querelle* poets who make their manner of having it out with the *Rose* a principal focus of their texts, the spectre cannot (and must not) be wholly forgotten. The transformation performed must remain visible or, as I suggested earlier, 'there', like Bouchet's Dido's near-forgetting-yet-remembering of her *infelix* ancestor. In other words, marrying these spectral ideas with the intertextual activity of appropriation that I showed Le Franc and Bouchet to valorize as an agent of rhetorical invention, the antagonistic, interpretative activity of the new text does not seek to supplant or efface the foregoing mastertext, the vernacular *auctor* Jean de Meun, but strives instead to pronounce its difference from it through hermeneutic remodelling.

This complex hermeneutic-rhetorical process brings us back to the second meaning of 'deffaire' in Milet's *Forest*: it is a question of 're-making' (*re-ffaire*) achieved through 'un-making' (*de-ffaire*), of rhetorical reinvention through hermeneutic dismantling.[78] Related lexemes of refashioning frequently form prominent patterns in *querelle* texts' pro-feminine discourse and seem consistently to call attention to the task of repairing misogynist rhetorical damage, whether actual or attempted. Le Franc's Acteur describes emblematically the assault upon Vérité attempted by Malebouche and his cohort, depicting an attack upon a statue of this personified virtue:

> Car aucuns avoyent sa bouche
> Voulu tout aultrement refaire
> [. . .]
> Car de jour en jour s'estudie

---

[78] Cf. Copeland 1995: 151–78.

A la couvrir, celer et taire.
Pour aultre chose il ne plaidie
Que pour la destruire ou desfaire.

(*CD*, vv. 2570–1, 2581–4)

(Certain individuals had wanted to reshape her mouth quite differently [. . .]
For every day he [= Malebouche] strives towards covering, obscuring, and
silencing it/her. He campaigns for nothing other than its/her demolition or
destruction.)

The terms of physical perversion he proposes intersect with terms of
rhetorical violence.[79] Whilst at loggerheads with Vilain Penser ('Ignoble
Thought'), Franc Vouloir depicts similarly his opponent's nefarious
interpretation of woman's being:

En quelque guise, en quelque fourme
Qu'elles se puissent comporter,
Tantost sault sus qui les refourme,
Qui mal y scet interpreter.

(*CD*, vv. 7809–12)

(In whatever way, in whatever form women may behave, he [= her opponent]
immediately leaps up to express it otherwise and interpret it *in malo*.)

He exposes the artifice of this false hermeneutic activity—'your false
illusion' (v. 7842)—whilst acknowledging that the malicious misrep-
resentation of a woman's character can destroy her reputation: 'By
falsifying (*contrefaisant*) you destroy (*desfaictes*)' (v. 8496). Through
the imagery of rhetorical refashioning—unmaking and remaking—Le
Franc's pro-feminine speaker implies that misogynistic 'damage' is
recoverable through a strategic recycling of the very linguistic procedures that are deployed to women's detriment. Michault's Vray Rapport
makes this quite clear when he describes his own rhetoric's capacity to
dismantle Faux Parler's falsity:

Et n'y a chose touchant prez
Qu'on ne puisse par motz exprez
Fondre et tantost anientir.

(*PHF* 54)

(There is nothing you can say on this matter that one cannot destroy and
demolish immediately with carefully chosen words.)

---

[79] I address this intersection in Chapter 2, pp. 100–1, 109–13.

Defence against the *Rose* can be made all the more potent and rhetorically spectacular by a sort of subversive fulfilment of the obligation to 'pass through' Jean de Meun's discourse in order to refute it. Through resistant hermeneutic performance of the *Rose*, pro-feminine writers engage in a revolutionary intertextual relationship with Jean de Meun in order to fight him on his own territory and with his own verbal weapons.

This intertextual war of words, like its intratextual counterpart that I explore in Chapter 2, is dynamic in its detailed attention to language, and requires a degree of textual precision and intellectual investment redolent of the earlier, and partially concurrent, *querelle de 'la Belle Dame sans mercy'*.[80] Certain offending phrases are repeatedly picked over, phrases that are first addressed at the turn of the fifteenth century in the literary debate over the *Rose*'s morality, the *'Rose' querelle*. They are addressed in documents by Christine de Pizan and by the eminent theologian and Chancellor of Paris Jean Gerson, both fierce critics of Jean de Meun.[81] Christine attacks the anti-feminine utterances of Jean de Meun's two main misogynistic characters—the Mari Jaloux and Genius—as the direct product of the author 'en sa persone',[82] and subversively appropriates two of their key phrases. First, she responds to the Mari Jaloux's categoric misogyny:

> Toutes estes, serez ou fustes
> De fait ou de voulenté, pustes!
>
> (*RR*, vv. 9159–60)[83]

(They all are, will be, or were, in deed or in thought, whores!),

by refashioning it to become an equally authoritative affirmation of feminine virtue:

---

[80] See Taylor 2003.

[81] As critics have often noted, misogyny is not the only, or indeed the principal, grounds on which Christine and Gerson oppose the *Rose*. For the theologian especially, the central question is Jean de Meun's immoral use of language, of which the misogynistic utterances of his personified voices are seen as an offshoot or symptom: see Desmond 2003. Nonetheless, it is these offshoots that are picked up by later *querelle des femmes* writers, who thereby retrospectively make of the *'Rose' querelle* a debate about women.

[82] 'In his own person': Hicks 1977: 62. By overriding the *Rose* supporters' claim that Jean de Meun's use of personified voices ('personnages' (ibid. 132)) relieves him of the responsibility for the Mari Jaloux's and Genius' misogynistic utterances, Christine and Gerson promote the author in person, not simply his text, as their chief target of criticism. See Chapter 2, pp. 137–40.

[83] The Mari Jaloux's tri-temporal statement has its own intertextual dimension as a perversion of scriptural formulae for describing the sacred mystery of God 'qui est et qui erat et qui venturus est': Rev. 1: 4.

Ja a esté, est et sera moult de plus vaillans femmes, plus honnestes, [. . .] et dont plus grant bien est ensuivi au monde que onques ne fist de sa personne.

(There have been, there are, and there will be more virtuous women, more honourable, [. . .] and from whom more great good has come forth into the world than ever did from his person.)[84]

Her hermeneutic reworking is, in fact, all the more authoritative as she transforms his universalization into a comparative ('plus honnestes'), thereby liberating it from the mode of generalization that Christine elsewhere classifies as a pernicious, misogynistic form of discourse.[85] Secondly, Christine revises Genius' injunction to man to shun woman:

> Fuiez, fuiez, fuiez, fuiez,
> Fuiez, enfanz, fuiez tel beste!
>
> (*RR*, vv. 16586–7)

(Flee, flee, flee, flee, flee, my children, flee from such a monster!),

by transforming it explicitly into an imperative to any morally upright reader to shun the poisonous content of the *Rose*'s flimsy fiction:

Mais si comme dit son prestre Genius: 'Fuiéz! Fuiéz femme, le mal serpent mucié soubz l'erbe!' puis dire: 'Fuiéz! Fuiéz les malices couvertes soubz umbre de bien et de vertu'.

(Thus if his priest Genius can say, 'Flee, flee woman, the evil serpent hidden in the grass'; I can say, 'Flee, flee the malice concealed in the shadow of goodness and virtue'.)[86]

Christine here exploits the facility of flexible quotation in order to refashion more spectacularly, more dexterously, and more effectively Jean de Meun's text.[87] She amalgamates Genius' initial injunction with his later imperative to flee 'li froiz serpanz en l'erbe':

> Fuiez, enfanz, car il enherbe
> Et empoissone et envenime
> Tout homme qui de li s'aprime.
>
> (*RR*, vv. 16595–8)

(Flee, my children, for it enchants, poisons, and envenoms every man who comes near it.)

---

[84] Hicks 1977: 19; Baird and Kane 1978: 52–3. This tri-temporal phrase haunts Christine's *œuvre*, notably her *Epistre au dieu d'amours* (1990: vv. 423–5) and the *Cité des dames* (1997: 324).

[85] See Richards 1996; cf. Blamires 1997: 11–15.

[86] Hicks 1977: 21; Baird and Kane 1978: 54–5. [87] Cf. Laennec 1993: 41.

The encounter with the snake in the grass (i.e. woman) that is explicit in Genius' speech thus haunts implicitly Christine's shrewd appropriation of the metaphor to underpin the analogy she makes between the concealed serpent and the poison secreted under the veil of the *Rose*'s fiction. Furthermore, Genius attributes these words to Virgil such that a further 'strand' of intertextuality is set in play here: Christine effectively rewrites both Jean de Meun and Virgil, killing two misogynist ghosts, as it were, with one rhetorical stone.[88]

Querelle des femmes writers' diegetic speakers hermeneutically rework the two phrases targeted by Christine in successive instances of rhetorical performance. The reduplicated imperative and the tri-temporal formula they take from Genius' and the Mari Jaloux's discourses in the *Rose* contain memorable forms of repetition; this makes them prime candidates for intertextual pick-up, since they are both easily recognizable and open to modulation. I offer the example of Le Franc's *Champion*,[89] where the spectre of Genius' imperative is spectacularly dispersed through the discourses of the text's various diegetic speakers: it appears, in modulated form, in three different speeches. Its misogynistic spectre is raised by Vilain Penser, one of Malebouche's henchmen, who conjures it up approvingly in his most vitriolic invective against women:

> Fuy les dedens, fuy les dehors!
> Des dyables sont acompaignies:
> Fui les. . . .
>
> (*CD*, vv. 6197–9)[90]

(Flee them inside, flee them outside! They keep company with devils: flee them . . .)

Contrariwise, on two occasions, the spectre is con*jured*. First, its characteristic form of the reduplicated imperative to flee, which signifies, in Genius' speech, misogynistic social divisiveness, is revolutionized in Book I by Dame Charité. As abbess superintending the chapel of true Love, she is the ideal foil to Jean de Meun's despicable, false priest:[91]

---

[88] Derrida comments that spectres *of* Marx are not only the spectres *derived from* Marx but also the spectres *by* which Marx himself was haunted: *SM* 162.

[89] See also *PHF* 42.

[90] It is likewise Vilain Penser who enlists the Mari Jaloux's misogynistic generalization as a view authorially endorsed by Jean de Meun: vv. 6367–8.

[91] Le Franc's Acteur observes approvingly that 'she never ceases preaching (*sermonner*) Love's commandments' (*CD*, vv. 1725–6), as if countering ironically the nefarious, interminable 'sermon' delivered by Jean de Meun's Genius (*RR*, vv. 16573–710).

Amez Amours, amez, amez!
[. . .]
Tous ensemble vous entramez,
N'ayez n'a vous n'a aultre noise.
A l'autel d'Amours chascun voise!

(*CD*, vv. 1705, 1707–9)

(Love Love, love, love! [. . .] All together, love each other, don't pick a quarrel with yourself nor with anyone else. Let everyone come to the altar of Love!)

Her exhortation to love calls for interpersonal, social, and religious harmony instead of division since the figure of Amour in the *Champion* embraces many levels of application from the political to the divine, as the God of Love is revealed to be assimilable to the Holy Spirit (vv. 1758–60).[92] Charité's imperative resonates not only intertextually, but also on a transtextual axis with the Christian Bible's greatest Commandment, which scans the *Champion*—and especially Book I—like a refrain: for example, it first appears inscribed on the pillars of Love's Chapel, where Charité is officiating:

A l'environ du pillier dextre
En lettre d'or fin escript voy:
De tout cueur Dieu aime. Au senestre:
Ton prochain aime comme toy.

(*CD*, vv. 1673–6)

(Around the pillar on the right I saw written in gold lettering: *Love God with all your heart*, and on the left: *Love your neighbour as youself*.)

A similar, double axis of hermeneutic activity operates on the *Champion*'s second recuperation of Genius' injunction, which, echoing Charité's imperative, is an invitation to unite that is antithetical to Genius' call for social dislocation; the Champion cries:

Venez au puy d'Amours, venez,
Venez y . . . !

(*CD*, vv. 4161–2)

('Come to the *puy* of Love, come, come along . . . !')

He invites all assembled to participate in a poetic competition, a *puy*, which is traditionally associated with praise of the Virgin, and thus

---

[92] This range of levels is summarized here by Charité: 'Love God and the king and the dauphin, and dukes and princes and neighbours': vv. 1717–18.

assimilable to a sort of pro-feminine agenda. I shall explore more fully in Chapter 2 the way in which the figure of the *puy* in the *Champion* functions as a court, and concludes in Book V with the staging of a diegetic exchange of *chansons* in praise of the Virgin Mary. For the moment, I wish to consider it as an arena for highlighting poetic interaction and rhetorical rivalry, as a diegetic echo, therefore, of the type of creative, competitive intertextuality in which I believe Le Franc to be engaging with Jean de Meun. In this sense, Franc Vouloir's invitation to unite may be seen specifically as an exhortation to unite against the foe; he throws down the gauntlet to Jean de Meun through his cry's reappropriation of Genius' injunction, calling his inscribed audience to congregate in order to celebrate woman's virtue, not to flee her falsely alleged vice.

Le Franc's deployment of a double axis of intertextual and transtextual relationships confirms an important aspect of *querelle* works' meticulous appropriation of the *Rose*'s misogynist discourse: it is not merely a decorative feature, but is integrated in—and integral to—the meaning-creating processes of the works themselves.[93] Hence the necessity that both the spectre and its living appropriation be perceived by the reader, who is thus able to engage in 'filling out' what Riffaterre calls the intertextual 'gap' between text and model[94] that the *querelle* writer creates through his own interpretative rereading of the *Rose*. To borrow Taylor's felicitous phrase describing successive poets' intertextual exchanges in the *'Belle Dame' querelle, querelle des femmes* writers attack the *Rose*'s offending discourse with 'exegetical relish'.[95] The textual precision of their reworkings, achieved by ghostly echo of a telling formula or by flexible quotation, demonstrates how these writers confidently anticipated their readership's familiarity with the *Rose*. A veritable network of intertextualities is established which is valuable to the modern critic seeking to understand how these works were received: how popular they were, and how they were intended to be read in their contemporary context.

Querelle poems do not only 'have it out with' Jean de Meun's *Rose* through isolated, transformative ghostings of fragments of speech. Their imaginative engagement with the *Rose* operates also on larger structural units, tackling whole episodes—as we saw at the outset of this chapter—or rewriting personifications from the *Rose*'s cast of

---

[93] Cf. Pasco 1994: 12.

[94] He describes how the perception of such a 'gap' provokes an intertextual drive to fill out its meaning: 1990: 57.

[95] Taylor 2001: 11.

characters. I examine in detail here two instances of such thoroughgoing, innovative negotiation with Jean de Meun's legacy: the recuperation of the *Rose*'s conclusion in the *Champion*, and the careful crafting of the characters Raison, Entendement, and Malebouche in an anonymous, early sixteenth-century poem known as the *Giroufflier aulx dames*. That this engagement is with textual units much greater than a single phrase does not mean that their attention to detail or the intellectual investment they require is at all compromised; on the contrary, each instance both manifests the writer in question's subtle skill and demands equally acute attention from the text's audience.

At the end of the *Rose*, the Lover's sexual penetration of the rose-maiden is communicated through the supposedly oblique metaphor of a pilgrim worshipping at the shrine of his beloved saint and kissing her relics. The allegorical structure of this conclusion was a notable bone of contention in the '*Rose*' *querelle*. Both Gerson and Christine condemned its impropriety, deeming its fictional veil to be an outrageous admixture of 'choses saintes' and 'ordure',[96] according to the theologian, or, in Christine's case, to be an inflammatory way of pointing up, rather than disguising, the sexual act.[97] Similar moral outrage is expressed by Le Franc's Champion when, in debate with Trop Cuidier, he states that the fiction is too transparent and that Jean de Meun should simply have said the lovers kissed, and left it at that (*CD*, vv. 12425–40). The subject is not dropped; at the end of Book V, it re-emerges in the poem's concluding *puy*, where it is taken up in a peculiarly specific defence of woman's honour. This so-called *puy* consists of a sequence of *chansons* in praise of the Virgin that are ostensibly composed and performed by eleven feminine virtues. Indeed, the entirety of Book V's debate is devoted to Mary, and specifically to a theological justification of the doctrine of the Immaculate Conception, which, to Le Franc's delight as a supporter of doctrinal reform, had recently been ratified by the Council of Basel in 1439 (*CD*, vv. 23425–32). It is in this light that the reader should approach the recuperation of the *Rose*'s conclusion that is performed most aptly by the song of Dame Virginité: she rewrites it both as a hermeneutic recovery of the rose-maiden's defloration, and as a theologically oriented defence of one holy woman's honour:

> Vierge, il entra ta chambre close,
> Close, reclose et close arriere.

---

[96] Hicks 1977: 62.   [97] See Swift 2004: 69.

Pas ne pouoit estre desclose,
Je le sçay, devant ne derriere.
[. . .]
Ainsy nonobstant la barriere
Entra ton clos sans flour corrumpre.

(*CD*, vv. 24161–4, 26167–8)

(Virgin, he entered your private room, closed, shut, and locked behind. It couldn't be opened, I know, at the front or at the back. [. . .] Thus, notwithstanding the barrier, he entered your chamber without damaging a flower.)

Her song is a rhetorical *tour de force* of verbs of closure and concealment. Her virtuoso manipulation of interlaced antitheses ('close'/'desclose' with 'devant'/'derriere') and synonyms ('arriere'/'derriere'), together with extended use of *traductio* ('reclose'/'close'/'desclose'/'clos') make her song a masterful interpretative performance to be applauded. It is, after all, a contribution to an intratextual poetic competition as well as being, on an intertextual axis, a spectacular piece of one-upmanship in Le Franc's competitive engagement with Jean de Meun. It is Virginité's specification of entry 'sans flour corrumpre' (v. 26168) that can be seen to trigger the twofold intertextual context of her song, especially as Marian floral symbolism has been played up particularly prominently throughout Book V.[98] The two rose-maidens—that of the *Rose* and the Virgin Mary as 'the white rose' (v. 22419)—intersect in this passage, which thereby conjures with multiple ghosts: the inimical spectre of the *Rose*'s sexual conquest, and the positive spectre of the Immaculate Conception.

In Virginité's song we may detect intertextual pressure points similar to those discussed earlier in the epitaph of Bouchet's Dido: points at which the spectre of the nefarious *Rose* continuation is being strenuously resisted but is still felt to be 'there'. The profusion of lexemes of closure, insisting upon miraculous penetration without rupture of any 'barrier', is evidence of such pressure; they counter the violent, forced access gained to the supposed 'sanctuary' by Jean de Meun's Lover, who burrowed frantically with his 'tool' (*hernois*) in order to break and enter:

[98] Mary is 'the white rose' (*CD*, v. 22419), 'the bud' (v. 23576), 'the flower [= best] of flowers' (v. 24069). Virginité's song can be appreciated as a depiction of the Immaculate Conception to varying degrees in different manuscripts of the *Champion*: it is only in *B1*, *P1*, and *A* that Book V's theological debate is extant; it is excised in all other copies up to v. 23433. It is, in essence, only the specific topicality of the Council of Basel's ratification of the doctrine that is obscured by this excision; the imagery of Mary's purity 'whiter than the lily flower' (v. 24106) remains clear.

Par ou le passage quis ai,
Le paliz au bourdon brisai.

(*RR*, vv. 21643–4)

(I managed to find a way through by breaking down the paling with my staff.)

This particular pressure point also resonates with the lexical insistence upon unforced, miraculous entry found in certain Old Testament texts that anticipate typologically both the Immaculate Conception and the Annunciation. The image of Mary as an impregnable castle was common currency in exegetical and homiletic tradition as an amplification of lines in Luke (10: 38) that are understood to evoke the incarnate Christ's miraculous entry into the intact Virgin's womb: 'Intravit in quoddam castellum.'[99] Virginité's depiction of a miraculous consummation not only draws on this general metaphor, but also, with Le Franc's characteristic textual precision and complexity, interweaves other, specific spectres: the Song of Songs and the book of Ezekiel prefigure the virginal womb in terms of miraculous opening and secure enclosure which resonate strikingly with Virginité's song.[100] By interlacing echoes of the *Rose* and scriptural models, Virginité redeems the body of the rose-maiden to represent a miraculous conception: either St Anne conceiving the Virgin, or Mary herself at the Annunciation.

Whereas the *Champion* acts to rehabilitate the figure of the 'rosier', the anonymous *Giroufflier aulx dames* supplants it as a flower that is semiotically tarnished beyond redemption; the rose is replaced by a red wallflower bush, 'un giroufflier vermeil' (*GD* 249), as the dramatic and thematic *point de repère* around which the poem's action is centred. Composed at some point before 1521,[101] the *Giroufflier*'s allegorical narrative describes the events heard and seen by a first-person narrator (l'Acteur), who is initially concealed behind the eponymous wallflowers. Having overheard a voice reading aloud from the *Rose*, he then witnesses a series of conversations between Raison and 'the writer (*facteur*) of the *Rose*', and Raison and Entendement. Entendement suddenly vanishes and l'Acteur then sees a large number of

---

[99] '[Jesus] entered into a certain village.'　　　[100] S. of S. 5: 2–6; Ezek. 44: 1–3.

[101] Three quarto editions are extant, produced in Paris by Michel Le Noir, hence a *terminus ad quem* of 1521, the year of Le Noir's death. At the poem's conclusion l'Acteur dedicates his work to an unnamed 'princesse yssue du hault lys' (*GD* 271). Baudrier (1914: 33) records an octavo edition published by Barnabé Chaussard in Lyons, which is probably datable to some time after 1523. English translations are my own.

personified ladies gathered together under a pavilion whom Raison also interviews. The narrator transcribes her ensuing dialogues with la Princesse des Fayes, Envie, Fortune, Jalousie, Prudence, and Noblesse, before Jeunesse steps up to ask Raison why ladies still put up with the *Rose*'s malicious misogyny; Patience intervenes and counsels patient endurance. At this point the crowd disperses and the narrator concludes by reaffirming his support of women's maligned honour. According to contemporary floral symbolism, the *giroufflier* behind which l'Acteur stands seems to represent the 'fidelity in adversity' that he shows towards the female sex.[102]

It is the *Giroufflier*'s presentation of the characters Raison, Entendement, and Malebouche on which I shall focus here as particularly innovative points of intertextual dialogue with the composite *Rose*. At the poem's opening, the narrator depicts himself

> A l'ombre basse d'un giroufflier vermeil,
> Cueillant pencées deux à deux à pareil
> Et maintz soulciz, dont je suis tant fourny.
>
> (*GD* 249)

(In the low shade of a red wallflower, gathering pansies/thoughts two at a time and many marigolds/cares, with which I am well stocked.)

The concentration of floral imagery and the introduction of this chain of images by an unusual, and thus striking, substitute for the conventional rosebush draw attention to the way that the author is exploiting the punning potential of *pencées* and *soulciz* as 'thoughts' or 'pansies', and 'worries' or 'marigolds'. These puns not only express the narrator's amorous distress, a conventional lyric conceit, but also serve as a literary reflexive vehicle to allegorize the creative process that the poet will deploy in the course of the poem. Literary invention is portrayed as flower-picking, an apt means of expressing the *Giroufflier*'s intertextual relationship with that most troubling poetic flower of the later Middle Ages, the *Rose*. The first 'literary graft', to use Pasco's phrase,[103] that the poet takes from the *Rose* is the character of Raison, and the reader is made to see this graft in the very act of its being taken in a dynamic and surprising way. The *Giroufflier* stages a diegetic performative reading

---

[102] Alongside this folkloric meaning, the wallflower also has a Christian significance as a symbol of the Virgin.

[103] 1994. The metaphor of floral grafting to represent intertextual activity is also used by Derrida 1982: 320.

of the *Rose* as l'Acteur overhears a squire reading aloud 'a new dream' (*GD* 249); it is implied that this character reads the book in its entirety, from the familiar rhyming couplet that appears in the work's title at the start of Guillaume de Lorris's portion:

> Et le nommoit *le Livre de la Rose*,
> Disant en luy toute l'amour enclose
>
> (*GD* 250)

(He called it *The Book of the Rose*, and said that the whole of love was contained within it),

through to Jean de Meun's allegedly misogynist continuation, where, to the Acteur's outrage, the voice he overhears 'was uttering vehement vituperation of ladies' (ibid.). When the reading concludes, Raison leaps up to challenge the reader:

> Je vy tantost d'ung giroufflier saillir
> Dame Raison, qui le vint assaillir.
>
> (*GD* 251)

(I saw Lady Reason suddenly leap out from a wallflower and accost him.)

Raison does not spring up out of a rose bush, an apparition which would have reflected how her character was conjured up by the squire's performance of the *Rose* text, but out of an alternative flower. The *Giroufflier* poet thereby demonstrates that the character he has plucked from the *Rose* is to be differentiated from Jean de Meun's personification even though it is ultimately from the *Rose* that Raison's character derives.[104] The new Raison arraigns the squire, assuming him to be the writer of the 'cursed book' (*GD* 251), and thus responsible for its villainous defamation of women. She closes her harangue by making explicit the substitution of the *giroufflier* for the *rosier* that was implied by the poem's opening and by her own emergence from a wallflower bush; she berates the presumed *Rose* author's villainy:

> Et l'as trouvé en ton villain rosier,
> Pas n'a serché en nostre giroufflier,
> Où est enclos honneur et gentillesse.
>
> (*GD* 255)

---

[104] The personification of Raison thus encapsulates the tension between *dérive* and *dérivation* that I discussed above, pp. 35–6.

(You found it [= defamation] in your ignoble rose bush; you didn't search in our wallflower bush, which contains only honour and graciousness.)

As in the poem's opening lines, the literary reflexive significance of the flowers is spotlighted: the *rosier* is the *Rose*, the writer's past composition, while the *giroufflier* may be understood to denote the work that Raison is effectively in the course of composing through the interviews she is about to undertake with several characters, amongst whom will be numbered many feminine virtues akin to *honneur* and *gentillesse*. Furthermore, Raison performs here her own corrective reading of the *Rose*, which she, like l'Acteur, has just overheard: she reappropriates the keyword *enclose*, grafted from the *Rose*'s famous title-incipit: 'ou l'art d'amours est toute enclose' (*RR*, v. 38), to depict the new, virtuous floral dominion of the *Giroufflier*, which seeks to supplant the *Rose*.

As the writer, now identified as Entendement,[105] turns to respond to Raison's accusations, it becomes evident to the *Giroufflier*'s extradiegetic reader that this poem's author is playing with time. Entendement introduces himself as the one who started the *Rose* (its 'commençant' (*GD* 256)), namely Guillaume de Lorris, and who is, by his own admission, already dead, and thus a literal ghostly presence in the *Giroufflier*'s text:

> L'ay commencé et ne l'ay peu parfaire
> Pour la cause de la fragilité
> De tout mon corps qu'est à debilité,
> Et me convint devant heure mourir
> Et plus n'ay peu ma matière suyvir.
>
> (p. 255)[106]

(I started it and then couldn't finish it on account of my physical frailty; as a result of infirmity I died prematurely and wasn't able to pursue my subject matter any further.)

It appears that the *Giroufflier*'s author, wishing to mark a distinction between the contributions of the two *Rose* poets, has resurrected the unquiet spirit of Guillaume, victim of an untimely death ('devant

---

[105] Unlike Raison and Malebouche, this personified abstraction does not feature in the *Rose*. Entendement often represents 'Thought' or 'Understanding', but, as will become clear below, 'Intention' is perhaps the most appropriate translation here.

[106] Entendement's account is consonant with the transfer of authorship from Guillaume to Jean that is described at the *Rose*'s midpoint: *RR*, vv. 10530–98.

heure'), through the rhetorical artifice of prosopopoeia[107] into the spectral mode of personification allegory, namely the character of Entendement, who bears all the traces of Guillaume and carries his voice. The poet accords Guillaume/Entendement the opportunity to set the record straight: he states that he has been unjustly persecuted after his death, since blame for the *Rose*'s dishonourable discourse should lie solely with its continuator:

> Et se après que j'eu finé ma vie,
> On a mis reprouche par envye,
> Le reprocher seroit à l'achevant,
> Selon tout droit, non pas au commençant.
>
> (*GD* 256)[108]

(And if, after I died, the book was reproached out of envy/hatred, the reproach should, by rights, be directed at the one who completed it, and not at the one who started it.)

He describes how his departed spirit has been troubled by the perversion he sees to have been performed on his work by Jean de Meun. He is racked with regret at not having been able to complete the task he started in the way he had intended:

> Et Dieu sçet bien comme j'en eu remort,
> Après que fu de cestuy monde mort,
> Que je ne l'eu de premier commencé
> Affin que l'eusse aultrement avancé
> Et declairé à quoy j'avoye tendu.
>
> (Ibid.)

(God knows how much remorse I felt after I died from this world, wishing that I hadn't been the one to start it so that I could have continued it differently and made clear in what direction I'd been leaning.)

Apparently believing that Guillaume's authorial intentions were honourable, the *Giroufflier* poet gives him the posthumous chance—like the opportunity for self-defence that Bouchet grants his deceased ladies—to fulfil his aim and complete 'his' *Rose*:

---

[107] One of the established functions of this device in Classical rhetoric is the legitimate 'raising of the dead' (*inferos excitatare*): Quintilian 2001: IV, 9.2.31.

[108] Persons guilty of such mis-accusation would appear to include Christine de Pizan, who, in her letter to Pierre Col as part of the *'Rose' querelle*, deems the bad egg of the *Rose*'s conclusion to rot the whole barrel of the composite work: Hicks 1977: 56.

> Mais, à conclure selon mon sentement,
> La fin seroit que en dame parfaicte
> N'eut oncques mal ne villanie faicte.
>
> (Ibid.)[109]

(To conclude as I'd intended, the final message would be that perfect femininity was never tainted by vice or villainy.)

The conclusion Entendement appends is, however, only virtual; it remains in the domain of speculation ('seroit') and can in this sense be assimilated to the sort of spectrality at work in the *Giroufflier*. Haunted by Jean de Meun's *Rose*, the unquiet ghost of Guillaume de Lorris returns as a *revenant* in pursuit of justice, a justice that is only available through rhetorical artifice since the alternative conclusion he voices cannot, in reality, supplant Jean de Meun's ending. The diegetic layering of voices here is quite complicated and the acts of performative interpretation are multiple. Within the *Giroufflier*'s allegorical fiction, Entendement is rewriting the end of the *Rose* by imposing what would have been its original ending had he, the poem's first author, been able to carry through his initial authorial intention. The nature of the rewrite he proposes can be seen as a diegetic echo of the *Giroufflier* author's overall aim in his poem: to substitute a new text for the *Rose* which is pro-feminine (adhering to the symbol of the *giroufflier*) rather than misogynistic (tainted by the *rose*). Entendement/Guillaume's stated intention appropriates his *Rose* contribution for the pro-feminine cause, retrospectively making the main thrust of his poetic argument a defence of women, as opposed to the allegory of love that was originally proposed by his *Rose* commencement: 'ou l'art d'amours est toute enclose' (*RR*, v. 38). The way that Entendement/Guillaume portrays his continuator as a misogynist thus reflects the manner in which the *Giroufflier* poet refigures the *Rose* 'commençant', effectively his own literary ancestor, as a defender of the case for women, appropriating him for the pro-feminine camp of late medieval authors.

Satisfied with having vindicated himself, Entendement/Guillaume proceeds to lay his own ghost:

> A celle foys celluy s'evanouyt
> Que oncques puis nul de nous ne le vit,

---

[109] The *Giroufflier* poet seems here to be responding to Guillaume's unfulfilled promise to conclude the *Rose* with 'a very fine ending' (*RR*, v. 2063) that will reveal the 'meaning' (*senefiance*) of the dream (v. 2069).

Car Attropos le tenoit soulx la lame
D'ombre de mort; Jesu-Crist en ay l'ame.

(*GD* 255)

(At this point, he [= Entendement] vanished, and no one saw him again, for Atropos held him in the shadow of death; may Christ Jesus have his soul!)

He vanishes without trace, returning whence his spectre came to a quasi-Dantean kingdom of shades, whilst his soul, presumed now to be at rest, is commended to Heaven by l'Acteur. L'Acteur responds to this disappearance by setting out with his writing implements ('plume et papier pour escrire' (p. 257)) to take up the pro-feminine mantle he perceives Guillaume to have worn. L'Acteur embarks on his own intertextual engagement with the *Rose* through his transcription of Raison's conversations, which will become the text of the *Giroufflier* itself.

In the *Giroufflier*, both the poet and his character (Entendement) can be seen to engage in what Harold Bloom has called 'intrapoetic' revisionary relationships with the dead.[110] In his work on poetic influence, Bloom makes a distinction between 'strong' and 'weak' poets that is singularly appropriate for articulating intertextual activity in the *Giroufflier*, where the personal authority of Jean de Meun is felt to press in anxiety-inducing fashion upon his predecessor-cum-successor, Guillaume.[111] It is, Bloom claims, only 'strong poets' who possess the capacity to exert a lasting anxiety of influence, and such a one, I argue, is Jean de Meun.[112] Bloom describes in emotive and embodied terms the 'trace' left by a prior writer in his heir: 'The strong dead return [. . .] and they do not come back without darkening the living.'[113] The effect of Jean de Meun's spectral return is evident from the very outset of the *Giroufflier* through Entendement's performance of the *Rose*;

[110] I return to Bloom's terminology in Chapter 2 since his term 'intrapoetic' enables me to evoke as one, complex unity the interrelation of intertextuality and interpersonality that I believe underpins *querelle* writers' conception of their misogynist forebears.

[111] Guillaume de Lorris maintains a double temporal relation to Jean de Meun here: he is his predecessor but, in the way that he returns in the *Giroufflier* to appraise the continuator's work, is also his successor.

[112] Bloom's theory has come under fire from feminist scholars for its 'more or less Freudian and Oedipal' structures, which automatically exclude women from poetic history: Delaney 1990: 88–103. However, it is precisely his privileging of paternal roots that makes his theory so useful for interpreting the tension staged by the *Giroufflier* poet between Guillaume and Jean. I limit myself here to the general terms of Bloom's thesis, as opposed to the detailed 'revisionary ratios' he contrives to classify different types of intrapoetic relationship: 1997: 14.

[113] Bloom 1997: 139.

the villainous continuation immediately eclipses Guillaume's portion in Raison's harangue. However, the *Giroufflier* allows Jean de Meun's dark shadow to be dispersed by reviving Guillaume—a 'weak' poet in several respects, as Entendement confesses his 'fragilité' (*GD* 255, cit. above)—and empowering him to become, albeit briefly, a 'strong' poet, who is able to revise and seemingly overthrow Jean's continuation. Although troubled by the activity of the *Rose*'s 'achevant', Guillaume retroactively tames his continuator and momentarily accords his own work precedence; but his moment soon passes: his shade rapidly fades such that the shadow of Jean de Meun is left to 'darken' the rest of the *Giroufflier*. After Entendement's disappearance, a new character pops up: Malebouche, the prime mover of literary misogyny amongst personification allegories, who

> . . . dames et demoiselles
> Va blasonnant en paroles cruelles.
>
> (*GD* 262)

(. . . [he] goes about mocking both married women and young virgins with cruel words.)

As the *pendant* to pro-feminine Entendement, Malebouche stands implicitly as the personified representation of Jean de Meun. By a neat intertextual irony, therefore, Guillaume de Lorris is here defeated, Frankenstein-like, by a monstrous, misogynistic mutation of the personification that his own *Rose* commencement created.[114] Through considerable allegorical wit and ingenuity the *Giroufflier* poet demonstrates how animated, parasitic, and power-hungry a process of intertextual transformation can be. She or he enables us to see how modern theories of influence and of the 'psychic battle' between successive authors are far from anachronistic as strategies for reading pre- or early modern texts.[115]

Bloom's notion of revisionary relationships is not only applicable to the quirky fiction of the *Giroufflier*; it makes a more general and valuable contribution to the dynamic, spectral theory of *querelle* intertextuality that I postulate here. It emphasizes 'the immense anxieties of indebtedness'[116] that I showed earlier to afflict Milet's 'chief des

---

[114] Like Raison, Malebouche has 'drifted' somewhat from her original role as porter in Bel Accueil's prison: *RR*, v. 2833. Malebouche's assimilation to misogyny is traceable back to Christine's *Epistre au dieu d'amours*, where she lambastes Jean de Meun and Co., as 'villainous slanderers': Christine de Pizan and Hoccleve 1990: v. 423.

[115] Bloom offers his theory as being applicable only to post-1700 literary activity.

[116] 1997: 5. For the interrelation of Bloom and Derrida, see Orr 2003: 63–7.

dames', and the dialectical relationship it identifies between poets.[117] The sorts of intertextual 'revision' that I have explored in the *Champion* and *Giroufflier* occur through the hermeneutic dismantling of the *Rose* continuation and the rhetorical reconstruction of, in these instances, the poem's conclusion and the entirety of Jean de Meun's continuation. A living appropriation of dead material is made possible, whether this entails the literary resurrection of Guillaume de Lorris's ghost or the reactivation of the metaphor of the Virgin as a rose or a castle as a means of rewriting sexual consummation. In other words, the 'strong dead', in this case Jean de Meun, are not allowed to return intact; as Bloom notes: '*How* they return is the decisive matter, for if they return intact, then the return impoverishes the later poets.'[118] I argue that *querelle* writers deliberately foster the *Rose* continuator's return so as to 'trump' this most prestigious late medieval best seller through subtle reinvention. They can be seen to allow themselves to be haunted by the spectre of Jean de Meun so as to enrich, rather than impoverish, the hermeneutic interest of their works: 'The mighty dead return, but they return in our colours, and speaking in our voices, at least in part, at least in moments.'[119] They conjure up his text in order to refute and reappropriate it in ways that 'have it out with' the *Rose*'s ghost on their own terms.[120]

So far in this chapter I have suggested new ways of reading *querelle* texts which highlight their authors' strategies of intertextuality as dynamic and diverse hermeneutic manoeuvres rather than static, monotonous repetitions of 'stock repertory'. The *Champion, Forest*, and *Giroufflier* engage in exciting, revisionary relationships with their *Rose* inheritance, which remains, I emphasize, a chosen inheritance. These writers undertake to lay the *Rose*'s ghost through radical rewriting of its discourse, dismantling its verbal body and incorporating it into their own texts. This spectropoetic process of conjuration is played out, to quote Derrida, as a hermeneutic operation 'à la fois puissante et, comme toujours, inquiète, fragile, angoissée'.[121] In other words, whilst the *Rose* is just another text, whose rhetoric is always open to appropriation and metamorphosis, it is also played up by the new author's diegetic characters to be a totemic, inescapably looming authority to which one remains double bound. Any 'radicalization', such as Virginité's recasting of the *Rose* defloration, 'est toujours endettée auprès de cela même qu'elle

---

117 Bloom 1997: 91.   118 Ibid. 140.   119 Ibid. 141.
120 The ghost of Boccaccio might be explored in similar terms. Cf. Kolsky 2005: 1.
121 *SM* 88. 'Both powerful and, as always, worried, fragile, anxious': *SoM* 50.

radicalise';[122] thus, over two centuries after its composition, in the literary cemetery of Octovien de Saint-Gelais's *Séjour d'honneur* (1494), the *Rose* continuation is still seen to belong to its author: Saint-Gelais's narrator recounts:

> Peu demouray en ce sejour commun
> Ou tout plaisir et leesse est enclose.
> Si apperceu lors maistre Jehan de Meun,
> Tenant encor son Rommant de la Rose.[123]

(I stayed a short while in this shared resting place where one finds every joy and pleasure. I then caught sight of Master Jean de Meun, still holding his *Romance of the Rose*.)

As if cued into the text by the keyword *enclose* in rhyme position, Jean de Meun once again looms large. It is the possessive adjective that is significant here: the master is envisaged still holding onto *his* book, the implication being that acts of poetic challenge, judicial trying, and hermeneutic revision have not succeeded in wrenching the *Rose* from its author, from whose indomitable spectre the book is indissociable.[124] If the *Rose* cannot be separated from its author, then the inheritors of this book can no more write independently of its author's influence when they engage with his text.

For the *querelle* writer, this image of the inescapable 'mighty dead' is an essential element of his compositional art, but in a positive sense: being so well known, the *Rose* can be relied upon to form part of an audience's intertextual competence,[125] and can thus be used to fuel new literary creation by engaging this audience in the hermeneutically exciting process of intertextual reading. *Querelle* writers seem to take the real anxieties about repeating and propagating the *Rose* that were expressed in the *'Rose' querelle*, and transpose them into the fictional conflicts they stage between pro- and anti-feminine speakers. Their aim is twofold: to enliven their own *débats*, and to direct the audience's

---

[122] *SM* 152. 'Is always indebted to the very thing it radicalizes': *SoM* 92.

[123] 2002: III. xii.109–12. English translation is my own.

[124] Saint-Gelais's narrator confirms my earlier conjecture that the relationship between Jean de Meun and his *Rose* is exceptional in the way that it was perceived by his immediate successors as one of literary property at a time when, according to most modern scholarship, such a concept was virtually unknown: see Brown 1995: 17–59.

[125] The *Rose* survives in some 320 manuscripts and 21 printed editions before 1538. See Huot 1993a and Bourdillon 1906. I use Bourdillon as my main source for information on the printed editions; recent, as yet unpublished research by Martha Driver indicates that some revision of Bourdillon's data may be necessary.

attention towards issues of inheritance in order to focus them on the intricate rewriting and appropriation performed by the current poet. These writers retrospectively establish the *Rose* as the arch-misogynistic authority. For the pro-feminine cause to be sustained it must continue to entertain and 'have it out with' Jean de Meun's ghost in successive resistant performances; these are no less dynamic for the frequency with which they raise his ghost since each writer (however temporarily) makes it his own. In conclusion, the *Rose* can be seen as the spectre that 'il ne faut pas chasser, mais trier, critiquer, garder près de soi et laisser revenir';[126] it is the force to be reckoned with in the *querelle des femmes*.

FROM CRITICAL READING TO CONTEMPORARY RECEPTION: TEXT AND PARATEXT

In this part of Chapter 1 I should like to turn my attention from modern critical readings to the contemporary reception of *querelle* texts; this will, I hope, bear out the validity of my postulated 'spectropoetic' approach as a reading strategy that is consonant with late medieval perceptions of intertextual activity. A central question must be addressed here: how can we know that contemporary readers of these works were not only sensitive to the hermeneutic manoeuvrings and intertextual dialogues that I have described, but, moreover, that they found this activity a principal source of interest, and that it was seen by *querelle* writers (and publishers) as one of the main stakes of literary composition? Evidence is supplied by features of both text and paratext[127] that readers were, to quote Huot, 'reading for the intertext' in its fullest sense: reading one text in dialogue with another, engaging intellectually with the weaving of the textual fabric itself.

This section will explore two aspects of paratextual apparatus—illustrations and marginal labels—across the production history of the *Champion des dames* as ways of discerning how at least some readers understood the work's complex intertextuality. Sustaining the central metaphor of Derrida's theory of 'inheritance', I shall consider, therefore, how the scribes, miniaturists, and later publishers and printers, of

---

[126] *SM* 144. 'one must not chase away but sort out, critique, keep close by, and allow to come back': *SoM* 87.

[127] I use the term as understood by Genette to embrace all features of a text's presentation as a book (1987: 7), including, for my purposes, illustrations and marginal annotation.

this sample *querelle* work acted as heirs to the text they presented in manuscript and print, and not only to this text, but also to its principal model, the *Rose*. We shall identify several ways in which they conjured with these spectres in the materiality of the text's presentation. My understanding of the roles played by labels and miniatures in these 'manuscript matrices'[128] and imprints will be informed here by Herman Braet's notion that such paratextual elements constitute a reading of the text:

Rappelons que dans un manuscrit illuminé, les miniatures forment avec les rubriques un support de la lecture: elles ponctuent et articulent, elles sélectionnent et mettent en évidence certains éléments. Bien plus riches parfois que l'écrit, les gloses visuelles permettent de clarifier, d'expliquer, de commenter. Les choix et les rapprochements opérés par les imagiers peuvent faire ressortir les perceptions variées dont un texte a fait l'objet; la lecture participative de l'artiste contribue à nous renseigner sur l'intelligence et sur la réception de l'œuvre.[129]

(Let us remember that, in an illuminated manuscript, the miniatures conjoin with the rubrics to assist the reading process: they punctuate and articulate the text, they pick out and highlight certain features. Often more rich than the written text, visual glosses allow for clarification, explanation, and commentary. The choices and connections made by illustrators can bring out the different interpretations that a text has received; the participation of the artist in the reading process helps give us information about the ways a given work was understood and received.)

Marginal labels are appended to the revised *Champion* codex, *P1*,[130] in which they are contemporary with the copying and illustration of the text.[131] They serve principally an indexing function as a sort of

---

[128] I borrow Nichols's coinage denoting the relationship between the text and other visual signs in 'the material specificity of medieval texts': 1990: 4.

[129] 1994: 111. English translation is my own. That manuscript images are readings and rewritings of texts is a founding premiss in much recent work on visual studies, such as Desmond and Sheingorn 2003. The interpretative value of other paratextual apparatus (rubrics and glosses) is explored by Huot 1987b.

[130] I use the sigla noted in Appendix 2A to refer to the different manuscripts of the *Champion*.

[131] Huot 1987b: 70. These marginal labels do not, to my knowledge, occur in any other *Champion* manuscript. The original, apparently rejected copy, *B1*, lacked any such indexing features and contained only one illustration in addition to a presentation miniature. In this light, the sixty-six miniatures of varying size punctuating *P1* were perhaps intended, together with its marginal labels, to improve the *Champion*'s chance of success by making the 24,000-line work more 'reader friendly'; to this pragmatic end, labels also occur in *P1* within illustrations to identify the characters featured. A further reason for the rejection of *B1* may quite simply be that its paucity of decoration did not live up to the sumptuous standards of book production expected by Philip: see Desmond and Sheingorn 2003: 84.

titulus, demarcating episodes in this massive debate poem. Technical labels also occur, indicating, for example, where the Champion digresses from his main argument (for example, fol. 22^v: 'incident'), as do *nota* marks and *maniculae*, which highlight certain 'maxims' (*sentences*) or significant lines. These labels also serve to indicate how the other texts with which the *Champion* engages were treated: whether they were remarked upon, how frequently, and with what selectivity. The main body of the *Champion* (Books II to V) takes the form of a scholastic debate, in which, as one would expect, textual *auctoritates*—ancient and modern, biblical, patristic, historical, and literary—are enlisted at every turn. What is striking about *P1*'s marginal labels is that they flag up exclusively and selectively contemporary, medieval texts by naming the author as a signifier for their work: Christine de Pizan and Dante are both highlighted in this fashion (fols. 114^r, 12^r), but none of Chartier, Machaut, Charles d'Orléans, or Froissart is named in the margin despite each being discussed at some length in the text.[132] The greatest frequency and concentration of labels is accorded to Jean de Meun. At every point that he is cited within the debate in Books II and III his name appears in the margin. The distribution of these labels is interesting. There is one isolated note on fol. 76^r ('Contre maistre Jehan de Meun ou livre de la Rose')[133] which corresponds to Franc Vouloir's criticism of the author's 'wicked treachery' in exposing the *Rose*-Lover's sexual 'manoeuvrings' (*CD*, vv. 12100–3). The marginal label seems here to play up the sort of ironic tensions highlighted above as a consequence of the *querelle* writer's double bind to his misogynist ancestor, needing to conjure him up in order to conjure him. At this point in the debate, Franc Vouloir issues his imperative against reading the *Rose*: 'True lovers, don't read his book' (v. 12113), advising instead the study of a 'healthy' allegorical courtly narrative, the *Horloge amoureux* by 'the learned Master Jean Froissart' (v. 12121). The marginal

---

[132] I suggest that the annotator's selection of names for labelling might correspond to the writers represented in Philip the Good's book collection. This hypothesis is especially tempting if we accept Charron's theory (2000: 23) that Le Franc himself supervised the compilation of *P1*. Such selective labelling could be seen as a way of targeting his intended audience, whose attention the author would be all the keener to attract, having (apparently: see Swift 2006) failed to do so with the first codex, *B1*. In which case, it is logical that Christine, as the most numerously represented vernacular author in the ducal library, should be flagged up, together with the continuator of the *Rose*, of which Philip possessed three copies at this time: Bousmanne et al. 2003: 49–53, 141–4, 210–13.

[133] 'Against Master Jean de Meun in the book of the Rose.'

labelling of this passage can thus be seen to undermine the Champion's counsel by according the *Rose* publicity (however adverse) and by eclipsing—by omitting to flag up—Froissart as preferred reading matter.[134]

Marginal labels appear to be deployed in *P1* to promote an awareness of the *Rose*, not just as the *Champion*'s main model, but as a major source of hermeneutic interest for the reader of this text. It seems to be important that Jean de Meun is flagged up as much as possible; two other passages that address his *Rose* (but also other authorities as well) display a remarkably dense concentration of labels, which highlight him, and him alone.[135] The first passage, in Book II, concerns woman's alleged untrustworthiness: her wifely wiles and her use of cosmetics to deceive men. Vilain Penser's initial enlistment of '. . . Jean de Meun whom everyone loves' (v. 6750) to support this argument is signalled in the margin by the comment: 'Cy allege maistre Jehan de Meun contre les femmes' (fol. 43ᵛ).[136] The *Rose* continuator is thus branded a misogynist, and it is in this capacity that he is labelled five times in the following ten pages,[137] twice in conjunction with Matheolus (fols. 44ᵛ, 47ᵛ). The first pairing of the two arch-misogynists highlights Franc Vouloir's rejection of their anti-matrimonial views (fol. 44ᵛ); in the stanza they flag up, it is not their texts that the Champion dismantles, but the names of the writers themselves:

> Car de quel pié Clopinel cloche
> Et que Mathieu ne se faint mie
> De sonner l'envieuse cloche
> Par fin despit de bigamie,
> On voit, on oit. . . .
>
> (*CD*, vv. 6921–5)

---

[134] I am assuming here that the annotator is labelling from a perspective on the text which accords with the expressed authorial intention to defend women and oppose Malebouche (i.e. Jean de Meun). The labels were, after all, designed to support the book's presentation to Philip the Good as a compliment to the Duke's supposed high regard for women (*CD* 8). Such a perspective does not, however, preclude an element of play and ambiguity: see Blanc et al. 1999: 483–508.

[135] Authorities named in the text but which receive no marginal label here include John of Salisbury (v. 6985), Augustine (v. 6962), Alain Chartier (v. 6915), and Machaut (v. 6917).

[136] 'Here he invokes Master Jean de Meun against women.'

[137] The page references of these labels in *P1* and their corresponding passages in the text as edited by Deschaux are as follows: fol. 44ᵛ (vv. 6913–36), fol. 47ᵛ (vv. 7489–536), fol. 48ᵛ (vv. 7641–8), fol. 51ʳ (vv. 8113–20), fol. 54ʳ (vv. 8665–72).

(We see and hear quite clearly on which foot Clopinel limps, and that Mathieu isn't pretending when he rings the bell of ill will for the despicable purpose of bigamy.)

The Champion plays punningly on Jean's sobriquet ('Chopinel')[138] and on Matheolus' reputation as a bigamist in order to perform a hermeneutic perversion of both authors' identities. Through a polyvalent pun on the senses of *clocher* ('to limp, hop, proclaim'), supported by the effect of alliteration (*cl-*), the Champion rhetorically cripples Jean de Meun, and this crippling can be seen as a potent image for the way Franc Vouloir's discourse, throughout the *Champion*, authoritatively refutes and radically reappropriates the nefarious *Rose*.

This focus on the authorial person is pertinent to the second passage in *P1* where marginal labelling of Jean de Meun is particularly concentrated, namely the episode with which I opened this chapter where the Champion restages La Vieille's indoctrination of Bel Accueil. On fol. 87^r three separate annotations flag up this episode: 'De la vieille Clopinel qui aprent Bel Accueil'; 'Contre maistre Jehan de Meun'; 'Comment la Vieille aprent Bel Accueil'.[139] The difference in phrasing between the first and third labels is noteworthy. In the first, responsibility for the *Rose* personification's discourse is located unequivocally in the voice of Jean de Meun; extradiegetic author and diegetic character are identified as one, as occurs likewise in the text, through the Champion's censure of the *Rose* continuator (vv. 14498–500, cit. above), as well as in the chapter heading for this section: 'Le Champion respond a l'adversaire en reprenant maistre Jehan de Meun, lequel a mis Bel Accueil a l'escole de la Vieille comme sous bon docteur' (preceding v. 13729).[140] In the third label, however, which accompanies Franc Vouloir's own impersonation of La Vieille, the old woman's speech is recognized as having been wrested from its original author.

The contemporary reader's apprehension of Jean de Meun's authorial presence in this episode seems to be confirmed by its accompanying illustrations in two copies of the *Champion*: one manuscript and one incunable. I use this episode's visual representation to introduce illustration as the second aspect of paratextual apparatus to be explored as evidence for

---

[138] In the central passage of the *Rose*, Jean de Meun identifies himself as '. . . Jean Chopinel, with gay heart and lively body': vv. 10569–70.

[139] 'Of Clopinel's Old Woman who instructs Fair Welcome'; 'Against Master Jean de Meun'; 'How the Old Woman instructs Fair Welcome'.

[140] 'The Champion responds to his adversary by taking to task Master Jean de Meun who set Fair Welcome to school under the Old Woman, as if under a learned teacher.'

the way certain late medieval readers conceived of the intertext for which they were reading. I am following here Braet's notion of the 'lecture participative de l'artiste', a theory that Salter and Pearsall also promote when they explain how illustrative evidence is valuable for offering 'an immediacy of imaginative response to the significance of a literary text which will enhance [the reader/viewer's] understanding in a unique way'.[141]

The first printed edition of the *Champion*, produced in Lyons in 1485, contains fifty-nine woodcuts that were specially designed to accompany this text.[142] Illustrating the chapter addressing Jean de Meun's mistreatment of Bel Accueil is an image of a young woman standing before an aged crone.[143] The figure of Jean de Meun stands between these two women as a palpable presence presiding over their interview: he places the girl's wary palm into La Vieille's outstretched hand as if physically putting her to school (the phrase used in the chapter heading is 'mettre a l'escole') under the old woman's tutelage (fol. O3^v: Plate 1.1). In an earlier, manuscript copy illustrating the same episode, Jean de Meun strikes an imposing presence as he is visualized standing between the debaters who are discussing the *Rose*'s characters (*P2*, fol. 98^r: Plate 1.2).[144] His active involvement in the debate is signalled here by the pointed finger of his raised right hand, a standard iconographic gesture for denoting speech. In this way Jean de Meun seems to be identified by visual means as the governing voice behind this scene's dialogue.

[141] 1980: 103. For Braet, see above, pp. 68–9.

[142] This total includes a number of repetitions of the same images. Physical similarities to the third edition of the *Rose*, published by Guillaume Le Roy *c.*1487, have led to Le Roy being designated as the editor of the *Champion* incunable. This attribution is debatable as the book bears no identifying mark; the typeface used in the *Champion* does not match that in any other imprint produced by Le Roy that I have seen, although Van Praët finds the characters used for the book's title page in Le Roy's 1485 edition of *Le Doctrinal de sapience*. I accept the attribution here for expediency, given that my principal focus below will be the second printed edition, published by Galliot Du Pré in Paris in 1530.

[143] We recall that the Champion envisages Bel Accueil as a 'young girl': *CD*, v. 14405.

[144] We should consider here the filiation of the *Champion*'s illustrated manuscripts. Charron proposes that four manuscripts, *B2*, *G*, *P2*, and *Z*, constitute a family: copied from a common exemplar which lacked the passage justifying the Immaculate Conception, they are destined for members of the Burgundian court circle: 1996: 123–4. Charron compiles a table comparing the miniatures of the most heavily illustrated manuscripts, namely *G*, *P1*, *P2*, and *Z*. She notes numerous parallels in the iconographic cycles for *P2* and *Z*; I record these, where necessary, relying on her table for this evidence (1996: 458–76) and also on the catalogue description of *Z* provided by Hindman © 1993: 68–78. The published version of Charron's study (2004) does not include the codicological and bibliographical details I discuss here.

HAUNTED IMAGES: WRITING AGAINST
THE GHOST

These two illustrations evoke an issue on which I shall focus in more detail in Chapter 2, namely the way that *querelle* reading practices seem to have embraced a cult of the author perceived as a personal identity alongside their perception of his text: interpersonality complementing intertextuality. The aspect of this cult of personality that I wish to isolate for discussion here is the way that this perception of an author enlivens the intertextual reading dynamic. In illustrations for the *Champion*, the phenomenon of showing the prior text's author as an active presence in dialogue with the characters that the *querelle* writer has inherited, or indeed with the writer himself, is not exclusive to portrayals of Jean de Meun. Miniatures devised for the *Champion* in *P1*, *P2*, and *G* show how a writer's reworking of his or her precursor was understood, at least in part, as a conversation between two people, rather than a disembodied interaction between two texts. This interpersonal intertextuality can ultimately be married with this chapter's spectropoetic theory of the misogynist writer as a ghostly presence haunting the text and paratext of his pro-feminine heir's *œuvre*. That said, we should insert an important caveat here: one of the essential aspects of Derridean spectral presence is that the ghost is never visible; its presence is detected, but it gazes upon us from a position in space and time in which we are unable to see it (*SM* 26–7). This is the paradoxical nature of spectral 'thereness' that I attempted to articulate above in relation to Jean de Meun's discernible presence, and the pressure exerted by his presence, in the texts of several *querelle* works: he is never seen directly, though he is addressed directly (*Forest*), invoked (*CD*), or even represented allegorically (*Giroufflier*). It might seem, therefore, a most un-Derridean gesture to propose that images representing spectral presences as visible entities can be married with his theory of spectrality. However, my point here is that such visualizations actually reinforce the case for a spectral reading of *querelle* intertextuality; the various artists are, as we shall see, responding to the strongly detectable yet unperceivable sense of presence exerted by the spectre in the text, and are making that presence visible in their illustrations. It is almost as if they, the illustrators, feel a pressure operating upon them to 'have it out with' the spectre by trying to fix it in a visible dimension. It is interesting in this light to note that, in the illustrations discussed above showing Jean de Meun present at the interview between La Vieille and Bel Accueil, the spectral interloper is represented looking on whilst the two speakers seem to proceed without actually seeing him: his is the controlling presence, though not perceptible to the human eye, and that is the nature of his 'thereness': 'cette Chose nous regarde [. . .] et nous voit ne pas la voir même quand elle est là.'[145]

The cycle of miniatures devised for *P2* (which is largely duplicated in *Z*)[146] privileges the representation of debate situations, both intratextual confrontations between the Champion and his diegetic adversaries and intertextual dialogue between different authorial persons. Both axes of textual relations are characterized by the same sort of animated, interpersonal exchange. For example, at one point in the *Champion*'s text, Franc Vouloir states that he disagrees with the way in which the poet Guillaume de Machaut concluded his popular *dit, Le Jugement du roy de Behaigne*, declaring: 'Je ne m'acorde au jugement | Machaut' (*CD*, vv. 12737–8).[147] To illustrate this episode, the miniaturist shows the Champion in conversation with another party (*P2*, fol. 83ʳ),[148] who may be understood to represent the poet Machaut. This third character is shown standing alongside the two diegetic debaters, Franc Vouloir and Trop Cuidier, and the latter appears to have turned away from his opponent, as if excluded from the principal line of communication, which is here effectively inter- rather than intratextual, that is, between the Champion and Machaut. Both the Champion and this third party are depicted making hand gestures indicative of speech to point up the dynamic nature of their dialogue.

One other episode should be considered here whose illustration in *P1*, *P2* and *Z*, and *G* portrays intertextuality as haunted acts of hermeneutic performance that are congruent with my earlier, theoretical, spectropoetic approach to *querelle* intertextuality. The episode in question is the Champion's *exemplum* of Proba (*CD*, vv. 18577–92), a woman lauded for her Christianizing rewriting of Virgil's works, since she saw that 'ex illis omnem Testamenti Veteris hystoriam et Novi seriem [. . .] posse describi'.[149] Her legend is ubiquitous amongst

---

[145] *SM* 26. 'This thing that looks at us, that concerns us [. . .] and sees us not see it even when it is there': *SoM* 6.

[146] See above, n. 144.   [147] 'I don't agree with Machaut's judgement.'

[148] Charron notes a similar image on *Z*, fol. 82ʳ.

[149] Boccaccio 2001: 412. 'From his poems one could easily compile the history of the Old and New Testaments.'

querelle writers from Christine de Pizan to Jean Bouchet.[150] She is often singled out by modern critics as a *vita* whose key significance in catalogues of women is literary reflexive, especially in her portrayal by Christine de Pizan: she functions as a *mise en abyme* of the author as *compilator*,[151] and/or as a model for Christine's relationship with Boccaccio in the way that she authoritatively revises a prior, male-authored work.[152] Proba does feature as a positive example in *De mulieribus*, but is praised in a way that still keeps the main focus of glorification on Virgil, not on her appropriation of his works:

tam compte composuit, ut huius compositi ignarus homo prophetam pariter et evangelistam facile credat fuisse Virgilium.[153]

(So neatly was it done that a person unacquainted with this work would easily believe Virgil to have been both prophet and evangelist.)

It is not surprising, therefore, given the contemporary popularity of her story, that the two stanzas devoted to praising Proba in the *Champion* receive particular attention from each manuscript's artist. What is striking, though, is how these artists represent her act of performative interpretation in three different yet equally dynamic ways. *P1* and *P2* embody and as it were dramatize the process of textual appropriation: on *P2*, fol. 131ᵛ (Plate 1.3), Franc Vouloir and Proba are depicted standing together, looking across at Virgil suspended in a basket;[154] Proba gestures towards him, and Virgil waves back. The miniature thus not only portrays Proba's rewriting of Virgil's text as an interpersonal form of communication, but, moreover, emphatically locates the superior authority and dignity with the female *re*writer, Proba, through the artist's innovative, visual allusion to the legend

---

[150] See Christine de Pizan 1997: 156–8; *Vies* 142–3; *NDV*, fol. Lᵛ (he calls her 'Centone', presumably after the title of her work, *Cento*); *JP*, vv. 2678–89.

[151] Blanchard 1992.   [152] Phillippy 1986: 179.

[153] Boccaccio 2001: 412.

[154] The popular legend of Virgil made ridiculous by love—a story often cited as a cautionary tale against woman's wiles by misogynists like the *Champion*'s Vilain Penser (*CD*, vv. 6097–120)—tells how the Emperor's daughter, with whom Virgil was infatuated, claimed to reciprocate his love; however, one night, when she was supposed to winch him up to her room, she left him hanging in his basket such that, the following day, he was made a public object of ridicule in Rome. See Smith 1995: 156–7, 186–95. Contrary to my own findings, Smith claims that the tale 'seems exclusively to have been used to poke fun at the follies committed by supposedly wise men in love': ibid. 157.

of Virgil as a fool, suspended in constrained circumstances in his cradle.[155] On *P1*, fol. 112ʳ, Proba is shown to wield similar authority over her pagan precursor: she stands in conversation with Virgil himself between two statues representing the Synagogue and the Church (that is, the Old and New Testaments). She points towards the Church, thereby indicating by a visual gesture how, by her own interpretative agency, she has rewritten the Classical writer's work in a Christian idiom. The third illustration of Proba's performative literary act is equally dynamic, but in a different way from the other two: *G*, fol. 373ᵛ (Plate 1.4). She sits upright behind a desk, her left hand holding a knife, and her right arm raised with a pen gripped in its hand. That this is the sole miniature in the tradition of *Champion* manuscripts to show Proba engaged in the act of writing is remarkable, for two reasons: first, *G* is diverging here from the visual template followed by the other manuscripts in its family (*P2* and *Z*); secondly, it is precisely in the pose of a writer at a desk that Proba is most commonly featured in contemporary illustrated manuscripts of the *Cité des dames* or of a popular vernacular translation of *De mulieribus claris*, *Le Livre de Jehan Boccace des cleres et nobles femmes*.[156] The Grenoble miniaturist seems deliberately to revert to conventional type on *G* fol. 373ᵛ in order, I argue, to introduce a subtle but significant innovation to this convention. Furthermore, it may even have been the illustration of *Nobles femmes* manuscripts that he had in mind. In the *Nobles femmes* image (Paris, BnF, MS fr. 598, fol. 143ᵛ),[157] Proba is shown bent to her task, writing into her own book with two other volumes open on a stand and one other closed. These three latter presumably represent the *Bucolics*, *Georgics*, and *Aeneid* from which Proba drew for her adaptation. In other words, Virgil is still visually present alongside Proba, just as he is highlighted in the text of her *exemplum* in *De mulieribus*. In *G*, however, Proba is in command of only one book: she is not writing in it here, but looking up at the pen she wields,

---

[155] This allusion appears to be the artist's own innovation. The only mention of the legend in the *Champion* occurs back in Book II, in Vilain Penser's misogynistic tirades (see above, n. 154). A similar image occurs on *Z*, fol. 129ʳ. By diminishing Virgil's status, the *Champion*'s illustration proposes a more radically pro-feminine perspective on Proba's achievement than is implied by Le Franc's text, where she is represented more conservatively as her Latin ancestor's equal: '. . . she had the same spirit (*le meisme courage*) as Virgil who wrote about Aeneas': vv. 18591–2. Cf. Jordan 1987: 30.

[156] See Appendix 2B for the manuscript tradition of French versions of *De mulieribus*. I address the text of these translations in Chapter 3.

[157] See also Paris, BnF, MS fr. 12420, fol. 147ʳ.

symbolically brandishing the tool of her creativity as a writer.[158] As a *re*writer, she also holds a knife, which she may be using, we deduce, to scratch out her illustrious predecessor's words to inscribe her own in their place, effacing and demoting Virgil to accord herself precedence and primacy.

The miniatures discussed above highlight the two key aspects of the *querelle*'s spectropoetic intertextual activity that I have identified in this chapter: a valorization of the gesture of (re)writing as a potent means of negotiating with a troublesome ancestor, and the dynamic, interpersonal dialogue with one's precursor that this (re)writing process entails. The dialogues these illustrations represent place in the same moment historically distant parties: Virgil and Proba, Guillaume de Machaut and Le Franc's Champion. In this respect, they can be seen as visual equivalents of the process of intertextual interaction practised by those *querelle* poets who enlist the spectre of the *Rose*; they imply a dynamic of response across time that was recognized explicitly in a late sixteenth-century *art poétique* by the Avignonnaise writer Pierre de Deimier:

> Jehan Clopinel dit de Meun a fort offencé
> La raison en se desbordant contre
> L'honneur des dames . . .
> [. . .]
> . . . *Mais en contre carrant*
> *Les opinions dudit pöete françois,*
> *Il luy fut respondu environ deux cens*
> *Ans aprés par un Martin Franc*, natif de la
> Comté d'Aumale, prévost et chanoine
> De Lausane en Savoye, lequel en composa
> Un livre à ce sujet intitulé le Champion
> des dames, qu'il adressa à Philippes.[159]

(Jean Clopinel, known as de Meun, has greatly offended reason by speaking out so excessively against women's honour [. . .] *But, contradicting the views of the aforementioned French poet, he was answered about two hundred years later*

---

[158] There is perhaps an intericonic dialogue here between the *Champion des dames* Master and the unusual iconography of Proba found in one, late fifteenth-century *Nobles femmes* manuscript, now Paris, BnF, MS fr. 599 (fol. 83ʳ), where she is represented as an astronomer, holding up a wand to the heavens. The iconographic programmes of these two manuscripts merit further close comparison.

[159] 1610: 529, 532–3 (my italics). English translation is my own. The *Académie* is dedicated to Marguerite de Valois.

by one Martin Franc, native of the county of Aumale, Provost and canon of Lausanne in Savoy, who wrote a book on this subject entitled the *Champion of Ladies*, which he addressed to Philip.)

Moreover, in the dictionaries of vernacular French writers compiled by the sixteenth-century bibliographers François de La Croix du Maine and Antoine du Verdier, Le Franc is cited principally in his capacity as respondent to the *Rose*: 'Il a escrit un livre contre le *Roman de la rose*, intitulé le *Champion des dames*.'[160] It is in this line of literary descent that his *Champion* was appreciated as a development, as it were, of Christine de Pizan's first contribution to the *'Rose' querelle*, her courtly narrative poem *L'Epistre au dieu d'amours* (1399), which was printed in the sixteenth century under the new title of *Le Contre rommant de la rose nommé le Gratia Dei*.[161] The *Champion* would have been especially striking as a 'contre-roman': amongst *querelle* texts, it manifests the most thoroughgoing engagement with Jean de Meun's work, and does so at exceptional length as the only poem to exceed the *Rose*'s 21,000 lines. Was Le Franc himself perhaps vying with the late *Rose* continuator to establish himself as the vernacular *auctor* of a new mastertext for the late Middle Ages?

Alongside sixteenth-century critical reception of the *Champion* as a work in textual dialogue with the *Rose*, a certain Parisian *libraire*, Galliot Du Pré, produced a material dialogue between the two texts when he chose to publish them in a series of editions, printed by Pierre Vidoue around 1530, which share the same woodcuts and format. As a result of this sharing, interesting iconic intersections connect the two editions. These intersections, which I shall address in detail below, can potentially be used as evidence to sketch out a contemporary publisher's perspective on the question of *querelle* intertextuality. A publisher/printer's[162] intervention in the distribution of images within and between editions may be seen as a further stage of intentionality and agency shaping a work's inheritance of

---

[160] 'He wrote a book against the *Romance of the Rose*, entitled the *Champion of Ladies*': La Croix du Maine 1584: 314; cf. Du Verdier 1585: 679.

[161] Hult 1997a: 154. An edition appeared in Paris in 1529 (printed by Julien Hubert) during the peak period for publication both of Marot's *Rose* and of *querelle des femmes* texts dealing with the *Rose*, like *Le Champion des dames* (1530) and *Le Monologue fort joyeulx* (*c.*1529), for which, see Conclusion, pp. 240–2.

[162] I acknowledge here the complex web of relationships between the agencies involved in producing an edition. The *libraire* (for whose 'protean function', see Winn 1997: 38) was sometimes also the printer, but she or he also employed the services of other printers, proof-readers, editors, artists, copyists, and writers: see Gaskell 1972: 40–56.

its literary forebears. I suggest, albeit from limited evidence, that we may see the circulation of a series of woodcuts as a printer's means of acknowledging some sort of thematic filiation between the works they illustrate and, moreover, as an advertising strategy to promote this interrelation in a material way in order to serve the publishers' commercial ends.[163] It is certainly striking that the print tradition of the *Champion* straddles the length of the *Rose*'s early printing history; some twenty-one editions of the latter appeared between 1481 and 1538.[164] More specifically, as Picot notes, the Lyons *Champion* bears physical similarities to Guillaume Le Roy's *c*.1487 edition of the *Rose*,[165] whilst the Paris *Champion* belongs to the same series of editions as the *Rose*, the *Oeuvres de feu maistre Alain Chartier*, the works of Guillaume Coquillart, and Villon's *Oeuvres* that were published contemporaneously by Du Pré.[166]

Galliot Du Pré's publishing career spans some sixty years (*c*.1511–*c*.1561), during which time he produced 330 editions. His editorial policy and his significant role as a publisher in shaping the literary tastes of an expanding public readership have received recent attention from Charon-Parent, whose findings are supported by the documentary evidence of an extant inventory of the *libraire*'s stock compiled upon his death in 1561. Of particular relevance to the present study are

---

[163] Gray sees the coincidence between the sudden popularity of pro-women literature and the advent of printing as a sign that the opposition between misogynistic and pro-feminine works was a phenomenon engineered by publishers for commercial gain: 2000: 19. We should bear in mind, though, that such a publishing phenomenon was not new; it was building on a long-established mode of circulating *pro* and *contra* texts, which were frequently grouped together in manuscript anthologies: see above, n. 60.

[164] This total includes editions of Clément Marot's recension and Jean Molinet's prose version, *Le Roman de la rose moralisé*. The '*Rose*' *querelle*, by contrast, did not survive into print as a complete dossier; Gerson's *Traité* continued to circulate, either on its own or in anthologies of devotional works, and was printed (in Latin translation) with Gerson's *Œuvres* from 1502. Christine's only surviving *querelle* contribution was her *Epistre au dieu d'amours*: see above, n. 161.

[165] Picot and Lacombe 1884: 251. Picot is mistaken in believing this to have been the first—rather than the third—printed edition of the *Rose*. The *Rose*'s print history begins in Lyons with Ortuin and Schenck (*c*.1481) then Jean Syber (*c*.1485–6) before Le Roy's version appears: Bourdillon 1906: 20–1.

[166] Tchemerzine 1932: 353. He refers here to the 1529 version of Marot's *Rose* (see below, n. 169), and to the edition of Chartier's *Oeuvres* produced in the same year. Both works are printed for Du Pré by Pierre Vidoue. Charon-Parent states that, when Du Pré took over from his father, Jean Du Pré, he discontinued the practice of printing to focus on editing and bookselling; Vidoue was the printer most frequently employed by Du Pré, for whom he produced forty-seven editions: 1988: 210.

her observations concerning the importance placed by Du Pré on the illustration of printed texts, and his cultivation of medieval vernacular literature, especially in the period 1528 to 1530.[167] Du Pré is, I believe, a central agent in fostering the revival in print of the *querelle des femmes* in Paris in the decade between 1525 and 1535,[168] a revival which appears to have been driven, in part, by the upsurge in popularity accorded to the *Rose* by Du Pré's commissioning of Clément Marot to update the text for a modern audience in 1526.[169] Marot's revised *Rose* comprises a corrected, modernized text of the *Rose* and a prefatory 'exposition moralle', which offers a number of recuperative, allegorical interpretations of the rose-figure that serve to rehabilitate Jean de Meun's authorial intention ('l'intencion de l'aucteur') from the accusations of wickedness brought against him in the *'Rose' querelle*. One such interpretation proposes the rose's possible symbolism of the Virgin Mary,[170] a reading also broached by Jean Molinet's moralized prose version of the *Rose*, published in 1500, 1503, and again in 1521.[171] In this light, we may recall the hermeneutic reappropriation of the rose-maiden performed by Le Franc's Dame Virginité, and may consequently see how, in the early sixteenth-century publishing sphere, the *Champion* may have been treated as simply a further variation on the current trend for rewriting the *Rose* through moralization: grafting new meanings onto the established matter in order to open up the field of

---

[167] Charon-Parent 1988: 209, 212.

[168] This revival should be read in the context of the general increase in printed output in Paris during this time: 235 editions were produced in the 1520s, and a further 295 between 1531 and 1535: Moreau 1996: 13.

[169] Attribution of the updated text to Marot is disputed, not least because his name appears nowhere in any of the editions: Hult 1997a. For expediency, I assume here that Marot is the reviser. The evidence for his commission is gleaned from his preface to the updated text, the 'Exposition moralle': [Marot] 1954–7: i. 89–92. Further editions of 'Marot's *Rose*' appear in 1529, 1531, 1537, and 1538, all printed by Pierre Vidoue for a number of publishers: Bourdillon 1906: 207. It is also for Du Pré, perhaps on the back of the success of the updated *Rose*, that Marot undertakes his project of correcting and revising Villon's *Oeuvres*, printed in octavo by Pierre Vidoue in 1533. The publisher's active sponsorship of such programmes of modernization sits well with the editorial policy that Charon-Parent claims Du Pré to have observed; from the evidence of the prefaces he often adds to the works he publishes, she concludes that utility and user-friendliness were key tenets of this policy: 1988: 213–14.

[170] See [Marot] 1954–7: i. 91.

[171] Hult rightly points out the great difference between these two moralizations of the *Rose*: whilst Marot's allegorical rehabilitation of the work is confined to a prologue, Molinet's engagement with moralization is more thoroughgoing; he punctuates his text with 107 *essais* proposing allegorical readings of each episode: 1997a: 150–1.

interpretation.[172] Indeed, it is those pro-feminine *querelle* contributions which ground (at least part of) their defence of women in an attack on the *Rose* that appear in print around 1530, either with Du Pré or with fellow Parisian *libraires*, together with re-editions of certain catalogues of exemplary women.[173]

The particular iconic interplay I consider here is the sharing of woodcuts between the 1530 edition of the *Champion* and the 1529 edition of Marot's revised *Rose*, both printed by Pierre Vidoue (Table 1). The shared illustrations, from the series of woodcuts Bourdillon classifies as P.V.i,[174] originate in the 1529 *Rose*, pass into the *Champion*, and recur again in the folio format of the 1531 *Rose*,[175] an edition shared between Du Pré and another Paris publisher, Jean Petit.[176]

The cuts in question illustrate, for example, Zeuxis painting a naked Lady Nature or Genius preaching from his pulpit to an assembled crowd.[177] The latter is readily integrated into the *Champion* to accompany the sermonizing character of Faux Semblant in Book V, who delivers his 'preschement' (*CD*, v. 20516) to the Champion (fol. 346ᵛ: Plate 1.5) against the doctrine of Immaculate Conception; the image of voluptuous Nature is aptly appropriated to represent l'Acteur's encounter with the goddess Venus in Book I (fol. 19ʳ: Plate 1.6).

172 Ibid. 152–4.

173 Du Pré compiles an anthology of *pro* and *contra* texts including the *Purgatoire des mauvais maris* (1532: see Chapter 2, pp. 142–3). He also has printed by Pierre Vidoue the *.XXI. Epistres d'Ovide* (= *Heroides*) in 1528, and stocks the first French translation of Agrippa's *De nobilitate*, which appears in Anvers in 1530. These editions all occur in octavo format or smaller, as part of a new trend for smaller books: Moreau 1996: 16; 1972–92: iii (1985) and iv (1992); Shaw 1977; Parent 1974: 248–9.

174 1906: 89. This programme of 33 cuts is influenced in part by illustrations devised for Antoine Vérard's quarto edition of the *Rose* in *c.*1500 (series V.ii).

175 Interestingly, the single 'new' cut that is added to P.V.i when the series reappears in 1531 is one which features already in the 1530 *Champion*; this seems to suggest that the printer used the *Champion*, whether simply on a material level, redistributing available images, or with some regard to interpretation of the text, when compiling the new *Rose* edition.

176 Du Pré and Petit (succeeded in 1530 by his son, Jean Petit II) very frequently shared editions with other Paris *libraires*: Parent-Charon 1996: 17; Renouard 1965: 340. Since neither Du Pré nor Petit was a practising printer, both required the services of a third party; Pierre Vidoue is known to have been employed by both, so it is likely, especially in light of the evidence of repeated illustrations, that he was responsible for printing the 1531 *Rose*.

177 *Le Rommant de la rose* (Paris: Galliot Du Pré, 1529), fols. 305ᵛ, 362ᵛ; (Paris: Jean Petit, 1531), fol. 99ʳ and fols. 71ᵛ, 75ʳ. Both cuts are innovated by the designer of the 1529 programme, and show little or no likeness to Vérard's earlier series: Bourdillon 1906: 89–90.

Table 1. Editions printed for Parisian publishers by Pierre Vidoue using the woodcut series P.V.i or its derivative P.V.ii

Text	Date	Publisher	Format	Woodcuts
Oeuvres . . . Alain Chartier	1529	Galliot Du Pré	in-16	Series P.V.i
Marot's *Rose*	1529	Galliot Du Pré	in-8	Series P.V.i
Le Champion des dames	1530	Galliot Du Pré Jean Petit	in-8	Series P.V.i
Marot's *Rose*	1531	Galliot Du Pré	in-folio	Series P.V.i
Marot's *Rose*	1537 1538	(various: 5) (various: 11)	in-8	Series P.V.ii[a]

[a] Bourdillon describes the series used to decorate later versions of the 1529 octavo as 'a set of poor and coarse recuttings from the series P.V.i': 1906: 91–2. English translations are my own.

This pattern of recycling in the printed editions of the *Champion* and *Rose* can, on the one hand, be seen to support the intertextual connections forged by Le Franc's text. However, on the other, viewed as part of an overall publishing strategy for repopularizing the *Champion* on the back of the success of Marot's *Rose*, it seems to serve a hermeneutically contrary function. Rather than opening up Le Franc's text, it potentially restricts the *Champion*'s significance to certain aspects of its moments of intersection with the *Rose* and its *Rose*-associated themes. Rather than privileging visually the *Champion*'s engagement with Jean de Meun's alleged misogyny, the series of woodcuts highlights the 'amorous fictions' (*CD* 5) that Le Franc's prologue misleadingly claims to be the substance and pith of his work. The editor selects as it were a different spectre of the *Rose* that he desires to haunt the new work and, as Charon-Parent notes, he uses illustration as the favoured means of promoting a particular understanding of the text.[178] Thus, in the 1530 edition's cycle of woodcuts, the defence of women is subordinated to the theme of love, and love in a purely secular, amorous vein as opposed to the complex, politically and divinely inflected concept present in the text of the *Champion*. For instance, the illustration for the opening siege on Love's castle of ladies rereads this attack in line with the popular earlier medieval allegory of seduction as besiegement, showing a lady at her window addressed in

[178] 1988: 214. She observes that Du Pré highlights in his editorial prefaces the role illustration is to play in certain texts by promoting the visual dimension of the edition as a work to be 'seen' (*veoir*).

wooing fashion by a single, armed knight (*CD* 1530, fol. 1^r: Plate 1.7),[179] as opposed to the scenes of full-scale military attack by Malebouche and his horde that feature in previous representations of this scene in both manuscript and print.[180] The God of Love himself is repeatedly represented (fols. 5^v, 204^v, 210^v: Plate 1.8) in the very iconography of Cupid as lustful son of Venus, wielding bow and arrow, from which Le Franc's Acteur seeks explicitly to distance his anagogical figure of Amour:

> Tel ne le vis comme on le paint
> Maintenant, car on le figure
> Que dards de tous costez empaint.
>
> (*CD*, vv. 305–7)

(I didn't see him in the guise in which he's depicted nowadays, for he's now represented shooting out arrows from all sides.)

Furthermore, when illustrating the catalogue of exemplary women detailed by the Champion in Book IV, the imprint accords a single image, as opposed to a series of portraits,[181] to the representation of women skilled in the arts and the ten sibyls (fols. 288^r, 319^v: Plate 1.9).[182] Rather than display their independently achieved crafts or simply a congregation of women,[183] it pictures six ladies gathered around a man in seductive manner as one lady is shown reaching to kiss him.

It appears that the sixteenth-century reading of the *Champion* that underpins its republication strategy reduces it to the sole dimension of 'amorous fictions', which, as we have already seen in this book, is far from being the pith of Le Franc's text. Its surface fiction has l'Acteur being guided by Valentine around the castle of Love, though this is really only a vehicle for broaching controversial, contemporary political and theological issues: a defence of Joan of Arc, and of the

---

[179] The cut features appropriately in the 1531 *Rose* to illustrate Bel Accueil's enclosure in a tower built by Jalousie to protect 'her' from assault by l'Amant (Jean Petit, fol. 24^v).

[180] *B1*, fol. 4^r; *P1*, fol. 3^v; *G*, fol. 7^r; *P2*, fol. 3^r; *Z*, fol. 2^r; Lyons incunable, fol. A4^v.

[181] *P1* has a sequence of miniatures to illustrate the skills of Hypsipyle, Arachne, Tamaris, Irene, and Marcia (fols. 104^r, 104^v, 104^v). The 1485 incunable bears a cut showing women carrying the tools of various trades (fol. R4^r), and depicts the sibyls each holding a banderole to represent their prophetic utterances (fol. T2^r).

[182] *Rose* 1531, fol. 21^r. This cut, together with six others drawn from the series P.V.i present in the 1529 *Rose*, is repeated in the contemporary edition of Chartier's *Oeuvres*, where it accompanies the opening of *Le Livre des quatre dames* (1529: fol. 212^r).

[183] *P1* (fol. 115^r) and *G* (fol. 384^v) show a congregation of ten sibyls.

Immaculate Conception.[184] In the 1530 imprint, these more weighty issues specific to Le Franc's pro-feminine argument are overlooked in two ways. First, the edition lacks the presentation miniature which introduces the poem's prologue in every previous illustrated copy, including the 1485 imprint. This omission can be seen to divorce Du Pré's edition from the political context of the work's composition, whereas the other, fifteenth-century versions sought to maintain the connection with Duke Philip's court visually as well as textually. They enabled the *Champion*'s historical time of insertion into the *querelle* to inform or 'ghost' subsequent readings/viewings of the book long after the death of its original patron.[185] Secondly, the guiding influence on the Paris edition's presentation seems not to have been its earlier imprint, but instead its principal intertextual model. The appearance of Du Pré's *Champion* seems to have been influenced in two significant respects by its publication in connection not just with the *Rose*,[186] but with a particular interpretation of the *Rose*; this can be understood by reference to the *Champion*'s newly amplified title in its 1530 edition:

Livre plaisant copieux et habondant en sentences, contenant la Deffence des Dames contre Malebouche et ses consors, et victoire d'icelles. Composé par Martin Franc, secretaire du feu pape Felix V, et nouvellement imprimé à Paris.

(An entertaining and copious book, abounding in moral teachings, containing the Defence of Ladies against Ill Speaking and his cohort, and the ladies' victory. Composed by Martin Franc, secretary to the late Pope Felix V, and newly printed in Paris.)

First, we note that Le Franc's massive work, equipped, for the first time it seems, with a prefatory table of chapter headings,[187] seems to be

[184] Franc Vouloir defends Joan as France's saviour in Book IV. Her subject is controversial given the *Champion*'s dedicatee, namely the Burgundian duke who had been responsible for handing her over to the English.

[185] It seems clear that presentation miniatures in copies after 1451 are intended to represent Philip and his advisers as opposed to new dedicatees; we recall that *G* contains, appended to the *Champion*, an epitaph of Philip the Good. A maintained image of Philip would surely be all the more meaningful given that, as far as we know, the circulation of the *Champion* in manuscript remained within Burgundian court circles: Charron 2000: 9. See also McKendrick 2003a: 71.

[186] The series of cuts on which P.V.i is based, namely V.ii, is itself copied from the woodblocks for the second Lyons series of illustrations (L.ii) which adorned the *c*.1487 folio edition of the *Rose* published by Guillaume Le Roy shortly after his edition of the *Champion*.

[187] A feature shared by every edition of Marot's *Rose*, starting with the 'briefve recollection des matieres' prefacing the 1526 copy.

valued principally here as an anthology of moral teachings embedded in an entertaining narrative, thereby combining two principles of Galliot Du Pré's editorial policy for vernacular literature: that a work should be easy to use, and that it should be useful.[188] Such a mode of reception is congruent with early sixteenth-century habits of reading the equally vast *Rose*, either in its original form or as a moralized version, as a sort of glorified compilation of traditional moral soundbites: 'comme livre plaisant et rempli de beaux traits de doctrine', to quote Du Verdier.[189] Secondly, it is the 'plaisant' aspect of the *Champion*'s fiction, such as l'Acteur's journey in Book I through the respective castles of Venus and Amour, that is privileged as a source of interest by its new title as well as by its shared woodcuts.[190] The work's *mundus significans* is confined to the single domain of amorous pleasures, haunted, as it were, by only one spectre, and this spectre is itself carefully selected and shaped out of the *Rose*'s complex mass of themes and discourses. Running somewhat contrary to the principle of proliferating meanings that is advocated by Marot's 'moralizing' preface to the updated text, the illustrative programme inserted by Vidoue for Du Pré limits the *Rose*—as well as, subsequently, the *Champion*—to what La Croix du Maine calls its 'discours amoureux'.[191]

A strongly nostalgic, we might say conservative, reading of both works is encouraged, in a way that neutralizes topical or moral controversy—whether the *Champion*'s political subtext[192] or the *Rose*'s misogyny, immoral language, or heresy—and harks back, in fact, to a more courtly mode of allegory characteristic of Guillaume de Lorris's original *Rose* portion.[193] The 1530 *Champion* thus serves as a sort of nostalgic presentation of *Rose*-related amorous themes, a role that is

---

[188] Another aspect of this 'user-friendly' policy is, of course, the linguistic project of updating the *Rose* text for a sixteenth-century audience. The publisher thus seems to combine a concern for linguistic modernization with literary nostalgia in his republication of 'classic' medieval vernacular texts.

[189] 'An entertaining book filled with fine nuggets of doctrine': 1585: 679.

[190] The phrase 'moult plaisant et delectable' appears frequently in Du Pré's prefaces for vernacular works: Charon-Parent 1988: 214.

[191] 1584: 246.

[192] Cf. Jordan's view that Le Franc's poem is 'the most conventional of all the defences printed in France in [the sixteenth century]': 1990: 93 n. 29. Her perspective holds true for the *Champion*'s printed edition of 1530, but could not stand as an overall judgement of the work when considered in its mid-fifteenth-century historical milieu.

[193] Cf. Bourdillon's contrary view that the 1529 edition's new woodcuts signify 'an almost entire breaking away from the old traditions' of *Rose* illustration: 1906: 89. I argue, rather, that the new series marks a deliberate re-inscription of that 'old tradition',

also suggested by the evidence Du Pré's inventory provides of the very temporary success enjoyed not only by the *Rose* and *Champion* editions, but also by other 'old-fashioned' vernacular literature produced in large quantities by Du Pré at this time.[194] Through its association with the *Rose*, the *Champion* responds to a quasi-antiquarian interest in late medieval fiction amongst its secondary—as opposed to its primary—historical audience.[195] We recall here the way that certain later sixteenth-century readers—Du Verdier, La Croix du Maine, and Deimier—identify the *Champion* uniquely by reference to its status as a response to the *Rose*. Furthermore, we note how La Croix du Maine highlights the almost antiquarian nature of interest in Le Franc as a writer confined to the past, 'highly rated in his day (*pour son temps*)'; regarding Le Franc in this light, he actually overstates how long ago the *Champion* was published in print: 'in Paris more than sixty years ago'.[196]

The question of the redistribution of illustrations between editions introduces new agents of influence into the book production process. The heirs to the *Rose* are not only those writers who inherit Jean de Meun's text, but also those publishers, woodcutters, and printers who mediate between the writer and his (secondary) audience in early

for example in the iconography of Fortune's rotating wheel (*RR* 1529: fol. H1^r; see *RR*, vv. 3984–90) or the besiegement scene that I discussed above.

[194] At his death, Du Pré had in stock an average of fifty copies of each of his editions, a figure indicating that his editorial decisions in judging the demands of his market were, for the most part, sound, given the average figure for print-runs in the period of 1,000 to 1,500 copies: Gaskell 1972: 161. However, the inventory records 454 unsold copies of the *Champion*, 161 of Marot's *Rose*, 183 of Chartier's *Oeuvres* and 293 of the *Traictez singuliers*, a small anthology of *rhétoriqueur* poetry: Charon-Parent 1974: 244–8. Du Pré produced publications of this kind in large quantities, reckoning that they were reliable titles that would sell steadily over a longish period; the *Rose* and *Champion* were, after all, best sellers of the early generations of printing. But in some cases, as with the *Champion* and *Traictez*, the public's tastes simply changed more quickly than he could sell his stock; flourishing sales of his political and juridical texts, especially around 1550, rapidly eclipsed vernacular literature in Du Pre's *boutique*. We recall also that, after 1538, no further edition of the *Rose* appeared until 1735. I am grateful to Adrian Armstrong for his advice on bibliographical issues.

[195] Strohm 1983: 142. The earlier *Champion* imprint might be seen to participate, back in fifteenth-century Lyons, in what McKendrick calls 'a *fin de siècle* retrospection and antiquarianism that revived interest in the *Rose*' (2003a: 74), especially if, like Tchemerzine (1932: 350), we propose a later date for this imprint, between 1490 and 1500.

[196] 1584: 314; a more accurate temporal expression would be 'just over fifty years ago'.

print culture.[197] Their intervention often comes, as in the case of the *Champion*, long after the *querelle* writer's death so that they are, in fact, juggling a number of ghosts, performing their interpretation of these ghosts' works through the material presentation of their texts. Whereas, in manuscript production, the illustrator designs an image to suit (or deliberately not suit) a pre-assigned place in a book and fixes it there in relation to the surrounding text, the arrangement of a woodcutter's designs for a text rests in the hands of the printer, both in the work for which they were first intended—here the 1529 *Rose*—and in any subsequent work into which he may choose to introduce them, such as the *Champion*. When the two works are thematically related and are printed contemporaneously for distribution by the same publisher, it seems likely that a certain spectrality effect was intended by the printer: that the images in the later work could be seen to be ghosted by the role these cuts played in the previous book's layout.

There is an interesting question of influence here between critical reception and publishing policy: did the apparent publication strategy practised by Vidoue/Du Pré of promoting the *Rose*'s and *Champion*'s intertextual links through the sharing of paratextual features between editions influence the sixteenth-century reception of Le Franc's work as a 'contre-roman de la rose', a particular elaboration of the trend for 'moralizing' the *Rose*? Or was it such an interpretation, sprung from a reading of the *Champion*'s text, which shaped editorial policy? The answer to this question is impossible to determine, but two other points are clear. First, linking the bibliographical focus of this part of Chapter 1 back to the literary semiotics of the first part, we may conclude that the haunting of one text by another has a very material as well as a theoretical presence in *querelle* works' acts of performative interpretation. *Con*juring and con*juring* the spectre of the *Rose* pertains not only to the tasks of author and audience,[198] but also to the mediating influence and intentionalities of additional agents in the book production processes of both manuscript and print cultures. Scribe, miniaturist, coordinator of production, woodcutter, printer, and editor/bookseller, intervening at various stages of production, can each be seen to engage with the

---

[197] For the less scrupulous aspects of Parisian printers' and booksellers' influence, see Brown 1995. Whereas Brown addresses tensions between printers and living poets, my own study deals principally with the posthumous republication in print of earlier, now deceased authors, hence the applicability of my 'haunting' model.

[198] I leave aside here the question of a performer or praelector of the text: see Chapter 2, n. 14.

ghosts of Jean de Meun and of Martin Le Franc.[199] The second point brings me back to the omission of the *querelle des femmes* from critical discussion of medieval intertextuality. It brings me specifically to Floyd Gray's contention of the 'perfunctory' treatment of 'standard themes' practised by *querelle* writers, a point he develops by asserting how *querelle* debate belongs in the fictional domain of 'rhetorical happening' rather than the fact of 'historical reality'.[200] This chapter has demonstrated, on the contrary, that a sophisticated level of intertextual engagement is evident at many stages in the production of *querelle* works, enabling us to see that these very processes of book production themselves constitute a grounding of the debate about women in 'historical reality', namely the editorial and commercial actuality of the late medieval book trade.

CONCLUSION: THE DYNAMICS OF INTERTEXTUAL PERFORMANCE

This chapter has probed both the literary and bibliographical dimensions of the *querelle*'s story of intrapoetic relationships. Its intertextual dimension not only shapes the *querelle* as an endemic feature of its poetics, but is taken up creatively by its authors, miniaturists, and publishers as a vital source of rhetorical invention, iconographic innovation, and hermeneutic engagement. I have emphasized throughout how modern critical approaches to intertextuality and theories of inheritance are congruent with late medieval concepts of rewriting and may be deployed to articulate more fully the interpretative energy and appropriative verve with which I believe *querelle* poets and readers engaged with the *Rose* in acts of resistant hermeneutic performance. To illuminate the particular dynamics of this engagement, it is possible to postulate a theory of spectropoetics. Its discourse of paradoxical conjuration and its emphasis on the anxiously experienced spectral presence of a prior author are fruitful tools for pinpointing the peculiarities of *querelle* works' involvement with Jean de Meun: their necessary debt to him, and their

---

[199] The interactions between authors, scribes, illuminators, miniaturists, binders, booksellers, readers, advisers, and librarians in manuscript production are discussed by McKendrick 2003a.
[200] 2000: 19.

peculiarly embodied, interpersonal conception of their misogynist fore-bear. Focusing on editions of Le Franc's *Champion* introduced evidence of contemporary reception to this study, together with a diachronic dimension of response which suggested how the poem's print tradi-tion's intersection with editions of the *Rose* was a double-edged sword. Such intersection advertised points of contact, but also obscured the specificities of the pro-feminine, politically engaged work since the *Champion* was no longer read in the context of its original historical milieu.

This chapter has shown, above all, that modern scholarship's view of *querelle* intertextuality as an arid, monotonous rehearsal of stock mate-rials must be revised. Sophisticated reading techniques were expected of contemporary audiences and are made manifest in the manuscript matrices and print history of the *Champion* in particular. I argue, therefore, that such strategies need to be reinstated by modern readers in order to appreciate the dynamic, intricate, and innovative nature of *querelle des femmes* intertextuality. This chapter's theoretical frame-work of performativity, exploring how pro-feminine poets' responses to misogynistic authority can be seen as acts of hermeneutic perfor-mance, has focused on defining the dynamic relationships entertained *between* texts. Equally dynamic dialogue may be identified *within* individual works whose narrative framework highlights the poten-cy of the spoken word as a verbal act carrying performative force, namely debates between pro- and anti-feminine spokespersons. The following chapter investigates different manifestations of verbal 'doing', with particular attention to those *querelle* debate poems that take the form of *jugements*. In these judgement poems, verbal activity assumes a legal weight, and the dynamism of rhetorical exchange encourages an appreciation of their debates as imagined dramatic performances. Reasons for the popularity of courtroom fictions for staging *querelle* debates will also be proposed, and will return us to the troubling double bind which the present chapter demonstrated to be the besetting dilemma of pro-feminine discourse: the inextricable bind to misogyny.

Et quil est bel perfaictement
Et mesmement vaillant es armes.

Ho dit le champion leaulx
Or voy ie que folement femme
Les roses devant les porceaulx
Et nestes dignes que de femme
Lon vous parle: que se mon esme
Ne fut de la dame parler
Du ciel et de la terre gemme
Tost men vertiez vous en aler.
Que vault parler: que vault science
Si non pour verite scavoir
Et honnourer en conscience
Quant on la peut appercevoir
Et que vault proces esmouvoir
Et puis faire la figue au iuge
Dissimuler contre le voir
Certes cest ung vaillant refuge.
Verite comme archesillas
A dit: on ne la voit pas goute
Nest au fons du puis ne plus bas
Car se voulez la verez toute
Mais chescun de vous la deboute
Et na cure de sa presence
Car elle a pleine veue redoubte
Le remors de sa conscience.
Pithagoras chescun entende
Disant apres dieu tout mortel
Parfait amour et honneur rendre
A verite son mot est tel
Je vous conseille et bien et bel
Car sans elle vous ne povez
Plaire a nostre dieu immortel
Lequel vous ames et louez.
Or la suyvez tant que vouldrez
Je scay quen la conclusion
De menterie vous vouldrez
De la male obstinacion
Engin et cavillacion
Ne peut verite agueline
Vaincre: et mettre a confusion
Dit tulle contre catheline.
Quant iamais on ne parleroit
Delle encontre toute nature
En labysme on la celleroit
Si viendroit elle a ouverture
Car comme le pre sa verdure
Liver passe sans desgeler
Ainsi elle qui tousiours dure
Certain temps ne se peut celer.
Se tu ne veulx oreille ouvrir
A raison et a verite
Et es tant beste que couvrir
Le te laisses a faulsete
Le doit comparer la bonte
Des dames et des damoiselles
Que vault ce que tu as conte
Nom pas deux petites noiselles.
Quant appolo qui estoit dieu
Entendit marcias vanter
En toute place et en tout lieu

Plate 1.1. Jean de Meun puts Bel Accueil 'a l'escole de la Vielle': Martin Le Franc, *Le Champion des dames*; Paris, BnF, RES YE-27, fol. O3v

Et puis faire la figure au Juge
Dissimuler contre le voir
Certes cest vng villain refuge

Verite comme arevlisas
Dit car Il ne veoit goutte
Nest au fons du puis ne plus bas
Car se vouloit la voye toute
Mais chun de vous la deboute
Et ma cure de sa goute
Car elle aplain veut redoubte
Le remord de sa conscience

Pitagoras chun entende
Disant apres dieu tout mortel
Parfaitte amour en honneur rende
A verite son mot est tel
Je vous conseille et bien et bel
Car sans elle vous ne poet
Plaire a nre dieu immortel
Lequel mal amez et loez

Ou la finez tuit q voulores
Je stay quen la conclusion
De menteuz vous doubtes
Et de malle obstination
Encion ne camilation
Ne veult verite aquesine
Vaincre ou mettre a confusion
Dist tulle contre cathelline

Lors frere vollorr leua le col
Et me ressemble proprement
Celui chant bastard de saint pool
Dont chun parle haultement
Pour ce que tousiours leaument
Il est porte enuers les dames
Et quil est bel par faittement
Et mesmement vaillan et armes

Ho dit le champion leaux
Or voy que ie follement seine
Mes loste deuant les pourtraux
Et nostre diuine q de feme
Len vous parle que se mon ame
Ne fist de la dame parler
Du ciel et de la terre chiere
Tantost men vervoie aller

Que vault parler q vault faire
Si non pour verite sauoir
Et cognoistre en conscience
Quant on le peult appchenoir
Que vault proces esmouvoir

Quant Tamais on ne parleroit
Delle ou contre toute nature
En Labisme on la chuleroit
Si vendroit elle a ouuerture
Car come le pre sa verdure
Hiuer passe ferust descheler
Ainsi elle qui tousiours sure
Certain temps ne se peult celer

Se tu ne veulx loreille ouurir
A raison et averite
Et est tant beste que conurir
Le te laissez a faussete

Plate 1.2.   The Champion, Jean de Meun, and Trop Cuidier : Martin Le Franc,
Le Champion des dames; MS *P2*, fol. 98ʳ

Plate 1.3. The Champion, Proba, and Virgil: Martin Le Franc, *Le Champion des dames*; MS *P2*, fol. 131ᵛ

Plate 1.4. Proba at her writing desk: Martin Le Franc, *Le Champion des dames*; MS *G*, fol. 373ᵛ

Plate 1.5. Faux Semblant speaks 'pretending to be a most virtuous and holy man': Martin Le Franc, *Le Champion des dames*; Paris, BnF, RES YE-4031, fol. 346ᵛ

Plate 1.6. L'Acteur encounters Venus: Martin Le Franc, *Le Champion des dames*; Paris: BnF, RES YE-4031, fol. 19ʳ

Plate 1.7. The assault on the castle of ladies: Martin Le Franc, *Le Champion des dames*; Paris, BnF, RES YE-4031, fol. 1ʳ

Plate 1.8. The God of Love: Martin Le Franc, *Le Champion des dames*; Paris, BnF, RES YE-4031, fol. 5ᵛ

Plate 1.9. Ladies 'who discovered many arts necessary to mankind': Martin Le Franc, *Le Champion des dames*; Paris, BnF, RES YE-4031, fol. 288^r

2

Performing Conflict: The Drama of Debate

Pour ce que ne pourroie avoir par guerre aucun remede contre
mes ennemis, [. . .] par le conseil d'aucuns saiges homes j'ay fait
adjourner et convenir iceulx mes ennemis par devant dame Raison
pour illecq faire debatre ma cause par Vray Rapport, mon advocat.
(*PHF* 27)

(Because I couldn't make any headway against my enemies on
the battlefield, [. . .] on the advice of certain learned men I've
had my enemies summoned by writ and assembled before Lady
Reason in order to have my case defended here by True Report,
my barrister.)

In the introduction to Pierre Michault's allegorical verse debate, *Le
Procès d'Honneur Féminin*, the wounded personification of woman's
reputation, Honneur Féminin, brings his cause against misogynists in
from the battlefield to be fought out in the courtroom. The relationship
between military arms and forensic discourse as instruments of combat
appears quite imbricated here. Honneur Féminin describes to the poem's
narrator how a legal wrong committed without cause against him ('un
tort inféré sans cause') was performed on his person in the form of an
ambush ('embusche') by the misogynist Malebouche's lackeys ('bringans
et souldoyers'): he was 'batu et deschiré par eulx d'aucuns bastons qu'il
portent nommés Faulses Langues'.[1] This graphic depiction of how his
body was beaten by the defamatory force of their tongues melds together
in a striking way the discourses of warfare and legal rhetoric.

---

[1] *PHF* 27. 'Beaten about and torn apart by those weapons of theirs known as False
Tongues.' English translations are my own.

The intersection of physical and verbal aggression is sustained by two rhetorical metaphors that can be seen to underpin the terms in which Honneur portrays his new injury ('nouvelle lesion et blechure'), which, it is revealed, consists of some recently composed misogynistic poetry ('aucuns vers en latins') (*PHF* 27). First, according to figurative representations used in Classical rhetoric and transmitted to the late Middle Ages, the sudden introduction of new arguments is represented as 'a surprise breakout or an attack from an ambush (*ex insidiis*)'.[2] Second, when Honneur describes how his gown 'avoit esté par force perchee en plusieurs lieux',[3] he can be seen to evoke the metaphor of linguistic piercing, since it was held that figures of reduplication (*conduplicatio*)—here represented by the repeated gashes inflicted by misogynistic Faulses Langues—inflict a major wound upon the opposition, as if 'a weapon (*telum*) should repeatedly pierce (*saepius perveniat*) the same part of the body'.[4] Furthermore, when Honneur describes his grievous wounds—'sur mon corps j'ay plus de playes que ung eschequier n'a de poins'[5]—the vocabulary and choice of simile that he deploys highlight the parity of 'playes' as physical injuries (*plaies*) and forensic arguments (*plaits*), as well as introducing the image of a site of ludic conflict, the chessboard.[6] The involved rhetorical imagery of Honneur's introduction—itself constituting a sort of juridical self-defence as he seeks to secure his addressee's support[7]—seems designed to set the stage for the *Procès*'s ensuing legal debate between Vray Rapport, advocate of Honneur Féminin, and Faux Parler, barrister for the anti-feminine camp. It evokes the dynamic and performative nature of language, and specifically of forensic rhetoric, and fuses together the discourses of warfare, law, and play—in both ludic and dramatic senses—in a sophisticated way.

To complement the previous chapter's exploration of how pro-feminine poets responded intertextually to misogynistic authority, the current chapter focuses on the sort of responsive acts that occur in the intratextual context of *querelle* debate poems which take the form

---

[2] Quintilian 2001: III, 6.4.14.

[3] *PHF* 27. '[His gown] had been pierced violently in several places.'

[4] [Cicero] 1981: 4.28.38. For images of words as swords in medieval treatises, see, for example, Bouchet 1969: fol. E2ʳ.

[5] *PHF* 27. 'I have more wounds on my body than a chessboard has squares.'

[6] See Cayley 2006: chapter 4, part II.

[7] As his addressee is l'Acteur, Michault might be playing here on the Classical connections maintained by the vernacular *acteur* with the Latin term for 'litigator' (*actor*): see Brown 1995: 205.

of *jugements*. A first section pinpoints performative aspects of the rhetoric of defence deployed in *querelle* debates in text and image, according special attention to the *Champion des dames*. A second section focuses on courtroom fictions in several works which demonstrate a thoroughgoing engagement with the terminology, procedures, and apparatus of contemporary judicial systems, both historical and literary. It seeks to identify how these fictions appropriate the discourse and courtroom framework of legal practice in ways that serve purposes specific to the literary defence of women.

The above analysis of the *Procès*'s prologue identifies a hitherto unexplored source of poetic interest in late medieval verse debates written in the tradition of the *querelle des femmes*: it uncovers the dynamism invested by writers and, as we shall see later, manuscript illustrators in the debating process itself. It evokes what I shall call the twofold nature of rhetoric as performance. This concerns first the performative force of language, akin to what early speech-act theorists call its 'illocutionary' and 'perlocutionary' forces, which are harnessed by *querelle* writers' refreshment of the vigour of debate; the above depiction of Honneur Féminin's ambush foregrounds the power of language that the pro-feminine speaker has to counter by striking out with his own rhetorical weapons. Secondly, it involves the way verbal conflicts are staged in *querelle* manuscripts, in both text and image, as performances in a dramatic sense. I shall focus on Martin Le Franc's pro-feminine debate poem the *Champion des dames*. In its text, there is a close attention to the pragmatics of performance: aspects of voice, gesture, and audience reaction. In the miniatures of the manuscript illustrated by the so-called *Champion des dames* Master, the verse debate's verbal dynamism and acoustic liveliness find their visual equivalent in striking images of animated disputation.

As a preface to the main body of this chapter, it is appropriate to explain briefly how an interface between dialogue and drama operates in *querelle* debates, and how I understand 'debate' itself as the term denoting the basic form of these poems' verbal exchanges. My approach to the theatrical dimension of rhetorical performance is informed by Jody Enders's investigation of late medieval French theatre's exploitation of the latent theatricality (or 'protodrama') of scholastic, and especially forensic, rhetoric. She proposes that medieval rhetoric's focus on vocal and gestural delivery—aspects of rhetorical performance or *actio*—fostered an 'aestheticization' of legal discourse into theatrical performance. The dramatic character of conflictual forensic debate became a model for actual dramatic invention on the part of medieval dramatists because it lent a new and spectacular dynamism to theatrical dialogue.[8]

My own study problematizes Enders's approach in two respects: first, I understand rhetorical performance as a quality possessed equally by *non*-dramatic literary texts' representations of *actio*, such as the verse debates composed by Le Franc and Michault; secondly, I propose specific reasons for different *querelle* poems' appropriation of 'the legal protodrama' which go beyond the desire that Enders identifies to dynamize and spectacularize the activity of debate. An example is useful here. I shall be highlighting especially Martin Le Franc's focus on debaters' voice, mien, and gesture—the three components of *actio*[9]—in passages of narrative commentary that punctuate the debate running throughout the *Champion des dames*. This emphasis on features of delivery becomes paramount in the work's sequel, the *Complainte du livre du Champion des dames à maistre Martin Le Franc son acteur*, in which it is understood that the Book (Livre) performed itself aloud before the Burgundian court, before being rejected by Philip the Good's entourage.[10] It is not just a scenario of public reading or *praelectio* that is evoked here—as Livre is said to have desired to '. . . vouloir en chaiere lire | Publiquement' (*C*, vv. 173–4)[11]—but an act of dramatic delivery, on which the Book's Author insists most vehemently when he criticizes Livre's performance:

> Or comme poi endoctriné
> Tu as volu trop hault parler.
> [. . .]
> Tu as cuidié du premier sault
> Que l'en cryast a la trompette:
> *A l'assault, dames, a l'assault!*
> Ha! Mors ta langue & ta lippette.
>
> (*C*, vv. 165–6, 177–80)

---

[8] Enders 1993; 1992.

[9] As identified, for example, by the *Ad Herennium* author: 'voce et vultu et gestu': 1981: 3.11.19.

[10] See Introduction, n. 2.

[11] '. . . [to] want to be declaimed publicly from the chair'. The phenomenon of 'prelection' in late medieval French and Burgundian courts is discussed by Coleman 1996. She proposes the popularity of 'aurality'—the reading aloud of a written text to one or more listeners—as a preferred mode of textual reception in the fourteenth and fifteenth centuries.

(So, like an unskilled orator, you wanted to speak too loudly. [. . .] You thought you should cry out from the outset, trumpet-like: 'Take arms, ladies, take arms!' Ha! Bite your tongue and your little lip!)

Informing his disappointed Book that it is no heralding horn— 'Trompette n'es tu ne herault' (v. 273)—its Author reprimands the unsuitably bombastic way in which Livre went out as it were all rhetorical guns blazing to deliver with excessive vigour and trumpet blast the text's first line. The Book should instead have observed the accepted rhetorical decorum of tempering one's tone and pitch, especially at the start of a speech. According to contemporary doctrine, as found in *Li Livres dou tresor*, one should

atenpler ta vois & ton esperit [. . .] et mander les paroles a l'issue de ta bouche [. . .] si que chascune [letre] ait son son, & cascun mos son accent entre aut & bas; et neporquant tu dois comencer plus bas que a la fin.[12]

(. . . moderate your voice and tone [. . .] and control the words as they come out of your mouth [. . .] in order that each [letter] may sound properly, and each word may have its appropriate pitch between high and low; however, you must always pitch lower at the beginning than at the end.)

Le Franc's focus on this performative dimension of his Book's rhetorical construction certainly serves to dynamize the *Complainte*'s lament of the *Champion*'s failed reception. More significantly, however, it is a strategic hermeneutic manoeuvre: according to the traditional, fivefold scheme of composition—*inventio, dispositio, elocutio, memoria*, and *actio*—*actio* is the only stage of a work's construction that can be separated from authorial intention and can thereby displace blame for the *Champion*'s failure onto the Book itself.[13] Conversely, therefore, the Book, who seeks precisely to locate responsibility firmly in the creative intention of its Author, blames its lack of success on inadequate *inventio* or *elocutio*. Alluding to an alleged 'poison' lying in the moral message of the work's content, the Book remonstrates:

> Se bouté m'eusses en mon sain
> Maint brocard et mainte sentence

---

[12] Latini 2003: 222. English translation is my own. The *Livres* (1260–7) is a prose encyclopedia in three volumes; rhetoric and politics are addressed conjointly in the third volume. The work enjoyed sustained success, surviving in over seventy manuscripts; it was first printed in Lyons in 1491 and in Paris in 1539.

[13] Both the essential role played by *actio* in the composition of a speech and this stage's separability from the preceding four stages of rhetorical construction are noted in the *Ad Herennium*: 3.11.19.

> Dont on a entendement sain
> Gaignié j'avoye l'audience.

(*C*, vv. 201–4)

(If you'd stuffed me with lots of healthy commonplaces and palatable proverbs that are readily accepted, I'd definitely have won over my audience/gained a hearing.)

Notwithstanding Le Franc's fictionalization of his Book's public delivery, I do not propose that any of the debates considered here was designed for actual dramatic performance.[14] My use of the terms 'theatre' and 'drama' thus remains figurative; they are useful metaphors for highlighting how *querelle* poets reinvigorate debate by pointing up features of *actio*,[15] and how, as I shall show, the *Champion des dames* Master deploys the manuscript page as a stage for communicating the dynamism of a debate's *déroulement*.

The term 'debate' is employed ubiquitously by modern critics to refer to the sort of versified, stanzaic dialogues composed by late medieval poets from Machaut to Villon. A recent *mise au point* of the term is provided by Emma Cayley, who sketches out the intellectual and literary influences on late medieval debate; she concludes that judicial trial models and earlier poetic forms such as the *demandes, joc-partits*, or *tensos*, combined with the scholastic model of the *disputatio*, shape the late medieval debate poem.[16] Subtending my study of later debates in the *querelle des femmes* is a similar assumption that their rhetorical

---

[14] With the possible exception of *MFJ*: see Conclusion, pp. 240–2. I here avoid conflating *praelectio* with dramatic performance, although Le Franc's evocation of the histrionic *actio* of his Livre could derive from the poet's knowledge of the current practice of *praelectio* at the Burgundian court. Coleman (1996: chapter 5) and Doutrepont (1909: 465–8) offer evidence that Philip the Good's recreational reading was both a private (i.e. silent) matter and a public affair, where the book was read aloud to a group. Provided we accept these contemporary testimonies at face value, as records of actual practice as opposed to strategic comments designed to flatter the Duke's literacy and/or his cultivated bibliophilia, it seems probable that the *Champion* would have been read aloud before the court to determine its merit. Cf. Doutrepont 1909: 311–12.

[15] I here make a distinction that appears blurred in several critical discussions of the 'theatralization' of discourse in non-dramatic works caused by the use of features of *actio*, which 'stages speech': Compagnon 1979: 149. For a series of essays that reach differing conclusions about a postulated late medieval continuity between 'dialogue as a bookish genre' and 'dramatic dialogue', and the idea of a non-dramatic work's 'dramatic potentialities', see Bordier 1999: I quote here in my own English translation his introduction: 11–12. An excellently nuanced discussion of the problem is offered by Taylor 1990.

[16] 2006: 20.

practice is coloured by a juridical model. The disputations in which pro- and anti-woman speakers participate carry as an endemic part of their rhetorical baggage a forensic use of rhetoric. For example, in the *Champion*, the first speech by Brief Conseil ('Hasty Thought'), the first delegate of Malebouche, is prefaced by a chapter heading that introduces him and his action in legal terms:

Cy Bref Conseil comme *advocat*, par le commandement de Malebouche, entre en *debat* et en *plaidoyrie* contre Franc Vouloir le champion des dames. (*CD*, preceding v. 2617 (my italics))

(Here Hasty Thought, acting as barrister, on the orders of Ill Speaking, enters into debate and pleading against Free Will, the Champion of ladies.)

Although, as Pierre-Yves Badel recognizes in his useful typology of French medieval debate,[17] 'debate' was not clearly defined as a genre, it seems clear that the *Champion*, at least, accepts as a given its interface with some form of judicial procedure in the context of *querelle des femmes* disputation. It is, after all, the topic of gender, of arguing the case for women, which inscribes all *querelle* texts in a tradition of forensic oratory.

Cayley nuances Badel's typology in three ways that are pertinent to my own use of the term 'debate'. First, she foregrounds the essentially performative nature of literary dialogue since 'it is always mediated by a third agent, be it the authorial subjectivity (possibly in the guise of a narrator) or the reader/listener. In other words, the literary dialogue can only ever be experienced via a performance, either reading or hearing.'[18] Cayley's use of 'performance' relates to my application of the term to the dramatic situation of juridical debate experienced by an audience; we shall see later in this chapter how the mediating role of Le Franc's Acteur contributes in an innovative way to the theatricalization of dispute in the *Champion*. However, my own study diverges here from both Badel and Cayley. While Badel insists upon the written nature of debate, and while Cayley's mediating third person is usually engaged in writing down the debate he overhears, the *Champion*'s narrator figure will be shown playing a different role, which works to privilege orality over written aspects of the dispute.

The second way in which Cayley contests Badel's typology is by refining his categorical distinctions between *dialogue, jugement*, and *débat*. She introduces as a subcategory of *jugement* the *songe* or dream-vision

---

[17] 1988: 98.   [18] 2006: 29.

in which the narrator is transported to an oneiric landscape where he observes the debate unfolding. In Cayley's useful subcategory we could situate the *Champion, Forest,* and *Procès,* the three principal trial texts that are to be discussed in the second part of this chapter. A further refinement is necessary, however. Badel's *jugement/débat* distinction is founded on the latter's organization of dialogue into short, responsive stanzas rather than longer units of discourse; such an arrangement emphasizes, he states, the 'conflictual element' of disputation.[19] My own treatment of *jugement-songe* works will dissolve Badel's distinction in two ways: first, longer, though still stanzaic, speeches can provide greater, rather than less, focus on conflict by the manner in which they sustain intricate and finely developed refutations of an opponent's argument; secondly, narrative intervention punctuating longer speeches can be used to point up this attention to the art of verbal warfare. Cayley's third refinement refutes Badel's underestimation of debate as simply a sort of 'parlour game' that does not carry any *senefiance.*[20] I respond similarly by recalling here how the *Champion*'s debate mobilizes controversial political and theological arguments in a potent historical context.[21]

One point on which Badel, Cayley, and I concur is the immense popularity enjoyed by debate form in late medieval French vernacular writing, especially when couched in an allegorical 'judgement' structure, where a presiding authority, such as Justice or Reason, intervenes to decide a dispute's outcome, having heard the arguments presented by both sides. Such a form lent itself ideally to the vogue for setting off pro- and anti-feminine arguments against each other in the same text. The circumstances of the *querelle*'s inheritance of debate form could seem, at first sight, to militate against any innovativeness. In the case of the *Champion,* one critic notes that 'Martin Le Franc is, of course, a highly traditional writer. He invented neither the method that he follows, nor the examples that he gives.'[22] This comment encapsulates a view of *querelle* texts as derivative, and thus lacking in poetic interest, that this chapter, and this book in general, endeavours to overturn. Vital hermeneutic interest lies, I argue, in the manner in which established matter is recycled, whether this matter pertains to content or to structure, such as debate form. For example, there is

---

[19] 1988: 104. English translations are my own.   [20] 2006: 30.
[21] See Introduction, n. 2, and Chapter 1, pp. 84–6.
[22] Dembowski 1989: 276 n. 25.

evidence of innovation in the structure of each judgement scenario. A typical *jugement* presented two opposing parties speaking on their own behalf and submitting their case to a single judge figure, as in Machaut's *Jugement* poems or Froissart's *Plaidoirie de la rose et de la violette*. *Querelle* texts nuance this paradigm by enlisting advocates to represent the parties in question: Michault's Vray Rapport, for instance, defends the embodiment of feminine honour against misogynist writers championed by Faux Parler. One might claim, though, that the *déroulement* of each *querelle* debate can hardly sustain interest in any suspenseful way since its outcome is predetermined to fall in the pro-feminine camp's favour;[23] the *Champion*'s narrator himself acknowledges, 9,000 lines before the end, that the pro-feminine advocate will ultimately win, whatever happens ('gaignera comment qu'il aille' (*CD*, v. 14792)). However, this lack of unpredictability does not entail a lack of dynamism in the debating process,[24] especially in the *Champion* where disputation is sustained for some 22,000 lines; on the contrary, the way the poem's narrator deliberately anticipates the final verdict draws attention to the fact that it is the manner in which he wins that is interesting. We need only compare briefly the presentation of the *Champion* with a contemporary (prose) debate, the anonymous *Dispute entre le sexe masculin et le feminin, autrement Bouche Mesdisant et Femme Deffendant*,[25] to appreciate the innovative way in which Le Franc's presentation of debate develops the protodrama of debate rhetoric. The *Dispute*'s author flags up the personified mode of debate that this defence of women treatise adopts as a way of enlivening its subject matter:

[P]our mieulx la matiere de ce present traictié deduire, entendre, et concevoir, je introduiray deux personnaiges: l'un aura nom Bouche Mesdisent; l'autres sera dit Femmes Deffendant.[26]

(So that the subject matter of this treatise may be better presented, received, and understood, I shall introduce two characters: one will take the name Slandering Mouth; the other will be called Defender of Women.)

---

[23] This rule applies to the corpus of texts addressed by this book; I have yet to discover an exception.

[24] Cf. Badel 1988: 109. Whilst I argue here that *querelle* debates are teleologically determined, I do not mean that their resolution is necessarily clear-cut: see below, pp. 144–52.

[25] Paris, BnF, MS fr. 1990, fos. 1^r–106^r. The rest of the manuscript consists of a list of proverbs: *Cent proverbes moraulx* (fos. 106^v–112).

[26] Ibid., fol. 2^r. English translation is my own.

The debate proceeds, however, in a relatively unanimated fashion: within the text there is little attention paid to the mechanics of disputation or delivery, nor is any fictional scene-setting evoked, unlike the *Champion*'s College of Envy or the *Procès*'s Court of Reason.[27] Paratextually, the *mise en page* does not highlight any form of dynamic interchange since the debate is set in continuous text, broken only by red ink indicating a change of speaker.[28] We shall see later how *mise en page* and illustration in a certain *Champion* manuscript seem designed specifically to encourage a reading of the text focused on aspects of dramatic verbal conflict and rhetorical delivery.

IMAGINING DEBATE: VERBAL ATTACK AND VERBAL DISPLAY

The revitalization of debate as dynamic conflict is an essential element of *querelle* judgement poems. The intersection of warfare, law, and play that I identified in this chapter's opening analysis of the *Procès* suggests how the imagery of physical conflict is used to represent the particularly potent, performative quality of the *querelle*'s rhetorical weapons. Interaction between the discourses of physical and verbal conflict is a common feature, not only of *querelle* judgements set in a courtroom fiction, but also of *querelle* texts which present simply as a treatise or monologue a forensic defence of women. Jean Marot, father of Clément Marot, prefaces his pro-feminine poetic monologue *La Vraye disant advocate des dames* (*c.*1506) with a prose description of how he undertook to

[27] For similar reasons, disputes such as Guillaume Alexis's *Debat de l'omme et de la femme* (1896: 121–44) do not find a place in my current study. Whilst, unlike the *Dispute*, the *Debat*'s exchange, set in alternating stanzas, is lively, it does not engage with the *jugement* structure that I postulate here: it both lacks a mediating, narrative voice and has no evident enlistment of a legal framework or discourse. For Alexis, see Conclusion, n. 11.

[28] Armstrong includes *mise en page* as a feature of paratextual organization: 2001: 63. An indication of what sort of reading the *Dispute*'s *mise en page* did foster is provided by the way that Latin quotations in the speakers' arguments—themselves divided into thematized chapter divisions—are underlined in red ink to enable ready reference to their substance as 'sentences'; this is a common practice in the late fifteenth century: Hasenohr 1990: 289. The *Dispute*'s juxtaposition with a list of proverbs in MS fr. 1990 can be seen to support this theory of the work's reception as a sort of compendium of commonplaces. Cf. Chapter 1, pp. 84–5.

forger et marteller sur l'enclume [*ed.*: enclu clume] de mon insuffisance les harnoys, estocz, lances et escuz servans à la defence, louenge et victoire de l'honneur des dames. (*VDA*, p. 94)[29]

([to] forge and hammer out on the anvil of my insufficiency the arms, swords, spears, and shields that serve the defence, praise, and victory of women's honour.)

Marot's metaphors of rhetorical weapons of pro-feminine defence that will ensure victory can be seen to respond to misogynists' verbal swords of attack, like the Faulses Langues used to assail Honneur Féminin in Michault's *Procès*.

It is Le Franc's *Champion* which engages most fully with this military imagery of debate. Not only, like the *Procès*, does it present a transition from hand-to-hand combat—in this case a joust between the Champion and Cruel Despit—to tongue-to-tongue disputation; it also sustains the imagery of jousting during the verbal debate so as to project the vigour of forensic procedure. Warfare, law, and play intersect when Malebouche nominates Trop Cuidier to continue the anti-woman case:

> Malebouche tout sangmeslé
> Ne sçavoit plus de qui juer
> Quant ung Trop Cuidier appellé
> Vint en champ son gage ruer.
>   (*CD*, vv. 11097–100)[30]

(Malebouche, all het up, had no one else to put in play, when a certain Too-Ready Belief entered the field to thrown down his gauntlet.)

The Champion greets this new adversary or 'bold jouster' (v. 11113) with a call to join arms in order to determine the debate's outcome: 'By joining battle we'll see who'll win!' (v. 11110). Illustrations in the poem's various manuscript copies set in relief this confluence of discourses through apparently deliberate literalizations of the military metaphor.[31] For example, *P1* (fol. 68ᵛ) offers a splendid image of Trop Cuidier throwing down his gauntlet. Elsewhere, in a chapter heading introducing the entry into verbal combat of another adversary, Vilain Penser, figurative reference is made to 'lices', the medieval term for a tournament ground: 'Malebouche [. . .] met es lices ung aultre combatant appellé Villain

[29] English translations are my own.

[30] Marot's Advocate uses the same image to depict an intervention made on behalf of women by personified Noblesse: *VDA*, vv. 31–2.

[31] See Appendix 2A. The visual literalization of a textual metaphor is a common artistic device.

Penser' (preceding v. 4313). Miniatures in three manuscripts (*Z* (fol. 33ʳ), *P2* (fol. 35ʳ), and *G* (fol. 90ᵛ: Plate 2.1) showing how Vilain Penser entered the field ('entra en champ') depict instead a literal joust between the two opponents before an audience of ladies.

What end does this convergence of discourses serve? In what way does the *querelle*'s depiction of rhetorical activity through military imagery distinguish it from the general confluence of war and law, combat and dispute in other medieval texts? Pierre Bec notes as a commonplace the way that adversaries in medieval disputations sometimes call each other *jonhedors* ('jousters'), whilst, in the sixteenth century, the jurist Jean Bouchet embraces the analogy between warfare and forensic practice when he depicts the role of an advocate in his *Epistre de justice* (1524):

> Non moins pourvoient a tout humain lignage
> Par leur scavoir doulx, & orné langage
> Que gens de guerre avec lances [&] escuz
> Car par eulx sont tous debas conuaincuz.[32]

(They serve the needs of the whole human race with their calm wisdom and ornate language no less than warriors with spears and shields, since it is through their efforts that all disputes are closed.)

Bouchet goes on to assert the superiority of legal eloquence ('beau parler') over fisticuffs ('forte main') in achieving a desired outcome. This superiority, understood as both efficacy and moral supremacy, lies in the skilful wielding of language and can be seen to underpin the *Champion*'s and *Procès*'s movements from misogynist-induced physical violence to the order of the courtroom. The superiority of verbal over physical conflict is not new to the late fifteenth century; it derives ultimately from Classical oratory and is cited as a Ciceronian inheritance in the late fourteenth century by the literary commentator Évrard de Conty in his definition of rhetoric:

> . . . disoit Tulles que on a aucunefois aucunes choses fait par beau langage et par beles paroles que on ne peust par force, naïz d'armes ne par autres voies quelconques, autrement avoir faict.[33]

(. . . Cicero stated that things have often been achieved by fine rhetoric and by fine words that could not be achieved otherwise by force, by arms, or by any other means.)

---

[32] Bouchet 1969: fol. E2ʳ. English translation is my own.
[33] 1993: 103. English translations are my own. De Conty presents his views in the context of a 'moralization' or amplified commentary on the allegorical and mythological narrative poem *Le Livre des échecs amoureux* (*c*.1370–80).

Indeed, the main thrust of de Conty's discussion of the third science of the scholastic *trivium* plays up its martial associations in order to give prominence to rhetoric as conflictual verbal engagement:[34]

Ceste aussi ramenee des anciens a la tierce planete, c'est assavoir à Mars, et la cause y peut estre car Mars de sa nature segnefie batailles et riotes, plaiz et controversies et toute autre maniere de discorde [. . .] Or n'est mie doubte que on voit souvent en ceste rethorique moult de debas, de contencions et moult de grans discordes entre gens esmouvoir, [. . .] et semble que ce soit aussi come une maniere de bataille.[35]

(Classical authorities also relate it to the third planet, that is Mars, and this may be because Mars by nature signifies battles and riots, arguments and disputes and all other manner of discord [. . .] And so it is that one often sees in this rhetoric many debates, contentions, and great disagreements flaring up between people, [. . .] and this seems like a sort of battle.)

He evokes here precisely the sort of disputational activity that characterizes *querelle* debates.

The most general, and perhaps the most important, significance of the intersection of verbal and physical conflict in the *querelle des femmes* is the particular vigour this overlap of discourses gives the spoken word as a performative or 'doing'. I have already indicated that the *Vraye disant advocate*'s narrator perceives words as potent defensive weapons; Marot's monologue harnesses this potency in order to counter the almost palpable venom of misogynistic discourse. In his poem, a work dedicated to Anne of Brittany, Marot ventriloquizes the voice of an anonymous lady Advocate addressing her adversaries:

> . . . Voz parolles basilicques,
> Iniques et dyabolicques
> Sont tant infaictes de venin,
> Qu'ilz sont grosses comme ydropicques,
> Pour destruyre à grans coups de picques
> L'honneur du sexe femenin.
>
> (*VDA*, vv. 20–5)[36]

---

[34] In this respect, his portrait of rhetoric seems to derive from Martianus Capella's armour-clad Lady Rhetoric: see Enders 1992: 89–99.

[35] Évrard de Conty 1993: 102.

[36] For the political context and textual tradition of *VDA*, see Chapter 3, pp. 188–91, and Conclusion, p. 231.

(. . . Your poisonous words, iniquitous and diabolical, are so infected with venom that they're swollen up like dropsical limbs to destroy with great, beefy blows the honour of the female sex.)

She sustains this tactile imagery of misogynistic discourse's effect throughout her monologue, and insists upon the damaging consequences for women's reputation. She appeals to her detractors:

> Mesdisans vueillez reprimer
> Vostre langue, qui point et mort
>
> (vv. 371–2)

(Slanderers, please hold your tongue, which stings and bites),

and states also how the superior efficacy of language can be harnessed for evil intent as well as good:

> Ne doubtez point que le coup furieux
> De dague ou lance n'est point si dangereux
> Que coup de langue, qui tout honneur efface.
>
> (vv. 660–2)

(Have no doubt that the furious strike of a dagger or spear is not half so severe as the blow of a tongue, which destroys all reputation.)

The issue of woman's reputation, on which she insists, is central to the *querelle*. Reputation, it is implied, exists in the domain of representation, that is, discourse, and is thereby susceptible to infinite reconfiguration both *pro* and *contra*. This susceptibility is thus a double-edged sword. The pro-feminine camp in the *Champion* recognizes reputation's potential for manipulation when the Champion prefaces his nomination of certain ladies of noble character with the comment:

> Aulcuns t'en vouldray nommer,
> Lesquelles se mal ne les nommes
> Porras tres vaillans renommer.
>
> (*CD*, vv. 5854–6)

(I'd like to name a few [women], whom, if you don't speak ill of them, you can repute most highly.)

His rhetorical insistence through *traductio* upon verbs of naming, and the drift between 'name' and 'renown' (*polyptoton*), foreground the ready transformation of women's identity into a malleable unit of discourse. Releasing women's names into the public domain releases their potential to be honoured and commemorated, but also enables misogynist slanderers to malign their reputation.

In the *Advocate* and *Champion*, therefore, the war of words becomes a war of attrition over woman's reputation. It activates a certain performative and pragmatic 'force' of language that can usefully be considered through the lens of speech-act theory, which privileges speech as, to quote Austin, the 'performance of an act *in* saying something as opposed to performance of an act *of* saying something'.[37] Such illocutionary acts,[38] voiced alternately by woman's detractors and defenders, can be seen to un-make and remake her identity through verbal performance. One of the principal types of act demonstrating this particular force of language in the *querelle des femmes* is the *blason*, an epideictic offering of praise or blame, which Marot's Advocate identifies as one means by which Jalousie and Malebouche daily tarnish women's reputation:

> Car chascun jour ilz donnent quelque touche
> A nostre honneur . . .
>
> > (*VDA*, vv. 649–50)

(Since every day they [= blazons] add another stain to our reputation.)

In the *Champion*, an exchange of *blasons* between Brief Conseil and the Champion encapsulates the forcefully performative nature of debate rhetoric that I postulate here, as well as evoking an element of play and suggesting a specifically agonistic, dramatic context in which these verbal exchanges should be understood. The *blasons* in question take as their subject 'Amour', whose court, we recall, houses the ladies defended by the Champion. Brief Conseil offers his 'diffinicion' of Love by piling up oxymorons:

> Amours, Amours, joye ennuieuse,
> Amours, liesse enlangoureuse,
> Amours, charité envieuse,

---

[37] 1975: 99–100. Italics are Austin's own emphases. The primary purpose of performative utterance to do rather than to assert something removes it from a true/false dichotomy and thus renders it most pertinent to the construction and reconstruction of malleable reputation discussed here. The idea of verbal 'doing' is not, of course, something innovated by speech-act theory; in Classical forensic activity, the Elder Seneca makes a distinction between the performative act of legal oratory (*causas agere* or *pugnare*) and the imitation fighting of declamation (*ventilare*): 1974: III preface, 12–13. A relationship between 'doing' and dramatic performance is established by Aristotle when he considers the derivation of δραμα from δραν ('be active'/'do'/'perform'): 1995: III.

[38] Austin 1975: 99–100.

> Esperance desesperee,
> Amours, coulour descoulouree,
> Ris plourant, enfer glorieux.
>
> (*CD*, vv. 3609–14)

(Love, love, sorrowful joy; love, melancholic delight; love, mean kindness, desperate hope; love, discoloured colour, tearful laughter, glorious hell.)

The Champion sees these oxymorons as rhetorically vitiating the nature of Love, and he strikes back immediately to rehabilitate Amour in a more extended *blason* that I quote selectively:[39]

> Amours toute joye nourrit,
> Amours ennuy vaint et appaise
> [. . .]
> Amours en pacience danse,
> Amours en adversité chante,
> Amours en pleurs est a la danse
> [. . .]
> Amours, Amours, vraye prudence,
> Justice en bon pois mesuree
> [. . .]
> Esperence tres asseuree.
>
> (*CD*, vv. 3689–90, 3721–3, 3737–8, 3741)

(Love feeds every joy, love overcomes and eases sorrow [. . .] Love dances in suffering, love sings in adversity, love rejoices while weeping [. . .] Love, love, true prudence, justice meted out in good measure, [. . .] hope that is most assured.)

His response both un-makes and remakes the language of his adversary's accusatory *blason*. On the one hand, he unpicks Brief Conseil's oxymorons to expose them as falsifications of Love's essence: he separates out the antithetical poles of 'joye' and 'ennuy' that his adversary conflates, and requalifies 'esperence' as 'tres asseuree' instead of 'desesperee'. On the other hand, he introduces new expressions involving antitheses which communicate the positive attributes of Love as a life-sustaining force that finds joy in sorrow through faith, rather than being the negative, paradoxical state of 'tearful laughter' (*ris pleurant*).

The directness of the Champion's response to Brief Conseil is highlighted by formal echoes between the two *blasons*: the reduplicated

---

[39] The chapter heading introducing his response calls it a 'blason'.

'Amours, Amours' apostrophe as well as the anaphoric repetition of
'Amours' as a line-initial term. These structural similarities draw attention to the hermeneutic transformations performed by the Champion
on his adversary's discourse, as he trumps both form and content of
the misogynist's argument. In terms of forensic rhetorical procedure,
he demonstrates the sort of prompt reply recommended, through aptly
physical imagery, by Classical oratory: 'dicendum statim est et prope
sub conatu adversarii manus exigenda'.[40] Similarly, when Trop Cuidier
steps up to face him later, the Champion responds to his adversary's
challenge 'immediately' (*de tire*): 'de tire | Sault son propos entretenir'
(*CD*, vv. 11105–6).[41] The particular qualities he manifests correspond
closely, in Classical forensic terms, to those of a good altercator.[42]
Altercatio is the type of debate which, in Roman courts, followed the set
speeches and examination of witnesses; it was the stage of the fiercest
and most challenging verbal combat, as Quintilian describes: 'asperrima
in hac parte dimicatio est, nec alibi dixeris magis mucrone pugnari'.[43]
This analogy with Classical procedure is apt in two respects. First, the
rhetorician's metaphor of 'hand-to-hand fighting' and 'thrusts' evokes
the force implied by the Champion's utterance as a verbal 'doing'. The
performative force particular to his *blason* of Love is that of incantation,
the thrust of which seems to have been appreciated by the *Champion des dames* Master; his illustration of the Champion's panegyric
on *G*, fol. 75ʳ (Plate 2.2), shows him facing Brief Conseil with arms
outstretched in a gesture of invocation.[44] Between the two speakers,

[40] 'One has to speak there and then, and make one's thrust almost at the same
moment as the adversary makes his': Quintilian 2001: III, 6.4.8. For the circulation
of Classical treatises in late medieval France, see Meyer 1999: 99–107; Ornato 1992.
Quintilian's *Institutio* was recovered in its entirety only in 1416 by Poggio during the
Council of Constance. It is likely that some of its ideas were familiar currency to Le
Franc, a frequenter of Conciliar circles in the 1440s and a frequent presence at the
Burgundian court.
[41] 'He leapt up immediately to continue his argument.' See also vv. 19793–4.
[42] 'bonus altercator': Quintilian 2001: III, 6.4.10.
[43] 'The fiercest battle is in the Altercation; nowhere else, one might say, is there so
much hand-to-hand fighting': Ibid. 6.4.4–5.
[44] A similar image features on *Z*, fol. 28ʳ. The most extensive recent work on the
secular visual language of gesture is Garnier 1982. The weakness of Garnier's study, in
its attempt to produce an exhaustive taxonomy of gestures, is a lack of contextualization.
For a more contextualized study, thus more limited in scope, see Burrow 2002; see also
Buettner 1996: 67–71. The earliest descriptive typologies of gesture appear in Classical
rhetorical handbooks and were intended to advise an orator how to exploit the persuasive
potential of *actio*. A theatrical vocabulary of gesture is evidenced by illustrations for fifth-
century manuscripts of Terence's comedies: see Aldrete 1999: esp. 44–75. A number

pictured emerging from a scalloped nimbus, is the God of Love, as if his apparition were being conjured up by the force of the Champion's rhetoric as a perlocutionary, not just an illocutionary, act: an act that concerns, to quote Austin again, 'what we bring about or achieve *by* saying something'.[45] The choice of illustration highlights how qualities of both verbal attack and verbal display—two complementary aspects of rhetorical performance—are present in the Champion's argumentation; his pro-feminine forensic discourse combining with it features of deliberative and demonstrative oratory.[46]

The second aspect of Quintilian's concept of *altercatio* that is especially resonant with the episode of exchanged *blasons* is the competitive spirit in which the rhetorician depicts this verbal combat arising: 'hic patronorum inter se certamen'.[47] The *Champion's blason* and *contreblason* constitute an agonistic exchange, as my discussion of Franc Vouloir's dexterous manipulation of his adversary's verses has already suggested. Moreover, this particular confrontation seems to be set quite specifically within the context of the late medieval poetic competition known as the *puy d'amour*,[48] to which the Champion proceeds to invite all Love's supporters:

> Venez au puy d'Amours, venez,
> [. . .]
> La feste est huy, n'arrestez grain!
>
> (*CD*, vv. 4161, 4165)

(Come to the *puy d'amour*, come! [. . .] It's happening today, don't delay!)

By stressing the immediacy of the festival, specifying that it occurs 'today' (*huy*) and urging haste, Franc Vouloir seems to imply that he and his adversaries are already participating in the competition by dint of the versified arguments, and especially the *blasons*, they are exchanging on the subject of Love.[49] Allusion to the practice of *puys* furnishes a

---

of stock or 'emblematic' gestures seem to maintain a stable meaning right up to, and throughout, the Middle Ages; invocation is one such gesture and is originally described by Quintilian 2001: V, 11.3.115.

[45] 1975: 109.   [46] See Mathieu-Castellani 1998: 30.

[47] 'Here we have a competition between advocates': 2001: III, 6.4.21.

[48] The historical development of the *puy* tradition is documented by Hüe 2002 and Gros 1992.

[49] In terms of known, historical *puys* on the subject of Love, Franc Vouloir's incantatory *blason* would sit well in a Puy du Souverain Amour (Hüe 2002: 319–25), and he does, in fact, refer to 'le puy d'amistié souveraine' (*CD*, v. 4186).

dramatic conceptual framework, resonating with contemporary cultural practice, to showcase the two speakers' performances of performative rhetoric. This framework can be seen as a literary reflexive permutation of the judgement theme, a permutation that is sustained to the poem's conclusion, when the Champion, and, by extension the poet Le Franc, is crowned victor with a laurel wreath ('chappelet de vert lorier' (*CD*, v. 24312)), the token of literary merit par excellence.[50] The *Champion*'s various illustrators appear to have seized upon the dramatic potential of this framework.[51] In the Grenoble MS, fol. 80ᵛ (Plate 2.3), the Champion and Brief Conseil are pictured in the foreground debating the legitimacy of the *puy*, which the latter, blinkered by his inability to conceive of love as anything other than carnal lust, reproves as a '*puy* of the devil' (v. 3977). Juxtaposed in the background the artist shows a *puy d'amour* in full swing, picturing the silver crowns held aloft that are to be awarded to the winners of the poetic contest and depicting copyists busily engaged in transcribing the works being performed by a number of contestants. The artist thereby furnishes the decor, props, and cast for the dispute's stage,[52] as if visually representing the interface between poetic, juridical, and dramatic structures of performance.

DEBATE AS DRAMATIC DIALOGUE: ORALITY AND *ACTIO*

The war of words I have outlined consists of potent speech acts on the part of both pro- and anti-woman camps, showing the spoken word in *querelle* debates to be both a weapon and a building block, a potent tool of attack, defence, and rhetorical display. My focus on the poetic joust of the Champion's and Brief Conseil's *blasons* has shown how the ideas of performative rhetoric and of rhetoric as dramatic performance interact in the *Champion* in a way that engages imaginatively with the juridical setting of the poem's debate and, crucially, focuses the readers' (and illustrators') attention on acts of utterance. The manner in which these utterances are delivered—the performance that frames the performative, as it were—also receives detailed attention and is used to spotlight the contrast between the two camps. For example, Le Franc's Champion encapsulates the virtues of a great orator; he is a good man and therefore

---

[50] See Hüe 2002: 291–2; Mühlethaler 1992: 98–9.   [51] See Gros 1992: 27.
[52] For our knowledge of *puy* furniture, see Hüe 2002: 301.

an excellent speaker.[53] If Franc Vouloir's virtue as a man defending the cause of women's honour determines his rhetorical excellence, then Le Franc ensures that this excellence is expressed through his Champion's *actio*—his voice, mien, and gesture—by selecting descriptive terms that resonate with contemporary rhetorical doctrine on delivery. The Champion exemplifies good delivery in his manner of speaking:

> Puis en parler moult aourné
> Sa voix doulce ainsi couler laisse.
>
> (*CD*, vv. 4535–6)

(Then, in most ornate speech, he lets his dulcet tones stream forth.)

This manner is both 'ornate' (*ornata*) and 'sweet' (*dulcis*). These qualities, present in rhetorical instruction since Quintilian,[54] are recommended by a contemporary treatise, the *Art et science de bien parler et de se taire*, which advises a 'parolle doulce, simple et soefve',[55] and by de Conty's commentary on rhetoric, which highlights the importance in 'pronunciacion' of 'deues paroles, aornees et beles'.[56] The Champion's composure never falters, even when he feels himself being provoked by his opponent's anger:

> A ire qui est si patente
> Fureur arragié convendroit,
> Mais Dieu doint que je vous contente
> Par sens reposé et par droit.
>
> (*CD*, vv. 2805–8)

(I should respond with furious anger to such patent ire, but God knows I shall answer you with a measured manner and lawful action.)

The Champion's 'cool head' is made apparent through his mien and gesture (*corporis motio*) as well as his voice (*vocis figuram*).[57] The manner

---

[53] The Quintilian ideal of the orator as *vir bonus*, whose discourse reflects his virtue (2001: V, 12.1.1), had currency in early humanist France, and was sustained by Nicolas de Clamanges: Mühlethaler et al. 2001: 302.

[54] Quintilian 2001: V, 11.3.30–40.

[55] 'Sweet, straightforward, and gentle speech' 1875: 354. English translation is my own. This edition is based on a Rouen imprint from *c*.1500-1. The *Art et science* (*c*.1400) is a French translation of Albertano of Brescia's *De arte loquendi et tacendi*. The Latin treatise circulated widely in both manuscript and print, and was translated into most European vernaculars. Three manuscript copies of the rhymed *Art* survive: see Graham 2000. Specifically in a forensic context, Bouchet counsels advocates to use a 'doulce harengue': 1969: fol. E2r.

[56] 'Sweet words, ornate and fine': 1993: 99.   [57] [Cicero] 1981: 3.11.19.

in which he is described preparing to reply to Vilain Penser seems to align him with the Classical ideal of an exemplary orator:

> Franc Voloir bien endoctriné
> Son regard vers la terre baisse.
>
> (*CD*, vv. 4533–4)

(Well-schooled Free Will lowers his eyes to the ground.)

It is the allusion here to Franc Vouloir's rhetorical education ('bien endoctriné'), as elsewhere to his status as 'escolier' 'en plaine escole' (v. 4055), that invites an assessment of his conduct through the specific optic of Classical oratory. This particular echo of Quintilian's doctrine in the Champion's brief pause for reflection is striking: Quintilian's ideal orator, Ulysses, is described standing 'with eyes fixed on the ground', adopting the conventional posture of humility, before lifting his head to 'pour forth his "blizzard" of eloquence'.[58]

Most of the above observations regarding Franc Vouloir's voice and mien are made by l'Acteur, the observing first-person narrator. The presence of this mediating voice accentuates the degree to which the debate is construed as a performance event in that it is granted an audience: the eyes, ears, and reporting voice of l'Acteur, who becomes, in turn, the extratextual audience's window onto the text's diegetic disputations, like a sort of director or *meneur de jeu*.[59] Reported details of *actio* function like didaskales[60] directing, not the poem's action, of which l'Acteur is simply the critical spectator, but the reader's apprehension of this action. A reading of the text according to l'Acteur's punctuating commentary enables us to re-evoke the *déroulement* of the debate's stage business. Not only the words of the dialogue, but also the way these words are pronounced and the physical activity accompanying their delivery—in short, their dramatic performance[61]—become a significant aspect of the debate's interest.

---

[58] 2001: V, 11.3.157–8.

[59] On the narrator of debates as a *meneur de jeu*, see Thiry 1986: 243.

[60] See Ubersfeld 1977: 20–2.

[61] Travieso-Ganaza shows how late medieval dramatic works contain the conditions of their staging within the play's text when the manuscript lacks any extradiegetic performance directions: the text's *mise en scène* is 'hyperdetermined' by the incorporation into its speeches of what she calls 'matrices of didaskales': 1990: 67–9. English translation is my own. The *Champion* evokes the pragmatics of its debate's virtual performance in the imagination of its reader (and, in the case of the Grenoble codex, its illustrator) by similar means.

Hermeneutic interest is created in the art of disputation and this level of engagement renders l'Acteur an essential, though far from impartial, witness to the debate. His commentary generates new meaning by evaluating the interlocutors' activity; for example, l'Acteur intervenes intermittently to remark on Malebouche's cohort's reaction to Franc Vouloir's speech. The misogynists' reaction is a measure of the efficacy of the Champion's rhetoric, of what his words have brought about through their perlocutionary force.[62] Franc Vouloir's vehement defences of ladies and love are shown to be highly efficacious in moving (if not persuading) his opponents. L'Acteur uses a mythological analogy to depict the audience's perturbation:

> Comme Eolus lachant les resnes
> Aux vens impetueusement
> [. . .]
> Ung chascun s'esmut tellement
> Que je cuiday que tout fendit.
> [. . .]
> Et l'ung a l'aultre chacoustoyent
> Menassans de pié et de main.
>
> (*CD*, vv. 4313–14, 4319–20, 4325–6)

(Like Eolus giving free rein to the impetuous winds [. . .] each and every [slanderer] got so agitated that I thought everything would cave in [. . .] They jostled elbows with each other, lashing out with hands and feet.)

He emphasizes here the disorder of the misogynists' uncontrolled physical gestures. This potential for violence, for lashing out with their limbs as well as their intemperate tongues, is present in their visceral response to the Champion's *contreblason* of love: these 'hot-headed slanderers' (v. 3802) try to turn the Champion's and Brief Conseil's altercation into a general brawl, with verbal weapons giving way to fisticuffs:

> Bastu l'eussent de chaude cole
> Se l'adversaire au dur courage
> N'eust tantost repris la parole.
>
> (*CD*, vv. 3806–8)

(They would have beaten him up if the firm-minded adversary hadn't started speaking again at that moment.)

---

[62] In Classical terms, this force equates to the *pathos* of rhetorical presentation (Cicero 1939: 37.128–38.133), which was a particular concern of certain rhetoricians in the mid fifteenth century: see Meyer 1999: 103–7.

The adversary's verbal intervention obviates a descent into physical violence, but l'Acteur's observation of the cohort's desire to fight and the simmering potential for an assault heightens the tension of the debate by underscoring the precariously unstable threshold in *querelle* disputation between verbal and physical violence.

This threshold, together with the interfaces between dialogue and drama, performativity and performance, finds a visual equivalent in the miniatures of *G*, the most copiously and unusually illustrated of the *Champion*'s nine extant witnesses.[63] As the above textual analysis has shown, the text's debate does not need a pictorial dimension for its performative quality to be appreciated. However, a brief glance at some of *G*'s images helps to show just how significant the text's performativity was held to be by at least one reader/illustrator, the *Champion des dames* Master, who, I argue, orients his entire iconographic programme around his perception of the debate as a performance, and who thereby creates a codex that can be seen as a theatre of debate.

I consider here principally those images showing the Champion and his adversary in the cut and thrust of debate, such as that on fol. 127^v (Plate 2.4).[64] This series of fifty-five images out of a total of 182 is, I argue, remarkable for the way that it focuses the viewer's attention on the text as a dramatic performance. By strategic use of the manuscript page's layout, these images organize the text around its *dramatis personae*, extracting the activity of debate from the poem's narrative thread, and presenting the text as a kind of dialogue drama *mis en acte*. Picturing speakers rather than the content of their speech is not in itself a novel technique; moreover, it can also be seen to serve a purely functional as well as a poetic role in the context of the *Champion*'s immense length: such images provide a sort of frequent, visual punctuation of the debate's *déroulement*. Nevertheless, I argue

---

[63] See Appendix 2A for descriptions of these manuscripts.

[64] Excluding the presentation miniature, *G*'s images may be sorted into eight types, presented in the order '(type) description, number in MS *G*': (1) Scenes from l'Acteur's journey around the castles of Venus and Amour (Book I only), 14; (2) L'Acteur pictured alone, 10; (3) The Champion pictured alone or in conversation with other characters, 22; (4) An adversary pictured alone, 15; (5) The Champion and an adversary pictured debating (with or without audience), 55; (6) Miniature divided into two frames, left and right; one showing the Champion and an adversary debating, and the other picturing a scene illustrating an *exemplum* cited by one of the debaters, 21; (7) A scene illustrating an *exemplum* cited by one of the debaters, 33; (8) A lady virtue reciting her *chanson* (end of Book V only), 11. The images I consider here belong mostly to type five.

that the high proportion of the Grenoble codex's miniatures allocated to this level of diegetic activity,[65] together with the particular manner in which debate scenes are presented, both individually and collectively, throughout the manuscript, merits special attention. The sheer number of these images suggests that the miniaturist felt this level of engagement with the debaters' activity, showing simply the act of their interlocution and not the topic of their debate, was sufficiently interesting in itself to warrant much illustration. The sheer size of the Grenoble codex's images and their dominance over a single column of written text argues for a disjunctive, rather than an integrative text–image relationship,[66] and thus foregrounds all the more the figurality of these speakers' imagined poses.

There is a shifting balance between discursivity and figurality as the artist strives to promote the dramatic nature of these altercations. He supplements the equation between debate and physical conflict already made in the text when he illustrates the aggression described above, when Brief Conseil's cronies square up to the Champion (*CD*, vv. 3806–8). In the left-hand frame of *G*, fol. 78ᵛ (Plate 2.5),[67] the violent arm gestures made by Brief Conseil's supporters seem directly to translate l'Acteur's description of the 'mesdisans transis de rage' on the point of assaulting Franc Vouloir who are only stilled by their spokesman's resuming verbal argument. In the manuscript's layout, l'Acteur's commentary directly precedes the miniature so it is plausible that an integrative text–image interrelation was intended at this point by the artist, the viewer's reading of the image being informed by his appreciation of the text. The balance between discursivity and figurality is, however, tipped towards the latter in the case of those miniatures which innovatively find a visual equivalent for the 'doing' or performative force of the debaters' rhetoric. I mentioned above that the illustration of speakers in the heat of debate is not in itself novel. For example, numerous illustrated manuscripts of the *Roman de la rose* and of Guillaume de Deguileville's popular rewriting of the *Rose*, *Le Pèlerinage de vie humaine*,

---

[65] Compare *P1*, whose sixty-six miniatures illustrate primarily scenes conjured up by the different *exempla* cited by either party; they show the content of speech rather than the act of speaking.

[66] This becomes especially clear if we compare *G* with *P1*, where the majority of miniatures in the two-column page layout occupy only a few lines of the written space within a single column.

[67] This miniature belongs to type six (see above, n. 64). Its right-hand frame illustrates the tale of Ulysses' enchantment by Circe, which the adversary here enlists to demonstrate woman's treacherous wiles: *CD*, vv. 3809–48.

together with iconographical programmes accompanying texts involving disputation, such as the *Response au Bestiaire d'amour*, a literary response to Richard de Fournival's famous bestiary, show gesticulating characters in conversation or disputing with one another.[68] Early fifteenth-century copies of Terence's *Comedies* also display the performance of debate.[69] In each of these instances, however, there is a certain conservatism of gesture, little difference between illustrations of simple discussion and those showing antagonistic dispute, and no clear distinction between the speaking and listening parties in any given exchange. What is thus remarkable about the *Champion*'s debate miniatures is the degree of differentiation between parties, the visualized dynamic of antagonism, and the degree of physical animation accorded to the interlocutors, especially in the lower half of the body. It is by means of this more elaborate and exaggerated manner of illustrating debate activity that the miniaturist not only creates an entertaining spectacle, but also redirects the viewer's attention back into the performance presented by the text. The speaking and listening parties are often clearly defined by the way that one interlocutor is shown reacting violently against the words his opponent utters. On fol. 127ᵛ (Plate 2.4), depicting Vilain Penser speaking against marriage, Franc Vouloir turns his face away from, and seems also to push away with his hand, such anti-matrimonial discourse. A similar gesture occurs on fol. 102ᵛ (Plate 2.6), where Vilain Penser's own movement is also more animated: as he prepares to enumerate his points of argument on his fingers,[70] he steps forward and leans towards the Champion so that it is the physical presence of the adversary's person as much as the rhetorical force of his words that Franc Vouloir appears to be fending off.[71] On fol. 264ʳ (Plate 2.7), it is the adversary Trop Cuidier who leans backwards in retreat from the advancing figure of a

---

[68] For the *Rose*, see Blamires and Holian 2002: plates 38–43, and Huot 1993a; for the *Pèlerinage*, see Hagen 1990; and for the *Response*, see Solterer 1995: figs. 8 and 9 (pp. 103, 111). See also the scenes of discussion between Boccaccio and Petrarch in fifteenth-century manuscripts of *Des cas des nobles hommes*, the vernacular translation of Boccaccio's *De casibus virorum illustrium*, such as Paris, BnF, MS fr. 229, fol. 303ᵛ.

[69] See Meiss 1974: ii. 41–50.

[70] The adversary's gesture of raising his right forefinger to enumerate the points of his argument on his left hand is attested by both Classical and medieval rhetorical practices: Buettner 1996: 67.

[71] The *Champion* Master's emphasis on leg movement is arguably one of the Grenoble miniatures' most remarkable features; Buettner notes that 'the widest range of expression and communicative power' is normally imparted to the upper limbs: 1996: 67.

vociferous Champion, who 'lifted his head' (v. 13729) to declaim in exceptionally excited and exclamatory fashion:

> Ho, dit le champion leaux,
> Or voy que je folement semme
> Mes roses devant les pourceaux
> Et n'estes digne que de femme
> L'en vous parle! . . .
>
> (*CD*, vv. 13737–41)

('Ho!', said the faithful Champion, 'I see now that I'm casting my pearls pointlessly before swine, and that you're not worthy of being talked to about woman's virtue.')

The interlocutors' poses and gestures translate strikingly their respective positions at this point in the debate.

By evoking striking and clearly delineated relationships between speaker and listener, the artist represents figurally the direction of the text's verbal exchange. He reflects also the dynamic nature of these exchanges: on fol. 114^r (Plate 2.8), the adversary recoils from the Champion's outstretched arm as if physically struck. This gesture corresponds in the text to an insult verbally 'punched' at Vilain Penser by Franc Vouloir, who berates him for his misogyny: 'Shame on you, villainous and depraved man!' (v. 5586).[72] It is thus the miniaturist's own close attention, not only to details of *actio* described by l'Acteur, such as his depiction of Vilain Penser's exceptionally animated state just before the miniature featured on fol. 102^v, but also to the force of speech uttered by the debaters themselves which informs his dynamic, dramatic representation of the debate situation. These representations in turn cue the viewer to look equally closely at the text to explain why characters are depicted in so animated a relationship or performing a particular gesture. As Brigitte Buettner has argued, visualizations of gesture serve a double function: 'they dramatize the relationship between characters, all the while defining for the viewer the nature of that relationship.'[73] In the Grenoble manuscript, this manner of visual 'definition' seems designed to pose questions and open up meaning, rather than provide complete significance in and of itself. It 'defines' the text by staging its action as a dramatic event in a way that prompts a detailed study of the

---

[72] This is the second line of the speech positioned directly beneath the illustration on fol. 114^r.

[73] 1996: 67.

text on the part of the reader through the lenses of performance and performativity.

G's debate miniatures are not simply visualizations of rhetorical performance; they can themselves be understood as a rhetorical manoeuvre, that is, a persuasive as well as an inventive enterprise on the part of the artist.[74] He uses images to persuade the reader/viewer who engages actively with the manuscript's text–image relationships of the centrality of performance—linguistic, dramatic, and hermeneutic—as a key to reading the *Champion*: a way of appreciating to the full its dynamic and varied verbal activity of debate. In this respect, the artist disrupts what had previously been postulated in the late Middle Ages as the accepted relationship in secular manuscripts between *painture* ('image') and *parole* ('word'). This relationship is first formulated as a theoretical principle in the vernacular in the mid thirteenth century by Richard de Fournival. In the prologue to his *Bestiaire d'amour* he presents his target reader, his lady, with a sort of *mode d'emploi* for making the most of text and image in the book he offers her, and begins with the direction: 'Painture siert à oel et parole à oreille.'[75] He proposes a neat logic of correspondences between image and eye, word and ear. The *Champion des dames* Master creatively disrupts this correspondence by using his pictures to stimulate the ear through the eye, using images as signs of voices in order to convince a reader/viewer of the potency of the spoken word and the acoustic qualities of the poem's debate.[76] We recall also how the previous chapter demonstrated images functioning to reinforce instances of hermeneutic performance within the text. Through their visualizations of Jean de Meun, illustrators could be seen to be responding to the *Rose* continuator's spectral presence haunting his heir, Martin Le Franc, as well as Le Franc's diegetic characters.

THE THEATRE OF DEBATE: THE PAGE AS STAGE

I remarked above that *G*'s illustrations militate both individually and collectively for the performativity of the *Champion*. Their 'collective'

[74] For this dual understanding of rhetoric, specifically regarding the rhetorical use of images to persuade, see Carruthers 1998: 132–3, 224. I am also indebted here to Carruthers's explorations of the active nature of medieval reading practices.

[75] 'The picture is for the eye, and the word for the ear': 1860: 2. English translation is my own. Word and image are here in the service of memory, since he wishes his lady to use the book as a means of remembering him in his absence.

[76] Cf. Carruthers 1990: 221–30.

dimension relates to the way that the artist uses the space of the codex to contrive what we might call 'transiconic'[77] relationships between images strategically positioned on the manuscript page. For example, in two debate images placed in the upper half of the recto of fols. 137^r (Plate 2.9) and 245^r (Plate 2.10), the miniaturist uses the visual prop of a throne (*chaire*), denoting the seat of authority, to create a dialogue of shifting power relations between the two debaters. The layout or *dispositio* of the illustrations' interlocutors is identical: the speaking party, seated in each instance in the throne, leans and gestures forwards towards the listening party, who responds negatively, either by withdrawing (fol. 137^r) or by making a gesture of fending off his opponent (fol. 245^r).[78] In each case, the discursive control that the speaker exercises in the text is translated figurally in the miniatures into his authority as the enthroned party in the exchange. The only, but semiotically vital, difference between these images is that the speaker and the listener exchange identities: on fol. 137^r it is Vilain Penser who evidently has the upper hand; on fol. 245^r it is the Champion who has regained rhetorical control over his adversary (now Trop Cuidier).

The dialogue or semiotic communication[79] between these two illustrations can be seen to enact the dynamic movement of constantly shifting power relations which characterizes the debate's *déroulement*. That the images themselves constitute a performance within the space of the codex as a sort of theatre is suggested by two other pairs of miniatures which argue for a reading of the manuscript page as a stage for the dramatic performance of debate. In these pairs of images (*G*, fols. 369^v–370^r, 395^v–396^r), the artist innovates upon the simplest of textual rubrics, indicating a change in speaker, to contrive a call-and-response effect—*pro* and *contra*, attack and defence—between miniatures positioned in the upper half of the verso and recto of successive pages. Fol. 370^r (Plate 2.12) may thus be seen to 'answer' fol. 369^v (Plate 2.11) in a double spatial dimension: the Champion speaks from the facing folio of the codex as well as from the opposite side of the room

[77] I coin this term by adapting 'intericonic' relationships (the equivalent in visual studies of intertextuality) to suit connections between images that occur across one manuscript (like transtextuality), rather than between manuscripts.

[78] The adversary's raised hand can be seen to indicate both objection and, perhaps, defensiveness.

[79] I here apply to a transiconic axis of gestural interplay the phrase coined by Buettner to denote the relationship sparked by 'the repetition, opposition, or superposition of gestures' within the same image: 1996: 69.

that is represented within the illustrations as a continuous stage running across the double-page opening.[80] Just as striking is the interface with theatre that is suggested by these miniatures' relationship with the rest of the *mise en page*. The Grenoble codex's layout is unique amongst manuscript copies of the *Champion*; whilst all other codices present the text in two (or more) columns, the combination in the Grenoble manuscript of a small format (266 mm × 194 mm) and large, bastard script accommodates only one column of text per page.[81] In the call-and-response page-pairings, this feature of *mise en page* is innovatively turned to account. As the illustrations spread over more than half of the written space, little more than one stanza can be fitted beneath; in each case the single stanza corresponds to the speech of the character depicted in the image directly above. In this way, perhaps consciously imitating the layout of contemporary play texts, the double-page spreads come to affirm the performativity of the Grenoble codex in two ways: on the one hand, they represent the script or *livre de scène* that might potentially be used *for* a dramatic performance, with alternating speeches headed with the name of the character speaking;[82] on the other, the pages themselves function as a stage displaying one, imaginative enactment *of* that performance, whose *meneur de jeu* is a combination of the text's Acteur, its ultimate author Martin Le Franc, the illustrator (and compiler) of the codex, and, to some extent also, each new reader/viewer who engages in reading the text in this particular manuscript matrix. Between the facing folios is enacted a forensic debate pictured in the dimensions of space and time of an imagined room, within the virtual theatre of the manuscript.[83]

[80] On the effect of double-page illustrations, see Toubert 1990: 373.

[81] *G* is the smallest of the nine extant *Champion* manuscripts. Stones considers two or three columns of text to be the norm in late medieval secular manuscripts (1976: 93), but cf. Hasenohr 1990: 349. The large size of *G*'s miniatures could be seen, in light of the codex's probable Burgundian recipient, to bear the influence of contemporary Flemish illustration, where half-page miniatures were quite normal in vernacular manuscripts: McKendrick 2003b.

[82] Late medieval play texts often appeared in various types of manuscript copy. The most usual layout for any copy produced prior to performance was one column of text per page; afterwards, however, a luxury version was often produced, featuring the text set in two columns and accompanied by miniatures; this copy would be intended for reading: Runnalls 1990: 98–9, 105–9. If a play manuscript could be produced for reading, then a non-dramatic text's presentation could equally, I argue, be made to suggest performance by deliberately incorporating features of dramatic works' *mise en page*, even though no actual dramatic performance was intended. Cf. Hasenohr 1990: 335–40; Hult 1983: 58; Ubersfeld 1977: 20–1.

[83] Cf. the 'theatrical' quality of medieval books identified by Huot 1987a: 3.

We have seen above, both within texts and miniatures and in the material arrangement of words and images on the page, that the twofold nature of rhetoric as performance is made a prominent source of interest in manuscripts of *querelle des femmes* debates. The verbal 'doings' of disputation perform a lively and intricate war of words, constantly dismantling and rebuilding woman's reputation or love in an agonistic framework of poetic competition. This framework points to the equal significance of the debate's manner of performance: the voice and gesture of each speaker, and the way *actio* and also performativity are translated figurally into vibrant images of antagonistic exchange. To return to the quotation with which I opened this chapter, we can perhaps now see why Pierre Michault was so keen for Honneur Féminin to bring his case in from the battlefield to the courtroom 'pour illecq faire debatre ma cause' in an even more dynamic and dramatic theatre of debate.

G is not alone in drawing attention to, and providing figural representation of, the debaters debating in the *Champion des dames*, but is unique in the number and proportion of illustrations it assigns to this diegetic level of activity. We can use the interest manifested specifically in the forensic aspect of the *Champion*'s debate by the illustrator of an affiliated manuscript, *P2*,[84] to introduce the popularity amongst *querelle* writers of one particular theatre of debate, the theatre of law, as a fictional framework for presenting pro- and anti-feminine dispute. We have indeed come full circle in this chapter, arriving back here where we began with the interplay between armed struggle and legal procedure in pro-feminine writing, so it is now worth considering just why this interplay crops up so often in the *querelle*.

One aspect of the *Champion*'s debate that is foregrounded by *P2*, but somewhat obscured by the iconographic programme of *G*, is its juridical framework.[85] The transition from battlefield to courtroom, from misogynistic disorder to tempered, well-governed order, is articulated by successive miniatures: the site of conflict shifts from the mêlée of Malebouche's 'souldars' (*P2*, fol. 20ʳ) to a formal 'beau parlement' (fol. 21ʳ, v. 2475: Plate 2.13), where Franc Vouloir and his adversary are pictured standing before an enthroned judge. However, the legal order that *P2*'s miniaturist introduces is in fact too well structured when

[84] For this affiliation, see Chapter 1, n. 144.
[85] The constantly shifting location of debate in *G* between indoor and outdoor scenes, together with the variety of combinations in which the trial's protagonists are pictured, means that, although a sense of vibrancy is communicated, any sense of a fixed *locus* of judgement is lost.

compared with the text's activity at this point: whilst Franc Vouloir does indeed exhort his opponent 'Fourmez vostre cas devant juge' (v. 2502), the debaters rapidly realize that they lack any neutral party to preside as such a judge, so the throne of fol. 21ʳ (and later of fol. 29ʳ) should, in fact, be shown empty.[86] They eventually settle on appointing a nearby statue of Vérité as their quarrel's arbiter, and Franc Vouloir expresses his somewhat qualified agreement to this appointment in terms which colour the rhetoric of *disputatio* with the purpose of law:

> Se vostre Verité parlast,
> Dist le champion, tres content
> Fusse qu'elle determinast
> Du droit que chascun cy pretent.
> Mais elle ne parle n'entent,
> Dont n'est en jugement propice.
> Si est bien simple qui s'attent
> A elle sur fait de justice.
>
> (*CD*, vv. 2593–600)

('If your Truth were to speak', said the Champion, 'I'd be very happy for her to pronounce a verdict on the cause that each party is contesting here. But she can neither speak nor hear, so is not apt to judge. Whoever awaits a verdict from her is truly a simpleton.')

Contrary to the Champion's initial scepticism, Vérité ultimately provides her *determinatio* ('conclusion') at the end of Book V, when she crowns him with a laurel wreath. This 'chappelet de vert lorier' (v. 24312) is a polyvalent symbol: it denotes victory in battle, both a physical joust against Cruel Despit (from Book I) and the 'champ de bataille' of verbal debate (from Books II to V); it indicates poetic supremacy, acknowledging Franc Vouloir's superior rhetorical skill and gesturing metatextually to the authorial achievement of Martin Le Franc; and it evokes the successful forensic defence of the case for women. I list the forensic significance of the 'chappelet' last since, although Vérité renders judgement as a quasi-legal 'juge', the dominant rhetorical framework

---

[86] The 1485 edition similarly represents the debate occurring before an enthroned judge (e.g. fols. L4ᵛ and L8ᵛ: Plate 2.14). Its programme of woodcuts seems informed by the illustrations of both *P2* and *G* (for example in the presentation of the lady virtues equipped with their symbolic attributes at the end of Book V: fol. Z6ʳ). The text of the imprint must, however, have been taken from (a recension of) one of the presentation copies (*B1* or *P1*) since the defence of the Immaculate Conception, a section that was partially cut from all post-1451 manuscripts, here stands complete.

of the *Champion* remains that of *disputatio*. This scholastic exercise concludes with a *determinatio* pronounced by a *maître* that is certainly analogous to a legal verdict or *sentence diffinitive*;[87] it is the degree to which *jugements* enlist juridical terminology and procedure which variously differentiates their debate framework from that of *disputatio*. It is principally in subsequent *querelle* contributions by Milet, Michault, and Marot that the terminological and structural apparatus of a courtroom fiction is mobilized in a thoroughgoing fashion. Might we conjecture, therefore, that it was the currency of forensic fiction in the slightly later works of Milet and Michault which informed the illustrator of *P2* when he came to situate the *Champion*'s debate in a courtroom before a judge?[88]

THE THEATRE OF DEBATE: THE FORENSIC STAGE

> Entrons leans tout sagement
> Et montons en la haulte salle;
> Illec verrons beau jugement
> S'il fut oncques en court royalle,
> Et par ordre moult prouffitable
> Serront les arrestz prononcez
> En audience générale,
> Et tous leurs meffais anoncez.
>
> (*FT*, fol. 219ᵛ)

(Let us enter quietly [the castle of Love] and go up to the upper chamber; there we'll see as fine a judgement as ever was in a royal court. And the verdicts will be pronounced in a most commendable order in open court, and all their offences proclaimed.)

Thus the personified character of Subtilité introduces to the narrator of Jacques Milet's *Forest de Tristesse* the courtroom drama that is to play out in this poem's allegorized criminal action against misogynist activity. The pro-feminine case is here advanced by Noble Vouloir, before the court of Dame Justice, in the kingdom of Love. The 'meffais' in question are the writings of those arch-misogynists of late medieval literature: Matheolus,

---

[87] See Enders 1993.

[88] If, as Charron suggests, the iconographic programme of *G* informed the illustrations of *Z* and *P2* (cf. Chapter 1, n. 144), then the latter probably date from *c*.1470–5. Milet's *Forest* and Michault's *Procès* were written in 1459 and *c*.1461.

author of the anti-matrimonial *Liber lamentationum Matheoluli* (1295), which was translated into French in the 1370s by Jean Le Fèvre,[89] and Jean de Meun.[90] The *Forest*'s forensic fiction is not an isolated instance; we recall here this chapter's prefatory quote from Michault's *Procès*, describing how Honneur Féminin decided to 'adjourner et convenir' his enemies before Dame Raison's court 'pour illecq faire debatre ma cause' (*PHF* 27–8). A number of *querelle* contributions adopt the fictional framework of courtroom debate or engage in detailed and innovative fashion with contemporary legal procedure, modelled on that practised in juridical sessions in the Grand'Chambre of the Parlement of Paris: the 'audience générale'[91] in the 'haulte salle' of the 'court royalle' to which Milet's Subtilité refers.

What precisely do *querelle* poets gain by enlisting a courtroom fiction, and whence is it inherited? What specific aspect of *querelle* discourse does this framework help articulate, and how is it helpful for the modern reader to focus on this engagement with the law as a key to understanding each debate's artistic construction, and also, possibly, its reception? The following discussion will demonstrate how specific forensic fictions, and the general idea of judgement feeding these fictions, merit special attention in order to provide a fuller appreciation of *querelle* debates in their contemporary literary and cultural contexts. Combining the themes of both the previous and current chapters, the court constitutes a *locus* in which intertextual dialogue with misogynistic authorities and intratextual debate procedure fuse together spectacularly to create a hermeneutically exciting and complex *querelle* poetic.

As my above quotations from the *Forest* and *Procès* suggest, a juridical *agôn* was seized upon to refresh and enliven the presentation of pro-feminine arguments. The very name that Milet accords his narrator's

---

[89] The *Lamentations* present the ignominy that Mathieu de Boulogne felt he suffered unjustly for having infringed canon law in order to marry his wife, herself a widow. Stripped of his office and having had his name humiliatingly diminished twice over to 'Math-eol-ul-us', he laments that his wife was not worth the sacrifice and inveighs against women in general: see Le Fèvre 1892. Le Fèvre's translation was printed in both Paris and Lyons around 1500.

[90] Matheolus and Jean de Meun are first viewed together as partners in crime in Jean Le Fèvre's rebuttal of his *Lamentations*, the *Livre de leesce* (*c*.1373), where the pro-feminine author-persona names amongst his adversaries 'Maistre Mahieu' and 'maistre Jehan Clopinel': 1905: vv. 747–9. Cf. Pratt 1999: 433; Christine de Pizan 1997: 48.

[91] *Grande Audience* was the title given to the chief juridical session in the *Grand' Chambre*: Shennan 1998: 337.

guide, 'Subtilité', suggests artistic skill,[92] and can be seen to gesture metatextually to the way that Milet uses his courtroom fiction as a rhetorical showcase for performing the trial of Matheolus and Jean de Meun. Performative considerations also apply to Michault's deployment of a parliamentary framework. As Honneur Féminin seems himself to indicate, forensic procedure is a way of dynamizing the rehearsal of established arguments in a particular debate structure: an innovative way to 'faire debatre ma cause' by setting disputation on a legal stage. These two poets' use of juridical terminology—already apparent in Subtilité's reference to 'verdicts' (*arrestz*) and Honneur Féminin's allusion to the process of 'summoning' (*adjourner*) his detractors before the court—is not without hermeneutic interest; nor is the way that, for instance, Milet's presiding judge, Dame Justice, threatens the assembled parliament with imprisonment for all 'delays' (*delaiz*) incurred by rowdy behaviour. Delays in court procedure and disruptive audience conduct were bones of considerable contention in contemporary ordinances aimed at reforming legal practice.[93] Whilst neither Michault nor Milet practised law professionally,[94] unlike some other contemporary writers who deployed courtroom fictions,[95] their audience seems to have been expected to have some familiarity with forensic terminology and procedure. Moreover, going one step further down the line of transmission, both works feature in print in the famous poetic anthology entitled *Le Jardin de plaisance et fleur de rethorique* (1501), whose own legal/literary interface is established by its opening rhetorical treatise written for jurists and members of the legal profession: 'aucuns licenciez en lois',[96] who were likely to be amateur poets. Furthermore, according to Kovacs, the highly popular *Jardin*, reprinted six times between 1504

---

[92] See Huot 1993b. This particular personification seems to be unique to Milet and might, perhaps, be read, like the Traverseur in Bouchet's *Jugement* (see Chapter 1, pp. 24–5), as a diegetic representative of the author's creativity.

[93] Shennan 1998: 31.

[94] Although Michault did maintain legal connections in his role as chaplain to the Burgundian *protonotaire*, Artus of Bourbon, whom he probably continued to serve after Artus was appointed *maître des requêtes* for the Parlement of Malines in 1473. For his part, according to the bibliographer La Croix du Maine (1584: 191), Milet studied law at the University of Orléans.

[95] For example, Guillaume Coquillart, author of the burlesque trial *Le Plaidoié d'entre la Simple et la Rusee* (see below, pp. 154–5), was a practising jurist. We recall also that Bouchet was a *procureur* in Poitiers, and his understanding of juridical practice doubtless informed the trial episode of his *Jugement*—a trial quite different from the courtroom fictions I address in this chapter.

[96] *Jardin de plaisance* 1910–25: i (1910), fol. 2ᵛ.

and 1535, owed much of its commercial success to 'upper-middle-class readers—primarily members of the legal hierarchy'.[97]

My discussion of intrapoetic relationships in Chapter 1 began by identifying how intertextuality is endemic to *querelle* poems since each work sets itself up as a response to a prior misogynistic authority, whether named or unspecified. By the same token, every male-authored *querelle* poem is to a certain extent inherently inscribed in a tradition of forensic oratory by dint of its proclaimed purpose to defend women by advocating on their behalf.[98] Even those texts that do not in any other way engage with the theme or structures of judgement carry a statement in a prologue or dedicatory epistle which affirms their position as defender of women's honour. Jean Dupré prefaces his catalogue of virtuous women *Le Palais des nobles dames* ([1534]) with a declaration to his dedicatee, Marguerite de Navarre, that 'à voz parties refie defendre la querelle des honnestes femmes'.[99]

There is, however, a sticking point in this inherently judicial structural condition: the *querelle* work's position of defence finds itself caught up in the same hermeneutic tangle that I characterized in Chapter 1 as the 'double binds' bedevilling a pro-feminine text as an innately intertextual response to anti-feminine discourse: the predicament of involuntarily promoting a misogynistic work by conjuring it up in order to denounce it, and the ethical anxiety of being culpable for repeating anti-feminine statements even in the act of repudiating them. The former predicament is made evident in the *Palais* by the appearance of the arch-misogynist Matheolus alongside the other, prestigious authorities that Dupré cites in his prefatory table of acknowledgements 'des autheurs desquelz les histoires du present livre ont esté pour la pluspart tirees';[100] it is against the *Lamentations'* attacks that he mounts his 'querelle' in women's

---

[97] 2001: 13 n. 24; 1. Moreau (1996) records the increasing purchasing power of lawyers, and the diminishing role of the clergy as buyers of books in the early sixteenth century. Concerning the *querelle* more specifically, and especially the dissemination of printed editions of the *Champion*, we note that Galliot Du Pré's clientele base consisted above all of magistrates and lawyers, to whom he sold books from his shop in the Palais de Justice: Charon-Parent 1988: 210.

[98] Cf. Kelly 1984: 66–7.

[99] 'I vow sincerely to defend against your adversaries the case of honourable women': [1534]: fol. A3ʳ. As a writer, the *Palais* is Dupré's only known work; as regards his life, we know that he was a nobleman who fought under the great Jacques de Genouillac at the Battle of Pavia (1525).

[100] '[Declaration] of the authorities from which the tales included in the present book have for the most part been drawn': ibid., fol. A5ʳ.

defence.[101] As regards the latter anxiety, we may find it striking that it is those *querelle* texts which manifest the most thorough going engagement with courtroom structures which address the dilemma of culpability most explicitly. This is, I believe, because these poems, notably Milet's *Forest* and Michault's *Procès*, offer their legal framework as a way of overcoming this troubling responsibility: they enlist the forensic principle of *audi alteram partem*, which decrees that both sides of a case should be heard.[102] In the case of *querelle* courts, this rule thus requires that misogynists' words are cited if they are to serve as evidence against them; indeed, at least one medieval court register stipulates the necessary precision of this citation, following the established principle that *negavit verbum ad verbo*: 'la réponse devait contredire la demande mot pour mot.'[103] In Michault's *Procès*, therefore, Vray Rapport asserts with confidence the legitimacy of citing the texts of Jean de Meun and Matheolus to bolster his case against them:

> Dont, pour tous cuers a justice inciter,
> Et pour monstrer l'erreur de ses escrips
> [. . .]
> Je narreray cy aucuns de leurs escrips
> Presentement, comme devant le juge.
>
> (*PHF* 32–3)

(And so, in order to incite all hearts to justice and to show the error in his writings [. . .] I shall here recount presently some of their writings, before the judge.)

He justifies his action by the juridical need to hear the misogynists' precise words recited. A little later, it is the narrator who highlights this necessity when he commends Judge Raison's meticulous respect for established legal codes, insisting that both sides get a hearing: 'sans oyr partie adverse ne voult appointier aucune chose.'[104]

---

[101] Cf. Blamires 1997: 61.

[102] This much-cited principle of natural justice formed part of the Athenian judicial oath and is attested by Aristophanes, Euripides, and Demosthenes. Amongst medieval literary courts it is enlisted by Nicolas De La Chesnaye's *Condamnation de Bancquet* (1503–5): 1991: vv. 1923–4.

[103] 'The response should refute the petition word for word.' English translation is my own. This note is found in the registers of the early, oral trial proceedings of the *Échiquier de Normandie*: Ducoudray 1902: 409.

[104] 'She did not want to make any ruling without having heard the other side's argument': *PHF* 44.

The pro-feminine advocate is, however, equally caught up with his *pro*-feminine ancestors or, at least, with a literary context of court-room fictions being deployed to challenge controversial figures. I refer specifically here to the way that what Enders dubs the 'aestheticization' of legal rhetoric was already a valuable currency in related literary debates of the period, the *querelle du 'Roman de la rose'* and the *querelle de 'la Belle Dame sans mercy'*.[105] The following discussion aims to show how *querelle des femmes* trials were particularly apt to turn to creative account selected features of these earlier fictions. Its basic premiss proposes that a courtroom framework fosters a singularly appropriate way of dealing with misogynistic authorities by putting the authors themselves on trial since it is, especially in Jean de Meun's case, the question of authorial intention that is at issue regarding his responsibility for his characters' misogynistic arguments. A common feature of these trials is their inconclusiveness: in Milet's *Forest*, for example, the verdict ('arrestz') predicted by Subtilité is not definitive; Michault's Honneur Féminin finds himself facing an appeal by the anti-woman advocate, Faux Parler. We shall see how this curious irres-olution both reflects the indeterminable nature of authorial intention and manifests *querelle* writers' reflexive interest in the nature of *pro* and *contra* debate.

The way that Milet, Michault, and others address the legacy of misogynistic literature by staging judicial encounters with the authors of these works, especially Jean de Meun, remobilizes a strategy practised in the earlier literary debate about this author's intention, the *querelle du 'Roman de la rose'*. Amongst this *querelle*'s correspondence is the courtroom fiction of Jean Gerson's dream-vision *Le Traité contre 'le Roman de la rose'* (1402),[106] in which the dreamer-narrator is transported to the 'holy court of Christianity'[107] presided over by Justice Canonique. The court's 'advocat', Eloquance Theologienne, argues in detail the case

---

[105] Recent synopses of how the aestheticization of legal practice and the theme of judgement developed in medieval French literature are offered by Becker 1997, and, with particular regard to how judicial structures concretize literary debates' sense of theatricality, by Cayley 2006: 22–6. Both highlight the *'Belle Dame' querelle*, but neither mentions the *'Rose' querelle* in this context.

[106] The *Traité* is exceptional amongst Gerson's writings on the *Rose*; his other interventions against Jean de Meun and his supporters occur in Latin, in the form of sermons, especially the series known as the 'Poenitemini' sermons from Christmas 1402, and of a letter ('Ad scripta cuisdam') addressed to Pierre Col. These documents, or fragments thereof, are reproduced in Hicks 1977.

[107] Hicks 1977: 59.

against Jean de Meun, and makes the 'requeste' that the *Rose* be withdrawn from circulation and destroyed: 'osté et exterminé'. Gerson's anti-*Rose* advocate, herself a precursor to Milet's and Michault's pro-feminine barristers,[108] expresses anxiety about the double bind of her discourse, caught up in the viciousness of the very language that she seeks to reprove: 'Je pouroie cheoir ou vice que je reprens.'[109] She is eager to abridge ('abreger') her speech, but, significantly, she expresses this eagerness at the same time as asserting the legitimacy of setting forth the articles of her case:

Si abregeray ma parole et ne diray plus que des articles contenus en la supplicacion de Dame Chasteté presentés par Conscience.

(I shall, therefore, cut my words short and speak merely of the article contained in the petition of Lady Chastity laid forth by Conscience.)[110]

The principal bone of contention raised by Eloquance Theologienne is the authorial intention behind the immoral 'dissolute speech' voiced by Jean de Meun's characters: La Vieille, Venus, and l'Amant.[111] On the one hand, she imputes complete responsibility for the *Rose*'s content to its author, dismissing his 'maniere de [. . .] parler par personnaiges'[112] as a fallacious attempt at blame-displacement; thus, when she indicts the poem's 'Fol Amoureux', it is the lover-protagonist, Jean de Meun's *acteur*-narrator, and the author himself who are compositely condemned under this name, since 'tout semble estre dit en sa persone'.[113] On the other hand, Gerson's advocate seems ready to grant posthumous pardon to the author's soul because, she reflects, it is Jean de Meun's supporters who should be blamed for misrepresenting their client's intention: 'a la semblance [. . .] du nice advocat qui cuide aidier son maistre et il destruit sa cause.'[114] Were the author himself to be interrogated, she

[108] I refer to Eloquance Theologienne as 'she' to accord with her grammatical gender, although Gerson uses the pronoun 'il' to denote the advocate, clearly identifying his/her voice as the diegetic representative of his own, authorial position: cf. Pratt 2002: 116.

[109] Hicks 1977: 78. 'I could fall into the vice that I reproach': Baird and Kane 1978: 84.

[110] Hicks 1977: 78; Baird and Kane 1978: 84.

[111] Eloquance Theologienne reads Venus as 'Luxure', and thus Chastity's arch-enemy.

[112] Hicks 1977: 67. '[His] method of speaking through characters': Baird and Kane 1978: 77.

[113] Hicks 1977: 74. 'Everything seems to be said in his own person': Baird and Kane 1978: 81.

[114] Hicks 1977: 70. 'Like a foolish lawyer who thinks he helps his client but rather destroys his case at law': Baird and Kane 1978: 78.

conjectures, he would admit the error of his ways by renouncing his *Rose*: 'ynellement, volontiers et de cuer il confesseroit son erreur.'[115]

As several critics have noted, *intentio auctoris* is the crux of the '*Rose*' *querelle*'s correspondence in general,[116] and a crux which, I argue, results in the main focus shifting from an impersonal textual authority (*auctoritas*) to a personalized author, from Jean de Meun's text to the *Rose* continuator in person ('en sa persone'). What the *querelle*'s *Rose* detractors thereby spawn as their most significant legacy to the *querelle des femmes* is a negative cult of personality surrounding the figure of Jean de Meun, which entails, in the *Traité*, his literary resurrection to stand trial:

Je vouldré bien [. . .] que l'aucteur que on accuse fust present en sa persone par retournant de mort a vie.

(I would wish that the author who is here accused could himself come forward in his own person, by returning from death unto life.)[117]

Eloquance Theologienne wishes she could get to the bottom of his authorial intention by addressing him face to face.[118] Crucially, however, the fulfilment of her wish remains virtual, beyond the reach of time and space.

We are here led back into the domain of inheritance, haunting, and spectres that I explored in Chapter 1 as a useful metaphor for intertextuality. We come to appreciate just how in tune that metaphor is with late medieval poetic practice; the fictional resurrection of an author in person complements intertextuality with a particularly potent form of spectral interpersonality. The way Gerson's diegetic advocate has it out face to face with his (Gerson's) conjured-up ancestor shows that interpersonality is not only something implicit in an inheriting writer's acts of textual appropriation, as I discussed in Chapter 1; in the domain of courtroom fictions it becomes explicit in an imagined encounter with the dead author, Jean de Meun, in person. My spectropoetic principle,

---

[115] Hicks 1977: 66. 'Swiftly, voluntarily, and gladly he would confess his crime': Baird and Kane 1978: 76.

[116] Monahan 2002; Hult 1997b: 356.

[117] Hicks 1977: 66; Baird and Kane 1978: 76.

[118] A cult of Jean de Meun as an author in the modern sense of the term—as a personality—was nascent in the late fourteenth century. One striking manifestation of this is Honorat Bovet's *Apparicion Maistre Jehan de Meun* (1398), in which the ghostly apparition features in the role of social critic. In contrast to my *querelle* poems, Bovet conjures up the *Rose* continuator as a positive figure of authority, as opposed to a persecuted, indeed prosecuted, ghost.

adapted from Derrida, that a master-text like the *Rose* haunts its heirs, that 'un chef d'œuvre toujours se meut, par définition, à la manière d'un fantôme' (*SM* 42),[119] as a troubling, controversial, and yet prestigious burden upon their literary consciousnesses, is thus extended to include the author himself as well as, or as part of, his text.

Gerson takes up the idea of spectral return in his *Traité*. Whilst seeking, on the one hand, to suppress Jean de Meun's nefarious work, Eloquance Theologienne wishes, on the other, to revive his person 'de mort a vie' to be present in court 'en sa persone' to answer charges. Her wish can perhaps be seen to respond to an earlier allegation made in the '*Rose*' *querelle*'s correspondence that a verbal challenge to Jean de Meun constitutes improper conjuring with the dead: Jean de Montreuil reproves Christine's persecution of his 'maistre' as an illegitimate prosecution of the deceased: 'quasi in pretorio causam ageres, nudiustertius contra mortuum verba faciens.'[120] The juridical analogy he uses might be seen to refer to the courtroom fiction framing Christine's first literary assault upon the *Rose* author, her *Epistre au dieu d'amours* (1399), in which the God of Love, a character appropriated by Christine from the *Rose*, rehearses the complaints of women who seek redress against false lovers and slanderers. In his capacity as King of the Court of Love, the eponymous 'dieu' issues a verdict in the form of a letter, banishing such 'desloyaux', including Jean de Meun, from his kingdom. We shall see a related scenario and cast of characters remobilized in Milet's *Forest*, in whose judicial framework Jean de Meun's authorial intention becomes as it were the criminal *mens rea* for which he is made to stand trial.

Although Jean de Montreuil refers to Christine's act of prosecution being performed upon a man who is unequivocally dead ('mortuum'), in the legal arena of verbal activity that he evokes, and that is developed by Gerson's *Traité*, it appears that speaking *of* and especially *to* the dead seems to be a way of keeping them alive. Eloquance Theologienne's speech is punctuated by statements and conjectures that alternately affirm the impossibility of revivification and express a desire for such an impossibility to be realized. She declares Jean de Meun to be dead and gone: 'Il avoit ja trespassé le hault pas duquel nulz ne revient',[121] but,

---

[119] *SM* 42. 'A masterpiece always moves, by definition, in the manner of a ghost': *SoM* 18.

[120] Hicks 1977: 28. 'Just [the] day before yesterday as if arguing in the courtroom, you spoke against a dead man': Baird and Kane 1978: 42.

[121] Hicks 1977: 63. 'For he had already gone to that low place from which nobody returns': Baird and Kane 1978: 74.

whilst engaged in the very act of denying his return, she addresses his spectre directly:

Je parle sans cause a toy, qui n'es pas ycy et auquel desplaisoit tout ce fait et desplairoit, come j'ay dit, se tu estoies present.

(Superfluously and in vain I speak to you, who are absent, for this deed truly displeases you and would displease, as I said before, if you were present.)[122]

Gerson seems deliberately to have his advocate protest too much: the pragmatic sense of the person deixis 'tu', implying some sort of interaction between the speaker and her addressee,[123] enters into conflict with the semantic weight of her statement that Jean de Meun is not present, and therefore cannot be communicated with. At the same time, her insistent recourse to conjecture and hypothesis ('se tu estoies', and above: 'il confesseroit', 'que l'aucteur [. . .] fust present') holds her discourse on the cusp of the possibility that his presence might be actualized in the *Traité*'s fictional court. She seems to be battling here with the paradoxical phenomenality entailed by what Derrida calls *l'effet de visière*, meaning the way one feels observed by a ghost, and yet cannot meet the gaze of this figure directly since it is always concealed from us, as if by a visor:[124] it is both visible and invisible, tangible and intangible. Eloquance Theologienne senses Jean de Meun's spirit, but knows she cannot make present and phenomenal this spirit; and yet she tries to address him, projecting a spectral identity (*spectre*) through her conjectures that substitutes imperfectly for the spirit (*esprit*), which can never be seen face to face.[125]

Making present a spectre of Jean de Meun is precisely what Milet, Michault, and Le Franc proceed to do in the *querelle des femmes* when they stage his textual return 'de mort a vie' to stand trial in the imaginative fictions of their courtroom debates. They effectively realize, but also reappropriate, Gerson's advocate's wish to resurrect and try Jean de Meun, and it is important to note here the hermeneutic shift they perform on Eloquance Theologienne's conjuring of the *Rose* continuator: whilst she prosecuted him for being guilty of immoral

---

[122] Hicks 1977: 68; Baird and Kane 1978: 77.

[123] See Verschueren 1999: 18–21.

[124] 'To feel ourselves seen by a look which it will always be impossible to cross, that is the *visor effect* on the basis of which we inherit from the law': *SoM* 7.

[125] The distinction between *spectre* and *esprit* is central to Derrida's thesis: the 'Thing' by which one is haunted cannot be determined as any visible, tangible manifestation, even though one feels its weight bearing down as if it were tangible; what one chooses to, and is able to, identify is only a spectre of the spirit: *SM* 27.

discourse in general, Milet's and Michault's pro-feminine advocates resurrect his ghost specifically as a misogynistic authority. They amplify what was, in fact, Christine de Pizan's identification of Jean de Meun's misogyny[126] into the principal, objectionable trait of his personality, and hence of his authorial intention.[127] The act of literary resurrection is pointed up by Michault, who envisages the misogynists' advocate, Faux Parler, supported by a formidable defence team in the court's gallery:

acompaignié d'aucuns trespassés, come Matheole, Juvenal, Maistre Jehan de Meun, acteur de la Rose, et aucuns vivants. (*PHF* 29)[128]

(In the company of certain deceased parties, such as Matheolus, Juvenal, Master Jean de Meun, the author of the *Rose*, and some still living.)

This reported presence is not mere rhetorical decoration; its importance lies in the effect it betokens upon Faux Parler, who feels pressure exerted upon him by Jean de Meun and Co.—'mes maistres que sont cy presens'[129]—to perform adequately in defending the misogynist cause. He feels the burden of their influence, the presence of their spirit, in the language he uses when he cites their arguments; their imagined visibility is a sign of this force. In Milet's *Forest*, where Jean de Meun stands as a convicted criminal brought before the court for sentencing, his imagined bodily presence is made meaningful by being turned to account to serve the pro-feminine case. This presence helps Noble Vouloir draw attention to the identity he perceives between the diegetic and extradiegetic voices of the *Rose*. He addresses the convict directly:

> Jehan de Meun, veulx tu donner blasme
> A Sebille qui fut à Romme?

---

[126] The charge of misogyny does not feature in Gerson's *Traité* per se; it is but one of the charges laid against Jean de Meun by Christine, and an accusation she first makes in a letter to Jean de Montreuil: Hicks 1977: 16. It is in her other works, outside the *querelle* correspondence, that misogyny plays a greater role as the alleged offence of Jean de Meun, such as her *Epistre au dieu d'amours*, the *Dit de la rose* (1402), and, of course, the *Cité des dames*.

[127] We are reminded here of Jean de Meun's resurrection in the *Giroufflier aulx dames* in personified form as Malebouche, whom Entendement (i.e. Guillaume de Lorris) characterizes as, above all, a misogynist.

[128] It is striking how this literary trend for resuscitating and trying past authorities as a way of dealing with misogynistic inheritance coincides with a historical period of intellectual and popular fascination with death, judgement, and the afterlife: see DuBruck 1999; Taylor 1984.

[129] The appellation has specific legal resonance: as well as evoking the general authoritative status of his misogynist 'masters', *maître* or *magister* was the title given to a graduate in Roman and canon law: Shennan 1998: 337.

> [. . .]
> Metz tu ceste cy en ta somme
> [. . .]
> Les as tu telles rencontrees
> Lors que cheminoys sur terre?
> Certes non, dont toutes oultrees
> De dueil viennent vengeance querre.
>
> (*FT*, fol. 221ʳ)

(Jean de Meun, do you mean to defame the Sibyl who went to Rome? [. . .] You put this in your summa [. . .] Did you meet women like this when you were alive? Certainly not, and for this, racked with grief, they come to seek revenge.)

Like Eloquance Theologienne claiming that 'everything seems to be said in his own person', Noble Vouloir imputes all responsibility to Jean de Meun for the misogynistic arguments voiced by his *Rose*'s characters. The rhetorical force of the repeated second-person pronoun underscores Noble Vouloir's apportionment of blame to the authorial voice, as does his lively depiction of aggrieved women seeking revenge against the author's person.[130]

This concept of personality-oriented *auctoritas*, concerning primarily the ineffaceable yet intangible author behind the text, does not merely give literary authority a named identity; it projects a personal subjectivity onto a totemic image of shadowy 'Maistre Jehan de Meun', who is implicitly or explicitly revived 'en sa persone' in a more or less face-to-face encounter each time that his text is challenged.[131] We recall here the manuscript images discussed in Chapter 1 showing the *Rose* author looming over characters from his poem, La Vieille and Bel Accueil, to accompany Franc Vouloir's interpretation of this episode in the *Champion*; they too can be seen as spectres of Jean de Meun's spirit, fixing in their images visual tokens of the author's presence in the text.

The contentious question of Jean de Meun's authorial intention provoked the '*Rose*' *querelle*'s new, embodied, author-centred approach to literary authority; it is the same bedevilling question that his presence in court is convoked to resolve in the *querelle des femmes*. The difficulty of proof, of pinning guilt upon so debatable an issue as authorial

---

[130] A similarly incensed band of ladies, seeking redress against Jean de Meun, is depicted by Pierre de Brantôme (1991: ii. 371–2), and the same (probably fictitious) anecdote is recounted contemporaneously by Du Verdier 1585: 679.

[131] Compare in this light the virulent biographical criticism voiced by Livre in Le Franc's *Complainte*, as he holds the person of l'Acteur, the book's author, entirely to blame for its failed reception at Philip the Good's court: *C*, vv. 195–6.

intention, is dramatized by these poems' appropriation of forensic procedure. As a convicted prisoner in Milet's *Forest*, Jean de Meun has, it is reported, already confessed his crime;[132] however, in none of the *querelle* trials—with one exception—is the act of confessing staged. The exception occurs in an anonymous pro-feminine prose fiction *Le Purgatoire des mauvais maris* (before 1467). As the title suggests, the juridical dimension of the *Purgatoire* is anagogical: a narrator-*acteur*, guided by Dame Raison around nine torture chambers housing faithless husbands, discovers who, at the Last Judgement, has been found worthy of punishment in purgatory to expiate their sins committed against womankind. In the final chamber he witnesses the torture inflicted upon Matheolus for the *gouliardises* ('ridiculous views')[133] expounded by his *Lamentations*. As if in perfect realization of the prediction made by Gerson's Eloquance Theologienne that a resurrected author would swiftly confess his offences,[134] Matheolus repents his crimes:

J'ay conspiré par mes escriptures contre l'onneur des dames, laquele chose m'est venue de ma propre nature, car oncques n'eus amour a elles. [. . .] Je confesse ma coulpe, et me repentisse volentiers se ce ne fust trop tart.[135]

(By my writings I have conspired against ladies' honour, and this came entirely naturally to me, since I never bore them any love. [. . .] I confess my fault and would willingly repent, if it weren't too late.)

The *Purgatoire*'s sentenced criminal freely admits the misogynistic intention behind his literary activity, whereas, in all other *querelle* trials where literary resurrection of the author focuses attention on his biographical motivations,[136] such intention remains allegation only, and even then it is hotly contested. In Milet's *Forest*, Noble Vouloir's accusation of Jean de Meun's 'treacherous intention' (fol. 220ʳ) is challenged by one of the court's presidents, Dame Raison. Ostensibly speaking impartially,

---

[132] Noble Vouloir's deictic exhortation to the court: 'See here their confession!' (*FT*, fol. 220ʳ), suggests that he waves this damning transcript triumphantly before the magistrates. See Shennan 1998: 67.

[133] *Purgatoire* 1998: 519. English translations are my own. For the *Purgatoire*'s print history, see ibid. 492–5. In addition to the extant copies Colombo-Timelli cites, the work also appears in London, BL, C.107.a.9, fols. 82ʳ–86ʳ. See also Badel 1996.

[134] See above, p. 137.

[135] *Purgatoire* 1998: 519. Colombo-Timelli publishes the earliest known edition of the work, and also edits a later version which adds the epithet *doloreuses* ('shameful') before *escriptures*, seemingly to add vehemence to Matheolus' penitence: *Purgatoire* 2002: 206.

[136] Noble Vouloir proposes that Jean de Meun's lifestyle explains his misogynistic attitude; his prejudice stems from his deliberate ignorance of woman's virtue: *FT*, fol. 221ʳ.

Raison does not deny the misogyny of the defendants' writings, but
does contest the legitimacy of pinning responsibility for this defamation
on the writers themselves. She proposes that any legitimate reading of
the *Rose* should exculpate the author, 'who never spoke ill of women'
(fol. 222ᵛ), and incriminate only the diegetic character in question, here
the Mari Jaloux:

> Se nous voulons de droit user
> On devroit le Jaloux deffaire
> [. . .]
> Et fault Jehan de Meun excuser
> [. . .]
> Je m'en raporte à son escript.
>
> (*FT*, fol. 223ᵛ)[137]

(If we want to proceed justly, we should condemn the Jealous Husband [. . .]
and acquit Jean de Meun [. . .] I refer to his own writings.)

Raison thus buys into the 'maniere de [. . .] parler par personnaiges'
that Eloquance Theologienne and all subsequent pro-feminine advocates
reject. Raison is made to argue quite convincingly that one cannot pass
sentence without being able to identify the underlying intention:

> Le langaige voyons nous trop bien
> Mais de son vueil ne sçavons rien.
>
> (*FT*, fol. 224ʳ)

(We can see his words well enough, but we know nothing of his intention.)

The authorial voice remains, for Raison, an opaque instance quite
distinct from any intratextual utterance; in forensic terms, she separates
clearly the 'letter' (*scriptum*) from the 'spirit' (*voluntas*) of the writer's
deed.[138] However, she begins to trip herself up: by grounding her
defence of Jean de Meun in the surface of his text ('son escript',
that is, *scriptum*), she has herself presumed to know his intention, to
identify by face-value interpretation of his self-exculpation the 'vueil'
(*voluntas*) that motivated his writing; she helps herself to both the
letter and the spirit.[139] Raison reattributes to Jean de Meun the motive

---

[137] The 'escript' to which she refers is presumably the passage in which Jean de Meun,
speaking for the first and last time *in propria persona*, offers his apology for misogynistic
slander by stating that he merely quotes what others have said: *RR*, vv. 15237–8.

[138] Quintilian 2001: III, 7.6. Cf. Carruthers 1990: 190.

[139] Raison's line of argument is notably similar to the strategy of defending Jean de
Meun adopted by Pierre Col: see Hicks 1977: 86, 110–11.

or 'courage' (fol. 224^r) offered in the *Rose* by Guillaume de Lorris's narrator-persona, namely that he undertook the work 'in honour of his *amye*' (fol. 223^v);[140] such an intention, Raison reasons, could not possibly be reconciled with misogynous motivation, hence Jean de Meun is innocent.

DEFERRING VERDICTS: DEBATING GUILT AND CREATING DEBATE

All this uncertainty and indeterminacy surrounding misogynist writers' authorial intention is not only manifested in an apparent resistance to staging their confessions, but also, on a more global structural level, results in the peculiarly inconclusive outcomes of *querelle* trials. In Milet's *Forest*, the 'sentence diffinitive' (fol. 224^r) or final verdict of the death penalty against Matheolus and Jean de Meun, which is supposed to brook no appeal, is unexpectedly attenuated by a merciful, last-minute intervention by the King of Love.[141] He lessens Matheolus' sentence to incarceration in 'a strong and secure prison' (ibid.) in the eponymous Forest, and lightens Jean de Meun's punishment to banishment. This mitigated penalty is all the more striking in light of the arsenal of arguments legitimizing the prisoners' immediate execution that are marshalled during the hearing by Noble Vouloir. For example, he introduces the convicts' offence as a crime of *lèse-majesté* since their attack on woman's honour also constitutes, he states, an assault on the King of Love: he affirms

> . . . que ce sont traitres hommes
> Et qu'ilz ont fait des maulx grans sommes
> Au roy d'amours et la deesse.
>
> (*FT*, fol. 219^r)[142]

(. . . that they are treasonous men, and that they have committed a vast number of crimes against the King of Love and the goddess [Venus].)

---

[140] See *RR*, vv. 41, 44.

[141] The King's intervention is intriguing in the context of Milet's allegorical 'court royalle' being predicated upon the procedure of the Parlement of Paris, where the king of France (at this historical moment, Charles VII) was the supreme judge (Shennan: 1998: 4); Milet's King of Love seems to hold similar sway.

[142] The crime of slander was deemed worthy of the death penalty in Roman law, from Cicero's *De re publica* 1948: 4.10.12. See Solterer 1995: 250 n. 11.

Woman's advocate thus magnifies the offence of misogyny to a degree of severity that merits the ultimate punishment:

> Les droitz et loix imperiaulx
> Nous monstrent qu'à mort on les livre.
>
> (*FT*, fol. 222^r)[143]

(According to the Roman rule of law they should be sentenced to death.)

Convicted misogynists deserve no less than the death penalty.

Why does Milet build up such an overpowering case in favour of the misogynists' execution, only to have Dame Justice's *arrest* retract from this conclusion? If it is not to provide a means, in Derridean terms, of 'having the ghost's hide', of achieving closure by 'winning out over the spectre, putting an end to it' and 'putting the ghosts to death',[144] then how do we explain this elaborate enlistment of judicial apparatus? I argue that Milet contrives such a clanging bathetic irony to foreground as much as possible the fact that Jean de Meun especially is getting off remarkably lightly despite, we are told, having been proven a 'villainous writer' (fol. 220^r); whereas Matheolus' *Lamentations* are condemned to be burnt, the *Rose* escapes scot-free of any censorship.[145] Milet thereby invites reflection on two fundamental conditions of the *querelle*'s existence. First, he is acknowledging that the misogynist controversy sparked by the *Rose* can never be laid to rest because we can never know unequivocally how the author behind the text wanted it to be read. Milet emphasizes how Jean de Meun's authorial intention is infinitely debatable; as I discussed above, it is never possible to pin down the spirit behind the spectre. The second condition of *querelle* poetics that Milet underlines stems from the first: each pro-feminine case can never produce complete, irrefutable proof as to the *Rose*-continuator's guilt, so no definitive sentence can be passed; consequently, response from an opposing standpoint remains a possibility and risks reversing the trial's verdict. This possibility is, in fact, both necessary and desirable: it is a

---

[143] Their crime is also equated with murder since their 'most dishonourable books' so disturb contemporary women that they 'will die if they are not granted justice' (FT, fol. 220^r).

[144] *SM* 210; *SoM* 132.

[145] The pre-modern Parlement possessed extensive police powers, including the right to censor publications: Shennan 1998: 4. Censorship of the *Rose*—usually by burning—is recommended in several *querelle* courts, and derives from Eloquance Theologienne's denunciation of the book in Gerson's *Traité*. Noble Vouloir recommends that all misogynistic literature be burned: *FT*, fol. 221^r.

sort of precondition that keeps stimulating *querelle* defences' response to misogynistic attack. An analogy with a trend in codicology is useful here to explain this precondition. Contemporary poetic anthologies, in both manuscript and print, juxtapose pro- and anti-feminine texts, indicating that a popular medieval habit of reading was dialectical, reading for *and* against, bouncing one off another,[146] like the *blason* and *contreblason* I examined above. It is something like this reading habit that Milet points up in his poem's contrived irresolution. It is Jean de Meun's, rather than Matheolus', text to which the *Forest* is the more heavily indebted through its cast of personifications, its allegorical setting, and the arguments raised by Noble Vouloir and Raison. Therefore, if Milet's work's challenge to the *Rose* continuator is to be appreciated as fully as possible, then familiarity with the *Rose* must be sustained amongst his audience. Within the fiction of the *Forest*, Milet plays up this extratextual condition of reception: he ensures that, in the poem's diegesis, the *Rose* is not burnt and that Jean de Meun's resurrected ghost is as it were allowed to live on; his exile is, it is implied, a potentially recoverable state.[147] Viewed in spectral terms, his sentence may be expressed in terms of a paradoxical ghost hunt ('la *chasse paradoxale*'): 'On chasse quelqu'un [. . .] mais c'est pour le chasser, le séduire, l'atteindre et donc pour le garder à sa portée.'[148] Kept 'close at hand', Jean de Meun's spectre is always ready to fuel new poetic activity, whether this activity chooses to affirm or disavow the inheritance of the *Rose*.

Martin Le Franc also recognizes the possibility of a judgement's reversal, and exploits his poem's dream framework as a means of evading any firm conclusion. In manuscripts *G* (fol. 434^v: Plate 2.15), *P2* (fol. 148^v), and *Z* (fol. 149^v), the poem's concluding illustration shows the composite diegetic situation at the end of the *Champion*'s climactic forensic encounter between Franc Vouloir and Faux Semblant. In both image and text, the crown of victory remains suspended above Franc Vouloir's head in the hands of Dame Vérité, the dispute's arbiter:

---

146 See Chapter 1, n. 60. Cf. Mann 1990: 41 n. 59.

147 Jean de Meun's punishment might be seen to be calqued upon that of Ovid, famously exiled for his crime of slander in composing the *Ars amatoria*. Christine refers to Ovid's case in the '*Rose*' *querelle* in order to suggest that his punishment was inadequate since, although Ovid himself was banished, the influence of his work was sustained: 'the root of a bad plant always survives': Hicks 1977: 138; Baird and Kane 1978: 135. Milet's choice of sentence for Jean de Meun thus seems singularly apt.

148 *SM* 223. 'One chases someone away [. . .] But it is in order to chase after him, seduce him, reach him, and thus keep him close at hand': *SoM* 140.

Encores mis ne l'avoit pas
Sus le chief du preu combatant.

(*CD*, vv. 24313–14)

([Truth] had not yet placed it on the head of the valiant fighter.)

Meanwhile, Faux Semblant suddenly drops dead and the ensuing farcical chaos of the adversaries being swallowed up by the earth ('transgloutis dans la terre' (v. 24328)) distracts and awakens the narrator prematurely, before the Champion's victory is made certain and definitive by his crowning. This device for interrupting juridical proceedings could be seen to derive from Gerson's *Traité*, from whose court the narrator awakes 'sans riens oïr de la sentence'.[149] Gerson's motive for deferring judgement is similar to both Le Franc's and Milet's: he recognizes any verdict's susceptibility to reversal, and acknowledges the inevitability that Jean de Meun's *Rose* and the debate it provokes will rumble on regardless of any individual *arrest*.[150] The figure of Jean de Meun or the elements of his text that his inheritors challenge in their juridical fictions are merely their own projections of the *Rose* author; Le Franc's Malebouche and Faux Semblant are as it were simulacra (*spectres*) of the troubling spirit (*esprit*) of Jean de Meun 'en sa persone', who will always elude capture, but who always wants chasing.[151]

The persistent elusiveness of Jean de Meun, the possibility of a judgement's reversal, and the necessary precondition to *querelle* creativity of continued misogynist attack are thus focalized by the poems' inconclusive verdicts. The reversibility of judgement is, in fact, already present in the *querelle des femmes* from a point that would generally be considered to precede its 'official' beginning in the *œuvre* of Christine de Pizan. It is present in Jean Le Fèvre's ostensibly recuperative, pro-feminine rebuttal of his own vernacular translation of Matheolus' *Lamentations*. At the opening of his *Livre de leesce* (c.1373), he addresses his inscribed female audience, from whom he begs pardon for having promoted the misogynistic *Lamentations*:

---

[149] Hicks 1977: 87. 'Hearing nothing of the judgement': Baird and Kane 1978: 90–1. More generally, of course, sudden awakening was a device employed to conclude numerous medieval narrative poems (*dits*) structured around a dream-vision.

[150] We may note in this light the following codicological irony: the only extant manuscript in which Gerson's *Traité* appears with the rest of the *'Rose' querelle*'s correspondence (BnF fr. 1563, fols. 178^r–99^r) is dominated by the works of Jean de Meun, starting with the *Rose* (fols. 1^r–144^v), the very work that Eloquance Theologienne called to be 'osté et exterminé'.

[151] See above, p. 146–7.

> Car je suy tout prest que je face
> Un livre pour moy excuser;
> [...]
> Il n'est riens qui n'ait son contraire,
> Qui en voulroit les preuves traire
> Et penser justement aux choses:
> Les espines sont près des roses;
> [...]
> ...ay fait cest livre, pour complaire
> Par argument de sens contraire,
> Pour vous excuser loyaument.[152]

(I am quite ready to write a book to excuse myself; [...] There is nothing that does not have its opposite; whoever wishes to have firm evidence and think rightly about the matter: thorns grow alongside roses; [...] I have written this book to please you by arguing the opposite, in order faithfully to defend you.)

Taken at face value, Le Fèvre's persona here expresses his ethical motivation for writing a corrective response to the *Lamentations'* misogyny. On the other hand, the passage reads equally as a textually self-conscious statement about the nature of *pro* and *contra* disputation about women.[153] Repetition of the term 'contraire' draws attention to the fact that the *Leesce* is itself responding to a prior work, towards which Le Fèvre directs his audience's attention as a means of publicizing *both* poems, notwithstanding—or perhaps because of—their antithetical ethical perspective on women; he does not seek for the former to cancel out the latter, but to be its complementary *pendant*.[154] It is less the content of the response than the very art of response by reversal that is foregrounded here; he highlights how this possibility of overturning judgement ensures the future possibility of new poetic production.[155] Le Fèvre uses the dialectic of *pro* and *contra*, the same sort of imbrication

---

[152] Le Fèvre 1905: vv. 18–19, 21–4, 33–5. English translations are my own.

[153] Le Fèvre's reflexive focus on the mechanics of argumentation can be seen to have a juridical colouring: he instructs his female audience how to defeat slanderers in forensic terms: 'Make a good *protestacion* to demonstrate your intention, and then hold back in order to *dupliquer*, in case anyone chooses to *repliquer*': 1905: vv. 3958–61 (my italics).

[154] The repetition of 'contraire' and Le Fèvre's choice of floral metaphor (v. 24) seem to conjure up the *Rose*, the misogynistic authority that he interpolated into his own translation of Matheolus: Pratt 1999. It is thus sharply ironic that the *Rose* should be incorporated into an ostensibly pro-feminine response, and this irony flags up how Le Fèvre is appropriating here, for his own, self-publicizing purposes, Jean de Meun's famous logic of contrariety regarding the complementary nature of 'contraires choses': *RR*, vv. 21577–80. Cf. Solterer 1995: 132.

[155] Cf. Mann 1990: 25.

of antithetical poles of debate that I discussed in Chapter 1 in terms of the *querelle*'s 'double bound' discourse, to develop a principle of textual response that defers closure.

That Le Fèvre is consciously playing with the infinitely deferrable nature of any verdict in *pro* and *contra* debate on the subject of women can clearly be seen from his comments at the close of the *Leesce*:

> Atant fineray mon propos
> Jusqu'a tant que plus sage viengne
> Qui ceste matiere soustiengne.
> Si croy je que jamais finée
> Ne sera ne determinée;
> [. . .]
> Plus en diray a l'autre fois,
> A Dieu vous commant, je m'en vois.[156]

(And there I'll end my speech until a wiser man comes along to support this matter. Thus I believe that it will never be finished or decided; [. . .] I'll say more about it another time; I commend you to God, and now I'm off.)

This ludic epilogue, with its playfully bathetic conclusion ('I'm off'), highlights not only how the debate's verdict will never be fixed one way or the other ('determinée'),[157] but also how any outcome is only ever provisional or is deferred ('jamais finée') because another, pro-feminine poet can always take up the reins of defence again against the existing body of misogynistic discourse. It is interesting, in light of the *Leesce*'s own creative circumstances, to note that Le Fèvre apparently solicits only *pro*-feminine continuations of his argument; his poem surely also invites rebuttal and is susceptible to the same reversal of judgement that Le Fèvre himself performed upon the *Lamentations*.

A sort of collaborative community of writers, each seeking to provoke continuation so as to promote a fruitful literary tradition, seems to be postulated by Le Fèvre's *Leesce*, together with an intertextually expert audience to appreciate this interplay. The two types of unfinalizability that he pinpoints—the infinite alternation of *pro* and *contra*, and the invitation for continuation—are extensively deployed in the other important precursor, alongside the *'Rose' querelle*, to the *querelle des femmes*, namely the *querelle de 'la Belle Dame sans*

---

[156] 1905: vv. 3983–7, 3990–1.

[157] Le Fèvre uses here the scholastic term for providing closure: in university practice, the master would impose a *determinatio* ('judgement') upon a disputation performed by his students: see Bazàn 1985.

mercy'. The cycle of courtroom fictions provoked by Alain Chartier's polemical *Belle Dame* try and retry the eponymous lady's alleged crime of condemning to death a suitor by refusing to grant him her favour.[158] Each trial text's diegetic jury seeks to establish a definitive conclusion:

> Que le jugement ainsi fait
> Ne se muera ne changera
> Mais demourra en son effet
> Tant que le monde durera.[159]

(That the verdict reached thereby will never alter nor change, but will remain in force until the world's end.)

They urge a movement towards closure that is simultaneously resisted by the extradiegetic artistic construction of each poem. Resistance is effected by various expedient fictions: the absence of counsel to represent the Belle Dame, alleged procedural misconduct, or the oneiric interruption to proceedings that we saw deployed in the *Champion des dames*. As Adrian Armstrong and Emma Cayley have recently demonstrated,[160] this resistance to closure is a deliberate strategy designed to provoke revisitation of the *Belle Dame* material by always leaving the ending open to rewriting. Successive rewriters form a sort of collaborative textual community to which the manuscript tradition of the cycle of *Belle Dame* trials bears witness.

This collaborative game of intertextual response does not correspond precisely to the poetics of anti-closure practised in the *querelle des femmes* corpus, but it does mark a significant precedent for manipulating courtroom fictions in a way that promotes hermeneutic interest in the conditions of a work's artistic construction. The implied metatextual level of engagement shared by the two *querelles* perhaps suggests that, like the interacting poets of the *Belle Dame* cycle, the target audience of *querelle des femmes* trials was, to some extent, readers who were potential poetic continuators of the literary debate for and against women, who would reconvene the fictional court to take up their case once more.

---

[158] It is worth noting that the *'Belle Dame' querelle* is to some extent generated by the same bone of contention that fosters the unfinalizability of the *'Rose' querelle* and the *querelle des femmes*, namely the indeterminable nature of authorial intention. The *Belle Dame* sequels interrogate the motivations of both Alain Chartier's characters, the Lady and the Lover, and the author himself.

[159] *Les Erreurs du jugement de l'amant banny* 1905: vv. 993–6. English translation is my own.

[160] Armstrong forthcoming; Cayley 2003; Armstrong 1997.

The intersection of the *Belle Dame* cycle's use of inconclusiveness with *querelle des femmes* trial poems is both manifest and nuanced,[161] and reveals how what Armstrong has usefully dubbed the 'deferred verdict topos' is appropriated in innovative ways by the juridical fictions of later works. Both *querelles*' trials use tightly woven systems of intertextual reference that help foster continuity: where successive *Belle Dame* sequels explicitly take up and challenge the verdict of a prior trial within the cycle, *querelle des femmes* contributions, as I showed in Chapter 1, use their hermeneutic action upon previous works, especially the *Rose*, as a means of pronouncing judgement upon them. The conclusions to Le Franc's *Champion*, Milet's *Forest*, and Michault's *Procès* do not so much overturn a previous verdict as point up their own provisionality or incompleteness: the possibility that the diegetic ending to their trials might not yet impose closure on the framework of the poem. This distinction is suggested within the *querelle* by Jean Le Fèvre, who seems to propose that any conclusion, whether 'for' or 'against', is simply a piece of poetic artifice, a sort of illusion, when he remarks in the *Lamentations*:

> Si me pourroit on opposer
> Et au contraire proposer,
> En blasmant ma conclusion,
> Que je di de grant illusion.[162]

(And anyone could oppose me, and put forward an argument to the contrary, by finding fault with my conclusion, which I propose to be/by way of a great illusion.)

Le Fèvre takes himself at his word when he 'opposes' his own, anti-feminine 'conclusion' with the *Leesce*'s pro-feminine case, thereby breaking the 'illusion' of the *Lamentations*' verdict by, it is implied, replacing it with another illusory outcome at the end of the *Leesce*.

It has been demonstrated above how *querelle des femmes* writers appropriate a combination of contemporary legal practice and already-aestheticized forensic procedure from the '*Rose*' and '*Belle Dame*' *querelles* to represent their relationship with misogynistic authorities in dynamic and striking fashion. First, forensic procedure furnishes a discursive

---

[161] We may note, for example, that the personified character Franc Vouloir, who, in Le Franc's *Champion*, defends the Belle Dame by awarding her an honourable Christian burial, after the example of her heirs in *Les Erreurs*, features as a magistrate in several poems throughout the cycle: see Chartier et al. 2003: 122, 138, 190.

[162] 1892: ii, vv. 2589–92.

framework in which pro-feminine speakers can both address and over-come the double bind upon their discourse by citing anti-feminine authorities with impunity. Secondly, the court may function as a stage for the literary resurrection of (alleged) past misogynists who can be made to stand trial for their crimes; the refutation of their discourse is thereby dramatized in a way that draws attention to the problematic, persistent, and ambiguous presence of the 'mighty dead'. Thirdly, the inconclusiveness of *querelle* debates appears a deliberate strategy,[163] highlighted by the juridical framework's deferral or disruption of a final verdict. The ending that is represented resists complete closure; Jean de Meun and his *Rose* are never definitively *mis à mort* in consequence of *querelle* writers' paradoxical ghost hunt: they consistently 'chase away' their misogynistic spectres, but precisely in order to 'chase after' them, to keep them close at hand. This paradox nests with others: the impossibili-ty of con*juring* without conjuring, and the attempted visualization of an unseeable spirit. These paradoxes encapsulate the essence of spectrality within the *querelle des femmes*.

Querelle trials appropriate the malleability, indeterminacy, and slip-periness of the trial structure. These qualities are identified as the properties of late medieval *jugements* by the author of the *Arrêts d'amours*, a compilation of fictional judgements ('arrêts') on love, pronounced in a 'Parlement d'Amours',[164] that is a direct contemporary of Michault's *Procès*.[165] In his epilogue to the fifty-one 'arrêts', the narrator effectively undermines the security of the verdicts that conclude the preceding cases by declaring that

> . . . ceulx qu'i cuidoient pour eulx
> Eurent contre eulx, je vous affie:
> Helas! Jugemens sont douteux,
> Nul n'est pas saige qui s'i fie.[166]

(And those who believed the verdict would go in their favour found it to have gone against them, I assure you. Alas! Judgements are a questionable business; no one is wise to trust in them.)

---

[163] Cf. Pratt 2002: 132 n. 40; Lazard 1985: 11.

[164] 1951: prologue, v. 4. Becker states that the procedure of this 'Parlement' is modelled on that of the Parlement of Paris: 1997: 310–11.

[165] Authorship is generally attributed to Martial d'Auvergne. Becker (1997: 311) accepts a date between 1460 and 1465 for the composition of the *Arrêts*, and critics, such as Folkart, generally settle on a date shortly after 1461 for the *Procès*.

[166] 1951: epilogue, vv. 17–20. English translation is my own. If deliberate, the double negative of the final line serves further to destabilize the fixity and validity of judge-ment.

What the *Arrêts'* narrator sees as the lamentable condition of verdicts' susceptibility to change is positively valorized by *querelle* writers; it is precisely the infinitely manipulable, provisional, and unfixable nature of the trial framework which renders it an ideal vehicle for mobilizing *querelle des femmes* arguments.

EPILOGUE: THE CASE FOR WOMEN IN CONTEXT

Writing on the *Belle Dame* cycle's retrials of Chartier's Lady, Gretchen Angelo concludes that the role of the late medieval fictionalized legal court is 'deeply implicated in the greater misogyny of the period'.[167] This chapter has advanced an argument to the contrary, proposing that a juridical framework was appropriated in the *querelle des femmes* as a literary vehicle to promote the case *for* women. Moreover, the forensic structures deployed by Le Franc, Milet, and Michault convey the complexity of the *querelle*'s entanglement with misogyny, staging dynamically the refutation of misogynistic authorities and yet alluding through inconclusive trial verdicts to the necessary perdurance of Jean de Meun and Co., in order to sustain *querelle* responses. Nuancing Badel's understanding of the *jugement* frame, that 'il appelle un verdict, soit la condamnation d'une des deux positions qui s'affrontent',[168] the trial debates of the *querelle* corpus may well appear to enact this 'appel', but they also interrogate its necessity as an artificial or false closure of the case for women.

Alongside the literary and rhetorical contexts which help us appreciate *querelle* writers' decisions to deploy forensic fictions, there also exist cultural factors that may have fostered this preference, namely the increasing prominence of jurists as book buyers in late medieval France, as well as the legal background, albeit varied, that several *querelle* contributors share. A more specific connection between the domains of literature about women and law may be postulated in this period by reference to Guillaume Coquillart's *Plaidoié d'entre la Simple et la Rusee* and its sequel, *L'Enqueste* (*c.*1478–9). In the courtroom procedure of these two poems, the Simple Girl and the Sneaky Girl dispute their possession of a lover, le Mignon, as if it constituted a property

---

[167] 2003: 144.
[168] 1988: 109. 'It calls for a verdict, that is, the condemnation of one of the two opposing positions.'

right.[169] The fiction of these poems, contrived around the law of *cas de saisine et de nouvelleté*, was devised in a particular cultural milieu: the theatre of the Basoche, the law clerks of the Parlement of Paris who satirized courtroom proceedings in comic plays that they wrote and performed before one another.[170] The *Plaidoié* and *L'Enqueste* were written at a time when Coquillart, who went on to become *avocat* of the Châtelet in 1481, was probably associated with the Basoche, having graduated in canon law in 1477; the poems were intended for the carnivals (*festes*) of 1478 and 1479.[171] In their comic plays, the Basochiens creatively conflated forensic oratory and acting in a style that emphasized performative exuberance and theatrical spectacle.[172] Such performative pleasure in legal argumentation resonates strongly with the imaginative manipulation of, and dramatic delight in, trial procedure that we have seen in this chapter to be germane to an evaluation of *querelle* debates' poetics. Moreover, it is striking that the heyday of the Basoche, between 1450 and 1550, coincides with the peak time for both the composition and publication of *querelle* trials; this correlation may be viewed alongside my earlier conjectures that a significant constituency of Michault's and Milet's intended audience was involved in the law. A conjunction of interfaces between literature and law, law and theatre, and dialogue and drama, operative at different levels of the legal hierarchy—both Basoche clerks and bourgeois jurists—appears to have played some role in stimulating the *querelle*'s recourse to judicial structures as a stage for debating about women.[173]

The Basoche not only wrote and performed plays, they also staged mock legal debates or *causes fictives* after hours in the Grand'Chambre.[174] We can perhaps view their practice of inventing legal cases, in which the players impersonated great orators of antiquity, as a useful analogy

---

[169] See Enders 1992: 233–45; H. Harvey 1969: 71–164. This trial is inconclusive: in a later work, *Les Droitz nouveaulx* (1480), a parody of a law book, Coquillart invites La Simple and La Rusée to come forward and have their case reopened: 1975: 127–244, vv. 58–61.

[170] Although the clerks served lawyers in the Parlement, they were not themselves members, but were associated with the Palais de Justice or 'Basoche': Shennan 1998: 48.

[171] Sylvie Lefèvre, in Hasenohr and Zink 1992: 613.

[172] Enders 1992: 129–61.

[173] Zimmermann points out how *querelle* criticism has not yet explored the relationship between 'high culture' and 'popular culture': 1999: 84. English translations are my own. Probing the texts' interface between literature and law might be one way of pursuing this relationship. Cf. Krueger 2002; Deschaux 1998.

[174] See Enders 1992: 133–4.

for the way *querelle* writers turned imaginatively to account the *agôn* of the defence of women debate. Writers create their own 'fictitious cases' for a variety of reasons related both to literary precedent—their deliberate engagement with the *'Rose'* and *'Belle Dame' querelles*—and to historical actuality. For example, in Le Franc's debate between Franc Vouloir and Malebouche's cronies, a fictional nullification trial of Joan of Arc and a defence of the Immaculate Conception are counterpoised by the histrionic comedy of the poem's protodramatic disputation and its farcical conclusion. We may add to this admixture of serious and comic, historical and imaginative, the fact that, in the sixteenth century, the subject of 'la defense du sexe' was adopted in juridical textbooks as a paradox, the defence of which, under such propositions as 'l'excellence des femmes est plus grande que celle de l'homme', was designed to train young barristers in the art of defending difficult cases.[175]

The elaborate artistry of *querelle* debates explored in this chapter— their creative use of interfaces between law and literature, dialogue and drama, political actuality and imaginative fiction—brings us to address in the following chapter the bedevilling dichotomy of 'sincerity' and 'rhetoric' that I first tackled in my Introduction. Is the *querelle* truly about defending woman's virtue, or is it merely a pretext for flamboyant literary invention and rhetorical display? And does the sex of the author have any bearing on this (questionable) distinction? What role, in sum, do women and women's gender identity have to play in the *querelle des femmes*? Chapter 3 will also bring together the performative frameworks of the present and previous chapters. The representation of women concerns at least two performative acts: the constitutive nature of verbal performance enacting an identity, and, in the case of the cast-list of noble women recycled in *querelle* catalogues, the hermeneutic performance of a given representation, such as Dido, conjuring up, whilst conjuring away, the spectres of her ancestors. Gender theory's development of both Austinian and Derridean ideas on performance, notably in the work of Judith Butler, will be used to probe further how performative approaches to the *querelle des femmes* may illuminate our understanding of its representations of women.

---

[175] See Charles Estienne's *Paradoxes, ce sont propos contre la commune opinion: debatuz en forme de declamations forenses: pour exerciter les jeunes advocates en causes difficiles* (Paris, 1553), *Declamation* 24, cited by Berriot-Salvadore 1990: 351.

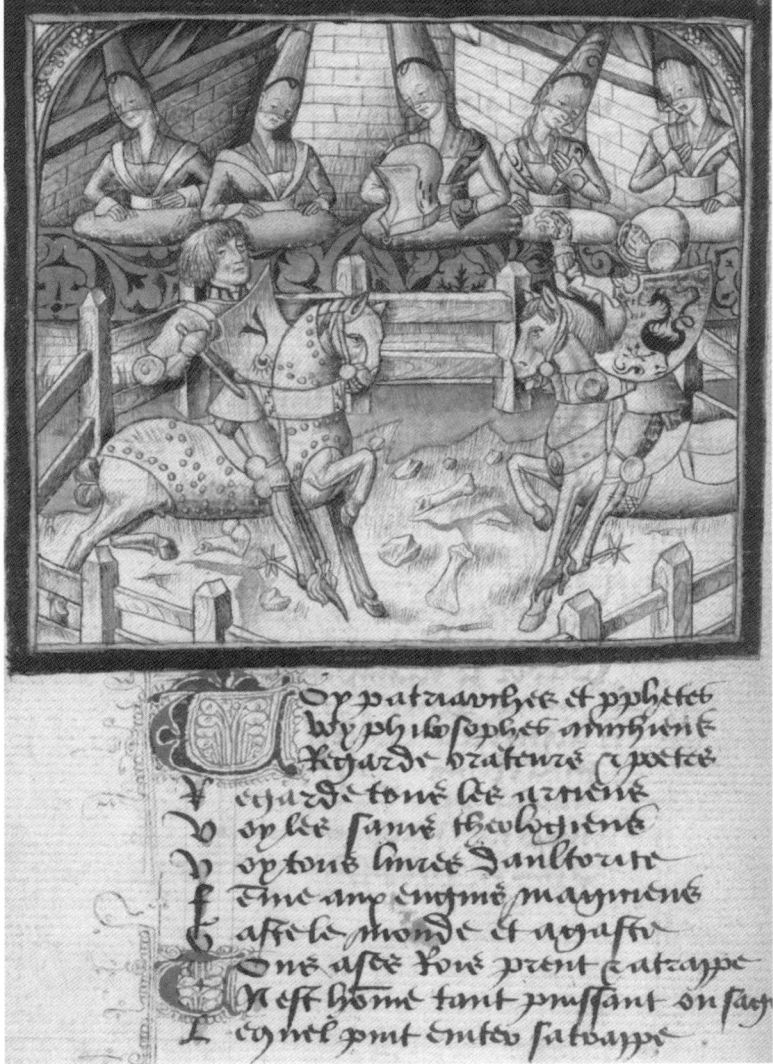

Plate 2.1. Vilain Penser enters the field: Martin Le Franc, *Le Champion des dames*; MS *G*, fol. 90ᵛ

Plate 2.2. The Champion invokes the God of Love: Martin Le Franc, *Le Champion des dames*; MS *G*, fol. 75ʳ

Plate 2.3. Debating the *puy d'amour*: Martin Le Franc, *Le Champion des dames*; MS *G*, fol. 80ᵛ

Plate 2.4. Rejecting Vilain Penser's argument against marriage: Martin Le Franc, *Le Champion des dames*; MS *G*, fol. 127ᵛ

Plate 2.5. (*Left*) The adversaries on the point of assaulting the Champion; (*Right*) Ulysses enchanted by Circe's song: Martin Le Franc, *Le Champion des dames*; MS *G*, fol. 78ᵛ

Plate 2.6. The Champion backs off from Vilain Penser: Martin Le Franc, *Le Champion des dames*; MS *G*, fol. 102^v

Plate 2.7. Trop Cuidier retreats from the Champion: Martin Le Franc, *Le Champion des dames*; MS *G*, fol. 264^r

Plate 2.8. Vilain Penser recoils from the Champion: Martin Le Franc, *Le Champion des dames*; MS *G*, fol. 114[r]

Plate 2.9. Vilain Penser enthroned: Martin Le Franc, *Le Champion des dames*; MS *G*, fol. 137^r.

Plate 2.10. The Champion enthroned: Martin Le Franc, *Le Champion des dames*; MS *G*, fol. 245ʳ

Plate 2.11. The adversary launches his verbal attack: Martin Le Franc, *Le Champion des dames*; MS *G*, fol. 369^v

Plate 2.12. The Champion responds with his verbal defence: Martin Le Franc, *Le Champion des dames*; MS *G*, fol. 370ʳ

Plate 2.13. The Champion and his adversary before a judge: Martin Le Franc, *Le Champion des dames*; *P2*, fol. 21ʳ

Plate 2.14. The Champion and his adversary before a judge: Martin Le Franc, *Le Champion des dames*; Paris, BnF, RES YE-27 fols. L4ᵛ, L8ᵛ

Plate 2.15. The Champion being crowned by Vérité: Martin Le Franc, *Le Champion des dames*; MS *G*, fol. 434ᵛ

3

Representing Women in the *Querelle des femmes*

Grand est le nom de moy Semyramis
Qui fuz regnant ès paÿs d'Assyrie:
J'eu l'esprit grand, couraige non remys,
[. . .]
Hardie fuz, saige en chevallerie,
Et deguisay mon estat femenin:
Car je portoys vestement masculin,
Pour mieux conduyre en armes mon affaire.

(*JP*, vv. 1680–2, 1685–8)

(Great is the name of me, Semiramis, who ruled over the kingdom of Assyria; I had a strong spirit, unflinching courage, [. . .] I was bold, and wise in military affairs; I disguised my feminine condition, as I wore masculine attire in order to advance my case better at arms.)

The first-person feminine subject of Semiramis' epitaph, housed in the palace of illustrious women in Jean Bouchet's *Jugement poetic de l'honneur femenin*, tackles directly the question of her gender identity through the discourse of transvestism.[1] She mobilizes the usual Middle French adjectives ('femenin', 'masculin') used to describe what pertains to each sex according to cultural convention—what we would call

---

[1] Like most other epitaphs in the *Jugement*, Semiramis' biography is based on Jacopo Filippo Foresti's *De plurimis claris selectisque mulieribus*. Foresti's catalogue, compiled in the 1490s, is heavily indebted to Boccaccio's *De mulieribus*. Bouchet's immediate source for Foresti is an anthology edited by Ravisius Textor (Jean Tixier), *De memorabilibus et claris mulieribus aliquot diversorum scriptorum opera* (Paris: Simon de Colines, 1521): Bouchet 2006: 53–5. All references to Foresti in this chapter will be to *De memorabilibus*.

gender issues—and employs them in a simply 'denotative', semantically neutral sense; there is no 'connotative'[2] value-judgement contained in her description of how she donned men's clothing in order to conceal her woman's body. We shall see in this chapter, however, that Semiramis' straightforward statements here belie the remarkable complexity which characterizes the representation of her actions, and those of other active women, by male authors writing in defence of her sex in the fifteenth and early sixteenth centuries. This heterogeneity arises from these writers' varied use of vocabulary—adjectives or collocative expressions that I shall explain more fully below—that valorizes her achievements in gendered terms: as those of a woman overcoming her nature to accede to a virile heroic ideal; as those of a woman surpassing the expectations of either sex; or as those of a woman for whom physical courage ('hardiesce') and 'chevallerie' are incorporated into a definition of femininity on woman's terms; for example, Semiramis features elsewhere in Bouchet's *œuvre* in the 'tabernacle of illustrious women' of his *Temple de bonne renommée* (1516), where her image is situated above Penthesilea and thereby thematically affiliated to this 'warrior woman'.[3]

The transvestism present in Semiramis' epitaph is not only vestimentary, but also linguistic, in the way her first-person speech is the product of a male author's imaginative ventriloquism. This second type of cross-dressing raises questions regarding both the writer's construction and the reader's perception of Semiramis' gender identity. Does an acknowledgement of the artifice of impersonation underlying Semiramis' epitaph affect the reader's interpretation of 'her' speaking voice, and does the author suggest that it should through the interactions of different levels of narrative voice in his *Jugement*? A consciousness of gender issues centred on the figure of transvestism can thus be seen to permeate Semiramis' epitaph at different levels: the verses' composition, their textual performance by a fictional, diegetic speaker, and their reception by contemporary and modern audiences. It is thus in terms of transvestism, understood here as the cross-dressing of her tongue as well as of her clothes,[4] that praise of her achievement and the representation of her gender identity may most fruitfully be analysed.

---

[2] I borrow this application of the standard semiotic distinction between orders of signification from Brown-Grant 2002: 155–69.

[3] 1992: v. 3989.

[4] Marjorie Garber (1992) supplies a useful taxonomy of terms for describing different degrees of 'transvestment'. Her 'cross-dressing' refers to instances of partial masquerade,

This chapter demonstrates how an awareness of feminine gender identity is central to the representation of women in the corpus of *querelle des femmes* texts investigated in this book. Such centrality can be detected on different textual levels and can be seen to entail a variety of relationships between the male author and his female subject, as this 'subject' denotes various feminine identities: the sex whose cause he is supporting, the individual exemplary women he portrays as case studies in his text, and the intended female audience of his work, whether this audience is construed through a general address to 'ladies everywhere', or whether the writer has a specific dedicatee in mind. We shall encounter first the necessary gender awareness shown by these writers' communication of their work to a female patron or hoped-for sponsor, especially as this extratextual contract is often represented through the incorporation of the dedicatee into the text's fictional framework. Secondly, I address two central hermeneutic issues of transvestism: how the male author defends woman's cause by impersonating her voice, and how he constructs her identity—her status as a woman worthy of honour—in gendered terms of 'wearing' masculine or feminine external or internal characteristics, from cross-dressing clothes to putting on a man's or woman's heart. This second transvestism of body and/or spirit will be the main focus of the rest of the chapter. In sum, we shall see how late medieval male authors writing in defence of woman consciously engage with what modern criticism would call the politics of gender identity through the rhetorical strategies and gendered terminology that they employ in her praise. In this way, we begin to see how women 'become' women of exemplary status, to use Simone de Beauvoir's term,[5] through their textual representation by male defenders of their sex.

while she uses 'passing' or 'cross-over' to denote the complete, even if episodic, assumption of the appearance of the opposite sex. While these distinctions may be helpful for discussing vestimentary transvestism, they prove problematic as regards ventriloquistic transvestism in literature, where a double level of awareness is always demanded of the reader: an acceptance of Semiramis' speech as a rhetorical performance by a woman, and a simultaneous recognition of this as an illusion. I explore this dual awareness in greater detail below.

[5] Her seminal work of feminist theory, *Le Deuxième Sexe*, is underpinned by the tenet that 'one is not born woman, one becomes it' (1949: ii. 13, English translation is my own), with this 'becoming' shaped by a whole range of cultural influences, just as the representations of women that I discuss here are shaped by the historical, literary, and linguistic influences informing each *querelle* writer.

WRITER AND PATRON: PRESENTATION
AND REPRESENTATION

Historical women occupy a key position in the production, reception, and circulation of many *querelle* works. In France, especially towards the end of the fifteenth and beginning of the sixteenth centuries, an environment in which works for and about women could flourish was fostered by a number of powerful and learned aristocratic women.[6] In his first literary foray into the Burgundian court, with the debate poem the *Champion des dames* (*c*.1442),[7] Martin Le Franc commemorates the death of Mary of Burgundy, Philip the Good's aunt, and also lauds the Duke's current wife, Isabel of Portugal, for her peace-weaving expertise in sealing the treaty of Arras between Burgundy and France in 1435.[8] When the *Champion* is initially rejected by Philip,[9] it is to Isabel, 'princess of virtue and honour' (*C*, v. 435), that the poet turns to negotiate an analogous, personal peace by interceding with the Duke on Le Franc's behalf. Her intercession in favour of his spurned book would, he states, ensure that its merits are justly rewarded with circulation:

> Car elle veult que renommée
> Soit donnee à ceulx qui le valent.
>
> (*C*, vv. 439–40)[10]

(Since she wishes that renown should be accorded to those who merit it.)

This female literary lineage continues, as Philippe Bouton's mini-treatise the *Mirouer des dames* is (probably) dedicated to a second Mary

---

[6] See Brown 2007b; Stephenson 2004; Driver and Brown 2001; Debae 1995; Berriot-Salvadore 1990.

[7] Mary forms a link between the courts of Le Franc's patrons, as the aunt of his prospective Burgundian patron and the late wife of his current, Savoyard sponsor Amadeus VIII: *CD*, vv. 1953–68. In a later manuscript of the *Champion*, possibly compiled for a member of the de Croy family after Philip's death in 1467, the poem is bound together with the *Lamentations d'Olivier de la Marche sur la mort de Marie de Bourgogne*, namely the Duke's granddaughter (d. 1482). A list of all extant manuscripts and early prints of the *Champion* can be found in Appendix 2A.

[8] *CD*, vv. 1848–64. See Charron 2000: 27–8.   [9] See Introduction, p. 1.

[10] Besides being dedicated in its prologue to the Duke, the *Champion* also addresses itself to a female audience at the poem's conclusion, where the narrator implores 'dames et damoiselles' (*CD*, v. 24361) to pray for him to the Virgin Mary. Isabel maintained a sizeable and diverse female entourage: Bousmar and Sommé 2000.

of Burgundy, granddaughter of Philip the Good and wife of Maximilian I, 'living and reigning illustriously' later in the fifteenth century.[11] Furthermore, both the rejected *Champion* codex and Bouton's *Mirouer* find their way further down the line of transmission into one of the most prestigious personal libraries of the early sixteenth century, that of Margaret of Austria, daughter of Maximilian and Mary.[12]

The increasing prominence and influence of female literary patrons in the early sixteenth century stimulates the composition and translation of texts on the subject of women's noble and virtuous ancestry. At the royal court of Louis XII, Anne of Brittany is said to have instituted 'la grand Court des Dames', what Brantôme calls a 'very fine school for Ladies'.[13] If it existed, its pedagogical programme, aiming at the moral and cultural education of ladies at court, may have informed some of Anne's literary commissions, notably her confessor Antoine Dufour's *Vies des femmes célèbres* (1504),[14] a catalogue of exemplary women modelled, at least in part, on Boccaccio's *De mulieribus claris*, a work which already featured in Anne's collection in the form of the vernacular translation made for her in 1493.[15] Anne also received favourably Jean Marot's *Vraye disant advocate des dames* (*c.*1506), a pro-feminine monologue, spoken by the eponymous woman barrister.[16]

Meanwhile, at the Moulins court of Anne of France, daughter of Louis XI and widow of Pierre II of Bourbon, Constable of France, the humanist physician Symphorien Champier failed in his attempts to find favour with his *Nef des dames vertueuses* (1503),[17] a complex

---

[11] *Le Mirouer des dames* 1882: 23. See also *Le Miroir aux dames* 1908: 8–9.

[12] It is estimated that her collection comprised some 400 books: see Debae 1995.

[13] 1991: i. 13. English translation is my own. The reliability of Brantôme's chronicles is often challenged: ibid., i, p. xlvii. Cf. Minois 1999: 429. Anne's establishment of a female court culture may be seen to implement recommendations for women's education offered by Christine de Pizan's *Tresor de la cité des dames*, a special copy of which was presented to the Queen in 1497 by the publisher Antoine Vérard: is it, perhaps, Anne's known possession of this work that inspires Brantôme to attribute to her a *Court des dames*?

[14] The presentation (and only extant) copy of the *Vies*, containing eighty-five miniatures, is now Nantes, Musée Dobrée, MS 17. Dufour, a Dominican, was the official preacher and royal confessor at Louis XII's court.

[15] [Anon.], *Le Livre de Jehan Bocasse de la louenge et vertu des nobles et cleres dames* (Paris: Antoine Vérard, 1493). See Brown 2007a.

[16] I discuss the publication history of *VDA* ('The true-speaking advocate of ladies') in my Conclusion, p. 23. For more detailed discussion of Anne's patronage of pro-feminine literature, see Brown 2007b.

[17] The dedication copy is now Paris, BnF, RES Vélins 1972.

four-part treatise intended, at least in part, as a *speculum dominarum*, a work of edification and instruction for the young princess Suzanne.[18] It may be that Anne already had in mind the more particular, practical manual that she herself would write for her daughter, her *Enseignements*, composed between 1503 and 1505, and that her own plan forestalled Champier's mistimed enterprise, thus resulting in his *Nef*'s rejection.[19] Although refused by its dedicatee, Champier's work was not a failure. Brown finds evidence that his decision to produce the *Nef* in print, rather than as a de luxe presentation manuscript, ultimately worked to his advantage by opening it up to a new audience. A letter from his friend Gonsalvo Toledo in 1508 attests to the work's success beyond aristocratic circles, amongst urban female readers. Alongside this reported success in Lyons, the *Nef* was later published in Paris in 1515, and again in 1531.[20]

Towards the middle of the century, another impetus to literary production on feminine topics was provided by several women associated with Louis XII's successor, François I. Jean Dupré dedicated his *Palais des nobles dames* ([1534])[21] to the King's sister, Marguerite de Navarre, herself active in composing as well as sponsoring literary works.[22] The *Palais* depicts a dreamer-narrator's journey around thirteen rooms of a palace which houses a vast number of women grouped according to their different virtues or skills. Dupré recognizes Marguerite's poetic skill within his *Palais* by honouring her expertise in the making of 'rondeaulx' and 'epistres' (*PND*, fol. D3^r) above the accomplishments of her historical, scriptural, and mythological predecessors in the liberal arts. Dupré's first-person narrator (l'Acteur) inscribes the author's extradiegetic patron within the diegesis of his palace's assembly of ladies by awarding her the prize in a poetic competition or *puy* that he sees enacted in the chamber

---

[18] The *Nef* ('Ship') comprises: a catalogue of women (*la fleur des dames*), a treatise on marriage (*le regime de mariage*), a book of *propheties des sibilles*, and a philosophical treatise (*le livre de vraye amour*). The first, third, and fourth books are dedicated to Anne, whilst the second is explicitly directed at Suzanne.

[19] See Matarasso 2001: 191–4; Jordan 1990: 95–104.

[20] Brown 2001: 153–60.   [21] See also Dunn 1976.

[22] Between 1509 and 1553 she receives more than seventy-five dedications. As a writer herself, her most famous work is the *Heptaméron*, a collection of *contes*, published posthumously, which developed the model for such *recueils* established by Boccaccio's *Decameron*.

housing women inventors.[23] L'Acteur addresses Marguerite in unctu-
ous style:

> Donc prens couraige à vouloir entreprendre
> De vous escripre au present catalogue
> Comme la dame qui a le bruÿt et vogue.

> (*PND*, fol. E2^v)

(And so I make bold to wish to undertake to inscribe you in the present
catalogue as the lady who has the greatest reputation and renown.)[24]

Dupré also pays tribute to the achievements of Marguerite's sister-
in-law, Queen Eleanor, and of Marguerite's mother Louise of Savoy,
particularly regarding the latter's role in assuring the political agreement
known as the 'paix des dames', the peace treaty negotiated at Cambrai
in 1529 between Spain and France that was seen to have been brokered
by the Emperor Charles V's aunt, Margaret of Austria, and Louise.

The strategy of deliberate slippage between extradiegetic patron and
diegetic representation, the actuality and fictionality of a historical
woman's identity, is also practised by Jean Bouchet, again touching
Louise of Savoy, whose death in 1531 he commemorates in his *Jugement
poetic de l'honneur femenin et sejour des illustres, claires et honnestes dames*
(1538). The *Jugement* narrates a fictional journey to the Underworld
where the deceased Louise's merits are assessed by three infernal judges
who determine whether she deserves a place in the palace of illustrious
ladies, the 'sejour' to which the work's title alludes, which already houses
the first-person epitaphs of 126 Hebrew, pagan, and Christian women
from Eve to Margaret of Austria; naturally, she is deemed sufficiently
worthy of honour. Having been presented to François I, the *Jugement*
was granted royal privilege for its printed edition in 1536.[25] Bouchet
addresses a later preface to Anne de Laval, the wife of François de La
Trémoille, one of Bouchet's patrons and correspondents amongst the
nobility of his native Poitiers. The preface is a long prose *Apologie* which
compiles and consolidates the principal theological and philosophical
arguments cited in defence of woman's honour in treatises of the period,
such as Henricus Cornelius Agrippa's *De nobilitate et praecellentia
foeminei sexus*.[26]

---

[23] For the late medieval tradition of *puy* poetry, see Chapter 2, pp. 117–18.

[24] English translations are my own.

[25] For discussion of the poem's success or otherwise in gaining patronage from the
French royal court, see Britnell 1986: 6.

[26] See Introduction, n. 11.

A male author frequently presents his work to a female patron whom he often represents within its literary frame. He is, moreover, engaged in representing women in the forensic sense of the term, providing a 'deffenssoir des dames' (*NDV*, fol. B3ᵛ) for a sex which, according to Champier, requires a voice to speak on its behalf since women have neither the learning nor the voice, the rhetorical ability nor the opportunity, to defend themselves. In his *Nef*'s prefatory *Apologie* to Anne of France, Champier reasons that women have been sitting targets for misogynists' attack on account of their helpless silence; he refers specifically to their inability to read those books of Scripture that could provide them with material to support the pro-feminine case:

. . . pour ce que les femmes sont comme les brebiz devant le loup et communement ne visitent pas les escriptures à eulx savoir deffendre et pour ce ne sonnent mot, on dit ces maulx estre venus d'elles. (*NDV*, fol. B4ᵛ)

(. . . because women are like sheep before the wolf, and generally do not read the Scriptures in order to learn how to defend themselves, and on account of this say nothing, they are then blamed for these ills.)

Champier's reasoning invites us to question the implication and effect of such male appropriation of the feminine voice. Are women really incapable of speaking out? Constance Jordan has suggested that, in Champier's case, this decision to speak for the persons he defends inscribes the self-professed promoter of women in an ambivalent discursive position: what may be implicit in Champier's decision 'is the fear that [women] may speak for themselves'.[27] I develop Jordan's reservations in light of arguments about women and speech made by Anne herself in the treatise that appears to have superseded Champier's *Nef*, the *Enseignements d'Anne de France . . . à sa fille Susanne de Bourbon*.[28] Writing shortly after her husband's death, and on the eve of Suzanne's marriage to Charles of Montpensier, future Duke of Bourbon, Anne here addresses her daughter as heir to the role of First Lady of the Moulins court, and sets out in no-nonsense terms a treatise of practical

---

[27] 1990: 104. Brown casts doubt on Champier's claim to be writing for a female audience, as much of the *Nef*'s third book is in Latin: 2001: 159.

[28] A de luxe manuscript copy was presented to Suzanne, but the work was also disseminated to a larger audience, being published in print in Lyons at Suzanne's request some time before her death in 1521, and later in Toulouse by Jean Barril in 1535: Berriot-Salvadore 1990: 403.

advice for the young woman.[29] Speech and the ability to communicate appropriately, confidently, and clearly are one of Anne's prime concerns: 'car la plus noble chose que Dieu aye mise en créature, c'est la parolle.'[30] Moreover, she openly criticizes the sort of pitiful, mute, sheep-like women whom Champier sees himself defending, advising her daughter:

Aussi, ma fille, en quelque lieu que soiez, ne faictes pas comme ces femmes nyces qui, en compaignie, [. . .] ne sçavent dire ne respondre ung seul mot, quant on parle à elles, et font semblant d'en riens ouyr, soit à leur honneur ou pour esbat.[31]

(Therefore, my child, in whatever circumstance you find yourself, do not act like those foolish women who, in company, [. . .] are not able to speak or answer a single word when spoken to, and pretend not to have heard anything, either for the sake of their honour or out of fun.)

A truly honourable woman who wants to fulfil her public role effectively should not resort to foolish feminine behaviour, but should have a tongue in her head for putting her virtue to use:

Aussi n'est-il pas beau à femme de façon estre morne ne trop peu enlangagiée. Car, comme dit Ovide, telz femmes, quelqu'autre perfection qu'elles aient, ressemblent à ydolles et ymaiges painctes, et ne servent, en ce monde, que d'y faire umbre, nombre et encombre.[32]

(Thus it is not fitting for a woman of stature to be dull and speak very little. For, as Ovid states, such women, whatever other perfection they possess, resemble idols and painted images; all they do is get in the way.)

A brief glance at the second book of the *Nef*, Champier's attempt at a *regime de mariage*, will suggest how his work failed to hit the right note with independent-minded, politically engaged Anne.[33] His chapter headings appear to espouse the woman's point of view, suggesting 'Comment la femme doit eslire le mari et pourquoi',[34] but their content

---

[29] We note that Anne presented her own work to Suzanne in place, not only of Champier's *Nef*, but also of Christine's *Tresor*, of which two copies were present in the Moulins library.

[30] 'Since the most noble gift that God has given mankind is speech': Anne de France 1878: 70–1. English translations are my own.

[31] Ibid. 112.   [32] Ibid. 67–8.

[33] We recall, for example, Anne's role as (unofficial) regent during the minority of Charles VIII. The *Nef*'s first book may have been found wanting for a similar lack of engagement with actuality, since only three *vitae* out of over 130 are taken from contemporary history: Joan of Arc, Joanna, Queen of Jerusalem and Sicily, and Queen Blanche, mother of Louis IX.

[34] 'How and why a woman should select a husband': *NDV*, fol. M[v].

rapidly reveals that the writer's main concern here is simply a rehearsal of woman's conventional position under customary and canon law: 'selon la loy des mariages et selon les constitutions du païs et des sacremens de mariage'.[35] That position circumscribes a wife's activity to the domestic sphere of procreation and child-raising since woman is given to man in marriage 'to multiply the human race' (fol. L3^v)[36] and to 'instruct the children in morality' (fol. O3^v).

Reading Champier's work in this light begins to suggest how a male author's presumed right to speak on women's behalf is a contentious issue: not only a subject of controversy when viewed through the lens of modern criticism informed by twenty-first-century feminist thinking, but also, and more significantly, a source of debate within the sixteenth century. Champier's assumption of an authorial, didactic position at odds with his hoped-for patron's agenda seems to have influenced the failure of his work to gain favour with this educated lady who did not hesitate to take up the pen herself, and who expected her daughter to speak out and act with a similarly assertive spirit.

The question of man's arrogation of the authority to defend women is addressed directly in one late sixteenth-century pro-feminine text, a treatise of uncertain authorship entitled *Le Triomphe des dames* (1599) and dedicated to Catherine Henriette de Joyeuse, Duchess of Montpensier. Although written almost a century after the *Nef,* and thus strictly lying outside the temporal parameters of the present study, the *Triomphe* is a useful text against which to read Champier's work and other defences known to have been written by men; it questions explicitly the validity of a male voice's appropriation of the female voice. The *Triomphe* embarks upon a defence of women that purports to be voiced by a woman; identifying herself enigmatically as an anonymous young woman ('une Pucelle sans nom'), the speaker addresses her female 'compagnes':

Ce que j'escry n'a autre but que la defense de la justice de vos querelles que le sexe a fait miennes.[37]

(What I write has no other aim than to defend the justice of your cause that sex has made mine.)

---

[35] 'According to matrimonial law, the constitutions of the kingdom, and the sacrament of marriage': ibid., fol. M2^r.

[36] Champier develops the obstetric dimension of his manual by including chapters addressing woman's ripe age for reproduction (fol. M2^v) and the best time of year for procreation (fol. N^r).

[37] [Pierre de Brinon] 1599: 3. English translations are my own.

This assertive, feminine voice concludes her treatise with a side-swipe at those men, however well meaning, who presume to speak her sex's part:

nous n'avons point mandié des hommes le retablissement de nostre reputation; nos fautes sont venues de l'infortune du temps, et nous les amendons par nostre propre prudence.[38]

(we have by no means sought from men the restoration of our reputation; our faults have come with the misfortunes of time, and we use our own good sense to correct them.)

But is it a woman or, with deliberately spectacular irony, a man who speaks here? I mentioned the treatise's uncertain authorship; its signature initials 'P.D.B' are generally attributed to Pierre de Brinon, whose other works were produced by the same publisher, but this attribution is not definitive. The possibility of female authorship should not be discounted, and it is a possibility worth probing in my reflections on the cross-dressing tongue of the ventriloquizing male author. Berriot-Salvadore highlights the *Triomphe* as an unusual *querelle* text, referring to its signature initials as 'the little enigma which gives it originality',[39] and which make the text interesting for modern readers. I argue instead that this 'enigma', rather than pointing to any particular originality, can serve as a springboard to raise the more general question of readerly preconceptions regarding male and female authorship in the *querelle*. It provides a spur to our thinking about the difference between the authorial voice and the text's speaking voice, and about how gender complicates this relationship. Is there a difference between a woman writing in her own name, like Anne of France, and a man writing in the name of a woman, what Pierre Bec usefully calls the distinction between 'féminité gynétique' (the extradiegetic woman author) and 'féminité textuelle' (the feminine diegetic voice),[40] and should these two cases be evaluated differently? The *Triomphe*'s anonymity leaves these questions open, but its speaker actively invites them to be posed; she launches a provocative attack on sexual difference:

Pourquoy appellerions nous ces choses differentes, qu'une heure, un moment, un mouvement peuvent rendre du tout semblables?[41]

(Why should we call these things different(ly), that an hour, a moment, a single movement can make absolutely the same?)

---

[38] [Pierre de Brinon] 1599: 341.
[39] Berriot-Salvadore 1990: 353. English translation is my own.
[40] 1979: 235–6. English translations are my own.
[41] [Pierre de Brinon] 1599: 7.

Her call for the abolition of different signifiers to designate man and woman as different entities can be seen to have a problematic literary reflexive dimension in light of her other comments, cited above, advocating women's speaking on their own behalf and rejecting the offer of representation by men. Is there or is there not a meaningful difference to be observed between the two 'choses' of male and female authorship of defences of women?[42]

Reflection on a gendered reading of authorship goes back to Plutarch, who, in his essay *De mulierum virtutibus*, poses the question:

Quod si poeticam facultatem, non aliam in viris atque mulieribus esse libeat ostendere atque ob hoc Sapphus carmina, cum Anacreontis versibus conferam [. . .] iure ne quisque hoc demonstrandi genus accusabit, si etiam oblectatione quadam & voluptate delinitum auditorem ad credendum inducat?[43]

(If we show, by comparing Sappho's poems with Anacreon's [. . .] that the art of poetry [. . .] is not one art when practised by men and another when practised by women but is the same, will anyone be able to find just cause for blame in our demonstration?)

In response to this question, Linda S. Kauffman concludes perspicaciously that 'Plutarch may be right that the art itself does not differ between the sexes, but the criticism does differ.'[44] Her conclusion is especially pertinent to my study because the texts she is considering in this light are Ovid's *Heroides*, twenty-one epistolary laments by mythological women abandoned by their lovers that the Latin poet ventriloquizes by impersonating each feminine voice.[45] Kauffman evokes the dilemma for criticism of what reading strategies should be applied to texts written *by* women compared to those written *as if* by women. Similarly, in the *querelle des femmes*, modern criticism has to wrestle with works that are known to use male impersonation of a feminine voice, speaking not only on behalf of, but also through the voice of, the woman being represented, such as the first-person epitaphs in Bouchet's *Jugement*

---

[42] The same debate rumbles on in modern criticism: the relationship between critical discourse and the gender of the critic, specifically with regard to male-authored feminist criticism, is explored by Boone 1990.

[43] I quote the Latin translation of Plutarch's treatise by Alamanno Rinuccini, *De claris mulieribus* (*c*.1464–5), in Ravisius Textor 1521: fol. 3ᵛ. I follow Kauffman's English translation: 1986: 50.

[44] 1986: 50.

[45] Like Plutarch's *De mulierum virtutibus*, Ovid's letters enjoyed considerable popularity in print during the peak period of the *querelle*, both in Latin (Moss 1982: 8) and in a French translation by Octovien de Saint-Gelais that was originally produced for Anne of Brittany: Winn 1997: 92–4.

poetic or the feminine persona of Marot's *Advocate*. This creative strategy, which Elizabeth D. Harvey has provocatively called 'transvestite ventriloquism' or 'ventriloquistic cross-dressing',[46] has, I believe, failed to gain adequate, positive attention in critical approaches to the *querelle*. It has been disregarded for one main reason, namely Christine de Pizan, who, since the 1970s, has been celebrated, to use Barbara Altmann's phrase, as 'the First Lady of the Middle Ages'.[47]

The well-documented existence of a writer known to be female writing in defence of her sex has stalled most attempts at assessing favourably the ostensibly similarly pro-woman output of her male contemporaries and immediate successors in late medieval France. It is assumed that only Christine's defence can be of serious interest since only she can have been writing sincerely 'like a woman' because she was biologically a woman.[48] As a corollary, it is often presumed that she can *only* have been writing sincerely and referentially; the mode of irony and strategies of artifice become the preserve of all male-authored defences, which are consequently devalued for their presupposed insincerity.[49] They are, after all, the products of a monolithic and oppressive patriarchy; a male (and thus automatically patriarchal) author's sincerity can only appear when he is writing against women, and even writers like Champier who intend to favour the female cause cannot help but slip into a misogynistic position which is, after all, more 'natural' for a man.[50] Modern criticism seems to be taking, not Christine, but her fictional persona's mentor in her *Livre de la cité des dames* (1404–5), Dame Raison, as its touchstone for reader response. Raison describes how women have been left unprotected by men, except for a few half-hearted, botched attempts at their defence:

sanz trouver champion aucun qui pour leur deffence comparust souffisemment, nonobstant les nobles hommes qui par ordenance de droit deffendre les deussent, qui par negligence et nonchaloir les ont souffertes fouler.[51]

---

[46] E. Harvey 1992: 2.   [47] 2002: 17–30.

[48] Matarasso 2001: 38. This assumption seems to underlie Richards's view that 'there existed before Christine no defence of women' (1983: 15), and Zimmermann's opinion that Le Franc's *Champion* represents a step backwards in relation to Christine's pro-feminine work as 'women are only presented in this text as an object of masculine discourse': 1999: 82. Cf. Lazard 1985: 11.

[49] See Woodbridge 1984: 4–6.

[50] Kelso remarks that 'we must believe [. . .] there was real antagonism' fuelling literary attacks on women: 1956: 10; more recently, Brown explains intrusions of misogyny into Dufour's *Vies* as signs of the author's 'ostensible defence of women' being 'contradicted by his latent misogynistic attitude': 2001: 159. I offer an alternative reading of Dufour below, pp. 217–20.

[51] 1997: 54. English translations are my own.

(without finding any champion who presented himself adequately in their defence, notwithstanding the noble individuals who by written order had to defend them, and who, through negligence and indifference, have allowed them to be dishonoured.)

Raison's long disquisition on different causes that 'have moved and continue to move many men to slander (*blasmer*) women' implies that the only whole-heartedness she recognizes in man lies, whatever his proclaimed intention ('quelque fust leur entente'), in the misogynistic generalization of femininity.[52]

The establishment of personal sincerity as a gynocritical or female-author-only prerogative, and the principal criterion for assessing a *querelle* text, is hermeneutically inhibiting in two key ways. First, it restricts our reading of male authors. How would one then deal with a writer like Jean Le Fèvre whose work straddles both sides of the pro-/anti-feminine divide, and enjoys considerable popularity in both manuscript and print?[53] Secondly, this criterion is also limiting to Christine and to Christine scholarship.[54] It is influenced, perhaps, by what Patrocinio Schweickart identifies in some feminist criticism of female-authored texts, as distinct from texts written by men, as a drive to 'connect' intersubjectively with 'the "voice" of another woman'.[55] Such a 'connection' need not, however, be transparent and referential.[56] Strategies of impersonation are equally open to the female author, and Christine provides a striking example of masculine transvestite ventriloquism which anticipates and complements the feminine verbal cross-dressing practised by *querelle* writers. In a now famous passage in her *Livre de la mutacion de fortune* (1403), a work commonly accepted to narrate autobiographically the twists of fortune in Christine's own

---

[52] Ibid. 66–72. See also Blamires 1997: 11–15.

[53] See my discussion of Le Fèvre in Chapter 2.

[54] Armstrong makes a similar point about the absence of critical readings of Christine's *Cité* which focus on the 'manner' of its construction rather than on its 'matter'; he suggests this lack to be a symptom of 'the (sadly persistent) received idea that women's writing is transparent, whilst rhetorical virtuosity is reserved for men': Bouchet 2006: 34 n. 1. English translation is my own.

[55] Schweickart reviews and compares the features of feminist readings of male- and female-authored texts. In the latter case, she notes the tendency 'to construe the text not as an object, but as the manifestation of the subjectivity of the absent author': 1986: 48–55.

[56] For two readings which do challenge, in different ways, a transparently referential and serious interpretation of Christine's writings in defence of women, see Blanchard 1992, and Fenster 1992.

life, her diegetic persona, Cristine, describes the sexual transformation
that she experienced following the death of her husband:

> Fort et hardy cuer me trouvay,
> Dont m'esbahi, mais j'esprouvay
> Que vray homme fus devenu.[57]

(I found in myself a strong and bold heart, which amazed me, but I felt that I
had become a real man.)

This apparent sex-change may be read, at least in part, as an instance of
creative play with categories of gender, voice, and the linguistic formulation of gendered identity.[58] Christine selects the masculine-encoded
qualities of 'force' and 'hardiesse' in order to concoct a discursive constel-
lation of exemplary masculinity, a sort of constructionist performance
of gender, consciously and wittily playing with pre-existing, culturally
mapped representations of the sexes:[59] if diegetic Cristine is going to
'become' a man, she might as well become a first-rate one!

   I pause briefly to analyse this controversial passage from Christine's
Mutacion[60] because she is juggling here with issues of gender identity
and authorial presence that will be germane to my analyses of *querelle*
texts in the second half of this chapter. When referring to her earlier
life as a woman and discussing her resemblance to her father, diegetic
Cristine makes a nuanced distinction between the natural (female)
identity determined biologically by her body and the equally natural
(male) identity defined by her mind and spirit, the rest of her being:

> . . . de toutes choses mon pere
> Bien ressamblay et proprement,
> Fors du sexe tout seulement.

(vv. 394–6)

---

[57] Christine de Pizan 1959–66: i (1959), vv. 1359–61. Subsequent references will
be incorporated into the text. English translations are my own. For expediency, I
differentiate orthographically between the authorial instance, Christine, and the voice of
her diegetic narrator, Cristine.

[58] We see again in this self-conscious strategy the difficulty of choosing between the
terms 'cross-dressing' and 'cross-over' to denote the transvestment of Cristine's voice: see
above, n. 4.

[59] I am indebted here to Diana Fuss's discussion of essentialism and constructionism:
1989: 2–6, and to Judith Butler's work on gender performativity: 2004; 1990a; 1990b.

[60] Recent scholars are divided over Christine's intention here: compare Desmond's
(1994: 195) and Richards's (2001: 240) performative readings with Nephew (2000:
532). Developing the performative approach, I argue that Christine's decision to have
Cristine perform a masculine voice actually highlights even more pointedly her female
subject-position through the deliberate artifice of ventriloquistic transvestism.

(. . . I resembled my father in every way, and rightly so, with the only exception being sex.)

Notwithstanding this remarkable similarity to a man, implying parity of reason and intellect, she remains sexually 'femelle' (v. 391). When narrating her 'transmutation' (v. 1336), biological reality appears again to be at stake, but this time it has transformed; she repeatedly emphasizes her good faith in affirming the reality of her sex-change:

> Or fus je vrays hom, n'est pas fable,
> De nefs mener entremettable.
>
> (vv. 1391–2)

(Then I was a real man—I tell no lie—employed in steering ships.)

However, in the same way that the second line of this couplet is intended as a nautical metaphor for her newly acquired command at steering a widow's path through life, so the affirmation of her masculinity as 'un-fabled' truth is also to be understood metaphorically as an expedient expression to denote her new social—though not sexual—role 'as a man'. This difference between sex and gender identity is pointed up by Christine in terms of another distinction, that between authorial and narratorial presence:

> Vous diray que je suis qui parle,
> Qui de femelle devins masle.
>
> (vv. 141–2)

(I shall tell you who I am, I who am speaking, who changed from a female into a male.)

The appended relative clause ('qui parle') identifies the transsexualized 'je' to be the text's narrative voice and not its authorial instance, thereby confirming diegetic Cristine's purported biological maleness ('masle') to be, in fact, an expedient masculine gender role that Christine's persona is assuming within the economy of the *Mutacion*'s fiction. This is Christine's act of 'transvestite ventriloquism': a fictional experiment in speaking 'like a man' which figuratively represents her entry upon her new career as a writer in the world of men. She uses imaginatively the vehicle of the first-person narrator to express, through its postulated masculinity, the concerns of a widow left, to use Christine's own metaphor, to steer the helm of her life's ship.

Christine's exercises in verbal masquerade throughout her *œuvre* not only counterpoint the ventriloquism of the *querelle*'s male-authored texts by cross-dressing to a masculine, rather than a feminine, tongue,[61] but also provide pertinent parallels. She, too, impersonates other feminine voices that feature in dialogue with her persona Cristine, most impressively the impassioned, euhemerized figure of Libera whose scribe she becomes in the *Livre de l'advision Cristine* (1405). The ventriloquisms of both sexes by both sexes are equally 'insincere' in the sense that each impersonated voice, regardless of gender, is a fictional projection intended to be held at a critical distance from, albeit in dialogue with, the authorial voice. In the wake of recent feminist theory, however, and its sensitivity to the definition of woman's voice, there remains a deep-seated suspicion surrounding the practice of ventriloquistic cross-dressing by male writers that is addressed in this study, and this suspicion risks restricting the critical treatment it receives to a question, once again, of sincerity. Scholarship on Ovid's *Heroides* points up this risk, having probed more fully than *querelle* criticism the workings of male-authored transvestite ventriloquism. Recent critics have been divided on the propriety of this rhetorical strategy, and Letter XIII, addressed by Sappho to Phaon, has proven a particular bone of contention. On the one hand, Kauffman argues for Ovid's sympathetic reconstruction of Sappho's lament, postulating his use of the letters in general to 'challenge conventional notions of tradition, of origins, of fathers, of paternity, of authority, of identity' by writing 'like a woman'.[62] On the other hand, Harvey, responding to Kauffman, reaches an impassable stumbling block of 'fundamental duplicity' undermining Ovid's ventriloquism and exposing it as mere 'masquerade': 'Ovid writes from the perspective of a woman because he is not a woman; he metaphorizes the figure of Woman.'[63] Whilst Harvey acknowledges Ovid's use of 'the metaphor of woman' for 'dismantling certain patriarchal values', she maintains that this endeavour is fatally flawed: 'Unlike the heroines he ventriloquizes, he simultaneously partakes of the very privilege he seeks to expose.'[64] The charges Harvey levels against 'cross-dressing the tongue' are twofold: it is essentially duplicitous and usurping, and it inhibits femininity by generating only a homogenized type or metaphor of 'Woman'.

I offer here a brief rebuttal of Harvey's gloomy perspective, applying her argument to Jean Marot's *Vraye disant advocate des dames*. As a sample text, this will illustrate how the dichotomy of female sincerity versus

---

[61] Blamires considers briefly in terms of gender Christine's use of the God of Love as her 'fictional mouthpiece' in her *Epistre au dieu d'amours*: 1997: 45.
[62] Kauffman 1986: 61.   [63] E. Harvey 1992: 39–40.   [64] Ibid. 40.

male insincerity is inappropriate to a reading of *querelle* ventriloquisms
that seeks both to recover the conditions of its contemporary reception
and to propose why these texts are still of interest to modern readers.
According to Harvey, transvestite ventriloquism is duplicitous in that it
unethically usurps women's tongue; in the case of Ovid's Letter XIII,
it parasitically exploits verse from Sappho's own poetry such that rights
of gender and property are transgressed. In the *Vraye disant advocate*,
Marot's impersonation of a female barrister speaking on behalf of
'nostre sexe'—the gender of his dedicatee, Anne of Brittany—seems,
far from being seen as unethical, to have been read according to a
certain contract of complicity between author and patron, writer and
audience.[65] Instead of being judged according to a criterion of sincerity,
the ventriloquizing act is understood as a rhetorical strategy: from the
poet's perspective, it forms part of the apparatus of his imaginative
fiction; for the reader, it is an element of the 'horizon of expectation'
that constitutes his or her hermeneutic engagement in the structure of
the *Advocate*'s monologue. In the *Advocate*'s prologue, Marot's persona
refers to his work as a 'traicté ou monologue' (*VDA* 94) and the double
appellation is perhaps significant for understanding the ventriloquism
it stages. As a monologue, the poem is a virtuoso solo performance, a
rhetorical *tour de force* worthy of purely aesthetic appreciation, like the
similarly ventriloquizing role-play of an anonymous *querelle* debate, *Le
Monologue fort joyeulx auquel sont introduictz deux avocatz et ung juge,
devant lequel est plaidoyé le bien et le mal des dames*, whose single speaker
impersonates three different (male) identities.[66] But the *Advocate* is also
a treatise, an aesthetic 'recreation, passetemps et délectation' that carries
underlying didactic profit for 'savoureuse digestion' (*VDA* 95), as befits
a poetic fiction in the medieval sense of the term. On the one hand, this
profit is the general 'deffence, louange et victoire' of woman's excellence,
and is itself contingent on the fictional gender of the speaker whose
rhetoric demonstrates as well as describes the intellectual prowess of 'ce
tres noble et magnifique sexe' (ibid.). On the other, the profit is also
a specific, political defence of Anne against the 'vicieuse machination'

---

[65] This 'contract' may be related to the sort of hermeneutic collusion between writer
and audience that Taylor perceives to be essential to the reappraisal of late medieval French
vernacular poetics: 'what is required is reading strategies which recognise "community"
and "cooperation" as guiding principles': 2001: 5.

[66] 'The most entertaining monologue, in which are introduced two advocates and
a judge, before whom the virtues and the ills of women are debated': 1876. English
translation is my own. See Conclusion, pp. 240–2.

of Pierre de Rohan, Maréchal of Gié, the Queen's personal enemy, who contradicted her wishes for the marriage of her daughter, and was subsequently tried, though unsuccessfully, for the crime of treason.[67] In this light, we may see the rhetorical activity of the Advocate to perform linguistically and dramatically, through an imaginative fiction, a form of revenge upon Gié. For instance, she mounts a vituperative assault on ungrateful 'seigneurs' who defame their own mothers:

> Ainsi que aspics et venimeux viperes
> De vos gueulles vomissez improperes
> Et vituperes, murtrissant nostre gerre.
>
> (*VDA*, vv. 52–4)

(Like aspics and venomous vipers you hurl out of your gobs insults and vituperations, murdering our sex.)

The stinging force of her voiced, fricative alliteration may also be directed metaphorically at the particular ingrate who aimed, according to Anne, at subverting the natural order of a mother's wishes for her daughter. The gender identity of the persona's voice becomes itself a sort of performance, with a political edge: by casting a woman, notionally Anne, in a litigating role, Marot uses his poem's fictional frame to accord her a measure of juridical authority that was denied women at this time, a privilege he points up when the Advocate declares:

> . . . Croyez certainement
> Que nous avons sens et entendement,
> Et force aussi, pour cy et tous endrois
> Le nostre honneur deffendre puissamment,
> Si permis fust par loix, canons et drois.
>
> (*VDA*, vv. 197–201)

---

[67] Marot 1999: 364. Pierre was the private tutor of François of Angoulême, the future François I. Against Anne's wishes, he wanted François to marry her daughter Claude of France, a plan which would ensure that the crown of France retained Brittany. In pursuing this project he acted against Anne, who wanted Claude to marry a Hapsburg (Charles of Luxembourg), and the Cardinal George of Amboise. Gié found himself isolated, and his opponents launched a legal action against him in 1504, but not before Gié had had a chance to extract from a weakened Louis XII an undertaking that Claude should marry François. His trial was deferred and referred from Paris to Toulouse. Even though the crime of *lèse-majesté* could not be proven, the marshal was dismissed from all his court offices, including the education of François of Angoulême. cf. Pierre de Brantôme 1991: i. 171.

(. . . Know for certain that we have the sense, understanding, and strength powerfully to defend our honour here and everywhere, if it were allowed by civil, canon, and customary law.)[68]

The caveat of her last line highlights the neat structural irony that the Advocate is already enacting through her monologue the possibility she states here to be pure hypothesis. Marot's Advocate can thus be seen to perform her legal authority through a sort of wish-fulfilment structure; she enacts a fantasy that transforms her legal defeat against Gié into imagined success, what would constitute for her, in Butler's terms, a more liveable possibility.[69] Marot also plays up the act of transvestite ventriloquism that constructs the Advocate's speech. Her discourse combines first- and third-person speech: she speaks in the first person in response to misogynistic slander of 'nostre honneur' by the 'seigneurs' to whom she addresses her pleading; she also speaks on behalf of 'l'honneur des femmes' as a third party. Thus her speech is both identifiable with and detachable from a woman's perspective. This hybrid composition is perhaps a strategic rhetorical manoeuvre on the part of Marot, one that opens up possibilities for the gender of this voice: woman and not woman. He does not appear concerned with establishing a layering of narrative levels corresponding to gender identity, distinguishing between a real male voice outside the text and the appearance of a female voice within; on the contrary, by maintaining a hybrid or an uncertainty, he allows the 'reality' of the Advocate's gender to be constituted by the performance itself, the embodiment that is the speaker's *je*.

This sort of performative play implies a relationship of complicity, a literary 'nod and a wink' between writer and patron. The female dedicatee obviously knows that her dedicator is male, but the literary text across which they communicate seems to be acknowledged as a locus in which the terms of this binary may be freed up, even contested. We recall here the paradoxical position of the *Triomphe*'s persona, asserting sexual identity with her subject whilst at the same time challenging the validity of sexual difference. Christine's ventriloquistic cross-dressing is also pertinent here: in her *Mutacion*, her repeated insistence upon her transformation into 'vray homme', far from affirming a straightforward gender split, raises question marks around the very notion of 'true' or 'real' gender. The *Triomphe* speaker's rhetorical question

---

[68] v. 201 may be seen to refer here to all three elements in French legal heritage; see Shennan 1998: 51–5.
[69] 2004: 216–17.

about gender identities being 'choses [. . .] semblables' proposes that there is no grading of gender reality: neither 'male' nor 'female' can be designated an individual's proper being; each is a position that is performed. Both Christine and Marot adumbrate a similar view through literary acts of ventriloquistic cross-dressing: the extradiegetic author and the diegetic persona are not presented in a binary opposition of real versus apparent gender identity. The literary embodiment that speaks as *je* manoeuvres in a malleable field of play which critiques essentialized gender presuppositions in the very act of constructing its own performance.

To return to Harvey, her assessment of Ovid's duplicity would invalidate any ventriloquizing author's claim to be pursuing his work with good intentions, to be writing 'like a woman' in good faith. The dedicatory epistles and prologues appended to several *querelle* texts invariably make such claims in the context of a conventional modesty topos. We encounter Jean Dupré's plea that Marguerite de Navarre should accept 'le present et geniture de mon debile entendement',[70] his *Palais*, which, however 'imperfaicte', is insured against failure by its well-intentioned motives:

> Car en matieres de grant et hault valoir
> L'on considere dessus tout le vouloir.
>
> (*PND*, fol. L6^v)

(Since, in matters of great and high importance, one considers above all the intention.)

On the one hand, Dupré's maxim offers a fair summary of the convention of as it were 'sincere insincerity' by which these defences were received. On the other, he can be seen to pinpoint here the key crux bedevilling both contemporary and modern readings of *querelle* texts that I identified in my Introduction to be authorial intention or 'vouloir'. *Querelle* writers consciously play with intentionality: we have seen here, and back in Chapter 1, how they contrive interferences between subject-positions on different narrative levels; in Chapter 2 we saw them take issue with their anti-feminine forebears by putting them on trial for the crime of misogynistic utterance such that the alleged authorial intention behind their utterance becomes the *mens rea*, so to speak, that determines their guilt. Thus, the modern reader needs to be alert to the flexibility, contingency, and sophistication involved

---

[70] 'The gift and product of my feeble understanding': *PND*, fol. A3^r.

in apparently straightforward declarations of 'vouloir' made by these medieval writers. On the question of gender and voice, Dupré is a case in point. In the dedicatory epistle to his *Palais*, he makes seemingly the most simple of statements affirming his position as woman's champion:

Maintenant, ma tresillustre maistresse, à voz parties refie[71] defendre la querelle des honnestes femmes et mienne. (*PND*, fol. A3^r)

(Now, my most renowned lady, before your adversaries I pledge myself to defend honourable women's case and my own.)

The addendum 'et mienne' is deliberately ambiguous: it signals how Dupré has made the pro-feminine case his own as spokesman on behalf of women, but also reveals that, in the very act of defending women, he is arguing his own case as a writer seeking Marguerite's patronage. That this double meaning was intended to be appreciated and approved by his dedicatee is indicated by a prefatory dialogue between the author and his book which features on the *Palais*'s title page:

> *L'autheur à son livre:*
> Petit livret, si tu gaignes la grace
> De la princesse à qui l'on te dedye,
> Heureux seras quoy que le monde dye;
> Mais aultrement il fault que l'on te casse.
> *Responce du livre à l'autheur*:
> Touchant à moy, je feray mon devoir;
> Et si la Dame se tient de moy contente,
> Pas ne convient encontre moy qu'on tente,
> Car me fera par tout le monde voir.
>
> (*PND*, fol. A^r)

(*The author to his book*: 'Little book, if you gain favour with the princess to whom you are dedicated, you will be fortunate, whatever the rest of the world says; but if you don't, you'll have to be sent packing.' *The book's answer to the author*: 'In all that concerns me, I shall do my duty; and if the Lady is happy with me, no one will have to attack me, as she will show me to everyone.')

The book anticipates explicitly the hoped-for consequences of the Duchess's sponsorship, namely promotion and circulation within and beyond her coterie, which would satisfy the 'vouloir' of its author, understood as both the pro-feminine intention of a lady's loyal servant

---

[71] I read this as an emphatic form (*re-*) of *fier*, in the sense of 'to swear': Godefroy 1969: iii. 787.

and the literary ambition of a vernacular writer.[72] We know that Dupré, a male writer, speaking through the masculine persona of his *autheur*, intends a certain irony or doubleness to subtend his declaration of woman's 'querelle' as his own ('mienne'). We should compare his statement with the similar declaration of solidarity made by the anonymous feminine speaker of the *Triomphe des dames*, as she asserted her defence of woman's 'querelles' 'que le sexe a fait miennes'. Is the *Triomphe* author, whether male *or* female, here indulging in a similar play to Dupré, by opening up the possible understandings of the speaker's professed identification with woman's cause? Both cases imply a questioning of the relationship between gender and voice: highlighting possible conflict between the gender of authorial and narrative voices, but also exposing the positionality of each instance. If we as readers depart from the easy distinction between sincerity and artifice as the predetermined, 'proper' qualities of female and male voices speaking in defence of women, we encounter a far more complex and intriguing set of questions concerning narrative play and the constructedness of gender positions. And these are questions to which we are directed by the texts themselves, through Dupré's complicitous 'nod' to his patron and the *Triomphe* speaker's ambiguous stance on sexual difference.

As a provisional conclusion to the knotty problem of gender, voice, and intention, it is already evident that, while the link between diegetic and extradiegetic voices is complicated by gender in transvestite ventriloquism, this relationship is not necessarily one of antagonism and unethical usurpation. It is, instead, a relationship full of creative possibility for the fictional representation of women, as illustrated by Marot's eloquent Advocate.

L'OPPOSITION MASCULIN–FÉMININ: WEARING CULTURAL SIGNIFICATIONS

The rest of this chapter will focus on a second question of transvestism raised by Semiramis' epitaph, and one which pertains to an especially knotty problem of representing feminine exemplarity in the *querelle*: how to praise a woman for fulfilling an active, often military office that is culturally defined as 'masculine', for example in the case of the Amazon Queen Penthesilea:

[72] See also Berriot-Salvadore 1990: 370.

vestoit armes et assailloit les plus grans [. . .], et selon le coustume des hommes chevaliers, non des femmes, montoit chars et chevaulx.[73]

(She put on armour and attacked the mightiest [. . .] and according to the custom of men warriors, and not women, she mounted horse and chariot.)

By contrast, throughout the *querelle*, the identities of similarly martially engaged figures (Semiramis, Hypsicratea, and Artemis) are constructed from gender vocabulary in ways that display an awareness of what we would now call a more flexible, performative conception of gender identity. This construction describes or implies an element of transvestment: whether figurative, through the use of gendered adjectives and the metaphoric donning/doffing of the heart of man/woman, or literal, vestimentary cross-dressing. In both cases, to use Butler's terms, these women are represented wearing certain cultural significations.[74] My analysis pursues a twofold argument: first, that particular applications of this ubiquitous vocabulary by certain *querelle* writers manifest an awareness, and a creative manipulation, of the value-judgements culturally ascribed to different gendered terms, such as the Latinate 'viril' (*virilis*) assimilating female achievement to a masculine heroic ideal; second, that these applications signal a frustration at the lack of any alternative discursive system allowing a valorization of woman's virtue in terms other than those of 'culturally intelligible gender',[75] constructed according to a patriarchal hegemony.

The principal type of *querelle* text from which I shall be drawing these examples of active women is catalogues of famous and infamous women, positive and negative *exempla* that are bound together by varying degrees of narrative development: from Christine de Pizan's *Cité des dames*, via Antoine Dufour's sequence of biographies without any connecting narrative thread, his *Vies des femmes célèbres*, to Jean Bouchet's *Jugement poetic*, whose series of 126 epitaphs transcribed by the Traverseur constitutes the catalogue component of his work. These writers were writing against the tradition of Boccaccio's *De mulieribus claris*, the fourteenth-century catalogue of women which was widely

[73] Taken from the anonymous translation of *De mulieribus* made in 1401, *Des cleres et nobles femmes*, recently edited by Baroin and Haffen 1993: i. 101, to which I refer hereafter as the *Nobles femmes*. English translations are my own. I list all fifteen extant manuscripts of the *Nobles femmes*, together with early prints of other French translations, in Appendix 2B.

[74] I refer here to her comments on gender, 'the act that embodied agents *are*', as an 'embodiment' or 'wearing' of 'certain cultural significations': 1990b: 276.

[75] The phrase is Butler's; I explain its context below, pp. 198–9.

transmitted (and also imitated) both in the original Latin and in French translation throughout the fifteenth century.[76] The Boccaccian tradition sets up 'masculine' and 'feminine' as symbolic positions, holding the masculine up as an ideal to be aimed at by the feminine, valuing women inasmuch as they were able to emulate the behaviour of men. Boccaccio's lexeme of choice for praising woman's accomplishments is *virilis*, a term implying that her supreme achievement as a woman lies in overcoming the expectations of her sex and entering another, superior, symbolic.[77] By contrast, fifteenth- and early sixteenth-century writers seem dissatisfied with this immasculating[78] viewpoint, which, by praising the man in woman, correspondingly denigrated the woman, the femininity, in her. *Femina* and its cognates connoted for Boccaccio effeminacy and weakness, aspects of character that were undesirable and must be suppressed if a woman wishes to earn praise. The later *querelle* bears witness to a concerted *mise en question* of the nature of gendered vocabulary used to define woman's achievements.

Gendered vocabulary is value-laden, an issue that Liliane Dulac has explored through a comparative analysis of the Assyrian Queen Semiramis, as she appears in *De mulieribus* and the *Cité des dames*,[79] for which Boccaccio's catalogue of famous and infamous women was Christine's principal souce.[80] Dulac structures her comparison of Boccaccio's and Christine's treatments of Semiramis around four categories: *fonction, récit, narration*, and *opposition masculin—féminin*; it is this last category that serves as my starting point here. Boccaccio's Queen is commended for her actions that, 'non seulement en femme, mais en quelconque homme de grant et noble courage sont merveilleuses et a loer',[81] whilst

[76] See also Stephen Kolsky's exploration of *De mulieribus* as '*architext*' in an Italian context of writing about women: 2005.

[77] See, for instance, the praise Boccaccio bestows on his dedicatee, Andrea Acciaiuoli: playing on the etymology of her name (from the Greek *andres*), he sees her to have so far exceeded womankind that she has been 'made man' by a miraculous, divine act: 2001: 4. Andrea's virility can thus be seen as the touchstone of the catalogue, although cf. ibid., pp. xiv–xv.

[78] I borrow Judith Fetterley's coinage for describing how woman must 'accept as normal and legitimate a male system of values': 1978: p. xx. In the present context, immasculation signifies her assimilation to a masculine ideal of virile behaviour.

[79] Dulac 1978. See also Armstrong 2004.

[80] Several critics have explored Christine's rewriting of Boccaccio through her erasure of ambivalence, and her recuperation of those women whom he brands notorious, including Brown-Grant 1995; Jordan 1987; Phillippy 1986.

[81] 'Not only in a woman, but also in a man of great and noble spirit, [they] are marvellous and praiseworthy': *Nobles femmes* 1993: i. 22. Underpinning Dulac's analysis

Christine, going a bit further according to Dulac, declares that 'nul homme en vigueur et force ne la surmonta'.[82] Dulac concludes that 'vertu' is gendered masculine by both writers since, while Christine evacuates Semiramis of all feminine qualities, Boccaccio maintains her feminine aspects only to denigrate them as factors which risked flawing her irredeemably—namely lubriciousness and vanity—had she not saved herself by denying her sex: acting 'against the nature of her sex', 'abandoning women's office', and taking up arms 'with noble and virile spirit'.[83] The situation seems straightforward, the correlation clear-cut: for Dulac, doffing all feminine attributes goes hand in glove with donning heroic dignity, and she concludes: 'Le modèle héroïque masculin est indispensable à l'éloge superlatif.'[84] She confirms this 'mythe didactique' of the desirability of 'becoming a man' by citing several other instances of the phenomenon of immasculated widows in Christine's *œuvre*, including the example of her *Mutacion* mentioned above.

My own discussion of authorial play with sexual and gender identities in the *Mutacion* advises caution in presupposing any straightforward *masculin–féminin* dichotomy in Christine's work, and two questions consequently arise out of Dulac's study. First, can one generalize across Christine's *œuvre* about the meaning of statements to the effect that a widow must take on 'cuer d'omme' in order to prove her virtue and gain the greatest honour? Among the instances Dulac cites are those of a chatelaine guarding her property in the *Livre des trois vertus*, and of the French Queen Fredegonde in the *Cité*. The particular ideological contexts of these transvestisms should be considered, since both women are taking on their 'cuer d'omme' as a sort of expedient identity, a means to a specific end. Christine imagines how the besieged Fredegonde might have addressed her troops on the eve of battle:

J'ay pourpensé un barat par quoy nous vaincrons [. . .] Je lairay ester toute paour femenine et armeray mon cuer de hardiece d'omme a celle fin de

is the assumption, now disputed, that Christine only knew Boccaccio in vernacular translation; for recent discussion of this controversy, see Chance 2002: 215. Dulac's assumption does not, however, invalidate her argument. For Boccaccio's Latin text, see Boccaccio 2001: 20–2, and see also Taylor's discussion of the 'journeyman translator' of the *Nobles femmes*: 2000.

[82] 'No man exceeded her in force and strength': Christine de Pizan 1997: 106.
[83] *Nobles femmes* 1993: i. 20–1.
[84] 'The masculine model of heroism is essential to superlative praise': Dulac 1978: 325, 323. English translations are my own. Cf. my own readings of Semiramis below, pp. 200–1.

croistre le courage de vous et de ceulx de nostre ost par pitié de vostre jeune prince.[85]

(I've worked out a strategy that will enable us to win [. . .] I shall leave behind all feminine fear and arm my heart with manly courage in order to raise your spirits and those of our troops out of pity for your young prince.)

She plans to perform masculinity in order to achieve a particular end ('celle fin'), to communicate more effectively with her (male) barons and thence proceed to victory; in doing so, she acts out of one of the most essentially feminine motives, namely maternal 'pitié' for the prince, her son.[86] She thus advances into battle as both warrior and mother, and Christine presents the iconic image of her riding forth as commander of her troops whilst carrying her son in her arms:

Elle fist bien et bel ordener tout l'ost, puis se mist devant, bien montee, son filz entre ses bras, les barons apres.[87]

(She set all the troops in good and fine order, then positioned herself in front, securely mounted, her son in her arms, the barons following after.)

The 'maleness' she puts on is no more than a contingently useful metaphor or expedient masquerade. She takes on 'hardiece d'omme' as a means to an end and not an end in itself, a route towards realizing an identity and not the identity itself.

It is similarly as a metaphor that 'cuer d'omme' features in the example Dulac cites from the *Livre des trois vertus*: the widowed chatelaine 'doit avoir cuer d'omme, c'est qu'elle doit savoir les drois d'armes'.[88] The appended explanation ('c'est que. . .') makes explicit how 'cuer d'omme' is simply a convenient shorthand notation *faute de mieux* for the taking up of a military role with a specific objective in sight. It is perhaps illuminating to see in Christine's rhetorical manoeuvres with collocative expressions of transvestment an adumbration of the sort of 'gender trouble' and 'undoing' of gender theorized by Butler. In this light,

---

[85] Christine de Pizan 1997: 144.

[86] For a discussion of Fredegonde's action that draws different conclusions, but from a linguistic line of argument similar to my own, see Brown-Grant 2002: 163.

[87] Christine de Pizan 1997: 144. Blamires points out the difficulty for *querelle* writers 'of asserting women's capacities to fulfil their talents in parity with men, without potentially undermining the status of the nurturing role': 1997: 95; Christine's portrayal of Fredegonde seems, however, to have no difficulty reconciling both aspects.

[88] '[She] must have a manly heart, that's to say she must know how to use arms': Dulac cites Paris, BnF, MS fr. 452, fol. 61ᵛ. English translation is my own.

we can see Christine's perspective on gender identity to have been constrained by what Butler calls a male-normative 'cultural matrix' through which gender identity becomes 'intelligible':

Regulatory practices [. . .] generate coherent identities through the matrix of coherent gender norms [. . .], the production of discrete and asymmetrical oppositions between 'feminine' and 'masculine', where they are understood as expressive attributes of 'male' and 'female'.[89]

Christine appears to be trying to disrupt this matrix of coherent binaries which opposes masculine to feminine, and which branches out to embrace gendered oppositions between qualities that are weighted in favour of a male hegemony: strong versus weak, brave versus meek, active versus passive, intellectual versus emotional, etc. Christine engages with the matrix's terminology in order to effect from within a critique of this culturally predetermined binary thinking and its manifestation in language. Her stumbling block is a lack of alternative gender vocabulary outside the *masculin–féminin* opposition to break down this dichotomous matrix; though wanting to oppose the Boccaccian normative system, she is still obliged to define her women's position in relation to it.[90] She seems to have very little room for manoeuvre; as Butler would remark:

A restrictive discourse on gender that insists on the binary of man and woman as the exclusive way to understand the gender field performs a *regulatory* operation of power that naturalizes the hegemonic instance and forecloses the thinkability of its disruption.[91]

However, such 'thinkability' is not entirely foreclosed for Christine. In the *Cité*, while reflecting on the relationship between gender and physical bravery, Christine's spokeswoman Dame Raison gestures towards a fracturing of the binary structure, and it is a reflection to which I shall return:

Pourtant se femmes n'ont mie toutes si grant force et hardiece corporelle que ont hommes communement, que ilz ne doivent mie dire ne croire que ce soit pour ce que du sexe femenin soit forclose toute force a hardiece corporelle.[92]

---

[89] 1990a: 17.
[90] See Butler 2004: 42, 197.   [91] Ibid. 43.
[92] Christine de Pizan 1997: 104. Boccaccio takes a similar view, which somewhat disrupts Dulac's analysis of his Semiramis as an immasculated figure: when the Queen casts off her male disguise, it is, he says, 'almost as if she wanted to show that spirit (*animum*), not sex (*sexum*), was needed to govern': 2001: 18; *Nobles femmes* 1993: i. 20. On reading inconsistencies in *querelle* portraits of women, see Armstrong 2003.

(Even if women don't all possess the same strength and physical boldness that men generally have, they absolutely must not say or think that this is because all strength and bodily courage are excluded from the feminine sex.)

Raison's argument is thus: physical bravery does not necessarily correspond to intelligible gender identity; there is space within the concept of 'sexe femenin' to accommodate, even appropriate, a virtue that is culturally mapped 'masculin'.[93] Whilst this sharing of virtues can be maintained conceptually, its representation in language is hampered by the oppositional terms of discourse the writer is obliged to employ, as well as by the slippage that occurs between the neutrally 'denotative' and positively or negatively 'connotative' adjectives *masculin* and *féminin*. It is in this light that we may understand Christine's preference for descriptive phrases involving noun collocation, like 'hardiece d'omme', rather than the adjective *masculin* or *viril*: as well as designating a quality intrinsic to men, the noun collocations denote a masculine gender role that women can adopt in order to achieve their own, feminine ends.[94] Such formulations also have the benefit of avoiding already value-laden terms which would hinder Christine's project of tearing down existing rhetoric for representing women's achievements in order to lay new foundations for defending her sex, to use the architectural metaphor governing the *Cité*.

The second question raised by Dulac's study is: are Boccaccio's and Christine's statements comparable? Christine's assertion that Semiramis exceeds any man is not just 'going a bit further' than Boccaccio, but is positing a far more radical achievement. In rewriting her source, Christine presents the woman as being not equal to, but greater than her male counterpart. Once again, she appears to be gesturing here towards what we might call a 'third term', a discursive position that woman's excellence in an active role might occupy outside the miry dichotomy of masculine and feminine gender terminology, but that she might attain by being a woman, by celebrating and not by casting off her feminine attributes, to adapt Dulac's phrase. Besides stating that Semiramis' accomplishments surpassed the expected abilities of both sexes, Christine insists upon the essential femininity of the warrior-woman seen by Boccaccio as a model of virility:

[93] Christine's argument appears to be grounded here in the Aristotelian concept of sexual identity as an 'accidental', rather than an 'essential', difference between man and woman.
[94] See Brown-Grant 2002: 163.

fu femme de moult grant vertu en fait de fort et vertueux courage es entreprises et excercice du fais des armes.[95]

(She was a woman of very great virtue as regards her strong and valorous spirit in the planning and execution of deeds of arms.)

Like Bouchet's epitaph for Semiramis at the head of this chapter, Christine's *vita* implies a subtle semantic slippage between the possible meanings of 'courage': the vernacular equivalent of the Latin *animus*, the 'courage' synonymous with Bouchet's Semiramis' 'esprit grand', and the term's collocative sense of physical bravery in the context of deeds of arms that Bouchet renders by reference to her being 'hardie' in matters of 'chevallerie'. The semantic slippage evoked by Christine's Queen's 'courage' thus appropriates linguistically for this woman's spirit a quality of heroism more conventionally gendered masculine such that it is precisely by being faithful to her nature as a woman that she excels and exceeds any man 'en vigueur et force'. Semiramis' portraits in the *Cité* and *Jugement* thus involve semantic negotiations between different frames of reference, and juggle constructionist and essentialist representations of feminine identity in an attempt to refeminize a woman's 'virility', as lauded by Boccaccio, and integrate her active 'cuer d'omme' into a properly, indeed exclusively, feminine virtue. It would be inappropriate to describe Christine's constructions of woman's identity as truly performative, in Butler's sense of the term, since Christine retains an essentialist sense of femininity which is expressed through her women's gestures, such as Fredegonde's maternity. What Butler's formulation of performativity helps us to appreciate, though, is how Christine is wanting to challenge the accepted realities of gender, that is, the supposedly predetermined limits of appropriate conduct for each sex. She tries to shake up the boundary between the binary terms. By integrating normatively masculine virtues, such as *hardiece*, into a discursive space of femininity she opens up femininity to new semantic possibilities that are determined by the woman's ability and potential to perform a broader range of gestures than previously deemed 'proper' to her sex. Furthermore, the essentialism Christine observes is itself a remodelling of previous, *anti*-feminine preconceptions: whilst Boccaccio deplores the weakness of *femina*, Christine valorizes it as woman's essential, and prestigious, virtue.[96]

---

[95] Christine de Pizan 1997: 106. Cf. Chance 2002: 220.
[96] See Fenster 2002: 366.

Two conclusions may be drawn from my critique of Dulac: first, the need on the reader's part for contextual sensitivity to determine whether taking on 'cuer d'omme' might be an expedient implemented by a woman, who remains very much feminine, and positively so, in her achievement of honour;[97] second, the need manifested on the late medieval writer's part to start breaking down gender terminology in order to define the role of an active woman on refreshed, if not entirely new, terms. Both these needs recur and are developed in the later *querelle des femmes* corpus. In his *Vies des femmes célèbres*, Antoine Dufour's position as reader of prior pro-feminine catalogues and writer of a newly commissioned work for Anne of Brittany is especially intriguing in its ambivalence. He uses repeatedly the formula identified by Dulac, the equation 'abandon femininity + acquire masculinity = virtue and renown', but its effect is often equivocal and, I argue, intentionally so. My analysis of gendered vocabulary in the *querelle*'s portrayal of active women pivots around four *vitae* drawn from Dufour that feature Dulac's formula employed to unusual or unexpected effect: Triaria, Hypsicratea, Artemis, and Maria Puteolina.

Before entering into close analysis of the *Vies*, it is helpful to explain briefly the complex use of source material in Dufour's text. We have established that the verbal construction of gender identity operates in the *querelle* as a carefully thought out negotiation within a limited vocabulary of gender-signifying terms.[98] We have also acknowledged, through Christine's remodelling of Boccaccio, that this negotiation is complicated by intertextuality: a writer's choice of vocabulary is not a selection of free-floating signifiers, but is necessarily an engagement with the literary context in which these terms have already been used. To redeploy the spectral metaphor I introduced in Chapter 1 to explore the effect of anxious negotiation with antecedents, the *querelle* biography of a given woman is haunted by previous representations of her; we saw this in action through the first-person epitaph of Dido in Bouchet's *Jugement*, where her reputation as virtuous widow was the intertextual pressure

---

[97] Alongside Fenster (see ibid.), Brown-Grant has shown how Christine resists the immasculation of women by men. She comments on Christine's semantic neutralization of adjectives such as *femenin* such that they 'carry no hint of value-judgement', whether positive or negative (2002: 163); I am indebted to her discussion of Christine's use of the vocabulary of gender.

[98] Hotchkiss reaches a similar conclusion regarding the baggage of cultural perceptions of gender roles carried by language: 1996: 125–7. Her study, however, concentrates only on literal instances of transvestism, and does not consider the metaphorical uses of cross-dressing rhetoric that I investigate here.

point of her speech. In the third-person biographies of Christine's *Cité*, it is the vocabulary of gender that constitutes particular flashpoints through which the spectre of Boccaccio's language is conjured up/conjured.[99] Christine stands as heir to a certain, dichotomous vocabulary, and is thus constricted in the choice of linguistic operations she can perform to represent her active women's achievements, to have it out with troubling spectres. This negotiation of gender identity becomes even more imbricated in Dufour's *Vies*, where the number of intertextual threads increases. Jeanneau's edition names *De mulieribus* as Dufour's principal model, but also notes that another influence, the 'chronique [. . .] des femmes vertueuses et vicieuses' by 'Frère Jacques Philippe', is mentioned in Faustina's *vita*.[100] Peter F. Sands subsequently identifies this latter as Jacopo Filippo Foresti's *De plurimis claris selectisque mulieribus*, published in 1497, which was essentially a reworking of Boccaccio.[101] Taking the example of Juno, Sands shows how closely Dufour follows this new Latin model; however, in a *reprise de parole*, Jeanneau argues the contrary, demonstrating, through the example of Diana, that Dufour remains distant from Foresti.[102] My own observations agree at once with both and with neither scholar since, while it is certain that Dufour's selection and arrangement of *vitae* as well as, for example, his concern for dating the biographies are informed by Foresti,[103] the terms in which he represents these women frequently adhere to neither source.

A further complicating factor, to which Brown draws attention, is Dufour's deeply ambivalent relationship with Boccaccio.[104] In his prologue, Dufour seems to invoke *De mulieribus* as his source when he refers to his own enterprise as an act of linguistic translation: ('ay bien

---

[99] One might also apply the spectrality effect to fifteenth-century vernacular translations of *De mulieribus*, in at least some of which there is a tendency to conjure up this spectre in order to reinforce its potency, rather than reject it as Christine does. As Taylor has noted, the earliest translations actually amplify the anti-feminine aspects of Boccaccio's text: 2000.

[100] *Vies*, pp. xxxi, 113.

[101] Sands 1977. For the nature of this reworking, and the context in which it was produced, see Kolsky 2005: 117–47.

[102] Jeanneau 1977.

[103] Not one of the women celebrated by Dufour is not found in *De plurimis*, and they follow in the same order. As regards dating, Dufour notes, for example, that Semiramis was a contemporary of Sarah (*Vies* 23), whereas this temporal contextualization is absent from Boccaccio's biographies.

[104] Brown 2001.

voulu translater ce present livre en maternel langage'[105]) but he does so, somewhat puzzlingly, having just condemned Boccaccio as a detractor of women in the prologue's opening sentence: his ghost is both conjured up approvingly and con*jured*. Moreover, we must consider precisely which version of Boccaccio's work, in Latin or vernacular translation, Dufour consulted.[106] Elements of his prologue appear to be modelled on that of the 1493 translation,[107] already present in Anne of Brittany's collection, which was thus, perhaps, presumed to be part of his dedicatee's horizon of expectation; however, the translated text's own variants on *De mulieribus* do not account for the peculiarities of Dufour's *vitae*.[108] I argue, in sum, that Dufour's enterprise is unusually eclectic, and it is, we shall see, in his innovative use of his source material's gendered discourse that the interest of his work's often perplexing representations of women lies. Although not following programmatically any single model, his literary endeavour is, at least partly, a linguistic translation; indeed, I believe Dufour uses his explicit self-identification as translator of an unnamed model as an opportunity to play, in the sphere of a vernacular text, on his habitual role as Anne of Brittany's translator of Latin religious works.[109] In his prologue, having situated his current project in opposition to Boccaccio, he then alludes with deliberately imprecise deixis to 'ce present livre' that he is to render; he thereby sets up from the outset the ambiguous relationship he wishes to entertain with his sources.[110] What is important for my present purpose is the

[105] 'I very much wanted to translate this present book into [my] mother tongue': *Vies* 1. English translations are my own.

[106] If it was the translation, Dufour's mention in the prologue of having himself translated a book could either be construed as disingenuous or, more likely, be understood to refer to Foresti's work since *De plurimis* was only available in Latin.

[107] *Vies* 1, 174.

[108] Having read closely several *vitae* in two copies of this translation (see Appendix 2B and References), I disagree with Callu's and Avril's conclusion that the translator 'made do with revising the old anonymous translation from 1401': © 1975: 71. Whether she or he had this version before him or her or not, she or he certainly depended also upon a copy of Boccaccio's original. The later fifteenth-century vernacular translations of *De mulieribus* merit further study.

[109] Anne commissioned Dufour to translate the Old Testament, and also six letters of St Jerome (*c.*1505). As Rita Copeland makes clear, any translation must always suppose a hermeneutic, being a rhetorical operation 'necessarily bound up with the deepest questions of interpretation, signification, and reception': 1995: 37.

[110] His use of *De plurimis* raises the question of his readership's expected competence; according to Jeanneau, Anne of Brittany herself read both Latin and Greek (*Vies*, p. ix; cf. Matarasso 2001: 178), but would her *Court des dames* be equally exceptionally educated? Was Dufour already aiming at an audience beyond the immediate court of ladies?

attention to detail of word and phrase that Dufour's eclectic approach
to the art of translation implies, since this care suggests that the nuances
of gendered description that I examine in the *Vies* are consciously
contrived effects.[111] I shall explain, where necessary and where of
particular interest, how each of the four *vitae* studied here relates to its
sources. This essential intertextual dimension to the representation of
women can perhaps be seen as a specifically literary manifestation of the
notion of gender performativity as a citational practice: the exemplary
woman in question is both reiterated and called into question in the
same moment when she is re-presented in the new *querelle* text. The
new text maintains a critical and transformative relationship with its
antecedents.[112]

First, in the biography of Triaria, who disguises herself in order
to follow her husband, Lucius Vitellius into battle, the acquisition
of 'cuer d'omme' is synonymous with vestimentary cross-dressing.
Dufour highlights this coincidence seemingly in order to emphasize the
transitory nature of the woman's transvestment:

Oubliant son sexe et fragilité [. . .] ceste femme de chair et homme de cueur
suivit son mari ingénieusement et bien armée.[113]

(Forgetting her sex and frailty [. . .] this woman in body and man in spirit
followed her husband ingeniously, wearing full armour.)

It is a transvestism undertaken for legitimate reasons:[114] her masculine-
encoded conduct in battle, 'there where she conducted herself so bravely
(*virillement*)', is approved since its ultimate aim is a return to domestic
tranquillity: 'love and honourable behaviour' towards herself from her

---

[111] This attention is itself eclectic; we shall see that, although he observes closely
nuances of language and style in his *vitae*'s sources, he sometimes appears careless with
their content. This is perhaps most striking in the case of Joan of Arc: *Vies*, 165 n. 319.

[112] See Butler 2004: 1–3, 218. This citationality highlights a problem of authorship
shared by Butler's performativity and Derrida's spectrality: one's gender/identity has no
single author: its performance is, on the one hand, regulated by norms that already exist;
on the other hand, though, it is a conscious and active calling into question of these
norms in the very moment of reproducing them in an innovative fashion, whether this
reproduction is embodied corporeally (for Butler) or in language (for the *querelle* and for
Derrida's 'conjuring').

[113] *Vies* 108–9. See Boccaccio 2001: 408–10; *De la louenge* 1493: fols. Q6ᵛ–7ʳ;
Foresti 1521: fols. 62ʳ–63ʳ.

[114] Whilst the wearing of masculine attire by women was generally condemned as a
transgression of Deuteronomy 22, medieval theologians, including Aquinas, condoned
certain cases of 'necessity' after the example of female saints who dressed as men in order
to protect their virginity: see Schibanoff 1996: 40–1. For the idea of 'legitimate' and
'illegitimate' gender performance, see Eckert and McConnell-Ginet 2003: 320–1.

husband and 'peace in her home'.[115] The logic of Triaria's action is that she behaves in both masculine and feminine modes at the same time, although the former is privileged since her manly heart is, somewhat incongruously for a woman supposedly acting out of wifely devotion, stated to be the essence of her identity. Attenuating this incongruous hybridity, however, is the fact that, unlike both his sources, Dufour omits to mention Triaria's supposed 'ferocity',[116] thereby distancing her from the stereotype of the *virago* or 'virile woman' that Foresti praises. It is as if Dufour wished to experiment here with different, not always compatible, solutions to defining Triaria's gender identity through different combinations of masculine and feminine elements.

Dufour's Hypsicratea, another devoted wife following her husband into war, is a further example of temporary vestimentary transvestism corresponding to the doffing/donning of gendered characteristics, but one where the masculine, rather than the feminine, part is the external element, thereby avoiding the incongruity present in Triaria's *vita*.

Ipsicrethea fut femme du grant roy Mithridates, laquelle, comme plaine de grant cueur, voyant son mary ainsi subjugué et banny par Pompée, s'en vint [. . .] cercher son bienaymé mary. Et pour ce que sa beauté donnoit à ung chascun envie et que deux ou troys foys, en allant par le pays, cuyda estre viollée, pour y remédier et garder la loyaulté à son mary, mua ses habillemens et coupa ses cheveulx [. . .], se armant de toutes pièces, affin de n'estre plus priée ne solicitée. Et, pour mieulx le trouver, en passant par les terres des Rommains, faignoit estre chevalier de Pompée, qui suivoit Mithridates [. . .]. Tant fist qu'elle le trouva [. . .] elle se déclaire estre sa femme et par ainsi se despoille pour prendre ses habitz fémenins, qui fut une si grande joye à Mythridates.[117]

(Hypsicratea was the wife of Mithridates the Great, who, filled with a mighty heart, upon seeing her husband subjugated and banished by Pompey in this fashion, went off [. . .] to look for her beloved husband. And because her beauty provoked desire in every man, and because, two or three times, passing through the kingdom, she thought she was going to be raped, in order to deal with this threat and to remain faithful to her husband, she changed her clothes and cut her hair [. . .], putting on full body armour, so that she would no longer be importuned or solicited. Moreover, the better to find him whilst passing through Roman lands, she pretended to be one of Pompey's soldiers who was

---

[115] *Vies* 109. This curious anecdote of the 'ransom' (*rançon*) to which Triaria holds her husband is unique to Dufour; in his version, she is thus allowed to strike a deal to her advantage, to ask for what *she* wants to gain out of saving her husband's life.

[116] *ferocitas*: Boccaccio 2001: 408; Foresti 1521: fol. 62^r.

[117] *Vies* 84–5. Note, however, her ultimate, cruel fate, poisoned by an ungrateful Mithridates.

pursuing Mithridates [. . .]. Eventually she found him [. . .] she declared herself to be his wife, and thus divested herself in order to put on her feminine attire, which was such a great joy to Mithridates.)

Dufour's innovation here is to inscribe a symmetry of transvestite acts in the narrative recounting Hypsicratea's pursuit of her husband on the battlefield. When she sets out, she 'mua ses habillemens et coupa ses cheveulx' for the respectable reason that she fears for her chastity; her transvestism is approved as the act of a loyal spouse, 'pour [. . .] garder la loyaulté à son mary'. Once reunited with her husband, therefore, she can divest herself freely and resume feminine attire: 'se despoille pour prendre ses habitz fémenins.' Hypsicratea's doffing and redonning of garments highlights her external transvestism not only as acts motivated by prudence and propriety, but also as an art of role-playing: she temporarily performs a male identity in order to get what she wants. This idea of performance is all the more significant as Dufour stresses the superficiality of her transvestment. Unlike his sources, he does not characterize the courtly wife's transformation into a warrior as an acquisition of the internal qualities of a manly spirit: *animus virili*.[118] Similarly, Dufour changes her motives for wanting to disguise herself. His sources held that it was a question of decorum: to appear as a woman on the battlefield would have been indecent.[119] In the *Vies*, Hypsicratea is motivated not by regulatory social norms, but by what we might see as the more positively feminine, pragmatic reason of wanting to protect herself from sexual attack in order to remain a loyal wife. Dufour's alteration here could, of course, be seen as a retrograde step: a way of circumscribing Hypsicratea's activity to her accepted social role as loyal wife. However, in the same way that Dufour's selection of vocabulary must be considered within his work's intertextual context, it is also necessary to consider any extratextual influence operating on his choices, specifically as regards his patronage. Given that he was writing his *Vies* as a commission from Anne of Brittany, his alteration of the motive of decorum could be seen strategically to delete any acknowledgement of female inferiority; such an acknowledgement

---

[118] 'animo virili predita', Boccaccio 2001: 324; 'virili animo insignita', Foresti 1521: fol. 49ʳ. Both expressions, but especially Foresti's term *insignita* ('marked'), draw attention to Hypsicratea's transvestment as a double cross-over, affecting both her internal and her external body.

[119] 'indecens lateri bellicosissimi regis incedere foeminam', Foresti 1521: fol. 49ʳ; Boccaccio 2001: 322.

would hardly be appropriate for a patron who was twice Queen of France, by Charles VIII and, subsequently, Louis XII.

As a point of comparison, we note that Christine's versions of both Hypsicratea and Triaria scrupulously avoid characterizing either woman's conduct in masculine/feminine gendered terms, preferring to refer instead to the function that each woman enables herself to fulfil by dint of being cross-dressed. When describing how Hypsicratea 'estoit convertie si comme en un tres fort et viguereux chevalier armé',[120] it is the military role she is to assume that affects the external state of her body and not this role's culturally mapped gender association. It is only when she quotes Boccaccio directly that Christine engages with gender-transformative language, citing his assertion that Hypsicratea advanced 'comme se fust homme'.[121] The isolated nature of this appearance of gender vocabulary within the *vita* perhaps supports the argument that Christine is using citation as a critical tool: her reuse of the normative form of representation, far from reaffirming the disguised wife's emulation of 'l'idéal héroïque masculin', deconstructs this supposed ideal, challenging or even undermining its value as a mechanism for defining woman's activity. The phrase 'comme se fust homme' seems evacuated of meaning, making the *Cité*'s modern readership recall the speaker of the *Triomphe des dames* who makes explicit this redundancy. Developing her argument for the instability of sexual difference, and having listed several examples of women transforming into, or being mistaken for, men, she concludes:

Mais je ne veulx étudier advantage à montrer que nous pouvons estre hommes—cela n'adjouste rien à nostre honneur; aussi n'enten-je pas m'en prevaloir.[122]

(But I don't want to spend any more time demonstrating that we can be men—that adds nothing to our honour, and so I don't intend to boast about it.)

The ability of a woman to act 'comme se fust homme', and thus to be portrayed in such immasculating terms, is denigrated as something utterly dispensable to feminine honour—quite contrary to the 'indispensable' masculine ideal posited by Dulac; 'l'éloge superlatif' is presented as being accessible to women on their own terms.

---

[120] '[She] was transformed into a very strong and vigorous armed knight': Christine de Pizan 1997: 258.

[121] Christine de Pizan 1997: 'Like a man'.   [122] [Pierre de Brinon] 1599: 11.

In the sixteenth century, Jean Bouchet seems to follow Christine's suit in his portrait of Hypsicratea. Her epitaph presents her negotiating her role without reference to gender-based terms of conduct.[123] What Bouchet valorizes is Hypsicratea's wifely (thus, implicitly, feminine) heart as the principal motive for following Mithridates into battle: 'J'eu telle amour, et coeur si bon, et franc' (*JP*, v. 2066).[124] This expression of desire is interesting. As in Dufour's portrait, there are intertextual and extratextual contexts in which we are invited to interpret the writer's remodelling of this woman's identity—contexts which prevent us from dismissing a male-authored representation of an active woman as an attempt to reinscribe her in a conventionally feminine, conformist wifely role. Reading intertextually, Bouchet's Hypsicratea departs from Christine's (and certainly Boccaccio's) in one, rather fascinating detail: whilst her motivation is love for her husband, she expresses her action first and foremost as a fulfilment of personal desire: 'mon désir' (v. 2069).[125] One other *querelle* text highlights this independence of spirit: Martin Le Franc's eponymous Champion of ladies acclaims Hypsicratea's 'perfect love' (*CD*, v. 16730), but concludes his portrait by emphasizing her autonomous, unconventional wish to take up arms:

> Mais elle voulut a son tour
> Les fais de guerre soustenir.
>
> (*CD*, vv. 16735–6)

(But she wanted, in her turn, to endure the deeds of war.)

Like a Shakespearian Desdemona *avant la lettre*, Hypsicratea is portrayed as a dutiful wife whose own desire as a woman leads her into the fray of battle. Whereas Christine's character appropriates military costume for her feminine purposes such that she remains only externally 'like' a knight, Le Franc's and Bouchet's Hypsicratea is also endowed with a 'cuer de chevalier' that associates her with the warrior women of the

---

[123] It is not impossible that Bouchet was drawing on the *Cité*, notwithstanding the fact that it was not printed in the sixteenth century. On the reception of Christine by the *rhétoriqueurs*, see Brown 1998. Cf. Bouchet 2006: 399, n. 410, and Berriot-Salvadore 1990: 347.

[124] 'I felt such love, and had a heart so fine and true': cf. Bouchet's Penthesilea: *JP*, vv. 1792–803.

[125] The extratextual context would concern how Bouchet calibrates certain exemplary women according to the sort of 'idéal' he represents as having been embodied by the historical noblewoman whom the *Jugement* commemorates, his patron's late mother, Louise of Savoy. See below, pp. 213–14.

querelle, including Joan of Arc, who are praised as feminine knights in body and mind through their appellation by the term 'chevaleresses' (*CD*, v. 17054).[126]

Dufour's gendering of woman's noble conduct is not confined to those examples where literal transvestism is undertaken, nor is his ambivalence in handling their active virtue. My third example, Artemis, is striking in this regard. Christine, Dufour, and Bouchet all address her as a hybrid example of virtue, resulting from a conflation of two distinct figures: Artemis devoted widow of Mausolus, and Artemis (or Artemidora) who fought on behalf of Xerxes.[127] Her character thus lends itself to definition in gendered terms: her immasculated role as a virtuous widow taking up arms, like Semiramis or Christine's chatelaine, succeeds her role as loyal wife. Boccaccio forges Artemis' hybridity by accepting that 'each undertaking was still that of a woman' ('opus quippe fuit femineum unumquodque'), but he uses this duality to point to a contradiction:

Sed quid [. . .] arbitrari possumus, nise nature laborantis errore factum ut corpori, cui Deus virilem et magnificam infuderat animam, sexus femineus datus sit?[128]

(What [. . .] can we think except that the workings of nature erred in bestowing female sex on a body which God had endowed with a virile and lofty spirit?)

Her virile spirit encased in woman's flesh is portrayed, as in the case of Dufour's Triaria, as a freakish anomaly; her femininity utterly at odds with her military accomplishment. The contradiction Boccaccio perceives in her gender identity works to the detriment of her femininity. In a *vita* that otherwise follows *De mulieribus* closely, the 1493 translation omits Boccaccio's comment that both roles played by Artemis were 'acts of women', perhaps seeing this to be somewhat at odds with the subsequent assertion of Artemis' virility or 'un-woman-ness'. The translation thereby irons out one of the interpretative creases, so to speak, that make Boccaccio's work so provocative of response.[129]

---

[126] Cf. Marot's Advocate's characterization of contemporary women as 'chevaleur-euses' who have Anne of Brittany as their 'emblem of honour': *VDA*, vv. 722–3.

[127] Christine de Pizan 1997: 137–40, 263; *Vies*, 73–5; *JP*, vv. 2000–15. Armstrong explains the sources of this hybridity: Bouchet 2006: 453–4. Champier addresses Artemis solely as a widow: *NDV*, fols. Eᵛ–E2ʳ.

[128] Boccaccio 2001: 240–2. The 1401 translation expands on the meaning of 'viril' ('force virile, c'est assavoir d'omme') so as to emphasize the paradox of Artemis' identity: *Nobles femmes* 1993: ii. 21.

[129] As Brown-Grant has made clear, *De mulieribus* itself is far from unitary or consistent in its manner of praising women: 1995: 473.

Subsequent *querelle* writers use Artemis' hybrid identity for the same purpose as Boccaccio, to open up the question of gendered conduct, but diverge from him in that they do not perceive Artemis' femininity to be at odds with her achievement. An even more complex perspective emerges in the *Vies*. Dufour concludes his *vita* with a curious homage:

tant virillement se monstra qu'elle chassa Xercès et sa grosse compaignie, qui en fuyant disoit: 'Je ne croy point que Arthémisie ne soit ung ange ou ung deable!' Après avoir pacifiquement son pays gouverné, mourut femme bien estimée et renommée.[130]

(She performed in so virile a manner that she put to flight Xerxes and his great army, who cried out whilst fleeing: 'I do not believe that Artemis is not an angel or a devil!' Having ruled her kingdom in peace, she died a well esteemed and renowned woman.)

Apparently unique amongst *querelle* biographies of Artemis, Dufour's concluding anecdote seems almost calculated to focus attention on the question not just of her gender, but of her very being. She fights as a man, dies as a woman, and, just to complicate further her ontological status, seems to exceed both male and female natures: her accomplishments make her supernatural. Although Dufour uses here the heavily loaded Latinate term 'viril', translating Boccaccio's lexeme of choice for describing woman's supreme achievement in surpassing her sex,[131] he uses it oddly: it appears in a context which suggests the transitory nature of Artemis' virility as an expedient performance rather than a permanent feature of her spirit that is at odds with her female nature. Moreover, Dufour omits the transsexualizing comment made in praise of Artemis which is present in all his sources, that she fought 'quasi cum Xerxe sexum mutasset'.[132] By opting not to impose this ultimate virility on Artemis, Dufour effectively follows Christine de Pizan's account of the warrior-queen, whom she consistently portrays in terms of her identity as a woman: 'chevaleureuse', 'ceste royne', 'la

---

[130] *Vies* 75. Dufour—like Christine and, later, Bouchet—errs in having Artemis fighting *against* Xerxes, perhaps on account of ambiguity present in *De mulieribus* and *De plurimis*: see Bouchet 2006: 453–4. Her alliance with the Persians is presented correctly by Le Franc (*CD*, vv. 16675–7), and also by Foresti's chronicle anthology of 1492, the *Supplementum supplementi cronicarum*: fol. 113ʳ. Armstrong (2004: 166) notes the *Supplementum* as a probable further source for Dufour and Bouchet.

[131] The *Nobles femmes* follows Boccaccio's usage of this lexeme, whereas Christine de Pizan eschews it entirely (Brown-Grant 2002: 167), except when explaining the meaning of 'Dido' as the Carthaginian equivalent of Latin '*virago*': 1997: 210.

[132] '[It was] almost as if she had changed sex with Xerxes': Boccaccio 2001: 240; *De la louenge* 1493: fol. K7ʳ; Foresti 1521: fol. 46ʳ.

vaillant Arthemise', concluding her *vita*, like Dufour, on an image of feminine glory achieved by 'celle vaillant dame'.[133]

Dufour's representation of Artemis seems to endow her with a fluidity of gender identity redolent of Christine's Fredegonde, proposing a configuration of masculinity-and-femininity that we might usefully consider in light of both Butler's performativity and the feminist critic Luce Irigaray's idea that woman practises a different logic of identity from man. In Dufour's account, not only Artemis' gender, but also her human status are illegible; she cannot be recognized, and Dufour resists the logic that that assimilates her conduct to a recognizable masculine ideal, thereby declining to impose such a normative view of gender behaviour. Artemis is presented as an indeterminable identity in terms of gender; her 'doings' do not add up to a coherent personhood, but she is still designated *elle*, a feminine 'she'. Irigaray postulates a positively valued position of uncertainty for femininity that may be seen to resonate with Dufour's biography of Artemis. This position is fundamentally plural and thereby resistant to any quantitative approach, thus also to any binary thinking that characterizes a masculinist system of gender classification:

Elle n'est ni une ni deux. On ne peut, en toute rigueur, la déterminer comme une personne, pas davantage comme deux. [. . .] Sa sexualité, toujours au moins double, est encore *plurielle* [. . .] 'elle' part dans tous les sens sans qu''il' y repère la cohérence d'aucun sens.[134]

(*She is neither one nor two.* Rigorously speaking, she cannot be identified either as one person, or as two. [. . .] Her sexuality, always at least double, goes even further: it is *plural* [. . .] 'she' sets off in all directions leaving 'him' unable to discern the coherence of any meaning.)[135]

In Dufour's *vita* of Artemis, therefore, Xerxes' stupefaction in the face of this woman's achievement and his inability to read her according to a heaven—hell binary can be seen as a diegetic echo of the way Dufour's authorial construction of her identity challenges (male) expectation: it critiques and innovates upon the received view of Artemis derived from the Boccaccian tradition. His depiction of her sexuality plays with the masculine—feminine binary, 'jamming its theoretical machinery', to

---

[133] Christine de Pizan 1997: 140. Christine reappropriates virtue-adjectives culturally mapped 'masculine' to describe Artemis' feminine identity: 'la preux et sage Arthemise' (p. 138).

[134] 1977: 26–8. Italics are Irigaray's own emphases.

[135] I follow Porter's translation: Irigaray 1985: 26–9.

quote Irigaray,[136] and rendering her illegible according to its terms. She is praised not only for her conduct when acting *virillement*, with 'cuer d'omme', on the battlefield, but equally for her subsequent peaceful government in a role, as ruler of her kingdom, that could still be culturally construed as masculine but is here remade for a woman.

A similar negotiation between codes of representation arises in Bouchet's epitaph for Artemis (LI). As a hybrid figure, she receives one of the longer epitaphs in the *Jugement*,[137] and the apportionment of its sixteen lines to the different aspects of her biography is revealing: the first thirteen lines relate to her fulfilment of her proper wifely duty, mourning the loss of Mausolus : '. . . que d'amour de mon espoux saisie | Fuz si tresfort . . .';[138] it is only in the final three lines that she speaks, summarily, of defeating Xerxes:

> Oultre je fuz aux armes tant propice,
> Qu'en excedant le femenin office
> Rendy Xersès fuyant, et despourveu.
>
> *(JP*, vv. 2013–15)

(Moreover I was so adept at fighting that, exceeding woman's office, I put Xerxes to flight and routed him.)

The gendered adjective is significant as a denotative term: it highlights Artemis' awareness of exceeding her culturally gendered 'office' in the legitimate context of political expediency—the necessity for the widow to take upon herself her late husband's duties, like Christine 'becoming' man in her *Mutacion*. However, Artemis is not only, or even principally, being honoured for overcoming her allotted role as a woman since the preceding, overriding emphasis in her epitaph on as it were her 'cuer de femme' ensures that she remains essentially and laudably feminine.

The delicate balance in Bouchet's portrait and the propriety of Artemis' conduct should be read in the context of the *Jugement*'s 'determining' female presence, the late Louise of Savoy, whose own conduct, as depicted during the poem's trial scene, operates as a sort of fulcrum for reading the palace's other occupants. For example, Fortune, a nymph summoned to bear witness to Louise's character, testifies that, like Artemis against Xerxes, she surpassed the strength of her sex ('elle passa de son sexe la force' *(JP*, v. 889)), noting that:

---

[136] 1977: 75: 'Autrement dit, l'enjeu [est] d'enrayer la machinerie théorique elle-même'.

[137] See Bouchet 2006: 100–3.

[138] '. . . I was overwhelmed with love for my husband': *JP*, vv. 2003–4.

> Je sceu tant bien son cas entretenir
> Que je l'ay faicte aux honneurs parvenir
> Non seulement femenins, mais virilles:
> [. . .]
> Mais tout conduict par temps, et par saison.

(JP, vv. 899–901, 908)

(I knew so well how to support her case that I bestowed on her, not only feminine, but also masculine honours. [. . .] But she always behaved with due propriety.)

We might be tempted to conclude here that Fortune's rhetoric is simply the usual hyperbole constituting, in Dulac's terms, a classic case of the hierarchical assumption about gender and praise: 'le modèle héroïque masculin est indispensable à l'éloge superlatif.' In this light, Fortune's subsequent comment that Louise always maintained due propriety in her conduct as a lady, notwithstanding her 'transgression' into virility, would merely be read as a bit of rhetorical padding to keep the royal lady in her culturally prescribed, 'proper' place. However, the terms Fortune uses in the above quotation are not those of the aforementioned equation: 'abandon femininity + acquire masculinity = virtue and renown'. Her terms are those of harmonious coexistence, privileging rather than rejecting femininity, and complementing it with masculine virtues in order to produce another, hybrid identity: 'not only feminine, but also masculine'. Through the voice of the nymph, Bouchet adumbrates a genuine complementarity of gender identity.[139] At the *Jugement*'s conclusion, Honour's eulogy of Louise restates this concept in terms which valorize more explicitly the broadened scope of activity deemed appropriate for honourable ladies:

> Elle fut femme, et œuvres d'homme feit:
> En quoy jamais au sexe ne meffit.

(JP, vv. 3686–7)

(She was a woman, and carried out the tasks of men; in this, she never acted against her sex.)

There is no mutual exclusivity, but instead an affirmation of non-contradictory coexistence that effectively confirms the conviction of

---

[139] However, Armstrong (2002: 179–81) rightly notes some 'play' in the system of Bouchet's *Jugement*: the proposition of complementary gender offices made by his diegetic speakers does not square with the normative statements about gender identity that he makes in his paratextual *Apologie* to Anne de Laval.

Christine's Dame Raison, quoted above, that one must not assume 'que du sexe femenin soit forclose toute force a hardiece corporelle'. Through the same device of the collocative phrase ('œuvres d'homme') preferred by Christine, Bouchet seems here to offer a way for a woman to expand the deeds judged congruous with her culturally ascribed 'office' without sacrificing her essential femininity in the process, and without committing any social impropriety.[140]

It is interesting to compare the way hybridity functions as a discourse of gender identity amongst *querelle* writers with Caroline Walker Bynum's investigations into hybridity as an image of change in personal identity in medieval writings. She acknowledges that the hybrid can destabilize expectation and boundaries, but proposes that it marks a resistance to change: what its 'rhetoric forces us to encounter is not change but contradiction'; instead of subverting a binary, it is 'often only a rather desperate—and ultimately only rhetorical—effort to wriggle out of the trap of either-or'.[141] By contrast, the sort of 'both . . . and' proposed by Christine and Bouchet aims to disrupt expectation by promoting *non*-contradictory coexistence, by representing conduct that would conventionally be classified masculine as something that is equally proper for a woman. Moreover, this change in signification is grounded in social reality, not just rhetorical play. Bouchet's proposition is applied to a contemporary, historical example, Louise of Savoy, and not only promoted in a distant, mythological past. We should acknowledge, though, that this distinction between reality and rhetoric is not clear-cut within the *Jugement*'s fictional frame: Fortune, herself a fictionalized goddess, magnifies the admirable nature of Louise's 'honours'

> Fort aprochans des honneurs magnifiques
> Qu'on feit jadis à tous les Heroïques.
>
> (*JP*, vv. 865–6)

(coming very close to the magnificent honours that used to be bestowed on all antique deities.)

By comparing the magnitude of her renown with the tributes accorded to antique deities, Fortune effectively mythologizes the sixteenth-century lady.

The sort of admiration these women's achievements excite may be seen to anticipate the wonderment inspired by the Renaissance 'femme

---

[140] Cf. *CD*, vv. 16641–4.   [141] Bynum 2001: 31, 187–8.

forte'. Ian Maclean notes how the paradox of the exceptional woman, in moralistic literature not unlike the *Vies*, carries a sting in its tail regarding gendered conduct: the impact of the 'femme forte' depends upon 'the assumption of female weakness [. . .]. Without such a contrast, the figure of the femme forte would lose much of its force.'[142] I bear in mind this sort of dependency on traditional, largely anti-feminine, gender stereotypes in turning to consider, as my final example of problematic gendered vocabulary, a woman who explicitly inspires Dufour's wonderment at the achievements of the female sex. Maria Puteolina (= Maria of Puzzuoli), a contemporary of Petrarch and a highly successful protector of her native Campania, lived

toute dédiée à des choses grandes et honnestes, évitant toutes modes féminines, usant d'une merveilleuse façon de vivre.[143]

(giving herself over entirely to great and honourable works, avoiding all feminine ways, practising a wondrous way of life.)

Her 'wondrous' way of life thus defines itself in opposition to the culturally defined expectation of a nobly born woman's lifestyle; it consists, we are told, of sobriety, little sleep, and constant activity. The term 'merveilleux' recurs throughout her *vita*; Dufour reports how Robert, King of Sicily, praised her:

'Nous sommes en merveileux temps là ou il fault qu'une femme en touz faitz certamineux passe les hommes.'[144]

(We are living in wondrous times when we see a woman surpassing men in all military deeds.)

What does this interpolated speech imply? Dufour omits to gloss his meaning: whether the imputation is that women have gone too far, or, conversely, whether he is using Maria's exceptionality as a woman to criticize a decline in masculinity. The paradox is clear, however: a woman has surpassed *both* sexes and her accomplishments are astonishing. Dufour cunningly avoids implicating himself in the misogynistic assumption of general feminine weakness that his wonderment at Maria risks entailing by using her *vita* as an *exemplum* to gesture to the potential

---

[142] Maclean 1977: 71.
[143] *Vies* 157. Maria's *vita*, which is not included by Boccaccio, features in Foresti (1521: fols. 134ʳ–134ᵛ), and is drawn from one of Petrarch's letters: 1974: i, 5.4, pp. 513–17.
[144] *Vies* 158.

in *all* women to succeed after her example. Maria can stand as the rule and not the exception, as Dufour cites the redoubtable lady:

'Tenez-vous seurs que, si les dames estoient en leur jeune eage exercitées es armes et faitz de guerre aussi bien que les homes, que bien peu on trouveroit de leurs semblables.'[145]

(Rest assured that, if ladies were trained in arms and deeds of war in their youth as well as men are, one would find very few [men] to match them.)

Maria enlists the familiar nature–nurture argument, which, as part of the arsenal of the pro-feminine case since Christine, underpins *querelle* writers' differentiation between female sex and feminine gender, and their claim for a more malleable understanding of the range of qualities and activities that may be judged 'proper' to women. She is arguing not that women should become more like men to the exclusion of their femininity, like Boccaccio's and Foresti's *viragos*,[146] but rather that, if offered the same opportunity and education, women would surpass, not merely equal, men and thereby perform 'faitz de guerre' as legitimate feminine activities.[147]

'BECOMING' WOMAN: CONTEXTUALIZING GENDER IDENTITY

The four problematic examples that I have discussed do not enable the reader, medieval or modern, to draw a universal conclusion about Dufour's approach to defining women's excellence in gendered terms. His *vitae* mobilize no unitary discourse on woman's status when exercising an active role that is contrary to her culturally ascribed 'femenin office': for example, he eschews reference to the virile ideal of behaviour already present in his sources' accounts of Hypsicratea and Artemis, but

---

[145] Ibid. Maria's speech, like Xerxes', is Dufour's innovation. Of interest with regard to the *merveilleux* is Bynum's discussion of wonder discourses circulating in the Middle Ages, according to many of which wonder is 'based in facticity and singularity' (2001: 73). The latter point is of especial note in the case of Dufour's Maria, since he both maintains that she is marvellous and evokes what Bynum views to be the opposite of wonder by offering her as an example to be imitated or generalized.

[146] Unlike Petrarch's and Foresti's Maria, she is not physically immasculated, but remains identifiable as 'femme' throughout: see below, n. 155. Cf. Boccaccio's description of how athletic, military training immasculated Amazon girls' bodies: 2001: 52.

[147] Unlike Dufour's King of Sicily, Foresti admires Maria's ability merely to compete with men, not to defeat them: 1521: fol. 134[v].

then chooses to introduce the term into biographies where no such lex-eme pre-exists.[148] Dufour is clearly not constrained by his sources, espe-cially in his most frequent innovation of introducing characters' speech, which often serves to project an imagined, contemporary perspective on the woman in question—such as Xerxes' and Robert of Sicily's reflec-tions—within the diegesis of the *vita* and thus, it is implied, within the particular ideological context in which the woman's conduct is to be understood. It almost appears to be Dufour's policy to surprise the reader by subverting their expectations of how a given *vita* from the established catalogue of exemplary women should be represented: martial women are refeminized, apparent victims are masculinized, and others present contradictions or perplexing ambiguities, such as Triaria and Artemis.[149]

I suggest that the apparent incoherencies in the gender identity of Dufour's ladies may be attributed in part to this desire to refashion. He thereby engages his audience in a sort of intertextual interpretative adventure, especially if we consider that Dufour may have been intending his work specifically to be played off against *De la louenge*. The *vitae*'s inconsistencies and peculiarities may also be explained by the historical context of Dufour's commission to compile a new catalogue of virtuous women perhaps for use by Anne as a *speculum dominarum* in her 'escole des dames'.[150] Dufour seems conscious throughout his *Vies* of orienting his *vitae* towards the interests and character of his patron; it is, after all, in this respect that his own 'translation' project can differentiate itself from the previous catalogue of ladies inspired by her, *De la louenge*, since he has greater room for hermeneutic manoeuvre. In the 1493 translation of *De mulieribus*, published by Antoine Vérard, it is principally the work's paratext that evokes the spirit and context in which the work should be received. Its prologue promises to disseminate the Queen's 'most famous name', and suggests how 'reading this present volume may arouse and awaken the noble spirit of many ladies'.[151] The woodcut at its head, which is repeated several times to introduce subsequent *vitae*, shows

---

[148] This occurs, for example, in the case of Sophonisba, whose gesture of noble suicide is praised for being performed 'virillement' (*Vies* 81). This immasculation is Dufour's own innovation upon Boccaccio (2001: 288–94) and Foresti (1521: fol. 47ᵛ).

[149] It is interesting to read this subversion of expectation in light of a recent definition of misogyny that Blamires adopts in his *Case for Women*: 'any presentation of a woman's nature intended to conform her to male expectations of what she is or ought to be': 1997: 11.

[150] As Brown notes, Dufour makes numerous references in his *vitae* to a 'mirror' in this sense of an exemplary model: 1999: 212 n. 16.

[151] *De la louenge* 1493: fols. A2ᵛ, A2ʳ.

an enthroned queen with her book to hand and several ladies seated before her in a relaxed manner suggestive of a private meeting, perhaps a session of Anne's 'escole'. Interestingly, the prologue and woodcuts are included only in the paper copies of Vérard's edition, intended for an unknown though presumably sizeable audience, and are absent from the vellum copies crafted especially for the kings of England and France.[152] This pattern of production suggests that the Queen's broader public image was Vérard's primary target in tailoring *De la louenge* through its paratext. In Dufour's *Vies*, the text itself, by not being tied to an individual source, can be manipulated more freely and creatively to curry favour with the Queen; it is here Anne herself, as commissioner and recipient of a lavish manuscript, who is the target audience.

Dufour's textual tailorings concern some of the retouchings and changes of emphasis made to the four *vitae* discussed above. The retouchings given to Triaria's and Hypsicratea's *vitae* to focus on their motivations for transvestment, acting out of wifely devotion, may be intended as a tribute both to Anne's devotion to Louis XII, her third husband,[153] and to her continued commitment to France itself via this marriage to her late husband's (Charles VIII's) successor. Similarly, Maria Puteolina's rigorous lifestyle, avoiding 'modes féminines', would be approved by a queen renowned for her exacting standards of conduct. We recall here Anne of France's criticism of feminine foolishness in her *Enseignements*, and her enlistment of negative *exempla* in order to instruct Suzanne. Should the prerogative for criticizing women by using 'feminine' as a negatively connoted gendered adjective within a rhetorical enterprise that is part conduct manual and part pro-feminine argument be reserved uniquely for female authors? Must it be encoded 'anti-feminine' when it appears under a male pen, especially when, as appears to be the case with Dufour, these negative images are directed to serving not so much his own didactic purposes as those of his female patron? We might also see Dufour's selection of Maria Puteolina as a strategic choice regarding Anne's public role: the Italian woman's relentless exertions to defend Campania parallel Anne's lifelong commitment to safeguarding the autonomy of her native Brittany within the kingdom of France. Dufour suggests this parallel by inserting mention of Maria's civic-mindedness into the list of her achievements that he copies from

---

[152] See Brown 2007a.
[153] Minois notes Anne's renowned wifely devotion in the face of her husbands' inconstancy: 1999: 429.

Petrarch and/or Foresti, highlighting her 'ardante' attention to 'la chose publique'.[154] A shift in emphasis is also apparent: whereas Petrarch's Maria is presented as a 'cross-over' case of transvestment, with Petrarch mistakenly offering her greeting 'as if to an unknown man', and is valorized primarily for her chastity and deeds of arms,[155] Dufour's refeminized figure is endowed with political acumen as well as physical strength, and is accorded a speech that sets her up as a champion of women's education, albeit martial rather than the moral and literary training offered by Anne's 'escole'.

There is a political edge to Dufour's literary project of adjusting the parameters within which a woman's identity qua *woman* may be performed. Like Marot and Bouchet, he as it were calibrates his biographies according to his target audience such that his patron becomes the dominant norm against which his exemplary tales are modelled.[156] His tales, in turn, stand as performances of aspects of her identity, intended to project a personhood that the Queen recognizes as her own performances, her own desired public image as an authoritative, strictly principled manager of court life, a devoted wife, a caring and educative mother.[157] Dufour imagines possibilities of woman's accomplishments being accomplished on woman's terms; these represent, in fact, the possibilities that are lived out, or are imagined to be liveable out, by Anne on *her* terms as his patron and his Queen. It is interesting to speculate whether Dufour's projected image corresponded to Anne's own image of herself. We may recall here Anne of France's rejection of Champier's *Nef*, which might be explained as the result of a *lack* of correspondence, of the Duchess not seeing herself in the same terms as those in which Champier wanted to present her.

It is possible to conclude that Dufour's subtle, even experimental, approach to representing gender identity, whether informed by stylistic, literary, or pragmatic concerns, frequently calls into question the universal model of feminine excellence proposed by Dulac's equation: 'abandon femininity' + 'acquire masculinity' = virtue and renown. He

---

[154] *Vies* 158.

[155] 1974: 515. Foresti's figure is similarly immasculated, with particular emphasis on her ferocity ('bellicosissima foemina') and on the impossibility of reconciling the positively valued virility she has taken on with the negatively valued femininity she has cast off: 1521: fols. 134^r–134^v.

[156] Cf. above, nn. 77, 125.

[157] Anne lost all her children by Charles VIII, and by the time of Dufour's commission she had only Claude (b. 1499).

appears, deliberately or otherwise, and as the effect of his insistence upon applying gendered descriptions to diverse contexts, to fracture any univocal understanding of femininity, and to propose, like Christine, that conventionally masculine qualities are by no means the preserve of masculinity. Moreover, Dufour also seems to adumbrate a sort of otherness, what I call a 'third term', to denote the capacity of certain women to surpass the expectations of either sex. Even though this third term remains definable only in relation to, or as an exclusion of, the established cultural matrix of intelligible gender identity, we may nevertheless view this term as a discursive gesture operating as a critique of the binary norm: interrogating the terms by which gender representation is constrained in order to open up different discursive possibilities.

CONCLUSION: REPRESENTATION AS NEGOTIATION

This chapter's study of transvestisms has focused on specific examples of women traced through different texts. It is consequently difficult to draw any general conclusion regarding different authors' approaches to representing women in gendered terms, and what this reveals about the nature of the feminine excellence they seek to promote in active women. Four possibilities are, however, identifiable: first, and most frequently, this feminine excellence is depicted in terms of a heroic, masculine model of virility; secondly, woman's achievements are often defined as surpassing the expectations of either sex; thirdly, intelligible gender categories are sometimes broken down to incorporate culturally defined masculine virtues into a femininity that defines woman more as it were on her own terms, following the direction in which Christine begins to point in her *Cité*; fourthly, a writer may reinstate the positive value of essential feminine qualities as wellsprings of supreme virtue that are uniquely woman's prerogative, and which elevate her rank in the hierarchy of Creation as a model of good conduct. Indeed, one of the effects I sought by selecting different examples from Dufour's *Vies* was to highlight the hermeneutic complexity present amongst a single author's portraits of active women. As Armstrong has highlighted with regard to Bouchet, it is crucially important not to suppress the heterogeneity present in *querelle* defences, especially those structured, like Dufour's *Vies*, as a catalogue of discrete *vitae* that do not seek to impose a homogeneous, coherent theory of, or a uniform code for, representing feminine identity.[158] The most profitable reading strategy for approaching these texts is thus one that recognizes each *vita* as a hermeneutic performance, a site of negotiation between a range of rhetorical and historical concerns.

I propose the following, tentative conclusions. Questions of transvestism, both vestimentary and figurative, are a prominent discourse in the *querelle des femmes*, especially in the use of gender adjectives to represent the doffing and donning of external and internal masculine or feminine characteristics. Through her 'neutralizing' rewriting of Boccaccio's positively loaded terms of virility and negatively loaded terms of femininity, Christine de Pizan forges new discursive possibilities for constructing gender identity. She favours collocations that can be used to designate women's taking on of a role, which, rather than opening up a contradiction with their femininity, suggests an enlarged scope of activity to be ranged beneath the banner of feminine identity. Aware of the limitations and pitfalls of gender vocabulary, Christine promotes a feminine subject who, in a manner akin to Judith Butler's concern with gender being constructed through performance as a 'doing' not a 'being', is 'performatively constituted' by verbal acts.[159] The innovative ways Christine deploys existing vocabulary signifying culturally ascribed norms of gendered conduct—'paour femenine' or 'hardiece d'omme'—create new linguistic configurations which fracture previously coherent notions of 'intelligible gender'. The figuratively cross-dressed, first-person narrator of Christine's *Mutacion* opens up new, creative possibilities for negotiating the linguistic representation of a woman's identity.

The use of gendered terminology in later catalogues of women is largely determined by the line of literary inheritance *querelle* writers choose to follow, as well as by extradiegetic, historically contingent considerations of patronage and audience. By following Boccaccio and Foresti, Dufour inevitably engages with value-laden gender adjectives but seems, unlike his predecessors, to wrestle with them in such a way as to fracture their coherence and thus gesture towards a feminine excellence that is not limited to the ideal of a woman needing to overcome her nature to achieve honour. Women such as Maria Puteolina act according to their feminine nature so as to exceed both sexes, while Artemis and Triaria manifest a sort of hybridity, however

---

[158] 2003: 228.   [159] 1990a: 25.

uneasy, between masculine and feminine identities. A more thorough-going complementarity underpins several of Bouchet's epitaphs; their representations of Semiramis, Hypsicratea, and Artemis appear to have been devised in dialogue with the writer's portrayal of Louise of Savoy's amalgamation of gender roles, and also seem informed (consciously or indirectly) by Christine's 'expedient' gender roles denoted by collocative phrases of the type 'cuer d'omme'.

The binary thinking endemic in structural misogyny and the poten-tially value-laden, connotative gender vocabulary that realizes this thinking in language does, as Alcuin Blamires remarks, give the medieval case for women very little discursive room in which to manoeuvre;[160] it haunts their case. However, right from Christine's careful reworking of Boccaccio's *De mulieribus*, beginning with Semiramis, attention to the vocabulary that constructs gender identity and commends women's achievements becomes itself an important ante in the *querelle des femmes*. The juggling of terms of transvestment and the contrivance of structural symmetries around gender identity in Dufour's *Vies* make the repre-sentation of gender identity a central concern of the poetics of *querelle* discourse. The prominent use of gender vocabulary provides a gauge for medieval and modern readers to appraise not so much a writer's ethical stance in the debate, his or her opinion on what makes an active woman laudable, but more his or her position in the debate's poetics: how his or her representation of women inserts itself into the rhetorical tradition of praising active women, whether she or he identifies explicitly a particu-lar, historical model against which his or her defence should be read, and how his or her use of gender vocabulary shows dexterity, innovation, or subtlety of approach in defining feminine achievements. In spectral terms, negotiations of vocabulary crystallize the writer's struggle to have it out, on his or her own terms, with the burden of anti-feminine binary thinking with which he or she, as heir, is weighed down.

An important feature of rhetorical dexterity is, as I suggested above at several points, the way that certain authors seem to express an awareness of the limitations of defining active women's accomplishments within the discursive constraints of a masculine–feminine binary, and gesture instead towards a notional 'third term', however ill defined this may be, so as to call into question the validity of the binary and experiment with new possibilities. These writers adumbrate a need for a restructuring of language—a genuine revolution—that allows woman to be defined

[160] 1997: 236.

on her own terms rather than being trapped in terms of a response to structural misogyny. Such a project, I have suggested, is susceptible to analysis in terms of Luce Irigaray's ambition as a feminist theorist, 'pas de faire une théorie de la femme, mais de ménager son lieu au féminin dans la différence sexuelle',[161] and, above all, within the *language* of this 'différence'. *Querelle* writers' need for linguistic revolution is felt and answered in 1555 by François Billon in his compendious chronicle of famous women, *Le Fort inexpugnable de l'honneur du sexe femenin*. Billon postulates an androgynous deity, 'la propre Verité', who presides over the writing of history as the feminine word/Word who seeks to correct the errors in a history that has been 'fardé de mondaine Virilité'.[162] As Jordan notes:

> By conceiving of the Word as androgynous [. . .], Billon clarifies the nature of a literary defence of women in a culture privileging males and the masculine. It requires an altogether new 'order of elements,' linguistic as well as physical, a second creation in and of language.[163]

Querelle writers' adumbration of such a new order in language entails considerable creative play with the possibilities for representing woman's gender identity. The optics of gender performativity through which I have analysed this representation in the current chapter: the linguistic tranvestism of a male author impersonating a woman's voice, and the descriptive cross-dressing of a woman's accomplishments being defined in relation to a masculine norm, may fruitfully be considered in light of the models of performance I postulated in my first two chapters. The undoing and redoing of gender, remodelling the verbal bodies of identities that carry with them their own genealogies, their traces of prior manifestations, may be seen as a particular thread of Chapter 1's spectropoetic theory of hermeneutic performance. In *querelle* works by Le Franc, Milet, and Michault that address Jean de Meun, his *Rose*, and Matheolus as the principal bones of pro-feminine contention, there is a double dynamic of citationality: conjuring up and conjuring literary spectres in order to have it out with these misogynistic ghosts. In *querelle* catalogues by Champier, Dufour, and Bouchet, which take

---

[161] 1977: 154. 'Not to create a theory of woman, but to secure a place for the feminine within sexual difference': 1985: 159.
[162] Billon 1970: fol. II^r: 'dressed in noble Virility'. English translation is my own. *Farder* may imply both 'decorate' and 'dissimulate'; the tone here is clearly ironic, highlighting the falsity of a history comprising only men's achievements.
[163] 1990: 204.

as their cue for defending women *De mulieribus,* Boccaccio becomes the dominant spectre: the ways in which Boccaccio's heirs respond to him (either directly or via reworkings or translations, themselves filterings of his spectre) testify to the troubling influence he was felt to exert over pro-feminine writing. The ambivalent attitude of Dufour, for example, selects, critiques, and filters the haunting presences of *De mulieribus* through each of his biographies, wherein the key intertextual pressure point is the gendered vocabulary used to praise women's achievements.

Chapter 2's focus on the intratextual linguistic performance of debate as verbal 'doings' informs the gender theory behind the present chapter's instances of transvestite ventriloquism. The imagined voice of a woman speaking out in her own defence is most often constructed as a self-consciously artificial position, given that it occurs most frequently in texts directed by a male author to a female patron: a certain complicity is implied between the two parties. The voice operates on an interface between rhetorical fiction and historical reality: Bouchet's epitaph for Louise of Savoy transposes retrospectively into a fictional form the lived experience of a historical woman; Marot's monologue, by contrast, entertains a more complex relationship with actuality, positing a fantasy of female juridical authority that nevertheless dramatically enacts the possibility of this authority, bringing about conceptually, if not actually, his patron's revenge over her enemies. There is a latent potency in the Advocate's speech that is both realized through violent rhetorical action, such as the vituperative force of her attack on 'venimeux viperes', and confined to the virtual realm of imaginatively projected vengeance. The tone of the *Advocate*'s performance might also bear scrutiny: should we appreciate the Advocate's tirade as a solemn indictment of her detractors, or does the complicity between poet and patron identified above admit of a comic edge, discernible perhaps in the exaggerated rhetoric of the prologue: l'Acteur's extreme servility contrasting with hyperbolic praise of his dedicatee that is excessive, even by contemporary standards of rhetorical flourish?[164]

This range of performative possibilities brings us to consider by way of conclusion the terms in which we should define the *querelle des femmes*: a body of texts unified by content, to be sure, as each proposes a

---

[164] Cf. Brown 2007b.

defence of woman's honour, but whose formal presentation embraces a diversity of rhetorical procedures, literary frameworks, intertextualities, tones, and registers, and whose material manifestation entails a variety of additional considerations: the politics of book production, whether manuscript illustration or strategies of printed publication, and the pragmatics of audience orientation.

Conclusion: A New Shelf-Life?

An anonymous late medieval trial debate introduces *Le Procès des femmes et des pulces, composé par ung frere mineur pèlerin, retournant des Hirrelendes, où il apprint la vraye recepte pour prendre et faire mourir les pulces, laquelle sera déclairée cy après à la diffinitive dudict Procès.*[1] The poem stages a dispute between a Woman and a Flea. The plaintiff, La Femme, submits to the jurisdiction of a Cordelier her case against La Pulce, recommending that the Flea should face the death penalty for his incessant torment of her tender skin. The Cordelier decides this 'matiere criminelle' in the Woman's favour and concludes proceedings by presenting his promised recipe for flea-repellent ointment.

This jolly little poem brings us to question the parameters of the *querelle des femmes*, to ask bluntly: 'what is the *querelle* really about, and how do we define its boundaries?' The principal subject matter of the *Procès* is obviously not a defence of women, but, when read closely, the poet appears to be enlisting elements of *querelle* argumentation that I identified in Chapters 1–3 as a means of presenting his cure for flea-bites in a subtly diverting manner, within the framework of a summary *jugement*.[2] The Woman couches her allegations against the Flea, to whom she refers generically as 'la beste cruelle', in terms that appear frequently in *querelle* texts to represent the monstrosity and aggressiveness of misogynist defamers of women. Fleas, the Woman declares,

---

[1] 'The Trial of the women and the flees, composed by a Franciscan pilgrim returning from Ireland, where he learned the true recipe for catching and killing flees, which will be revealed after the verdict of the aforementioned trial': 1875: 62. English translations are my own. De Montaiglon and de Rothschild reproduce an edition that they judge to have been published in Paris, *c.*1520. I have located neither the copy they cite nor any other.

[2] The forensic particulars of this judgement lie in the Cordelier's reference to the flagrant manner in which fleas bite ('trop oultrageusement' (p. 68)), thereby evoking a case of *present meffaict* (what we would call *in flagrante delicto*), which permits a summary trial by a judge: Boutillier 1603: 221–2.

> Par trahison, par grand desloyaulté
> Viennent à moy, mordant si asprement.
>
> (*PFP* 64)

(Through treachery and great faithlessness [they] come upon me, biting so keenly),

like the venomous, stinging tongues of the 'seigneurs' vituperated by Jean Marot's Advocate. United in 'une mesme alliance' they mount vigorous attacks ('assaulx') in similar manner to Malebouche's cohort besieging the *Champion*'s castle of ladies. Furthermore, the crime the Woman describes evokes, through scurrilous double entendre, an allegation of sexual assault against the Flea '. . . qui sault en la ruelle | Entre mes jambes'.[3] Her pleading is cast in a parodic tone; comic disjuncture is set up, not only between the implied discursive context of misogyny and the Flea's actual offence, but also between the Woman and the legendary ancestry of illustrious ladies to which she claims to be heir. She inscribes herself in a prestigious lineage of virtuous women by drawing a most inappropriate analogy between her esteem for the Cordelier and Penelope's wifely devotion to Ulysses:

> Pénélopé jamais tant Ulixès
> N'ayma de cueur que fois [*sic*] vostre personne.
>
> (*PFP* 66)

(Penelope never loved Ulysses as sincerely as I love you.)

I believe the poet deliberately opens up this intersection with *querelle* discourses, through the intertextuality of the Woman's rhetoric, in order to tap into a popular reservoir of literary creativity in the late medieval period.

This intention seems to be confirmed later in the sixteenth century by the way that a German writer, Jean Fischart, takes up the *Procès*. Fischart, a satirist and publisher who imitated several French texts, including Rabelais's *Gargantua*, considerably amplified the *Procès* to some 4,315 lines, and entitled his reworking *Floh Haz, Weiber Traz* (1573).[4] His amplification expands particularly the poem's legal framework, reversing the roles of plaintiff and defendant and elaborating the Woman's

---

[3] '. . . who leaps up in the alleyway between my legs': *PFP* 66.
[4] Noted by the editors of *PFP* 70. The title is quite gnomic, but might loosely be translated as 'The flea's feud against the defiant women'. I am grateful to Annette Volfing for her assistance with this translation.

replique, and engages more substantially with defence of women topics. He offers a long and convoluted verdict delivered by the Chancellor of Fleas which praises woman's mild, pacific nature, her maternity and her nobility, and regrets her abuse by faithless lovers. The Chancellor condemns fleas to death should they re-offend, except when they bite women's ever-wagging, nagging tongues

> Damit sie sehr die Mann betören,
> Wann sie nicht schweigen und aufhören;
> [. . .]
> Weil sie die üben spat und frü.[5]

(with which they totally captivate men, for they will not be silent and will not stop going on.)

The judge's arsenal of pro-feminine arguments is ironically and comically subverted by this anti-feminine sting in the tail, which plays off two misogynistic linguistic stereotypes: woman as treacherous seductress, and the haranguing wife.[6]

Fischart's poetic response to the *Procès* shows that, whatever else he thought the poem was about, its engagement with *querelle* discourse formed an important part of his reading and rewriting of the trial. For modern readers seeking to understand the poetics of texts that enlist the rhetorical stance of a defence of women—in ways as diverse as Champier's *Nef* and the *Girouflier aulx dames*—posing the question 'what is the *querelle* about?' is on the one hand useful and, on the other, somewhat irrelevant to an appreciation of these works. The question is not helpful in that it confines our focus to content, as opposed to the manner in which the given matter of *querelle* argumentation—its stockpile of exemplary women and its repertory of anecdotes and aphoristic tags—is shaped and reshaped in innovative ways. It is on this subtle shaping process that I have insisted throughout this book as our new focus of study. Asking what *querelle* texts are about *is*, however, fruitful to the extent that the act of posing the question indicates some recognition of the works' complexity and diversity; it suggests that we are searching for reading strategies that illuminate their formal characteristics, such as their fundamental intertextuality, in ways that engage with modern hermeneutic interests. This book's chapter divisions have been devoted to precisely

---

[5] *PFP* 72. I am grateful to Nigel Palmer for his assistance with this translation.
[6] See, for example, Le Fèvre 1892: ii, vv. 241–3.

such a search, whether addressing a number of texts grouped together according to a shared problem (how to commend the virtues of an active woman), a common form (debate, judgement, catalogue), or, within Chapter 1, taking a single work (the *Champion*) and probing its different manifestations in manuscript and print. This overall construction around different structural groups has three important consequences for a fruitful reading of the *querelle*. First and foremost, it orients critical attention directly towards the rhetorical apparatus through which texts perform their interesting interpretative manoeuvres. Secondly, by refuting the opinion mentioned in my Introduction that the *querelle* defies characterization in terms of shared formal traits, it proposes a more useful method of grouping texts for analysis than other systems supplied hitherto. Thirdly, my proposed strategy is just that: one possible approach enabling methodical and probing analysis to open up the texts to a modern audience. Other, equally valid possibilities could, for example, concentrate on the treatment of the narrator figure in a selection of texts, or could consider different patterns of innovation applied to the formal model of the catalogue.[7] One might also address the implications of literary form—prose, verse, or prosimetrum—for the way different texts represent pro-feminine arguments.[8]

This plurality of possible strategies highlights once again the polyvalence of *querelle* texts, a polyvalence that prevents any definitive 'poetics' from being concluded since no single set of laws governs the creation and function of literary defences of women; but neither is there artistic anarchy. What this book has done is simply open up some *pistes de lecture* based on shared formal characteristics. One of the most characteristic, and simultaneously most perplexing, features of *querelle* texts is what we might call their polytonal identity. This may concern the question of humour, as was suggested by the brief discussion in Chapter 2 of how the literary/legal interface served both 'comic' and 'serious' ends within the same text, and in Chapter 3 of how Marot's *Advocate* might be read with a nod and a wink. Alternatively, a work may present itself as having a finger in several discursive pies, for example the synthesis, in text and image of different *Champion*

---

[7] I begin to address both these issues in an article on reported discourse in the *Palais des nobles dames* (Swift forthcoming).

[8] This type of question is currently being addressed, though not specifically in relation to *querelle* works, by an AHRC-funded project on poetic knowledge in late medieval France, led by Sarah Kay and Adrian Armstrong.

editions, of political message, theological criticism, red hot polemic, a catalogue of women, personification allegory, and dramatic debate. The *Champion*'s publication history reveals a complex, hybrid composition that is, it seems, intended to be read as a dialogue between multiple discursive contexts. It would be false to the sophistication of Le Franc's poetics to conclude that a debate about women served him purely as a vehicle or pretext for mobilizing pungent criticism of Philip the Good's policies—such as his withdrawal from the Council of Basel—within the 'safety' of imaginative fiction. Three points are noteworthy in this regard. First, throughout the *Champion*, the particular is made general: Franc Vouloir's defence of Joan of Arc becomes a miniature mirror for princes, which, in turn, becomes a radical assertion of women's virtue in general as leaders of men (*CD*, vv. 16817–7168). Similarly, although Book V is devoted to the Virgin Mary alone—a very specific defence of an exceptional woman—the Champion makes clear from the outset his intention 'to praise all [women] for the love of one' (*CD*, v. 6888); she may be exceptional, but the Virgin's feminine excellence can yet be extrapolated as an exemplification of all womankind. Secondly, the *Champion*'s engagement with misogyny is, as we saw in Chapters 1 and 2, almost inextricable from Le Franc's project of refuting and rewriting the *Rose*. The *Rose*'s vital role in the interpretation of the *Champion* is reflected in the illustrations and paratextual apparatus of manuscript and printed editions of the poem in relation to editions of the *Rose*. A third point brings back in the sort of synthesis between serious and comic that I suggested above. Philip the Good, whom Le Franc's prologue celebrates as a stout defender of 'la querelle des dames', was notoriously lewd and fickle, fathering a host of bastard children and showing considerable lack of esteem towards his legitimate wife.[9] To what extent, therefore, was Le Franc's pro-feminine project simply a sop to the Duke, a flattering of the attitude of deep respect for women that was maintained by the Burgundian court in public, if not in private? Was Le Franc colluding in some sense with Philip, lauding lavishly the essentially specious image of a pro-feminine duke as a sort of ironic nod and a wink to his dedicatee, a sort of homosocial pact? Alternatively, we may equally, perhaps more likely, conclude that Le Franc, who had no ties of dependency upon Burgundy, was mounting a scathing, satirical assault on this court's anti-feminine practices; that the Provost

[9] See Vaughan 2002: 132–5.

of Lausanne undertook his project as an attempt to expose the hypocrisy operative in this milieu, and/or to reform the Duke's iniquitous mores.[10]

Marot's *Advocate* operates with similarly deliberate mobility. We recall from Chapter 3 that it has a double focus of specific, political satire and the general defence of woman's honour. This duality ensures both its topical, immediate success and its continued, broader dissemination on the bandwagon, as it were, of the early sixteenth-century print tradition of *querelle* works. Its success in both target zones is attested by the varied company the *Advocate* keeps in its manuscript and print witnesses. It appears, for example, in an illuminated, vellum presentation copy, probably for Anne of Brittany herself (Paris, BnF fr. 1704); in a compilation of historical writings in prose and verse (fr. 9225); and in a later, composite copy (Paris, 1535), in which it forges two significant transtextual relationships. It acts on the one hand as an encomium to a royal lady, since it is juxtaposed with a *Comploration* on the death of Louise of Savoy, François I's mother. On the other hand, it serves to present one side of the *querelle* polemic, for it features alongside, and as the complementary counterpoint to, Guillaume Alexis's republished misogynistic tirade, *Le Grant Blason des faulces amours*.[11] A similar argument may be advanced for Dufour's *Vies*, Dupré's *Palais*, or Bouchet's *Jugement*, in the ways that they synthesize concern for, dedication to, or orientation towards, an individual woman with a defence of women as a group. Each text could be said to perform differently according to the context in which it is read, the political frame that is placed around it by its manuscript or print context, the contemporary cultural context of its initial reception (to its primary audience), and the circumstances, both cultural and bibliographical, of

[10] By having his work eventually accepted by Philip, Le Franc could also be seen to be profiting from this hypocrisy. However, we might interpret his next Burgundian commission, the *Estrif de Fortune et de Vertu* (1447–8), to have been designed according to a similarly ethical agenda, as a suitable follow-up to the counsel for virtuous living present in the *Champion*. Was Philip himself simply toying with this virtue-expounding writer in order to promote a further public image of himself as sponsor of morally worthy books composed by an officially morally steadfast author? Did he perhaps find the Provost's earnest endeavours simply a source of amusement, though one from which his public image could benefit?

[11] Defaux and Mantovani describe this imprint in Marot 1999: 359. The *Grant Blason* was Alexis's most popular work in print, enjoying over thirty editions: see Bossy 1990: 23, 26. Of Alexis's life, we know nothing, although he tells us that he was a Benedictine and also a prior; he was active as a writer in the middle and later fifteenth century. His literary works all share a didactic element; as we saw in Chapter 2, he also achieved popularity with his *Debat de l'omme et de la femme*, a further engagement with *querelle* discourse.

later reappearances in print (to its secondary audience). We recall, for example, how the second appearance of the *Champion des dames* in print divorced the text visually from its Burgundian patronal history, substituting instead the literary context of courtliness and of the *Roman de la rose*; the parameters for performance were repositioned.

In conclusion, I propose that we might most usefully see the literary defence of women as a *topos*, in two senses. First, in accordance with the term's root in Aristotelian and Ciceronian rhetoric, it is a 'place' where arguments are found; its spatial implications can perhaps be seen to be concretized in the architectural structures framing the fictions of Dupré's and Bouchet's narrators' tours around palaces of virtuous women.[12] Secondly, this *topos* is a rhetorical 'storehouse' already filled with prefabricated themes, phrases, and examples.[13] It is in this second sense that the *querelle topos* has been summarily dismissed by most critics, who have addressed it only in its raw form as the subject matter of a work. They have neglected to observe the polyvalent potential of this material and the different ways that this potential was turned to account by the writers explored in this book. Reconsideration of the *topos*, therefore, in its primary, Classical sense helps re-orient critical interest towards the manner of poetic shaping, concerning how the arguments are represented, 'invented',[14] or reinvented: how they are designed to perform.

I close by offering a reading of perhaps the most ingenious, ambiguous, and polyvalent use of the defence of women *topos* that I have discovered within a single text in the late medieval *querelle* corpus: *Le Rousier des dames, sive le pèlerin d'amours* by Bertrand Desmarins de Masan.[15]

---

[12] Aristotle used τόπος to denote the 'region' of the mind where similar arguments are stored: 1958: 1.1. Cicero situates the topics in that branch of argumentation 'concerned with invention of arguments' (*inveniendi*) and develops the spatial metaphor, describing how one should track down (*pervestigare*) an argument by knowing the places or topics (*loci*): 1949: 2.6–8. Dupré's, and also Bouchet's, roving narrator-personae can similarly be seen to search out arguments to defend women as they tour the *loci* of palace rooms.

[13] Curtius appropriates the term in this sense for medieval literary studies, deriving his understanding of *topos* from Quintilian's 'communes loci': 1990: 70. cf. Smith 1995: 4–5.

[14] Cicero's *Topica* summarizes the rules for the invention of arguments: 1949: 18.71, 19.73.

[15] Neither place nor date of publication is marked on either extant early printed edition of 'The rose bush of ladies, or the pilgrim of love' (BnF, RES P YE-240 (in-12); RES YE-3840 (in-16)), although it is likely that the poem dates from around 1510 since Desmarins also wrote *Le Procès des deulx amans plaid[o]yant en la court de Cupido la grace de leur dame* (Montaiglon and Rothschild 1875: 170–92), whose sole extant copy is datable to between 1508 and 1514. There is a significant overlap of material between the two poems, which I note below where pertinent. These two works constitute our

The *Rousier*'s exceptionally innovative and sophisticated handling of intertextualities, its juggling of narrative voice, and its manipulation of perspectives on women will enable us to dismantle modern critical prejudice against the presumed insincerity and/or mere intellectual play of male-authored *querelle* works, and will allow us to advance a more fruitful approach to evaluating a male authorial instance in anti-feminine as well as pro-feminine texts.

The *Rousier* is a dense allegorical narrative structured around a sequence of dialogues and interspersed with the odd lyric insertion, such as the 'chanson du pèlerin', after the style of a late medieval *dit*. The protagonist, the eponymous pilgrim, embarks on a journey that may be divided into three stages according to the different roles he plays out and the various *loci* he visits. He first encounters a convent, then a house of love that increasingly resembles a brothel, and ultimately arrives in the garden containing the rose bush of the title; he is a pilgrim of God's love, a suitor in profane love, and, finally, an exiled and embittered lover. His perspective on women ranges wildly during his journey: from pro-feminine courtly adoration of women, to virulent misogyny, and then back to an ethic of pro-femininity grounded both in women's essential role in society and in their blessed state as epigones of the Virgin. His perspective is held in dialogue—in the Bakhtinian sense of true, polyphonic simultaneity—with several other characters' attitudes, including a similarly shifting viewpoint belonging to the poem's narrator, l'Acteur.

Such is the hybrid matter of the *Rousier*'s tale, but it is the manner in which it is told that arrests the reader's attention and invites careful scrutiny of both the text itself and its intertextual context. The poem triggers multiple intertextual connections from the outset, not least by the resonance of the *Rose* implicit in its title. This expectation of inter-sections with the *Rose* is, however, deferred since the opening passage is devoted instead to evoking a number of different intertextualities. We are invited on the one hand to situate the Pilgrim, described as being pensive and full of sadness, in the context of the medieval type of the dolorous lover-protagonist. On the other hand, we are called to identify him as an actual journeying pilgrim who travels onwards rather than pausing in his grief ('dueil') to drift off into a dream-vision. The Pilgrim's description of his initial landscape surroundings infuses the

knowledge of Desmarins's life and works, namely that he was a poet from Masan, near Carpentras.

narrative with an array, indeed an excess, of mythological allusions—to the tales of Paris and Venus, and Pyramus and Thisbe—such that the text can be seen at this point, to quote the Pilgrim himself, to be a space that is 'moult contaminé'. We shall see that this idea of 'contamination' or 'cross-pollination', to use a horticultural metaphor apt to the poem's appropriation of the *Rose*, may stand as a watchword, in its more neutral etymological sense of 'touching together', for the *Rousier*'s dexterous interweaving of different intertextual threads.[16] In the mythologically overloaded opening landscape, however, the reader's intertextual competence is being stretched to breaking point because there is, as yet, no indication of what the important elements are, and because, looking for the *Rose* in response to the work's title, the reader currently fails to find it.

The contamination only intensifies as the Pilgrim reaches a Carmelite convent and, desirous of seeing its infirmary, finds it to resemble a paradise (*RD* 169); the hospital scene is not developed, however, as the Pilgrim turns tail and moves on. He comes next to a fine residence frequented by lovers whose door is adorned with two knockers, one of which represents Cupid, Venus' arrow-firing son. A structural parallel seems to be implied between these two locations, the house of divine love and the house of erotic desire. A sort of 'descent' from holy mission to profane quest—from Guillaume de Deguileville-like pilgrimage proper to the amorous chase of a Jean de Meun-like Lover—is described by this transition and confirmed by the appearance of the Pilgrim's first interlocutor, l'Hostesse des Amours. As an avatar of the *Rose*'s Courtoisie, who first welcomed Guillaume de Lorris's lover-narrator into that poem's garden, the Hostess greets the Pilgrim for a friendly chat ('devisons'). Their interview remains in the courtly register of Guillaume's *Rose*-portion, though uneasily so: the Pilgrim's lament (*la chanson du pèlerin*) cites the familiar courtly figure of Doulx Espoir, but equates this character's spiritual aid with material wherewithal as the lover bemoans his indigence: 'I haven't any grace, gold, or silver' (*RD* 172).[17] Our suspicions are thus already aroused regarding the Pilgrim's trustworthiness as the loyal lover he claims to be.

Just as the Pilgrim is allowed to step over the threshold into this veritable pleasure garden ('vray clos de plaisance'), Malebouche suddenly

---

[16] The poet seems to be playing simultaneously on two connotations of the title-flower: its associations with the *Rose*, and also its use to denote a 'compilation' or 'anthology' (after the Latin *rosarium*), as in the contemporary manual of statecraft, Louis XI's *Rosier des guerres*.

[17] English translations are my own.

pops up to caution the Hostess against admitting the amorous wanderer, who is, Malebouche states, a 'traitor' and 'detractor' (*RD* 182) who means no good towards women. This familiar personification thus assumes the porterly role (s)he played in the *Rose* as guardian of Bel Accueil's tower, protecting the rose from amorous advances. This role stands in ironic counterpoint to his/her more recent incarnations in *querelle* texts as a male arch-misogynist, who is himself the principal 'detractor' of women.[18] Malebouche's long and varied performance history is thereby evoked by the role in which (s)he is cast by Desmarins; he conjures up different spectres to invite the reader to sift between these different traces of identity.[19]

The narrative voice of l'Acteur intervenes for the first time at this point to object to Malebouche's brutal dismissal of the pilgrim-lover, whom he rebaptizes 'l'amoureux'. Moreover, in l'Acteur's eyes, the Pilgrim is a pitiable 'pouvre amoureux' since, quite unexpectedly, the narrator adopts a staunch anti-woman stance in sympathy with the spurned lover, concluding that woman's heart deceives many (*RD* 182). Blame is placed squarely on woman's and not man's 'parlers [. . .] detracteurs' and deceptive wiles, and l'Acteur enlists the canonical, misogynistic *exempla* of Samson, Solomon, and David as instances of men humiliated by treacherous women. The *Rousier* poet creates a radical ambiguity here by obscuring the authorial instance behind the parade of voices pronouncing for and against women.[20] His actorial preface to the poem, in which he offers his work to ladies, begging their mild mercy ('clemente grace') should he offend them in any way, seems, on the surface, to suggest a pro-feminine stance quite contrary to the

[18] I note both possibilities of gender in the case of Malebouche: whilst, in the *Rose*, she stands guard as an aspect of the rose-maiden's personality, the *querelle*'s Malebouche is often represented as a cleric or a personified stand-in for Jean de Meun (as in the *Champion*), and thus appears in both text and image as a man.

[19] Bynum (2001) prefers the term 'shape' to identity or performance, as a term that encapsulates 'the sequence, the before and after of a self' (p. 181); she describes human selves as 'shapes with stories, always changing but always carrying traces of what we were before' (p. 188). My own discussion of performance, with regard to Malebouche here or to Dido in Chapter 1, converges with Bynum's notion of shape, since I highlight the historical dimension of performance as continual remaking that she seems to downplay. My articulation of identity politics in terms of spectropoetics reinforces the significance of such past traces being present in each hermeneutic performance.

[20] In Desmarins's *Procès*, the authorial instance is similarly ambivalent; its Acteur's blatant misogyny (1875: 179–81) is offset by a number of inserted *rondeaux* written from a pro-feminine perspective which function especially strikingly at the end of the poem to conclude the *Procès* on a positive note for women, in praise of 'the virtues you possess': ibid. 190.

deeply anti-woman position he adopts in alleging the pilgrim-lover's unjust banishment;[21] we shall see later just how ambivalent the stance projected by l'Acteur's preface proves. L'Acteur also assumes a double textual identity: he is both internal and external to the diegesis, serving as hermeneutic guide (whether reliable or otherwise) to both diegetic characters and the extradiegetic reader. On the one hand, the Pilgrim is shown by a sort of metalepsis to have 'heard' l'Acteur's tirade; he declares himself to have been swayed by the narrator's argument to embrace a misogynistic stance, exclaiming 'as l'Acteur has stated':

> Qui eusse dit, aussi pensé
> Des femmes la perversité!
>
> (*RD* 186)

(Who could have told of, or even conceived, the malevolence of women!)

The Pilgrim thereby assumes the role of a banished lover, seeing himself 'banni de Plaisance' (ibid.). On the other hand, l'Acteur addresses himself to an audience of spectators observing the interchange between Malebouche, the Pilgrim, and the Hostess from an extradiegetic vantage point:

> Ne voyez-vous icelle hostesse,
> Que le pellerin moult oppresse,
> Regetter hors de sa maison
> Par Malebouche la perverse?
>
> (*RD* 183)

(Do you not see this Hostess, who greatly torments the Pilgrim, throw him out of her house on the orders of malevolent Ill Speaking?)

The external viewpoint he invites us to adopt draws attention to the intertextual complexity of the *Rousier*'s engagement with the *Rose*. The poet turns to account what I called in Chapter 1 the plurality of the intertext's spectres: its different, sometimes contradictory threads of meaning. The *Rousier* uses the ambiguity already present in Jean de Meun's position on women to weave together in a single scenario conflicting aspects of his characters' discourse, juxtaposing the effectively pro-woman stance of the *Rose*'s Malebouche as protector of Bel Accueil with the anti-woman diatribe of Genius or the Mari Jaloux,

---

[21] The prologue to Desmarins's *Procès* offers a very similarly worded self-exculpation: 1875: 173.

whose perspective Desmarins's Acteur and, subsequently, his Pilgrim espouse.[22]

The long-anticipated intersection with the *Rose* that was suggested by the *Rousier*'s title is finally reached as the Pilgrim attains his third and final *locus*, the fine and sumptuous garden, where he stumbles across numerous lovers assembled

> Dessoubz l'ombrette d'une rose
> [. . .]
> Laquelle là estoit enclose.
>
> (*RD* 187)

(in the little shadow of a rose [bush] [. . .] that was therein enclosed.)

The tell-tale 'rose'/'enclose' rhyme triggers the reader's intertextual impulse and raises the spectre of the *Rose* in ways I discussed in Chapter 1 in the context of the *Giroufflier aulx dames*, a related rewriting of the *Rose*'s horticultural poetics. Having already subverted readerly expectations by deferring explicit reference to the rose bush and by according his Acteur an unexpected attitude to women, the subtle *Rousier* poet here contrives once again to shock by undermining the intertextual presuppositions of his target, *Rose*-informed reader: the garden is introduced to the Pilgrim by Vérité, who describes it as the demesne of Doulx Regard where 'la court des dames' used to congregate. The courtly vein of Guillaume de Lorris's *Rose*-commencement is thereby evoked,[23] but is rapidly undercut by Vérité's ensuing definition of Doulx Regard, which represents the figure as a tool of women's wiles:

> Par doulx regard et par œillades
> Femmes deçoivent maint amant.
>
> (*RD* 188)

(By their kindly look and by casting glances women mislead many a lover.)

Vérité is the second, supposedly neutral, authority after l'Acteur to defect to misogyny in the *Rousier*; the irony latent in l'Acteur's prefatory disclaimer that he will speak of women 'only inasmuch as I can know

---

[22] The Pilgrim's rhetoric is pure Genius as he shuns any relationship with women: 'Bon fait fouir amourettes | Et des femmes l'acointance': *RD* 198. Desmarins's *Procès* offers the same maxim: 1875: 189. Both texts thus recall Jean de Meun's Genius' oft-cited 'fuiez, fuiez' imperative: see Chapter 1, pp. 52–4.

[23] Guillaume's God of Love lists 'douz resgarz' as the third of three comforts to those in thrall to love: *RR*, vv. 2715–48.

the truth (*verité*) about them' (p. 164) here becomes apparent.[24] He and Vérité are far from being objective witnesses to the truth; indeed Vérité, whom we recall to have served as the neutral, ultimately pro-feminine judge in Le Franc's *Champion*, ends up espousing a viewpoint that would be more appropriate to Truth's usual arch-enemy in the *querelle des femmes*, Malebouche.

Vérité and the Pilgrim consolidate their misogyny and their implicit connection with the anti-feminine discourse of Jean de Meun's *Rose* by performing a 'description of the rose bush moralized (*moralisé*) on the subject of women' (*RD* 189). Vérité thus maps various significances onto woman by comparing her with the rose tree's attributes. However, her hermeneutic acrobatics appear subverted by irony: the authority of her moralization is undermined by its presentation as a random 'pick 'n' mix' of interpretations. They oscillate between complete antithesis:

> Au rosier n'a rien que bonté,
> *Mais* femmes n'ont qu'iniquité
>
> (*RD* 190 (my italics))

(In the rose bush there is nothing but goodness, *but* women know nothing but iniquity),

and absolute identity:

> *Tout ainsi que* certainement
> La rose au vent n'est permanable,
> Je vous promectz par mon serment
> Que la femme est variable
>
> (*RD* 193 (my italics))

(*In exactly the same way that* the rose is certainly not stable in the wind, I promise you, upon my oath, that woman is changeable),

but always work to woman's detriment. This opportunistic, scattergun approach to moralization enables Vérité to maintain the misogyny that underpins every comparison. I believe that the poet has his characters practise this dubious methodology as a sort of distorted, diegetic echo of the way the *Rousier* engages with its intertextual models; the distortion serves to highlight for the extradiegetic audience how acts of performative interpretation are required of them as readers of the poem's particularly creative intertextualities.

---

[24] L'Acteur's and Vérité's shared anti-woman perspective is reflected in the way both speakers enlist the tale of Samson and Delilah to illustrate woman's iniquity: *RD* 183, 195.

The greatest shock to the reader's already destabilized position in this curiously pro- *and* anti-woman response to the *Rose* is yet to come. It appears in the form of a surprise narrative intervention by a new character, Équité, who interrupts Vérité's moralization to address l'Acteur sternly:

> Sus le genre masculin
> Parle ung peu par equité,
> Car certes le femenin
> Tu as assez tourmenté.
>
> (*RD* 198–9)

(For equity's sake, speak a little about the masculine gender, for you've certainly tormented the feminine gender enough.)

Équité thus introduces an overseeing, authoritative if not authorial voice that is, for the first time, unlike the voices of l'Acteur and Vérité, not anti-woman; but is it pro-feminine either? What Équité proposes is not, in fact, equity as an ethical imperative, but simply balance or counterbalance as an artistic desideratum. The purely aesthetic concern of her command is reinforced by l'Acteur's poetic response: instantly 'converted' to the pro-feminine argument, he sets about countering Vérité's misogynistic *blason* generalizing woman's iniquity:

> Femmes sont cause de tous maulx;
> Par femme tout mal se deploye
>
> (*RD* 197)

(Women are the cause of all ills; by woman every ill is exposed),

with a *contreblason* that lauds her virtue in equally universalizing terms and imitatively inverts the anaphoric pattern of Vérité's litany:

> Par femmes nulz (ne) sont marris,
> Femmes donc fault soustenir.
>
> (*RD* 203)

(No one is made unhappy by women, and so we must defend women.)

And on this eulogistic note, the poem ends. My reading of the *Rousier* points up how the poem intersects with a number of this book's interpretative concerns: the performance of identity through the Pilgrim's shifting role; the multi-levelled role of l'Acteur; the hermeneutic performances implied by the intertextual malleability of figures like

Malebouche and Vérité; a deeply ambiguous and self-conscious intertextual relationship with the *Rose*; and the performative rhetoric of response through *blason* and *contreblason*. I hope that the preceding chapters can be seen to have furnished a number of hermeneutic tools to enable the modern reader of this late medieval *querelle* text to tackle, understand, and find interest in its astonishing pot-pourri of *querelle topoi*.

It is the *Rousier*'s most perplexing ambiguity on which I shall focus in conclusion, namely the absence of any overarching authorial instance. This is further complicated by the interventions of several actorial or 'substitute' authorities (l'Acteur, Vérité, Équité), which make the inevitable question 'is this male poet for or against women?' almost impossible to answer. The *Rousier*'s Acteur chimes in just as readily with Équité's pro-feminine rhetoric as with Vérité's misogyny; his selection of which side of the case to defend is portrayed as an expedient decision made on aesthetic grounds. A related notion of expediency is expressed by diegetic characters in other comic permutations of the *querelle*. The Acteur of an anonymous courtroom comedy, the *Monologue fort joyeulx auquel sont introduictz deux avocatz et ung juge, devant lequel est plaidoyé le bien et le mal des dames*,[25] one 'Verconus', states that his decision to have the Judge rule in favour of women was a well-advised strategy:

> En soustenant l'honneur des dames
> Je parle comme bien apprins.
>
> (*MFJ* 191)

(In defending the honour of ladies I speak as one who has been well taught.)[26]

In terms of his monologue's rhetorical time of insertion into *querelle* tradition, Verconus implies that his choice of perspective shows off his erudition and allows him to situate himself in the line of prestigious past and present pro-feminine writers currently in vogue, such as Martin Le Franc, whom the *Monologue*'s pro-woman advocate, Gentil Couraige, has already cited as an authority;[27] hence his choice will secure popularity for his work. A more pragmatic expedient may also inform Verconus's statement: if, as Petit de Julleville suggests, the *Monologue* was intended for performance at a *puy*,[28] namely a literary gathering

---

[25] The earliest extant edition was published by Jean Saint-Denis in Paris, *c.*1529. See also Chapter 1, n. 161 and Chapter 3, p. 189.

[26] English translations are my own.

[27] We recall that a new edition of the *Champion* was printed by Pierre Vidoue for Galliot Du Pré in 1530, just after the *Monologue*'s publication in Paris.

[28] Petit de Julleville 1886: 262.

implicitly underpinned by a pro-feminine agenda insofar as its poems
were composed in woman's honour, the *farceur* can be seen to have
made a prudent decision that is calibrated to satisfy his target audience.
Expedient choice is also thematized by Coquillart in his parodic *querelle*
trial, *Le Plaidoié d'entre la Simple et la Rusee.* At the hearing's close,
Coquillart's Acteur reflects on the nature of barristers' decision-making:

> Par ce l'en peult appercevoir
> Souvent en mainte plaidoirie,
> [. . .]
> . . . l'advocad qui plaidie
> Les causes, raisons et moyens,
> Pourveu qu'il ait la main garnie,
> Estre pour les deux abayans.[29]

(By this one can often see, in many a case, [. . .] the barrister who argues the
causes, reasons, and means, representing both parties, so long as his palm is
crossed.)

Although a more explicitly materialistic argument for how to select
one's *partie* than Verconus's attempts to curry favour with his audience, the financial motivation claimed for lawyers shares the same
order of pragmatism as the *farceur*'s defence of his decision to defend
women.

Within the three comic texts, the figures of l'Acteur (*Rousier*), the
performer-director (*Monologue*), and the lawyer (*Plaidoié*) stand, I
argue, as diegetic representatives of the author, expressing in humorous
vein the variety of considerations—poetic, aesthetic, political, and
financial—that may influence his decision to take a pro- or anti-
feminine standpoint in his work. Brief reflection on these different
contextual factors should bring us to see the reductiveness of many
modern critics' verdicts on male-authored *querelle* works: whether they
are dismissed for failing to be sincere, since all male writers are inevitably
contaminated by misogyny, or, more recently, are disregarded as mere
intellectual games to which the topic of gender is merely incidental.
Indeed, it should persuade us that the question of a committed ethical
perspective is somewhat irrelevant. As I suggested in Chapter 2, *querelle*
authors frequently colour their subject with both serious and comic
touches, and the game they play poetically by contributing to the

---

[29] 1975: vv. 802–3, 806–9. English translation is my own. See also Chapter 2,
pp. 154–5.

querelle is itself quite serious. It is clear from the sheer mass of literature devoted to debating the female sex that woman as an amalgamation of qualities and women as individual characters were important literary subjects in this period. In order to play this 'jeu sérieux', to use the phrase coined by Cerquiglini-Toulet to depict the nature of fifteenth-century poetics,[30] the writer, whether the author of a debate or of a catalogue, has to be qualified in both pro- *and* anti-feminine argumentation and *exempla*. As I showed on the intertextual and intratextual axes of dialogue in Chapters 1 and 2, both sides of the case are equally—we might say symbiotically—important in shaping a *querelle* text.[31] This symbiosis is acknowledged by the diegetic author-figures I discussed above: the *Rousier*'s Acteur proves his dexterity in handling the polemics and *exempla* of the case for and against women, and the *Monologue*'s Verconus expressly states that he is master of both sides of the argument—'Je sais le faict et le deffaict'[32]—while conveniently excluding himself from any *prise de position*: 'Qui a le tort? Je n'en sçays rien.'[33] Similarly, Coquillart's Acteur does not wish to implicate himself in, nor, on the other hand, entirely separate himself from, the mercenary decision-making of lawyers, and thus declines to offer comment on their practice: 'Mais toutesfois je n'en dis riens.'[34]

These comic protagonists reflect the way in which the notion of an authorial instance becomes, in several *querelle* poems, to some degree inscrutable, especially when, as we recall from Chapter 2's discussion of Jean Le Fèvre, a poet serves as his own respondent, countering his own anti-feminine work (*Lamentations de Matheolus*) with a pro-feminine text (*Livre de leesce*). This opacity is not, however, a reason for dismissing Le Fèvre's literary activity as a matter of 'mechanical'[35] rhetorical exercises. On the contrary, as I have argued throughout, *querelle* writers' focus on the art of response directs the reader's interest more keenly towards the poetic construction of each work and, potentially, especially in the case of Chapter 3's transvestite women and of Marot's *Advocate*, to the way that literary language and fiction are being used as imaginative spaces

---

[30] 1993b: 49.   [31] See Fenster and Lees 2002: 4; Blamires 1997: 61.
[32] *MFJ* 180.   [33] 'Who's in the wrong? I haven't a clue': ibid. 181.
[34] 'But all the same, I pass no comment': 1975: v. 810. The ability to handle arguments both for and against is perceived as a mark of artistic distinction by the sixteenth-century poet Clément Marot, when he discusses the art of composing *blasons* and *contreblasons*: 'I tell you willingly: whoever stretches his mind, here speaks of white and here of black; and what painter merits praise who does not know how to paint a devil as well as an angel?': 1922: 42. English translation is my own.
[35] Mann 1990: 30.

to experiment with alternative representations of women that critique existing discursive or cultural codes.

It is not, however, the case that the writer's personal opinion is wholly divorced from the verdict he stages in his poem; it is just that his individual investment in the *querelle* is of a more nuanced and contextually influenced nature than has hitherto been acknowledged. For example, we may deduce from the inconclusive trial verdicts explored in Chapter 2 that several writers had a complex understanding of how a pro-feminine opinion should be represented. There is, we might conclude, a performative dimension to the author's role, a contingent positionality or what Butler has called 'a practice of improvisation within a scene of constraint'.[36] This 'constraint' can be multiple, relating to political, cultural, and/or discursive contexts. One might argue that there is one contextual factor that 'automatically' overrules all other considerations, whether literary or pragmatic, namely the dedication of a work to a female patron which immediately determines the pro-feminine bias of a text. At least two instances of female patronage (one sought, one obtained) within the *querelle* corpus suggest the situation was more complicated. First, we saw briefly in Chapter 3 how Champier's *Nef*, with its wholly laudatory portraits of virtuous women, was rejected in favour of a more practical manual for educating a young princess, in which Anne of France was not averse to offering critical images of women as negative *exempla* for her daughter Suzanne.[37] Secondly, we saw in Dufour's *Vies*, dedicated to Anne of Brittany, how the writer's decision to engage with the rhetoric of gender-description employed by his main models, Boccaccio's *De mulieribus* and Foresti's *De plurimis*, was a prominent poetic concern that occasionally risked leading Dufour into misogynistic waters. The example of Dufour's *Vies* points to the fundamentally dialectical quality of the late medieval defence of women, whose poetics emerge from the dialogue it maintains with the other side of the case as a necessary and objectionable 'contaminating' presence, and from a negotiation between the writer (or, equally, the miniaturist) and the rhetorical, historical, and personal circumstances of his time of insertion into *querelle* tradition.

---

[36] 2004: 1.

[37] Besides the image of 'nyces' women who cannot conduct themselves properly in public, Anne cites the examples of duplicitous and scheming 'mad fools', who 'deceive and trick many people with their wretched and poisonous finesse' (1878: 12), and of melodramatic 'silly women' (p. 115).

This new way of approaching *querelle* texts breaks down any supposed dichotomy between sincerity and insincerity in order that male- and female-authored (and anonymous) literary defences of women may come to be considered on the same footing. As I proposed at the beginning of Chapter 3, our re-evaluated perspective on male-authored defences of women might fruitfully inflect our reading of the First Lady of the Middle Ages, Christine de Pizan, rather than, as has largely been the case until now, having *her* eclipse *them*. As my reading of the *Rousier* demonstrates, what is vital is not a known, authorial viewpoint orienting the text, but the experience for the reader of engaging with its serious game, of tackling with hermeneutic relish 'ung nouveau cas [. . .] pour recreation de [s]on curieux entendement'.[38] In some sense, we can consider the binary view of medieval writings about women, that a given writer was either for or against her sex, in parallel with the binary framework of gender identity that I showed certain writers to be disrupting in their *querelle* contributions. The attitude towards women developed by a particular author, his or her own gender, and the ways she or he represents women's identities are all aspects of *querelle* writings that modern criticism needs to reconsider in more performative terms, to deconstruct in order to appreciate the complex nexus of influences, agencies, and contingencies operative upon these writers, as they broached new rhetorical possibilities.

Close readings of this corpus of texts, together with an examination of the texts in their context, reveal the true poetic sophistication of many male-authored *querelle* works: their engagement with gender representation; their deployment of narrative strategies and fictional frameworks to enliven the presentation of established, pro-feminine arguments; and their creative response to the totemic influence of Jean de Meun in text, paratext, and image through detailed hermeneutic reappropriation of the *Rose*. A work's context is also historical, concerning the conditions of its reception, the political agenda potentially informing it, and, perhaps most significantly and strikingly in this period of transition from manuscript to print cultures, its path of transmission and dissemination: its (re-)appearance in print, its different illustrative programmes, and, in the case of the *Champion*, its publication in the same series as its problematic model, the *Rose*. These factors enable us to reconstruct a great deal about how these works were read and how we should go about reading them

---

[38] 'A new case [. . .] for the entertainment of [one's] curious mind': *RD* 193.

today in order to remove them from the neglected, dust-covered shelf and restore to them their significant position in late medieval poetics and twenty-first-century critical thought. As the theoretical framework of this book has highlighted, in many different contexts, these texts are essentially performances, and were conceived of as such by their medieval authors: transient events—as implied by the dream fiction framing the *Champion, Forest, Procès, Palais,* and *Jugement,* or by the artifice of transvestite ventriloquism—and yet crucial moments for asserting an individual interpretative imprint on the development of pro-feminine discourse, as in Dufour's particular recastings of women's identities, Le Franc's reworkings of Jean de Meun's *Rose,* or Marot's imaginary realization of Queen Anne's triumph over her enemies. These are performances grounded in the multiplicity of textual voices: the narrative layers within a given text, together with the intertextual voices driving a particular literary tradition; the paratextual contributions of rubricators, illustrators, and publishers, as well as the extratextual considerations of patronage and target audience. Viewed together, as this book has endeavoured to show, these performances constitute an engaging body of writings in defence of women, or, to quote Le Franc, 'la querelle des dames singulierement recommandee'.[39]

[39] 'the most highly esteemed case for women': *CD* 3. cf. Introduction, n. 3.

APPENDIX 1

Chronologies of *Querelle des femmes* Texts

A. CHRONOLOGY OF PRIMARY TEXTS

I include here works that are mentioned at least once in the course of this book, and which are to varying degrees connected to the defences of women which constitute the book's main corpus (indicated in bold type). Works are listed according to their known/presumed date of composition.

*c.*1240	Guillaume de Lorris, *Le Roman de la rose*
*c.*1245	Richard de Fournival, *Le Bestiaire d'amour*
1269–78	Jean de Meun, *Le Roman de la rose* (continuation of Guillaume's text)
1295	Matheolus, *Liber lamentationum Matheoluli*
1330–1	Guillaume de Deguileville, *Le Pèlerinage de vie humaine*
*c.*1337	Francesco Petrarca, *De viris illustribus*
1355	Guillaume de Deguileville, *Le Pèlerinage* (revised)
1355–74	Giovanni Boccaccio, *De casibus virorum illustrium*
1361–2	Giovanni Boccaccio, *De mulieribus claris*
*c.*1368	Jean Froissart, *L'Horloge amoureux*
1371–2	Jean Le Fèvre, *Les Lamentations de Matheolus*
*c.*1373	Jean Le Fèvre, *Le Livre de leesce*
1399	Christine de Pizan, *L'Epistre au dieu d'amours*
1401	***Le Livre de Jehan Boccace des cleres et nobles femmes***
	Laurent de Premierfait, *Des cas des nobles hommes et femmes*
1402	Jean Gerson, *Le Traite contre 'le Roman de la rose'*
1404–5	Christine de Pizan, *Le Livre de la cite des dames*
1405	Christine de Pizan, *Le Tresor de la cite des dames* = *Le Livre des trois vertus*
1409	Laurent de Premierfait, *Des cas* (revised)
1440–2	**Martin Le Franc, *Le Champion des dames***
before 1451	**Martin Le Franc, *La Complainte du livre du Champion des dames à maistre Martin Le Franc son acteur***
1459	**Jacques Milet, *La Forest de Tristesse***

[*c*.1460?]   Guillaume Alexis, *Le Grant Blason des faulces amours; Le Debat de l'omme et de la femme*

1460–5   [Martial d'Auvergne], *Les Arrêts d'amours*

c.1461   **Pierre Michault, *Le Procès d'Honneur Féminin***

before 1467   *Le Purgatoire des mauvais maris*

before 1477   *Le Chevalier des dames du Dolent fortune*

1477–82   Philippe Bouton, *Le Mirouer des dames*

c.1478–9   Guillaume Coquillart, *Le Plaidoie d'entre la Simple et la Rusee; L'Enqueste*

[*c*.1480?]   *Dispute entre le sexe masculin et le feminin*

1493   *Le Livre de Jehan Bocasse de la louenge et vertu des nobles et cleres dames*

1494   Octovien de Saint-Gelais, *Le Sejour d'honneur*

1496   Octovien de Saint-Gelais, *Le s.XXI. Epistres d'Ovide*

1497   Jacopo Filippo Foresti, *De plurimis claris selectisque mulieribus*

1500   Jean Molinet, *Le Roman de la rose moralise*

1501   *Le Jardin de plaisance et fleur de rethorique* (including *Le Procès d'Honneur Feminin; La Forest de Tristesse*)

1503   Symphorien Champier, *La Nef des dames vertueuses*

1503–5   Anne de France, *Enseignements d'Anne de France . . . à sa fille Susanne de Bourbon*

1504   Antoine Dufour, *Les Vies des femmes célèbres*

c.**1506   Jean Marot, *La Vraye disant advocate des dames***

1509   Henricus Cornelius Agrippa, *De nobilitate et praecellentia foeminei sexus* (published 1529)

c.1510   Bertrand Desmarins de Masan, *Le Procès des deulx amans plaid[o]yant en la court de Cupido la grace de leur dame*

[*c*.**1510?]   Bertrand Desmarins de Masan, *Le Rousier des dames***

before *c*.1520   *Le Procès des femmes et des pulces*

before 1521   *Le Giroufflier aulx dames*

1521   Ravisius Textor, *De memorabilibus et claris mulieribus*

c.**1529   *Le Monologue fort joyeulx***

1529   *De la noblesse et preexcellence du sexe foeminin* = translation of Agrippa, *De nobilitate*

[*c*.**1534]   Jean Dupré, *Le Palais des nobles dames***

1538   Jean Bouchet, *Le Jugement poetic de l'honneur femenin*

1551   *Boccace. Des dames de renom*

1555   François Billon, *Le Fort inexpugnable de l'honneur du sexe femenin*

1559   Marguerite de Navarre, *L'Heptameron*

B. EARLY PRINTED EDITIONS OF *QUERELLE DES FEMMES* TEXTS

Known editions of the core defences of women are listed together with those of selected ancillary works (the *Roman de la rose* and its re-editions, commentaries, or responses, and French translations of Boccaccio's *De mulieribus*).

1479–84	*Le Purgatoire des mauvais maris* (Bruges)
[*c.*1481]	Guillaume de Lorris and Jean de Meun, *Le Roman de la rose* (Lyons)
1485	Martin Le Franc, *Le Champion des dames* (Lyons)
[*c.*1485]	*Le Roman de la rose* (Lyons)
[*c.*1487]	*Le Roman de la rose* (Lyons)
1493	*Le Livre de Jehan Bocasse de la louenge et vertu des nobles et cleres dames* (Paris)
[*c.*1494]	*Le Roman de la rose* (Paris)
[*c.*1494–5]	*Le Roman de la rose* (Paris)
1497	Jacopo Filippo Foresti, *De plurimis claris selectisque mulieribus* (Paris)
[*c.*1497]	*Le Roman de la rose* (Paris)
[1498–1505]	*Le Roman de la rose* (Paris)
[1499–1500]	*Le Roman de la rose* (Paris)
1500	Jean Molinet, *Le Roman de la rose moralise* (Paris)
1501	*Le Jardin de plaisance et fleur de rethorique* (Paris)
*c.*1500–*c.*1519	*Le Purgatoire des mauvais maris avec l'Enfer des mauvaises femmes* (Paris)
1502	Jean Gerson, *Le Traite contre 'le Roman de la rose'* (Latin translation) (Paris)
1503	Symphorien Champier, *La Nef des dames vertueuses* (Lyons)
	Molinet, *Le Roman de la rose moralise* (Lyons)
1504	*Le Jardin de plaisance* (Paris)
1505	*Le Jardin de plaisance* (Paris)
[*c.*1510?]	Bertrand Desmarins de Masan, *Le Rousier des dames* (Paris?)
1515	Champier, *La Nef des dames vertueuses* (Paris)
	Le Jardin de plaisance (Paris)
	Le Roman de la rose (Paris)
1519	*Le Roman de la rose* (Paris)
[1520–1]	*Le Roman de la rose* (Paris)
before 1521	*Le Giroufflier aulx dames* (Paris)

1521	Ravisius Textor, *De memorabilibus et claris mulieribus* (Paris)
after 1523	*Le Giroufflier aulx dames* (Lyons)
1525	*Le Jardin de plaisance* (Lyons)
	Le Jardin de plaisance (Paris)
1526	*Le Roman de la rose* (Paris)
[1526]	[Clément Marot], *Le Roman de la rose* (Paris)
1527	*Le Jardin de plaisance* (Paris)
[1528]	*Le Roman de la rose* (Paris)
1529	[Clément Marot], *Le Roman de la rose* (Paris)
	Le Contre rommant de la rose nommé le Gratia Dei (Paris) = Christine de Pizan, *L'Epistre au dieu d'amours*
*c.*1529	*Le Monologue fort joyeulx* (Paris)
1530	Le Franc, *Le Champion des dames* (Paris)
[*c.*1530]	Desmarins de Masan, *Le Rousier des dames* (Lyons)
	Le Purgatoire des mauvais maris avec l'Enfer des mauvaises femmes (Lyons)
1531	Champier, *La Nef des dames vertueuses* (Paris)
	[Clément Marot], *Le Roman de la rose* (Paris)
[*c.*1534]	Jean Dupré, *Le Palais des nobles dames* ([Lyons])
1535	Jean Marot, *La Vraye disant advocate des dames* (Paris)
1537	[Clément Marot], *Le Roman de la rose* (Paris)
1538	Jean Bouchet, *Le Jugement poetic de l'honneur femenin* (Poitiers)
	[Clément Marot], *Le Roman de la rose* (Paris)
	Le Plaisant Livre de noble homme Jehan Bocace (Paris)
1551	*Boccace. Des dames de renom* (Paris)
1555	François Billon, *Le Fort inexpugnable de l'honneur du sexe femenin* (Paris)

Lists of Manuscripts, Incunables, and Early Printed Editions

Manuscripts and editions are listed chronologically (where known), and extant copies of imprints listed alphabetically according to the location of the current holding library.

A. MANUSCRIPTS AND EARLY PRINTED EDITIONS OF *LE CHAMPION DES DAMES* (*C*.1442)

Manuscripts:[1] information gleaned from: Bousmanne et al. 2003: 99–104; Charron 2000; 1996; Le Franc 1999: pp. xi–xvi; Avril and Reynaud 1995: 100–2, 205; Hindman *c*.1993: 70–8.

B1 Brussels, Bibliothèque Royale, MS 9466, *c*.1442; text of all five books complete; two miniatures attributed to Péronnet Lamy, with space for a further illustration (fol. 109^v): the 'rejected' presentation copy.

P1 Paris, BnF, MS fr. 12476, 1451; text lacking six stanzas on Joan of Arc, vv. 16921–68; includes *La Complainte du livre du Champion des dames à maistre Martin Le Franc son acteur*; sixty-six miniatures: the 'revised' presentation copy.

B2 Brussels, Bibliothèque Royale, MS 9281, *c*.1470; Books IV and V incomplete.

B3 Brussels, Bibliothèque Royale, MS IV 1127, *c*.1470; state of completeness unknown.

G Grenoble, Bibliothèque Municipale, MS 352 Rés., fols. 1^r–437^r, *c*.1470; Book IV lacking vv. 16921–68 and Book V incomplete, starting at v. 23433; rest of manuscript contains a verse epitaph for Philip the Good (d. 1467) (fols. 439^r–439^v), and *Les Lamentations d'Olivier de la Marche sur la mort de Marie de Bourgogne* (1482) (fols. A^r–G^r), which was presumably added at the front of the volume at a later date; 182 miniatures attributed to the *Champion des dames* Master: owned by Charles de Croy, grandson

---

[1] I am grateful to Roger Middleton for offering his bibliographic expertise to verify certain details of ownership and transmission.

of Jean de Croy, a member of Philip the Good's Order of the Golden Fleece.

P2 Paris, BnF, MS fr. 841, *c*.1470; Books IV and V incomplete; ninety-two miniatures.

Z Private Collection (Ex Bourg de Bozas), *c.* 1470; Book IV lacking vv. 16921–68 and Book V cut from vv. 20482–3433; 140 miniatures.

A Paris, Bibliothèque de l'Arsenal, MS 3121, 1481; text complete, except for vv. 16921–68.

V Rome, Vatican Library, MS Palatin Latin 1968, third quarter fifteenth century (?); text complete, except for prose prologue and vv. 16921–68.

Note: my information regarding the text's completeness is dependent for *B2, B3, G, Z, A,* and *V* on Deschaux (in Le Franc 1999: pp. xi–xvi).

Incunable and print: Le Franc 1999: p. xvi; Picot and Lacombe 1884: 251–3.

Le Champion des dames (Lyons: [Jean du Pré/Guillaume Le Roy?], 1485), in-fol.; text complete, except for vv. 16921–68; fifty-nine woodcuts.
Lyons, Bibliothèque Municipale, incunable 266.
Paris, BnF, RES YE-27.

Le Champion des dames. Livre plaisant, copieux et habondant en sentences, contenant la Deffence des Dames contre Malebouche et ses consors, et victoire d'icelles (Paris: Galliot Du Pré, 1530), in-8; text complete, except for vv. 16921–68; twenty-two woodcuts.
Grenoble, Bibliothèque Municipale, Rés. F28041.
Paris, BnF, RES YE-4028-4030.
Paris, BnF, RES YE-4031.

B. MANUSCRIPTS AND EARLY PRINTED EDITIONS OF THE FRENCH TRANSLATIONS OF BOCCACCIO'S *DE MULIERIBUS CLARIS*

Manuscripts: filiation, provenance, and ownership are documented by Buettner 1996: 100–1; Boccaccio 1993: i, pp. ix–xi; Bozzolo 1973: 23–5, 91–9. For clarity, I note here only those features most relevant to this study, namely date of composition and illustrative content.

Le Livre de Jehan Boccace des cleres et nobles femmes (1401)
P1 Paris, BnF, MS fr. 12420, *c*.1402, 109 miniatures.
P2 Paris, BnF, MS fr. 598, *c*.1403, 107 miniatures: identical programme to fr. 12420.
L1 London, British Library, MS Royal 16 G.V., *c*.1410, 103 miniatures.

L2 London, British Library, MS Royal 20 C.V., *c*.1410, 105 miniatures.

B1 Brussels, Bibliothèque Royale, MS 9509, 1410–15, thirty-three miniatures.

Li Lisbon, C. Gulbenkian Foundation, MS L.A. 143, 1410–15, forty-eight surviving miniatures.

Ph Philadelphia, Free Library, MS T 15/490, 1420–5: single leaf.

V Vienna, Österreichische Nationalbibliothek, COD. 2555, 1462–72.

P3 Paris, BnF, MS fr. 1120, before 1467.

N1 New York, Public Library, Spencer MS 33, *c*.1470, seventy-six surviving miniatures.

N2 New York, Pierpont Morgan Library, MS M 381, *c*.1475 (?), forty-one miniatures.

P4 Paris, BnF, fr. 133, third quarter fifteenth century, one miniature.

P5 Paris, BnF, fr. 599, text copied before 1467, illustrated *c*.1488–96, 103 miniatures.

P6 Paris, BnF, fr. 5037, fols. 223^r–305^v, third quarter fifteenth century: rest of manuscript comprises an assortment of historical texts concerning the reigns of Charles VII and Louis XI, including copies of royal correspondence, and Christine de Pizan's *Livre de la prod'ommie*.

C Chantilly, Musée Condé, MS 856, fols. 31^r–130^v, third quarter fifteenth century: rest of manuscript contains Lives of women saints and Christine de Pizan's *Livre de la cité des dames*.

P7 Paris, Private Collection (Ex Phillipps 3648), fols. 1^r–82^r, late fifteenth century: rest of manuscript contains Christine de Pizan's *Livre de la cité des dames* (fols. 83^r–150^r).

Incunables and early prints:

Le Livre de Jehan Bocasse de la louenge et vertu des nobles et cleres dames (Paris: Antoine Vérard, 1493), in-fol.

Bibliographical information detailing production and ownership is provided by Brown 2007a and Winn 1997.

London, British Library, G 1430: paper.

London, British Library, IB.41132b: vellum copy for Henry VII.

Manchester, John Rylands Library, 15883 Inc. 15^E.

Paris, Arsenal, F$^°$ H 4992: paper.

Paris, BnF, RES G 365: paper.

Paris, BnF, RES Vélins 1223: vellum copy for Charles VIII and Anne of Brittany.

Le Plaisant Livre de noble homme Jehan Bocace, poète florentin, auquel il traicte des faictz et gestes des illustres et cleres dames (Paris: Arnoul and Charles les Angelliers, 1538), in-8; uses the same, anonymous translation as Vérard's edition (above).

Paris, BnF, RES G 2238.
Paris, BnF, RES G 2239.

Boccace. Des dames de renom, nouvellement traduict d'italien en langage françoys
(Lyons: Guillaume Rouillé, 1551), in-8; from the Italian translation by Luca
Antonio Ridolfi.
Paris, BnF, RES G 20207.

References

References in the text to primary and secondary sources other than those named in the Abbreviations list have been abbreviated to provide the author's surname (or a shortened title, if the work is anonymous) and the date of publication.

BIBLIOGRAPHIES, DICTIONARIES, AND REFERENCE SOURCES

Baudrier, Henri (1914). *Bibliographie lyonnaise*, ctd. Julien Baudrier, 12 vols. (Lyons/Paris: Brun (i–xi), Brossier (xii)/Picard, 1895–1921), xi.

Biblia sacra iuxta vulgatam versionem (1975). Ed. B. Fischer, J. Gribomont, H. F. D. Sparks, W. Thiele, and R. Weber, 2nd edn., 2 vols. (Stuttgart: Württembergische Bibelanstalt).

Godefroy, Frédéric (1969). *Dictionnaire de l'ancienne langue française et de tous ses dialectes du IXe au XVe siècle*, 10 vols. (Paris: Vieweg/Bouillon, 1880–1902; repr. Nendeln, Liechtenstein: Kraus).

Hasenohr, Geneviève, and Zink, Michel (eds.) (1992). *Dictionnaire des lettres françaises: le moyen âge*, rev. edn. (Paris: Fayard).

The Holy Bible: King James Version (1990). (Cambridge: CUP).

Moreau, Brigitte (ed.) (1972–92). *Inventaire chronologique des éditions parisiennes du XVIe siècle d'après les manuscrits de Philippe Renouard*, 4 vols. (Abbeville: Paillart).

Omont, Henri (ed.) (1895–1918). *Bibliothèque nationale de France. Catalogue général des manuscrits français*, 13 vols. (Paris: Leroux).

Picot, Émile, and Lacombe, Paul (eds.) (1884). *Catalogue des livres composant la bibliothèque de feu M. le baron James de Rothschild*, 5 vols. (Paris: Morgand, 1884–1920), i.

Renouard, Philippe (1965). *Répertoire des imprimeurs parisiens: libraires, fondeurs de caractères et correcteurs d'imprimerie* (Paris: M. J. Minard).

Tchemerzine, Avenir (1932). *Bibliographie d'éditions originales et rares d'auteurs français des XVe, XVIe et XVIIe siècles*, 10 vols. (Paris: Plée, 1927–34), v.

PRIMARY SOURCES

Manuscripts and Contemporary Editions

Martin Le Franc, *Le Champion des dames*

Grenoble, Bibliothèque Municipale, 352 Rés., fols. 1^r–437^r (microfilm).
Paris, BnF, fr. 841 (BnF microfilm 422).

Paris, BnF, fr. 12476 (BnF microfilm 330).

Paris, BnF, RES YE-27 (Lyons: [Guillaume Le Roy?], 1485).

Paris, BnF, RES YE-4031 (Paris: Galliot Du Pré, 1530).

Boccaccio, *De mulieribus claris*

Le Livre de Jehan Boccace des cleres et nobles femmes.

Paris, BnF, fr. 598 (BnF colour microfilm 75).

Paris, BnF, fr. 599 (BnF colour microfilm 292).

Paris, BnF, fr. 5037.

Paris, BnF, fr. 12420 (BnF colour microfilm 96).

Le Livre de Jehan Bocasse de la louenge et vertu des nobles et cleres dames (Paris, Antoine Vérard, 1493).

Manchester, John Rylands Library, 15883 Inc. 15^E.

Paris, BnF RES G 365 (BnF microfilm 9711).

Other manuscripts

Dispute entre le sexe masculin et le feminin, autrement Bouche Mesdisant et Femme Deffendant, Paris, BnF, fr. 1990, fols. 1^r–106^r.

Other early printed editions

Boutillier, Jean (1603). *La Somme rurale* (Paris: [n.pub.]) (Oxford, Bodleian Library, 40 C 22 Jur).

Champier, Symphorien (1503). *La Nef des dames vertueuses* (Lyons: Jacques Arnoullet) (Oxford, Bodleian Library, Douce C subt. 141).

Chartier, Alain (1529). *Les Oeuvres de feu maistre Alain Chartier* (Paris: Galliot Du Pré) (Oxford, Bodleian Library, 8 || C 64 Art.Seld.).

Dupré, Jean ([1534]). *Le Palais des nobles dames* ([Lyons]: [n.pub.]) (Oxford, Bodleian Library, Douce D 68).

Du Verdier, Antoine (1585). *Bibliotheque d'Antoine du Verdier, seigneur de Vauprivas* (Lyons: Barthélémy Honorat).

Foresti, Jacopo Filippo (1506). *Novissime historiarum omnium repercussiones [. . .] que supplementum supplementi cronicarum nuncupantur* (Venice: Georgius de Rusconibus) (Oxford, New College Library, BT1.11.6).

—— (1521). *De plurimis claris selectisque mulieribus*, in Ravisius Textor, *De memorabilibus et claris mulieribus aliquot diversorum scriptorum opera* (Paris: Simon de Colines), fols. 14^v–160^r.

Guillaume de Lorris and Jean de Meun ([c.1487]). *Le Rommant de la rose* ([Lyons]: [Guillaume Le Roy]) (Oxford: Bodleian Library, Douce 194).

La Croix du Maine, François Grudé de (1584). *Premier volume de la bibliotheque du sieur de La Croix du Maine . . .* (Paris: Abel l'Angelier).

[Marot, Clément] ([1526]). *Cy est Le Rommant de la rose* (Paris: Galliot Du Pré) (Oxford, Bodleian Library, Mal. 12) (Paris, BnF, NUMM 70256).

—— (1529). *Cy est Le Rommant de la rose* (Paris: Galliot Du Pré) (BnF, NUMM 70257).

[Marot, Clément] (1531). *Cy est Le Rommant de la rose* (Paris: Jean Petit) (Oxford, Bodleian Library, Douce L 484).

Le Monologue fort joyeulx auquel sont introduictz deux avocatz et ung juge, devant lequel est plaidoyé le bien et le mal des dames ([*c*.1529]) (Paris: [Jean Saint-Denis]) (Paris, BnF, RES YE-3852).

[Pierre de Brinon] (1599). *Le Triomphe des dames* (Rouen: Jean Osmont) (Paris, BnF, microfilm R 24057).

Pierre de Courcelles (1557). *La Rhétorique* (Paris: Sebastien Nyvelle) (Paris, BnF, microfiche M 9585).

Pierre de Deimier (1610). *L'Academie de l'art poétique où [. . .] l'on peut parvenir à la vray et parfaicte connoisance de la poésie françoyse* (Paris: J. de Bordeaulx) (Paris, BnF, NUMM 88126).

Plutarch (1521). *De mulieribus claris*, trans. Alamanno Rinuccini, in Ravisius Textor, *De memorabilibus et claris mulieribus aliquot diversorum scriptorum opera* (Paris: Simon de Colines), fols. 3^v–14^v.

Ragueau, François (1704). *Glossaire du droit françois*, rev. Eusèbe de Laurière (Paris: Jean and Michel Guignard).

Ravisius Textor (Jean Tixier de Ravisy) (1521). *De memorabilibus et claris mulieribus aliquot diversorum scriptorum opera* (Paris: Simon de Colines) (Oxford, Bodleian Library, Meerm. 248).

Modern Editions

Agrippa von Nettesheim, Henricus Cornelius (1996). *Declamation on the Nobility and Preeminence of the Female Sex*, ed. and trans. Albert Rabil, Jr. (Chicago: University of Chicago Press).

Alexis, Guillaume (1896). *Œuvres poétiques*, ed. Arthur Piaget and Émile Picot, 3 vols. (Paris: Firmin-Didot, 1896–1908), i.

Anne de France (1878). *Les Enseignements d'Anne de France, duchesse de Bourbonnois et d'Auvergne à sa fille Susanne de Bourbon*, ed. Martial A. Chazaud (Moulins: Desrosiers).

Aristotle (1958). *Aristotelis Topica et Sophistici elenchi*, ed. William D. Ross (Oxford: Clarendon Press).

—— (1995). *Poetics*, ed. and trans. Stephen Halliwell (Cambridge, Mass.: Harvard University Press).

Les Arrêts d'amour de Martial d'Auvergne (1951). Ed. Jean Rychner (Paris: Picard).

L'Art et science de bien parler et de se taire (1875). In Anatole de Montaiglon and James de Rothschild (eds.), *Recueil de poésies françoises des XVe et XVIe siècles* (Paris: Jennet, 1855–78), x. 351–68.

Baird, Joseph L., and Kane, John R. (eds.) (1978). *La Querelle de la Rose: Letters and Documents* (Chapel Hill, NC: University of North Carolina Department of Romance Languages).

Billon, François (1970). *Le Fort inexpugnable de l'honnneur du sexe femenin*, ed. M. A. Screech (Wakefield: S. R. Publishers/Johnson Reprint Corporation/Mouton).

Boccaccio, Giovanni (1962). *De casibus illustrium virorum: A Facsimile Reproduction of the Paris Edition of 1520*, ed. Lewis Brewer Hall (Gainesville, Fla. Scholars' Facsimiles and Reprints).

—— (1993). *Boccace 'Des cleres et nobles femmes'*, ed. Jeanne Baroin and Josiane Haffen, 2 vols. (Paris: Les Belles Lettres).

—— (2001). *Famous Women*, ed. and trans. Virginia Brown (Cambridge, Mass.: Harvard University Press).

Bouchet, Jean (1969). *Epistre de justice*, in *Epistres morales et familieres du Traverseur*, ed. Jennifer Beard (Wakefield: S. R. Publishers/Johnson Reprint Corporation/Mouton), *Ep. Mor.*, ii.v, fols. D2^r–E6^r.

—— (1992). *Le Temple de bonne renommée*, ed. Giovanna Bellati (Milan: Vita e Pensiero).

—— (2006). *Le Jugement poetic de l'honneur femenin et sejour des illustres claires et honnestes dames*, ed. Adrian Armstrong (Paris: Champion).

Bouton, Philippe (1882). *Le Mirouer des dames*, in M. E. Beauvois, *Un agent politique de Charles-Quint: le Bourguignon Claude Bouton, seigneur de Corberon* (Paris: Laroux), 'seconde partie', 3–30.

Bovet, Honorat (2005). *L'Apparicion Maistre Jehan de Meun*, in *Medieval Muslims, Christians, and Jews in Dialogue: The 'Apparicion Maistre Jehan de Meun' of Honorat Bovet*, ed. and trans. Michael Hanly (Tempe, Ariz.: Arizona Centre for Medieval and Renaissance Studies).

Brantôme, Pierre de Bourdeille, seigneur de (1991). *Recueil des dames, poésies et tombeaux*, ed. Étienne Vaucheret (Paris: Gallimard).

Champier, Symphorien (2007). *La Nef des dames vertueuses*, ed. Judy Kem (Paris: Champion).

Chartier, Alain, Herenc, Baudet, and Caulier, Achille (2003). *Le Cycle de 'La Belle Dame sans mercy': une anthologie poétique du XVe siècle*, ed. and trans. David F. Hult and Joan E. McRae (Paris: Champion).

Le Chevalier des dames du Dolent fortuné: allégorie en vers de la fin du XVe siècle (1990). Ed. Jean Miquet (Ottawa: Presses de l'Université d'Ottawa).

Christine de Pizan (1959–66). *Le Livre de la mutacion de fortune*, ed. Suzanne Solente, 4 vols. (Paris: Picard).

—— (1989). *Le Livre des trois vertus*, ed. Charity Cannon Willard and Eric Hicks (Paris: Champion).

—— (1997). *La città delle dame*, ed. and trans. Patrizia Caraffi (Milan: Luni).

—— and Hoccleve, Thomas (1990). *Poems of Cupid, God of Love: Christine de Pizan's 'Epistre au dieu d'amours' and 'Dit de la rose'; Thomas Hoccleve's 'The Letter of Cupid'*, ed. and trans. Mary Carpenter Erler and Thelma S. Fenster (Leiden: Brill).

Cicero (1939). *Orator*, ed. and trans. H. M. Hubbell (Cambridge, Mass.: Harvard University Press/Heinemann).

—— (1948). *De re publica, De legibus*, ed. and trans. Clinton Walker Keyes (Cambridge, Mass.: Harvard University Press/Heinemann).

—— (1949). *Topica*, ed. and trans. H. M. Hubbell (Cambridge, Mass.: Harvard University Press/Heinemann).

[——] (1981). *Ad C. Herennium de ratione dicendi (Rhetorica ad Herennium)*, ed. and trans. Harry Caplan (Cambridge, Mass.: Harvard University Press/Heinemann).

Coquillart, Guillaume (1975). *Œuvres: suivies d'œuvres attribuées à l'auteur*, ed. Michael Freeman (Geneva: Droz).

Desmarins de Masan, Bertrand (1856). *Le Rousier des dames sive le pèlerin d'amours*, in Anatole de Montaiglon and James de Rothschild (eds.), *Recueil de poésies françoises des XVe et XVIe siècles* (Paris: Jennet, 1855–78), v. 162–203.

—— (1875). *Le Procès des deulx amans plaid[o]yant en la court de Cupido la grace de leur dame*, in Anatole de Montaiglon and James de Rothschild (eds.), *Recueil de poésies françoises des XVe et XVIe siècles* (Paris: Jennet, 1855–78), x. 170–92.

Du Pont, Gratien (1972). *Art et science de rhetoricque metriffiee* (Toulouse: Nycolas Vieillard, 1539; repr. Geneva: Slatkine Reprints).

Du Pré, Jehan (forthcoming). *Le Palais des nobles dames* (Lyons, 1534), ed. Brenda Dunn-Lardeau (Paris: Champion).

Dufour, Antoine (1970). *Les Vies des femmes célèbres*, ed. G. Jeanneau (Geneva: Droz).

Les Erreurs du jugement de l'amant banny (1905). In Arthur Piaget, 'La *Belle Dame sans merci* et ses imitations', *Romania*, 34: 375–428.

Évrard de Conty (1993). *Le Livre des échecs amoureux moralisés*, ed. Françoise Guichard-Tesson and Bruno Roy (Montreal: CERES).

Le Fèvre, Jean (1892). *Les Lamentations de Matheolus*, in *'Les Lamentations de Matheolus' et 'Le Livre de leesce' de Jehan le Fèvre, de Resson: poèmes français du XIVe siècle*, ed. A.-G. van Hamel, 2 vols. (Paris: Bouillon, 1892–1905), i.

—— (1905). *Le Livre de leesce*, in *'Les Lamentations de Matheolus' et 'Le Livre de leesce' de Jehan le Fèvre, de Resson: poèmes français du XIVe siècle*, ed. A.-G. van Hamel, 2 vols. (Paris: Bouillon, 1892–1905), ii.

Le Franc, Martin (1887). *La Complainte du livre du Champion des dames à maistre Martin Le Franc son acteur*, in Gaston Paris, 'Un poème inédit de Martin Le Franc', *Romania*, 16: 383–437.

—— (1999a). *Le Champion des dames*, ed. Robert Deschaux (Paris: Champion).

—— (1999b). *L'Estrif de Fortune et de Vertu*, ed. Peter F. Dembowski (Geneva: Droz).

Le Giroufflier aulx dames (1878). In Anatole de Montaiglon and James de Rothschild (eds.), *Recueil de poésies françoises des XVe et XVIe siècles*, (Paris: Jennet, 1855–78), xiii. 240–80.

Guillaume de Deguileville (1893). *Le Pèlerinage de vie humaine*, ed. J. J. Stürzinger (London: Nichols & Sons).

Guillaume de Lorris and Jean de Meun (1992). *Le Roman de la rose*, ed. Armand Strubel (Paris: Librairie Générale Française).

Guillaume de Machaut (1988). *'Le Jugement du roy de Behaigne' and 'Remede de Fortune'*, ed. and trans. James I. Wimsatt and William W. Kibler (Athens, Ga.: University of Georgia Press).

Hicks, Eric (ed.) (1977). *Le Débat sur 'le Roman de la rose'* (Paris: Champion).

Le Jardin de plaisance et fleur de rethorique: reproduction en fac-similé de l'édition publiée par Antoine Vérard vers 1501 (1910–25). Ed. Eugénie Droz and Arthur Piaget, 2 vols. (Paris: Firmin-Didot).

La Chesnaye, Nicolas de (1991). *La Condamnation de Bancquet*, ed. Jelle Koopmans and Paul Verhuyck (Geneva: Droz).

Latini, Brunetto (2003). *Li Livres dou tresor*, ed. Spurgeon Baldwin and Paul Barrette (Tempe, Ariz.: Arizona Center for Medieval and Renaissance Studies).

Laurent de Premierfait's 'Des cas des nobles hommes et femmes' (1968). Ed. Patricia May Gathercole (Chapel Hill, NC: University of North Carolina Press).

Marot, Clément (1922). *Les Blasons anatomiques du corps féminin*, in Frédéric Lachèvre, *Bibliographie des recueils collectifs de poésies du XVIe siècle (du Jardin de plaisance, 1502, aux Recueils de Toussaint du Bray, 1609)* (Paris: Champion), 41–9.

[——] (1954–7). *Le Roman de la rose, dans la version attribuée à Clément Marot*, ed. Silvio F. Baridon, 2 vols. (Milan: Istituto Editoriale Cisalpino).

Marot, Jean (1999). *La Vraye disant advocate des dames*, in *Les Deux Recueils Jean Marot de Caen*, ed. Gérard Defaux and Thierry Mantovani (Geneva: Droz), 93–119.

Michault, Pierre (1978). *Le Procès d'Honneur Féminin*, ed. Barbara Folkart (= *Moyen Français* 2).

—— (1980). *Le Procès d'Honneur Féminin*, in *Pierre Michault: œuvres poétiques*, ed. Barbara Folkart (Paris: Union Générale d'Éditions), 27–68.

Milet, Jacques (1910). *La Forest de tristesse*, in *Le Jardin de plaisance et fleur de rethorique*, ed. Eugénie Droz and Arthur Piaget, 2 vols. (Paris: Firmin-Didot, 1910–25), i, fols. 204^r–24^v.

Le Miroir aux dames: poème inédit du XVe siècle (1908). Ed. Arthur Piaget (Neuchatel: Attinger).

Le Monologue fort joyeulx auquel sont introduictz deux avocatz et ung juge, devant lequel est plaidoyé le bien et le mal des dames (1876). In Anatole de Montaiglon and James de Rothschild (eds.), *Recueil de poésies françoises des XVe et XVIe siècles* (Paris: Jennet, 1855–78), xi. 176–91.

Montaiglon, Anatole de, and Rothschild, James de (eds.) (1855–78). *Recueil de poésies françoises des XVe et XVIe siècles: morales, facétieuses, historiques*, 13 vols. (Paris: Jennet).

Ovid (1986). *Heroides and Amores*, ed. and trans. Grant Showerman, 2nd edn. (Cambridge, Mass.: Harvard University Press).

—— (2004). *Metamorphoses*, ed. R. J. Tarrant (Oxford: OUP).

Petrarca, Francesco (1974). *Le familiari*, ed. Ugo Dotti, 2 vols. (Argalìa: Urbino).

Le Procès des femmes et des pulces, composé par ung frère mineur pèlerin, retournant des Hirrelendes, où il apprint la vraye recepte pour prendre et faire mourir les pulces, laquelle sera déclairée cy après à la diffinitive dudict procès (1875). In Anatole de Montaiglon and James de Rothschild (eds.), *Recueil de poésies françoises des XVe et XVIe siècles* (Paris: Jennet, 1855–78), x. 61–74.

Le Purgatoire des mauvais maris (1998). In Maria Colombo-Timelli, 'Le *Purgatoire des mauvais maris*: introduction et édition', *Romania*, 116: 492–523.

Le Purgatoire des mauvais maris (2002). In Maria Colombo-Timelli, 'Le *Purgatoire des mauvais maris* et *L'Enfer des mauvaises femmes*: introduction', *Romania*, 119 (2001): 483–505, and 'Le *Purgatoire des mauvais maris* et *L'Enfer des mauvaises femmes*: édition', *Romania*, 120 (2002): 192–225.

Quintilian (2001). *The Orator's Education*, ed. and trans. Donald A. Russell, 4 vols. (Cambridge, Mass.: Harvard University Press).

Richard de Fournival (1860). *Le Bestiaire d'amour*, ed. C. Hippeau (Paris: Aubry).

Saint-Gelais, Octovien de (2002). *Le Séjour d'honneur*, ed. Frédéric Duval (Geneva: Droz).

Seneca (1974). *Controversiae I–VI*, ed. and trans. Michael Winterbottom (Cambridge, Mass.: Harvard University Press/Heinemann).

Valerius Maximus (2000). *Memorable Doings and Sayings*, ed. and trans. D. R. Shackleton Bailey, 2 vols. (Cambridge, Mass.: Harvard University Press).

Virgil (1978). *Aeneid*, ed. and trans. H. Rushton Fairclough, 2 vols. (Cambridge, Mass.: Harvard University Press/Heinemann).

SECONDARY SOURCES

Abensour, Léon (1979). *Histoire générale du féminisme: des origines à nos jours* (Paris: Delgrave, 1921; repr. Paris: Slatkine Reprints).

Albistur, Maïté, and Armogathe, Daniel (1977). *Histoire du féminisme français: du moyen âge à nos jours* (Paris: Éditions des femmes).

Aldrete, Gregory S. (1999). *Gestures and Acclamations in Ancient Rome* (Baltimore: Johns Hopkins University Press).

Altmann, Barbara K. (2002). 'Christine de Pizan, First Lady of the Middle Ages', in Kennedy et al. (2002), i. 17–30.

—— and Carroll, Carleton W. (eds.) (2003). *The Court Reconvenes: Courtly Literature across the Disciplines* (Cambridge: D. S. Brewer).

Angelo, Gretchen V. (2003). 'A Most Uncourtly Lady: The Testimony of the *Belle Dame sans mercy*', *Exemplaria*, 15: 133–57.

Angenot, Marc (1977). *Les Champions des femmes: examen du discours sur la supériorité des femmes 1400–1800* (Montreal: Presses de l'Université du Québec).

Armstrong, Adrian (1997). 'The Deferred Verdict: A Topos in Late-Medieval Poetic Debates?', *French Studies Bulletin*, 64: 12–14.

—— (1999). ' "Regardez bien tout au long les histoyres": Illustration and Self-Conscious Writing in Jean Bouchet's *Jugement poetic de l'honneur femenin*', *Bulletin of the John Rylands University Library of Manchester*, 81/3: 241–68.

—— (2000). *Technique and Technology: Script, Print, and Poetics in France 1470–1550* (Oxford: Clarendon Press).

—— (2001). 'Paratexte et autorité(s) chez les Grands Rhétoriqueurs', *Travaux de littérature*, 14: 61–89.

—— (2002). 'L'Active et la passive: deux modèles de vertu féminine dans *Le Jugement poetic de l'honneur femenin* de Jean Bouchet (1538)?', in Jennifer Britnell and Ann Moss (eds.), *Female Saints and Sinners: saintes et mondaines (France 1450–1650)* (Durham: Durham Modern Languages Series), 179–95.

—— (2003). 'Les Femmes et la violence dans le *Jugement poetic de l'honneur femenin* (1538)', in Jennifer Britnell and Nathalie Dauvois (eds.), *Jean Bouchet: Traverseur des voies périlleuses (1476–1557)*, *Actes du colloque de Poitiers (30–31 août 2001)* (Paris: Champion), 209–28.

—— (2004). 'Semiramis in *Grand Rhétoriqueur* Writing', in Michael Twomey and Alasdair MacDonald (eds.), *Schooling and Scholarship: The Ordering and Reordering of Knowledge in the Western Middle Ages* (Louvain: Peeters), 157–71.

—— (forthcoming). ' "Leur temps est; le mien est passé": Poetic Ingenuity and Competition in the *Querelle de la Belle Dame sans mercy*', in *The Virtuoso Circle: Competition, Collaboration and Complexity in Late Medieval French Poetry* (Tempe, Ariz.: Arizona Center for Medieval and Renaissance Studies), chapter 1.

—— and Adams, David J. (eds.) (1999). *Text and Image in the French Illustrated Book from the Middle Ages to the Present Day* (= *Bulletin of the John Rylands University Library of Manchester*, 81/3).

Atwood, Margaret (2002). *Negotiating with the Dead: A Writer on Writing* (Cambridge: CUP).

Aughterson, Kate (ed.) (1995). *Renaissance Woman: A Sourcebook* (London: Routledge).

Austin, J. L. (1975). *How to Do Things With Words*, 2nd edn. (Oxford: Clarendon Press).

Avril, François, and Reynaud, Nicole (1995). *Les Manuscrits à peintures en France: 1440–1520*, rev. edn. (Paris: BnF/Flammarion).

Badel, Pierre-Yves (1988). 'Le Débat', in Poirion (1988), 95–110.

—— (1996). 'Nouvelles Allusions au *Roman de la rose*', in Luciano Rossi (ed.) '*Ensi firent li ancessor*': *Mélanges de philologie médiévale offerts à Marc-René Jung*, 2 vols. (Alessandria: Edizioni dell'Orso), ii. 475–90.

Bazàn, Bernardo C. (1985). *Les Questions disputées et les questions quodlibétiques dans les facultés de théologie, de droit et de médecine* (Turnhout: Brepols).

Beauvoir, Simone de (1949). *Le Deuxième Sexe*, 2 vols. (Paris: Gallimard).

Bec, Pierre (1979). ' "Trobairitz" et chansons de femme: contribution à la connaissance du lyrisme féminin au moyen âge', *Cahiers de civilisation médiévale*, 22: 235–62.

Becker, Karin (1997). 'La Mentalité juridique dans la littérature française (XIIIe–XVe siècles)', *Moyen Âge*, 103/2: 308–27.

Benson, Pamela J. (1992). *The Invention of the Renaissance Woman: The Challenge of Female Independence in the Literature and Thought of Italy and England* (University Park, Pa.: Pennsylvania State University Press).

Bent, Margaret (2004). 'The Musical Stanzas in Martin Le Franc's *Le Champion des dames*', in John Haines and Randall Rosenfeld (eds.), *Music and Medieval Manuscripts: Palaeography and Performance* (Aldershot: Ashgate), 91–127.

Bérier, François (1988). 'La Traduction en français', in Poirion (1988), 219–65.

Berriot-Salvadore, Evelyne (1990). *Les Femmes dans la société française de la Renaissance* (Geneva: Droz).

Blamires, Alcuin (1997). *The Case for Women in Medieval Culture* (Oxford: Clarendon Press).

—— and Holian, Gail C. (2002). '*The Romance of the Rose' Illuminated: Manuscripts at the National Library of Wales, Aberystwyth* (Tempe, Ariz.: Arizona Centre for Medieval and Renaissance Studies).

—— Pratt, Karen, and Marx, C. W. (eds.) (1992). *Woman Defamed and Woman Defended: An Anthology of Medieval Texts* (Oxford: Clarendon Press).

Blanc, Agnès, Dang, Virginie, and Ostorero, Martine (1999). 'Martin Le Franc', in Martine Ostorero, Agostino Paravicini Bagliani, and Kathrin Utz Tremp (eds.), *L'Imaginaire du sabbat: édition critique des textes les plus anciens (1430–c.1440)* (Lausanne: Université de Lausanne), 483–508.

Blanchard, Joël (1992). 'Compilation and Legitimation in the Fifteenth Century: *Le Livre de la cité des dames*', in Richards (1992), 228–49.

Bloom, Harold (1997). *The Anxiety of Influence: A Theory of Poetry*, 2nd edn. (New York: Oxford University Press).

Bock, Gisela (2002). *Women in European History*, trans. Allison Brown (Oxford: Blackwell).

—— and Erler, Mary Carpenter (2002). 'The European *Querelle des femmes*', *Disputatio*, 5: 127–56.

Boone, Joseph A. (1990). 'Of Me(n) and Feminism: Who(se) Is the Sex That Writes?', in Joseph A. Boone and Michael Cadden (eds.), *Engendering Men: The Question of Male Feminist Criticism* (New York: Routledge), 11–25.

Bordier, Jean-Pierre (ed.) (1999). *L'Économie du dialogue dans l'ancien théâtre européen: actes de la première rencontre sur l'ancien théâtre européen de 1995* (Paris: Champion).

Bossy, Michel-André (1990). 'Woman's Plain Talk in *Le Débat de l'omme et de la femme* by Guillaume Alexis', *Fifteenth Century Studies*, 16: 23–41.

Bourdillon, F. W. (1906). *The Early Editions of the 'Roman de la rose'* (London: Chiswick Press).

Bousmanne, Bernard, Johan, Frédérique, and Van Hoorebeeck, Céline (2003). *La Librairie des ducs de Bourgogne: manuscrits conservés à la Bibliothèque Royale de Belgique*, 2 vols. (Turnhout: Brepols, 2000–), ii.

Bousmar, Eric, and Sommé, Monique (2000). 'Femmes et espaces féminins à la cour de Bourgogne au temps d'Isabel de Portugal (1430–1471)', in Jan Hirschbiegel and Werner Paravicini (eds.), *Das Frauenzimmer: Die Frau bei Hofe in Spätmittelalter und früher Neuzeit* (Stuttgart: Thorbecke), 47–8.

Bozzolo, Carla (1973). *Manuscrits des traductions françaises d'œuvres de Boccace, XVe siècle* (Padua: Antenore).

Braet, Herman (1994). 'Aux sources du *Roman de la rose*', in P. R. Monks and D. D. R. Owen (eds.), *Medieval Codicology, Iconography, Literature, and Translation: Studies for Keith Val Sinclair* (London: Brill), 110–19.

Britnell, Jennifer (1986). *Jean Bouchet* (Edinburgh: Edinburgh University Press).

Brown, Cynthia J. (1995). *Poets, Patrons, and Printers: Crisis of Authority in Late Medieval France* (Ithaca, NY: Cornell University Press).

—— (1998). 'The Reconstruction of an Author in Print: Christine de Pizan in the Fifteenth and Sixteenth Centuries', in Marilynn Desmond (ed.), *Christine de Pizan and the Categories of Difference* (Minneapolis: University of Minnesota Press), 69–85.

—— (1999), 'Textual and Iconographical Ambivalence in the Late Medieval Representation of Women', *Bulletin of the John Rylands University Library of Manchester*, 81/3: 205–39.

Brown, Cynthia J. (2001). 'The "Famous-Women" Topos in Early Sixteenth-Century France: Echoes of Christine de Pizan', in Mühlethaler and Billotte (2001), 149–60.

—— (2007a). 'Paratextual Performances in the Early Parisian Book Trade: Antoine Vérard's Edition of Boccaccio's *Nobles et cleres dames* (1493)', in E. Jane Burns, Eglal Doss-Quinby, and Roberta Krueger (eds.), *Cultural Performances in Medieval France: Essays in Honor of Nancy Freeman Regalado* (Woodbridge: Boydell and Brewer), 255–64.

—— (2007b). 'Le Mécénat d'Anne de Bretagne et la politique du livre', in Kathleen Wilson-Chevalier (ed.), *Les Femmes et les arts à la Renaissance: patronnes et mécènes, d'Anne de Bretagne à Catherine de Médicis* (Saint Étienne: University of Saint Étienne Press) (forthcoming).

Brown-Grant, Rosalind (1995). '*Des hommes et des femmes illustres:* modalités narratives et transformations génériques chez Pétrarque, Boccace et Christine de Pizan', in Liliane Dulac and Bernard Ribémont (eds.), *Une femme de lettres au moyen âge: études autour de Christine de Pizan* (Orléans: Paradigme), 469–80.

—— (2002). 'Writing beyond Gender: Christine de Pizan's Linguistic Strategies in the Defence of Women', in Kennedy et al. (2002), i. 155–69.

Buettner, Brigitte (1996). *Boccaccio's 'Des cleres et nobles femmes': Systems of Signification in an Illuminated Manuscript* (Seattle: University of Washington Press).

Burrow, J. A. (2002). *Gestures and Looks in Medieval Narrative* (Cambridge: CUP).

Busby, Keith, and Jones, Catherine M. (eds.) (2000). *'Por le soie amisté': Essays in Honor of Norris J. Lacy* (Amsterdam: Rodopi).

Butler, Judith (1990a). *Gender Trouble: Feminism and the Subversion of Identity* (New York: Routledge).

—— (1990b). 'Performative Acts and Gender Constitution: An Essay in Phenomenology and Feminist Theory', in Sue-Ellen Case (ed.), *Performing Feminisms: Feminist Critical Theory and Theatre* (Baltimore: Johns Hopkins University Press), 270–82.

—— (2004). *Undoing Gender* (New York: Routledge).

Bynum, Caroline Walker (2001). *Metamorphosis and Identity* (New York: Zone Books).

Callu, Florence, and Avril, François (c1975). *Boccace en France: de l'humanisme à l'érotisme* (Paris: BnF).

Carlson, Marvin A. (2001). *The Haunted Stage: The Theatre as Memory Machine* (Ann Arbor: University of Michigan Press).

Carruthers, Mary (1990). *The Book of Memory: A Study of Memory in Medieval Culture* (Cambridge: CUP).

—— (1998). *The Craft of Thought: Meditation, Rhetoric, and the Making of Images, 400–1200* (Cambridge: CUP).

Cayley, Emma J. (2003). 'Drawing Conclusions: The Poetics of Closure in Alain Chartier's Verse', *Fifteenth Century Studies*, 28: 51–64.

—— (2006). *Debate and Dialogue: Alain Chartier in his Cultural Context* (Oxford: OUP).

Cerquiglini-Toulet, Jacqueline (1993a). 'Cadmus ou Carmenta: réflexion sur le concept d'invention à la fin du moyen âge', in Cornilliat et al. (1993), 211–39.

—— (1993b). *La Couleur de la mélancolie: la fréquentation des livres au XIVe siècle, 1300–1415* (Paris: Hatier).

Chance, Jane (2002). 'Illuminated Royal Manuscripts of the Early Fifteenth Century and Christine de Pizan's "Remythification" of Classical Women', in Kennedy et al. (2002), i. 203–41.

Charon-Parent, Annie (1988). 'Aspects de la politique éditoriale de Galliot Du Pré', in Pierre Aquilon, Henri-Jean Martin, and François Dupuigrenet Desroussilles (eds.), *Le Livre dans l'Europe de la Renaissance: actes du XXVIIIe colloque international d'études humanistes de Tours* (Paris: Promodis), 209–18.

Charron, Pascale (1996). 'Le Maître du *Champion des dames*: un enlumineur du Nord de la France de la seconde moitié du XVe siècle' (unpublished doctoral thesis, Université de Paris-IV-Sorbonne).

—— (2000). 'Les Réceptions du *Champion des dames* de Martin Le Franc à la cour de Bourgogne: "Tres puissant et tres humain prince [. . .] veullez cest livre humainement recepvoir"', *Bulletin du bibliophile*, 9–31.

—— (2004). *Le Maître du 'Champion des dames'* (Paris: Institut National d'Histoire de l'Art).

Coleman, Joyce (1996). *Public Reading and the Reading Public in Late Medieval England and France* (Cambridge: CUP).

Compagnon, Antoine (1979). *La Seconde Main ou le travail de la citation* (Paris: Seuil).

Copeland, Rita (1995). *Rhetoric, Hermeneutics, and Translation in the Middle Ages: Academic Traditions and Vernacular Texts* (1991; repr. Cambridge: CUP).

Cornilliat, François, Langer, Ullrich, and Kelly, Douglas (eds.) (1993). *What is Literature? France 1100–1600* (Lexington, Ky.: French Forum).

Curtius, Ernst Robert (1990). *European Literature and the Latin Middle Ages*, trans. Willard R. Trask, 7th edn. (Princeton: Princeton University Press).

Davis, Colin (2005). 'Hauntology, Spectres and Phantoms', *French Studies*, 59/3: 373–9.

Debae, Marguerite (1995). *La Bibliothèque de Marguerite d'Autriche: essai de reconstitution d'après l'inventaire de 1523–1524* (Louvain: Peeters).

Delaney, Sheila (1990). '"Mothers to Think Back Through": Who Are They? The Ambiguous Example of Christine de Pizan', in Sheila Delaney (ed.), *Medieval Literary Politics: Shapes of Ideology* (Manchester: Manchester University Press), 88–103.

Dembowski, Peter F. (1989). 'Martin Le Franc, Fortune, Virtue and Fifteenth Century France', in Norris J. Lacy and Gloria Torrini-Roblin (eds.), *Continuations: Essays on Medieval French Literature and Language in Honor of John L. Grigsby* (Birmingham, Ala.: Summa), 261–73.

Derrida, Jacques (1982). 'Signature, Event, Context', in *Margins of Philosophy*, trans. Alan Bass (Chicago: University of Chicago Press), 307–30.

—— (1993). *Spectres de Marx: l'état de la dette, le travail du deuil, et la nouvelle Internationale* (Paris: Galilée).

—— (1994). *Specters of Marx: The State of the Debt, the Work of Mourning, and the New International*, ed. Bernd Magnus and Stephen Cullenberg, trans. Peggy Kamuf (London: Routledge).

Deschaux, Robert (1998). 'Sourires et joies dans le *Champion des dames* de Martin Le Franc', in Jean-Claude Faucon, Alain Labbé, and Daniel Quéruel (eds.), *Miscellanea mediaevalia: mélanges offerts à Philippe Ménard*, 2 vols. (Paris: Champion), i. 407–15.

Desmond, Marilynn (1994). *Reading Dido: Gender, Textuality, and the Medieval 'Aeneid'* (Minneapolis: University of Minnesota Press).

—— (2003). 'The *Querelle de la Rose* and the Ethics of Reading', in Barbara K. Altmann and Deborah L. McGrady (eds.), *Christine de Pizan: A Casebook* (New York: Routledge), 167–80.

—— and Sheingorn, Pamela (2003). *Myth, Montage, and Visuality in Late Medieval Manuscript Culture: Christine de Pizan's 'Epistre Othea'* (Ann Arbor: University of Michigan Press).

Diamond, Elin (1996). *Performance and Cultural Politics* (New York: Routledge).

Doutrepont, Georges (1909). *La Littérature française à la cour des ducs de Bourgogne* (Paris: Champion).

Driver, Martha W., and Brown, Cynthia J. (eds.) (2001). *Women and Book Culture in Late Medieval and Early Modern France* (= *Journal of the Early Book Society*, 4).

DuBruck, Edelgard (1999). 'Death: Poetic Perception and Imagination (Continental Europe)', in Edelgard E. DuBruck and Barbara I. Gusick (eds.), *Death and Dying in the Middle Ages* (New York: Peter Lang), 295–313.

Ducoudray, Gustave (1902). *Les Origines du parlement de Paris et la justice aux XIIIe et XIVe siècles* (Paris: Hachette).

Dulac, Liliane (1978). 'Un mythe didactique chez Christine de Pizan: Sémiramis ou la veuve héroïque (du *De mulieribus claris* de Boccace à la *Cité des dames*)', in *Mélanges de philologie romane offerts à Charles Camproux*, 2 vols. (Montpellier: Centre d'Estudis Occitans), i. 315–43.

Dunn, Brenda 1976. 'Recherches sur l'expression linguistique dans *Le Palais des nobles dames* (XVIᵉ siècle)', 2 vols. (unpublished doctoral thesis, University of Grenoble III) (BnF microfilms R-191453 and R-191454).

Eckert, Penelope, and McConnell-Ginet, Sally (2003). *Language and Gender* (Cambridge: CUP).

Enders, Jody (1992). *Rhetoric and the Origins of Medieval Drama* (Ithaca, NY: Cornell University Press).

—— (1993). 'The Theatre of Scholastic Erudition', *Comparative Drama*, 27/3: 341–63.

Fenster, Thelma S. (1992). 'Did Christine Have a Sense of Humour? The Evidence of the *Epistre au dieu d'amours*', in Richards (1992), 23–36.

—— (2002). 'Possible Odds: Christine de Pizan and the Paradoxes of Woman', in Kennedy et al. (2002), ii. 355–66.

—— and Lees, Clare A. (2002). 'Introduction', in Thelma S. Fenster and Clare A. Lees (eds.), *Gender in Debate from the Early Middle Ages to the Renaissance* (Basingstoke: Palgrave), 1–18.

Fetterley, Judith (1978). *The Resisting Reader: A Feminist Approach to American Fiction* (Bloomington, Ind.: Indiana University Press).

Foulet, Alfred, and Speer, Mary Blakely (1979). *On Editing Old French Texts* (Lawrence, Kan.: Regents Press of Kansas).

Franko, Mark, and Richards, Annette (2000). *Acting on the Past: Historical Performance across the Disciplines* (Hanover, NH: Wesleyan University Press).

Fuss, Diana (1989). *Essentially Speaking: Feminism, Nature and Difference* (London: Routledge).

Galand-Hallyn, Perrine, and Hallyn, Fernand (eds.) (2001). *Poétiques de la Renaissance: le modèle italien, le monde franco-bourguignon et leur héritage en France au XVIᵉ siècle* (Geneva: Droz).

Gallica, la bibliothèque numérique de la Bibliothèque nationale de France [website], http://gallica.bnf.fr/, accessed 27 January 2007.

Garber, Marjorie (1992). *Vested Interests: Cross-Dressing and Cultural Anxiety* (London: Routledge).

Garnier, François (1982). *Le Langage de l'image au moyen âge: signification et symbolique*, 2nd edn., 2 vols. (Paris: Léopard d'Or).

Gaskell, Philip (1972). *A New Introduction to Bibliography* (Oxford: Clarendon Press).

Genette, Gérard (1972). *Figures III* (Paris: Seuil).

—— (1983). *Nouveau Discours du récit* (Paris: Seuil).

—— (1987). *Seuils* (Paris: Seuil).

Goyet, Francis (1987). '*Imitatio* ou intertextualité? (Riffaterre Revisited)', *Poétique*, 71: 313–20.

Graham, Angus (2000). 'Albertanus of Brescia: A Preliminary Census of Vernacular Manuscripts', *Studi Medievali*, 41/2: 891–924.

Gray, Floyd (2000). *Gender, Rhetoric and Print Culture in French Renaissance Writing* (Cambridge: CUP).

Greene, Thomas M. (1982). *The Light in Troy: Imitation and Discovery in Renaissance Poetry* (New Haven: Yale University Press).

Gros, Gérard (1992). *Le Poète, la vierge et le prince du puy: étude sur les puys marials de la France du Nord du XIVe siècle à la Renaissance* (Paris: Klincksieck).

Guillerm-Curutchet, Luce, Hordoir-Louppe, Laurence, Guillerm, Jean-Pierre, and Piejus, Marie-Françoise (eds.) (1971). *La Femme dans la littérature française et les traductions en français du XVIe siècle* (Lille: Publications de l'Université de Lille III).

Hagen, Susan K. (1990). *Allegorical Remembrance: A Study of 'The Pilgrimage of the Life of Man' as a Medieval Treatise on Seeing and Remembering* (Athens, Ga.: University of Georgia Press).

Harvey, Elizabeth D. (1992). *Ventriloquized Voices: Feminist Theory and English Renaissance Texts* (London: Routledge).

Harvey, Howard Graham (1969). *The Theatre of the Basoche: The Contribution of the Law Societies to French Mediaeval Comedy* (Cambridge, Mass.: Harvard University Press, 1941; repr. New York: Kraus).

Hasenohr, Geneviève (1990). 'Traductions et littérature en langue vernaculaire', in Martin and Vezin (1990), 231–352.

Hindman, Sandra (ed.) (©1993). *Les Fastes du livre manuscrit du XIIIe au XIXe siècle* (Paris: Les Enluminures).

Hotchkiss, Valerie (1996). *Clothes Make the Man: Female Cross Dressing in Medieval Europe* (New York: Garland).

Hüe, Denis (2002). *La Poésie palinodique à Rouen (1486–1550)* (Paris: Champion).

Hult, David F. (1983). 'The Limits of Mime(sis): Notes Toward a Generic Revision of Medieval Theatre', *Esprit Créateur*, 23/1: 49–63.

—— (1997a). 'La Fortune du *Roman de la rose* à l'époque de Clément Marot', in Gérard Defaux and Michel Simonin (eds.), *Clément Marot 'Prince des poëtes françois' 1496–1996: actes du colloque international de Cahors en Quercy 21–25 mai 1996* (Paris: Champion), 143–56.

—— (1997b). 'Words and Deeds: Jean de Meun's *Roman de la rose* and the Hermeneutics of Censorship', *New Literary History*, 28/2: 345–66.

Huot, Sylvia (1987a). *From Song to Book: The Poetics of Writing in Old French Lyric and Lyrical Narrative Poetry* (Ithaca, NY: Cornell University Press).

—— (1987b). 'The Scribe as Editor: Rubrication as Critical Apparatus in Two Manuscripts of the *Roman de la rose*', *Esprit Créateur*, 27/1: 67–78.

Huot, Sylvia (1993a). *The Romance of the Rose and its Medieval Readers: Interpretation, Reception, and Manuscript Transmission* (Cambridge: CUP).

—— (1993b). 'Sentences and Subtle Fictions: Rereading Literature in the Later Middle Ages', in Cornilliat et al. (1993), 197–209.

Irigaray, Luce (1977). *Ce sexe qui n'en est pas un* (Paris: Minuit).

—— (1985). *This Sex Which is Not One*, trans. Catherine Porter (Ithaca, NY: Cornell University Press).

Jeanneau, G. (1977). 'Dufour et son modèle', *BHR* 39: 89–90.

Jordan, Constance (1987). 'Boccaccio's In-Famous Women: Gender and Civic Virtue in the *De mulieribus claris*', in Carole Levin and Jeanie Watson (eds.), *Ambiguous Realities: Women in the Middle Ages and Renaissance* (Detroit: Wayne State University Press), 25–47.

—— (1990). *Renaissance Feminism: Literary Texts and Political Models* (Ithaca, NY: Cornell University Press).

Kauffman, Linda S. (1986). *Discourses of Desire: Gender, Genre, and Epistolary Fictions* (Ithaca, NY: Cornell University Press).

Kay, Sarah (1990). *Subjectivity in Troubadour Poetry* (Cambridge: CUP).

Kelly, Joan (1984). 'Early Feminist Theory and the *Querelle des femmes*, 1400–1789', in *Women, History & Theory: The Essays of Joan Kelly* (Chicago: University of Chicago Press), 65–109.

Kelso, Ruth (1956). *Doctrine for the Lady of the Renaissance* (Urbana, Ill.: University of Illinois Press).

Kennedy, Angus J., Brown-Grant, Rosalind, Laidlaw, James C., and Müller, Catherine M. (eds.) (2002). *Contexts and Continuities: Proceedings of the IVth International Colloquium on Christine de Pizan (Glasgow 21–27 July 2000), Published in Honour of Liliane Dulac*, 3 vols. (Glasgow: University of Glasgow Press).

Kolsky, Stephen (2005). *The Ghost of Boccaccio: Writings on Famous Women in Renaissance Italy* (Turnhout: Brepols).

Kovacs, Susan R. (2001). 'Staging Lyric Performances in Early Print Culture: *Le Jardin de plaisance et fleur de rethorique* (*c*.1501–02)', *French Studies*, 55/1: 1–24.

Kristeva, Julia (1969). *Semiotikè: recherches pour une sémanalyse* (Paris: Seuil).

Krueger, Roberta L. (2002). 'Beyond Debate: Gender in Play in Old French Courtly Fiction', in Thelma S. Fenster and Clare A. Lees (eds.), *Gender in Debate from the Early Middle Ages to the Renaissance* (Basingstoke: Palgrave), 79–95.

Lack, Roland François (1990). 'Intertextuality or Influence: Kristeva, Bloom and the *Poésies* of Isidore Ducasse', in Worton and Still (1990), 130–42.

Laennec, Christine Moneera (1993). 'Christine Antygraphe: Authorial Ambivalence in the Works of Christine de Pizan', in Carol J. Singley and Susan

Elizabeth Sweeney (eds.), *Anxious Power: Reading, Writing, and Ambivalence in Narrative by Women* (Albany, NY: SUNY), 35–49.

Lazard, Madeleine (1985). *Images littéraires de la femme à la Renaissance* (Paris: PUF).

McKendrick, Scot (2003a). 'Reviving the Past: Illustrated Manuscripts of Secular Vernacular Texts, 1467–1500', in Thomas Kren and Scot McKendrick (eds.), *Illuminating the Renaissance: The Triumph of Flemish Manuscript Painting in Europe* (Los Angeles: J. Paul Getty Museum), 59–78.

—— (2003b). 'Painting in Manuscripts of Vernacular Texts c.1467–85', in Thomas Kren and Scot McKendrick (eds.), *Illuminating the Renaissance: The Triumph of Flemish Manuscript Painting in Europe* (Los Angeles: J. Paul Getty Museum), 223–311.

Maclean, Ian (1977). *Woman Triumphant: Feminism in French Literature 1610–1652* (Oxford: Clarendon Press).

McLeod, Glenda K. (1991). *Virtue and Venom: Catalogs of Women from Antiquity to the Renaissance* (Ann Arbor: University of Michigan Press).

Mann, Jill (1990). *Apologies to Women: Inaugural Lecture Delivered 20th November 1990* (Cambridge: CUP).

Martin, Henri-Jean (1959). 'Ce qu'on lisait à Paris au XVIᵉ siècle', *BHR* 21: 222–30.

—— and Vezin, Jean (eds.) (1990). *Mise en page et mise en texte du livre manuscrit* (Paris: Cercle de la Librairie-Promodis).

Matarasso, Pauline (2001). *Queen's Mate: Three Women of Power in France on the Eve of the Renaissance* (Aldershot: Ashgate).

Mathieu-Castellani, Gisèle (1998). *La Quenouille et la lyre* (Paris: Corti).

Meiss, Millard (1974). *French Painting in the Time of Jean de Berry: The Limbourgs and their Contemporaries*, 2 vols. (London: Thames and Hudson).

Meyer, Michel (ed.) (1999). *Histoire de la rhétorique des Grecs à nos jours* (Paris: Librairie Générale Française).

Minois, George (1999). *Anne de Bretagne* (Paris: Fayard).

Monahan, Jennifer (2002). '*Querelles*: Medieval Texts amd Modern Polemics', in Kennedy et al. (2002), ii. 575–84.

Moreau, Brigitte (1996). 'La Librairie parisienne du début du XVIᵉ siècle', in Frédéric Barbier, Sabine Juratic, and Dominique Varry (eds.), *L'Europe et le livre: réseaux et pratiques du négoce de librairie, XVIᵉ–XIXᵉ siècles* (Paris: Klincksieck), 13–16.

Moss, Ann (1982). *Ovid in Renaissance France: A Survey of the Latin Editions of Ovid and Commentaries Printed in France before 1600* (London: Warburg Institute).

Mühlethaler, Jean-Claude (1992). 'Les Poètes que de vert on couronne', *Moyen Français*, 30: 96–112.

Mühlethaler, Jean-Claude and Billotte, Denis (eds.) (2001). *'Riens ne m'est seur que la chose incertaine': études sur l'acte d'écrire au moyen âge offertes à Eric Hicks* (Geneva: Slatkine).

—— Cornilliat, François, and Dull, Olga A. (2001). 'Fonction éthique et sociale de la poésie au XVᵉ siècle', in Galand-Hallyn and Hallyn (2001), 301–46.

Murphy, James J. (2001). *Three Medieval Rhetorical Arts* (Tempe, Ariz.: Arizona Center for Medieval and Renaissance Studies).

Nephew, Julia A. (2000). 'Gender Reversals and Intellectual Gender in the Works of Christine de Pizan', in Eric Hicks, Diego Gonzalez, and Philippe Simon (eds.), *Au champ des escriptures: IIIᵉ colloque international sur Christine de Pizan. Lausanne, 18–22 juillet 1998* (Paris: Champion), 517–32.

Nichols, Stephen G. (1990). 'Introduction: Philology in a Manuscript Culture', *Speculum*, 65: 1–10.

Ornato, Ezio (1992). 'Les Humanistes français et la redécouverte des classiques', in Carla Bozzolo and Ezio Ornato (eds.), *Préludes à la Renaissance: aspects de la vie intellectuelle en France au XVᵉ siècle* (Paris: CNRS), 1–45.

Orr, Mary (2003). *Intertextuality: Debates and Contexts* (Cambridge: Polity Press).

Parent, Annie (1974). *Les Métiers du livre à Paris au XVIᵉ siècle (1535–1560)* (Geneva: Droz).

Parent-Charon, Annie (1996). 'Associations dans la librairie parisienne du XVIᵉ siècle', in Frédéric Barbier, Sabine Juratic, and Dominique Varry (eds.), *L'Europe et le livre: réseaux et pratiques du négoce de librairie, XVIᵉ–XIXᵉ siècles* (Paris: Klincksieck), 17–30.

Parker, Andrew, and Sedgwick, Eve Kosofsky (1995). *Performativity and Performance* (New York: Routledge).

Pasco, Allan H. (1994). *Allusion: A Literary Graft* (Toronto: University of Toronto Press).

Petit de Julleville, Louis (1886). *Histoire du théâtre en France: répertoire du théâtre comique en France au moyen âge* (Paris: Cerf).

Phillippy, Patricia A. (1986). 'Establishing Authority: Boccaccio's *De claris mulieribus* and Christine de Pizan's *Le Livre de la cité des dames*', *Romanic Review*, 77/3: 167–94.

Piaget, Arthur (1993). *Martin Le Franc, prévôt de Lausanne* (Lausanne: Payot, 1888; repr. Caen: Paradigme).

Poirion, Daniel (ed.) (1988). *La Littérature française aux XIVᵉ et XVᵉ siècles* (Heidelberg: Winter) (= *Grundriss der Romanischen Literaturen des Mittelalters*, viii/1).

Pratt, Karen (1999). 'Translating Misogamy: The Authority of the Intertext in the *Lamentationes Matheoluli* and its Middle French Translation by Jean Lefèvre', *Forum for Modern Language Studies*, 35/4: 421–35.

—— (2002). 'The Strains of Defense: The Many Voices of Jean Lefèvre's *Livre de Leesce*', in Thelma S. Fenster and Clare A. Lees (eds.), *Gender in Debate from the Early Middle Ages to the Renaissance* (Basingstoke: Palgrave), 113–33.

Richards, Earl Jeffrey (1983), 'Christine de Pizan and the Question of Feminist Rhetoric', *Teaching Language Through Literature*, 22: 15–24.

—— (ed.) (1992). *Reinterpreting Christine de Pizan* (Athens, Ga.: University of Georgia Press).

Richards, Earl Jeffrey (1996). 'Rejecting Essentialism and Gendered Writing: The Case of Christine de Pizan', in Jane Chance (ed.), *Gender and Text in the Later Middle Ages* (Gainesville, Fla.: University Press of Florida), 96–131.

—— (2001). 'Virile Woman and Womanchrist: The Meaning of Gender Metamorphosis in Christine', in Mühlethaler and Billotte (2001), 239–52.

Richardson, Lula McDowell (1929). *The Forerunners of Feminism in French Literature of the Renaissance from Christine of Pisa to Marie de Gournay* (Baltimore: Johns Hopkins University Press/PUF).

Riffaterre, Michael (1980). 'La Trace de l'intertexte', *La Pensée*, 215: 4–18.

—— (1981). 'L'Intertexte inconnu', *Littérature*, 41: 4–7.

—— (1990). 'Compulsory Reader Response: The Intertextual Drive', in Worton and Still (1990), 56–78.

Runnalls, Graham A. (1990). 'Towards a Typology of Medieval French Play Manuscripts', in Philip E. Bennett and Graham A. Runnalls (eds.), *The Editor and the Text* (Edinburgh: Edinburgh University Press), 93–113.

Salter, Elizabeth, and Pearsall, Derek (1980). 'Pictorial Illustration of Late Medieval Poetic Texts: The Role of the Frontispiece or Prefatory Picture', in *Medieval Iconography and Narrative: A Symposium* (Odense: Odense University Press), 100–23.

Sands, Peter F. (1977). 'Antoine Dufour, Jacques Philippe and "le racheter des hommes"', *BHR* 39: 81–7.

Schibanoff, Susan (1996). 'True Lies: Transvestism and Idolatry in the Trial of Joan of Arc', in Bonnie Wheeler and Charles T. Wood (eds.), *Fresh Verdicts on Joan of Arc* (New York: Garland), 31–60.

Schweickart, Patrocinio P. (1986). 'Reading Ourselves: Toward a Feminist Theory of Reading', in Patrocinio P. Schweickart and Elizabeth A. Flyn (eds.), *Gender and Reading: Essays on Readers, Texts, and Contexts* (Baltimore: Johns Hopkins University Press), 31–62.

Searle, John R. (1969). *Speech Acts: An Essay on the Philosophy of Language* (Cambridge: CUP).

Shaw, David (1977). *Provisional Short-Title Catalogue of Books Printed in Paris by Pierre Vidoue 1516–43* (Canterbury: University of Kent).

Shennan, Joseph. H. (1998). *The Parlement of Paris*, 2nd edn. (Stroud: Sutton).

Smith, Susan L. (1995). *The Power of Women: A 'Topos' in Medieval Art and Literature* (Philadelphia: University of Pennsylvania Press).

Solterer, Helen (1995). *The Master and Minerva: Disputing Women in French Medieval Culture* (Berkeley and Los Angeles: University of California Press).

—— (2002). 'The Freedoms of Fiction for Gender in Premodern France', in Fenster and Lees (2002), 135–63.

Sprinker, Michael (ed.) (1999). *Ghostly Demarcations: A Symposium on Jacques Derrida's 'Spectres of Marx'* (London: Verso).

Stephenson, Barbara (2004). *The Power and Patronage of Marguerite de Navarre* (Aldershot: Ashgate).

Stones, Alison (1976). 'Secular Manuscript Illumination in France', in Christopher Kleinhenz (ed.), *Medieval Manuscripts and Textual Criticism* (Chapel Hill, NC: University of North Carolina Press), 83–102.

Strohm, Paul (1983). 'Chaucer's Audience(s): Fictional, Implied, Intended, Actual', *Chaucer Review*, 18/2: 137–45.

Swift, Helen J. (2004). '(Un)covering Truth: Speaking "Proprement" in Late-Medieval French Poetry', *Nottingham Medieval Studies*, 48: 60–79.

—— (2006). 'Martin Le Franc et son *livre qui se plaint*: une petite énigme à la cour de Philippe le Bon', in Tania Van Hemelryck and Céline Van Hoorebeeck (eds.), *L'Écrit et le manuscrit à la fin du moyen âge* (Turnhout: Brepols), 329–42.

—— (2008). 'Points of Tension: Performing *Je* in Jean Bouchet's *Jugement poetic de l'honneur femenin* (1538)', in Elina Gertsman (ed.), *Visualizing Medieval Performance: Perspectives, Histories, Contexts* (Burlington, VT.: Ashgate) (forthcoming).

—— (forthcoming). '"Tresfort se plaignent de ce que sont frustrees/ d'immortel bruyt": des voix (dites) féminines rapportées par des voix masculines dans la *querelle des femmes*', *Verbum*.

Taylor, Jane H. M. (1984). 'Un miroer salutaire', in Jane H. M. Taylor (ed.), *Dies Illa: Death in the Middle Ages: Proceedings of the 1983 Manchester Colloquium* (Liverpool: Francis Cairns), 29–43.

—— (1990). 'The Dialogues of the Dance of Death and the Limits of Late-Medieval Theatre', *Fifteenth Century Studies*, 16: 215–32.

—— (1999). '*Le Chevalier des dames du dolent fortuné*: Image and Text, Manuscript and Print', *Bulletin of the John Rylands University Library of Manchester*, 81/3: 153–76.

—— (2000). 'Translation as Reception: Boccaccio's *De mulieribus claris* and *Des cleres et nobles femmes*', in Keith Busby and Catherine M. Jones (eds.), *'Por le soie amisté': Essays in Honor of Norris J. Lacy* (Amsterdam: Rodopi), 491–507.

—— (2001). *The Poetry of François Villon: Text and Context* (Cambridge: CUP).

—— (2003). 'Embodying the Rose: An Intertextual Reading of Alain Chartier's *Belle Dame sans mercy*', in Barbara K. Altmann and Carleton W. Carroll (eds.), *The Court Reconvenes: Courtly Literature across the Disciplines* (Cambridge: Brewer), 325–33.

Telle, Émile V. (1969). *L'Œuvre de Marguerite d'Angoulême, reine de Navarre, et la querelle des femmes* (Toulouse: Lion, 1937; repr. Geneva: Slatkine Reprints).

Thiry, Claude (1986). 'Débats et moralités dans la littérature française du XVᵉ siècle: intersection et interaction du narratif et du dramatique', *Moyen Français*, 19: 203–44.

Toubert, Hélène (1990). 'La Mise en page de l'illustration', in Henri-Jean Martin and Jean Vezin (eds.), *Mise en page et mise en texte du livre manuscrit* (Paris: Cercle de la Librairie-Promodis), 355–434.

Travieso-Ganaza, Mercedes (1990). 'Le Dialogue du *Jeu de la feuillée* comme matrice didascalique', in Jean-Pierre Bordier (ed.), *Langues, codes et conventions de l'ancien théâtre: actes de la troisième rencontre sur l'ancien théâtre européen: Tours, Centre d'Études Supérieures de la Renaissance, 23–24 septembre 1999* (Paris: Champion), 67–82.

Ubersfeld, Anne (1977). *Lire le théâtre* (Paris: Éditions Sociales).

Vaughan, Richard (2002). *Philip the Good: The Apogee of Burgundy* (Harlow: Longmans, 1970; repr. Woodbridge: Boydell Press).

Verschueren, Jef (1999). *Understanding Pragmatics* (London: Arnold).

Ward, John O. (1995). 'Quintilian and the Rhetorical Revolution of the Middle Ages', *Rhetorica*, 13/3: 231–84.

Winn, Mary Beth (1997). *Anthoine Vérard, Parisian Publisher, 1485–1512: Prologues, Poems and Presentations* (Geneva: Droz).

Woodbridge, Linda (1984). *Women and the English Renaissance: Literature and the Nature of Womankind, 1540–1620* (Brighton: Harvester Press).

Worton, Michael, and Still, Judith (eds.) (1990). *Intertextuality: Theories and Practices* (Manchester: Manchester University Press).

Zimmermann, Margarete (1999). 'Querelle des femmes, querelle du livre', in Dominique de Courcelles and Carmen Val Julián (eds.), *Des femmes et des livres: France et Espagne, XIVᵉ–XVIIᵉ siècles: actes de la journée d'étude organisée par l'École Nationale des Chartes et l'École Normale Supérieure de Fontenay Saint-Cloud, (Paris, 30 avril 1998)* (Paris: École des Chartes), 79–94.

Index

I list references to Jean de Meun separately from those to *Le Roman de la rose*, distinguishing thereby between references primarily to his authorial person, and references to the text or to Guillaume de Lorris. Italic numbers denote reference to illustrations.